ROUTLEDGE LIBRARY EDITIONS: COMMODITIES

Volume 5

COMMODITY POLICIES

COMMODITY POLICIES

Problems and Prospects

ALASDAIR I. MACBEAN
AND
D. T. NGUYEN

Routledge
Taylor & Francis Group

LONDON AND NEW YORK

First published in 1987 by Croom Helm Ltd.

This edition first published in 2024
by Routledge
4 Park Square, Milton Park, Abingdon, Oxon OX14 4RN

and by Routledge
605 Third Avenue, New York, NY 10158

Routledge is an imprint of the Taylor & Francis Group, an informa business

British Library Cataloguing in Publication Data
A catalogue record for this book is available from the British Library

ISBN: 978-1-032-69509-9 (Set)
ISBN: 978-1-032-69401-6 (Volume 5) (hbk)
ISBN: 978-1-032-69413-9 (Volume 5) (pbk)
ISBN: 978-1-032-69410-8 (Volume 5) (ebk)

DOI: 10.4324/9781032694108

Publisher's Note
The publisher has gone to great lengths to ensure the quality of this reprint but points out that some imperfections in the original copies may be apparent.

Disclaimer
The publisher has made every effort to trace copyright holders and would welcome correspondence from those they have been unable to trace.

COMMODITY POLICIES: Problems and Prospects

Alasdair I. MacBean and D. T. Nguyen

CROOM HELM
London • New York • Sydney

© 1987 A.I. MacBean and D.T. Nguyen
Croom Helm Ltd, Provident House, Burrell Row,
Beckenham, Kent, BR3 1AT

Croom Helm Australia, 44-50 Waterloo Road,
North Ryde, 2113, New South Wales

British Library Cataloguing in Publication Data

MacBean, Alasdair I.
    Commodity policies: problems and prospects.
    1. Commodity control 2. Raw material
    I. Title II. Nguyen, D.T.
    382.1'7   HF1051

    ISBN 0-7099-1708-2

Published in the USA by
Croom Helm
in association with Methuen, Inc.
29 West 35th Street
New York, NY 10001

Library of Congress Cataloging-in-Publication Data

MacBean, Alasdair I.
    Commodity policies.

    (Croom Helm commodity series)
    Bibliography: p.
    Includes index.
    1. Commodity control. 2. Developing countries —
Economic policy. I. Nguyen, D.T. II. Title.
III. Series
HF1428.M29   1987   382'.3'091724   87-9069
ISBN 0-7099-1708-2

Printed and bound in Great Britain by Mackays of Chatham Ltd, Kent

CONTENTS

TABLES AND FIGURES

Figures

To Marion and Geik Huan

LIST OF ABBREVIATIONS

SFT   Single Factoral Terms of Trade
UNCTAD   United Nations Conference on Trade and Development
UBEB   Union of Banana Exporting Countries

ACP	African, Caribbean and Pacific (Countries)
ARIMA	Auto-Regressive Moving-Average (Box-Jenkins forecasting method)
CAP	Common Agricultural Policy (EEC)
CFF	Compensatory Financing Facility (IMF)
CMC	Commodity-Mix Component (Shift-Share Analysis)
CMEA	Council for Mutual Economic Assistance
COMUNBANA	A Joint Marketing Company for Bananas
CPE	Centrally Planned Economy
DFTT	Double Factoral Terms of Trade
EC	European Community
ECU	European Currency Unit
EEC	European Economic Community
EPR	Effective Protection Rate
FAO	Food and Agriculture Organisation
GATT	General Agreements on Tariffs and Trade
GDP	Gross Domestic Product
GNP	Gross National Product
GSP	Generalised System of Preferences
ICA	International Commodity Agreement
IMF	International Monetary Fund
IPC	Integrated Programme for Commodities
ITA	International Tin Agreement
LDC	Less Developed Country
MAD	Mean Absolute Deviation (Index of Instability)
MDC	More Developed Country
MINEX	MINerals EXport Earnings Stabilisation Scheme (EEC) (also called SYSMIN)
NBTT	Net Barter Terms of Trade
NIEO	New International Economic Order
NTM	Non-Tariff Measure
OECD	Organisation for Economic Cooperation and Development
RC	Regional Component (Shift-Share Analysis)

RMSD	Root Mean Square Deviation (Index of Instability)
SDR	Special Drawing Rights (IMF Currency Unit)
SFTT	Single Factoral Terms of Trade
STABEX	STABilisation of EXport Earnings
SYSMIN	See MINEX
TNC	Trans-National Corporations
UN	United Nations
UNCTAD	United Nations Conference on Trade and Development
UPEB	Union of Banana Exporting Countries

This is the eighth volume in the Croom Helm Commodity Series. Other books which have been published in the series to date are Uranium by Marian Radetzki, Tin by William Robertson, The Modern Plantation Estate by Edgar Graham with Ingrid Floering, Commodity Models for Forecasting and Policy Analysis by Walter Labys and Peter Pollack, The International Grain Trade by Nicholas Butler, The Political Economy of Natural Gas by Ferdinand Banks, and my own contribution, International Commodity Control. A further imminent volume is International Commodity Agreements: A Legal Study by B.S. Chimni. Volumes covering a range of other subjects are also planned over the course of the next few years.

The aim of the Series is a general one: to advance the understanding of issues relating to the production and marketing of primary commodities. As a result, volumes in the Series deal with a range of subjects - from the examination of a fairly specialised commodity, such as uranium at one end of the spectrum, to a much broader subject, such as commodity price behaviour, at the other. Wherever possible, however, it is hoped that volumes in the Series will share a common form so that they may be useful for reference purposes. It is also intended that they should each be forward-looking rather than merely an historical account.

Contributors to the Series come from a variety of countries and backgrounds so that a variety of approaches have been adopted. In general, however, they are already established in their chosen fields and we are confident that this is being reflected in the quality of the Series as a whole.

The Series should appeal to anyone interested in commodity issues, whether their principal concern is with policy, marketing, trading or simply obtaining general background information. Both the publishers, Croom Helm, and myself, Fiona Gordon-Ashworth, as Series Editor, welcome any feedback that users of the Series may have.

Fiona Gordon-Ashworth
Series Editor

The Series is edited by Fiona Gordon-Ashworth, formerly of the University of Southampton, who now works at the Bank of England. (The views expressed in this book are not to be taken as those of the Bank of England.)

PREFACE

Exports of non-oil primary commodities remain the principal source of foreign exchange for most developing countries. Many of these countries still obtain most of their foreign exchange earnings from exports of no more than three commodities. Although exports of manufactures have been growing fast, only about 10 developing countries obtain more than half of their export earnings from manufactures. Since most of the developing countries depend for their growth on their capacity to pay for imports of capital goods, raw materials and/or fuels, they are understandably concerned about the trends and fluctuations in the prices and proceeds of their primary commodity exports. The fall in primary export earnings in recent years has contributed significantly to their present debt problem. This is exacerbated by the increased agricultural protectionism in the industrialised countries, for whom the main worries in commodity trade are the risk of shortages of key minerals, the embarrassing surpluses of food products and the pressure of commodity price instability on domestic inflation.

This book aims to give an objective examination of arguments and facts on commodity problems, policies and prospects. The main issues covered include agricultural protection, discrimination against processing in developing countries, world food prospects, world supplies of minerals, and the growth and stability of the export earnings of developing countries from commodities. In particular, the progress and difficulties in the implementation of UNCTAD proposals in the commodity field (under the so-called Integrated Programme for Commodities) are discussed. These proposals include a Common Fund for assisting a series of International Commodity Agreements, compensatory financing of commodity shortfalls, processing of raw materials in developing countries and access to the markets in industrialised countries for developing countries' exports of commodities or semi-manufactures. Trade in primary commodities remain crucial to the prosperity of both rich and poor nations. What will happen to it depends to a considerable extent on the outcomes of negotiations between governments. Negotiations have often failed because of misunderstandings, misleading or unreliable information and incorrect analyses, although the inability to reconcile the differences of interests between developed countries and developing countries and between developing countries themselves is probably the ultimate cause. It is hoped that the review and clarification of arguments and facts in this book will assist the commodity specialists, economists and governments to find new areas of common interest and new or improved practical proposals for dealing with problems in commodity trade.

We gratefully acknowledge the financial support from the British Overseas Development Administration (ODA) for the project on which this book is based. We are grateful to UNCTAD, FAO, the World Bank and various International Commodity Associations for making their statistics and documents available to us. Sincere thanks are due to Professor G. Adams, Dr A. Matthews and Dr A.J. Yeats for their valuable comments on various chapters of this book in earlier drafts and Mr J. Gregory (UNCTAD) for his effort to transfer data to us. We are greatly indebted to Professor J.R. Behrman and Dr Fiona Gordon-Ashworth for being most generous with their time in reading and giving us their helpful comments on the whole of an earlier draft of this book. Messrs R.J. Perkins, de Nigris, K. Becker, S. Zarqa, G. Wurdack and N. Alexandratos (FAO), Professors Ann Kreuger and G. Pyatt, Drs R. Duncan and D. Mitchell and Mr L. Alexander (World Bank), Drs T. Morrison, Ke-Young Chu and Ali Salehizadeh (IMF), Mr J. Carr and Dr P. Jumpasut (International Rubber Study Group), Mr P.O. Ononye (International Cocoa Organisation), Mr A.C. Hannah (International Sugar Organisation) and Mr M.H. Farrow (International Tin Council) have discussed the works of their organisations relevant to our enquiries and clarified many practical issues. To all these people we wish to express our special appreciation. We also wish to thank Mr G. Stark for providing much of the needed research assistance, Dr M. Yolles for setting up the Commodity Data Base at Lancaster, Mrs Janice E. Jacklin for her help in running difficult computer jobs and Mrs Geik Huan Nguyen for her patience and effort in obtaining copies of a large number of articles and documents and compiling a comprehensive list of references on commodities. Finally we wish to commend and thank Mrs Sylvia Truesdale for her excellent typing of the whole manuscript, Mrs Heather Watt and Miss Julie Taylor for their patience and stamina in coping with our handwriting in earlier drafts of chapters. Responsibility for errors is of course ours alone.

A.I. MacBean
D.T. Nguyen

Chapter One

THE MAIN ISSUES

No one seriously questions the strategic or economic importance of oil either to importers or exporters. But the case for the non-oil primary commodities is less clear cut. Over the past twenty years changes in the structure of world trade reveal a fall in the share of food and raw materials in world exports and imports. The share of primary commodities has declined relative to manufactures. Within that declining share the proportion exported by the less developed countries (LDCs) has fallen while that of the industrialised nations has increased (See Chapter 2 below).

As a group, the non-oil developing countries have become less specialised in primary commodity exports. The share of manufactures has increased sharply. However, it remains the case that most of these manufactures are concentrated in the exports of a relatively few LDCs. Hong Kong, Singapore, South Korea and Taiwan between them accounted for just over 40 per cent of exports of manufactures from LDCs excluding the oil exporters. (World Bank, 1983) For several large LDCs manufactured exports are increasingly important:

Table 1.1:   Manufactures as a Percentage of Merchandise Exports

	1960 %	1980 %	Population (millions) Mid 1981
India	45	59	690
Pakistan	27	50	85
Brazil	3	40	121
Argentina	4	23	28
Mexico	12	39	71

Source: World Bank, World Development Report, 1983, Tables 10 and 1

1

Although this rapid growth of manufactured exports is a dominant trend, primary commodity exports still constitute the major source of foreign exchange for the majority of LDCs. In many of them almost all of their export earnings come from three or less primary products. For Burundi, Ghana and Zambia over 70 per cent of export earnings come from one commodity. (World Bank, 1983, p. 10) Clearly the fate of such countries is tied to trends and fluctuations in the proceeds from the particular commodities which they export. For developing countries as a whole exports of food and raw materials are about 55 per cent of total exports excluding mineral fuels. (UNCTAD, 1983, Table IV)

From the viewpoint of the industrialised nations, non-oil commodity trade causes concern mainly in terms of the risk of shortages of key minerals on the one hand and embarrassment of surpluses in many of the food products on the other. There are secondary worries about the effects on internal price stability of wildly fluctuating commodity import prices. If fluctuations in import prices have a ratchet effect upon domestic prices and wages this could be a significant factor in the inflationary process in the industrial nations. (Behrman, 1977; Kaldor, 1976)

Probably the major concern is with security of supplies of minerals which are essential to their manufacturing industries but worries about cartel action by LDC suppliers taking a leaf out of the OPEC book have lessened since the 1970s. The conditions for successful cartel action to restrict supply and enhance prices seem to be lacking for most of the minerals. Too many sources of supply, availability of natural and synthetic substitutes, lack of political cohesion among suppliers together with the world recession have largely eliminated the threat of other cartels, just as the last of these has produced a crumbling of the structure of OPEC's control over oil prices. But the industrialised nations do continue to have real fears about the threat to the security of their supplies of several key minerals: chromium, molybdenum, manganese and cobalt, implied by political instability in Southern Africa. The dependence of the USA, the European Community (EC) and Japan upon import of minerals is illustrated in Table 1.2.

As far as trade in food is concerned the protectionist policies pursued by most industrial nations result in serious distortion in resource allocations among the more developed countries (MDCs) and between them and the LDCs. The European Community produces grains, meat and dairy products which could be imported from North America and Australasia at much lower cost. All the industrial nations grow beet sugar, most of which could be replaced at lower cost by imports of cane sugar from LDCs. Their subsidies to butter production also discriminate against exports of vegetable oils from the LDCs. To add still more injury to world agricultural exporters the EC supports domestic agricultural

Table 1.2: Import Dependence 1979-80 in Percentages
Imports as a Percentage of Domestic Consumption
plus Exports

	United Kingdom	European Community	Japan	United States
Aluminium (inc. bauxite and alumina)	78	45	70	73
Antimony	100 (a)	92 (a)	100 (a)	63
Asbestos	100	84	98	82
Barytes	71	18	36	47
Cadmium (refined)	68	32	–	56
Chromium	100	97	99	90
Cobalt (a)	100	100	100	100
Copper	75	80	80	20
Fluorspar	10	29	100	86
Germanium (refined)	100	2	100	under 13
Iron Ore	86	87	89 (b)	25
Lead	53	44	47	13
Lithium	100	100	100	–
Magnesium Metal	75	over 61	9	2
Manganese	100	99.5	99	100
Mercury	100 (a)	91 (a)	28	30
Molybdenum	100	100	99	–
Nickel	100	87	100	88
Niobium	100	100	100	100
Phosphate	100	100	100	1
Platinum Group	100 (a)	100 (a)	100 (a)	93
Potash	64	19	100	69
Rhenium	100	100	100	88
Selenium	100	100	100	63
Silicon	100	44	43	20
Silver	100	58	57	43
Sulphur	92	31	–	16
Tantalum	100	100	100	100
Tin	71	93	99	94
Titanium	100	100	100	80
Tungsten	100 (a)	78 (a)	85 (a)	48
Uranium	100	70	100	..
Vanadium	100	100	100	40
Zinc	81	57	48	49
Zirconium	100	100	100	68

(a) Before allowing for secondary recovery
(b) Most of balance from stocks

Source: Philip Crowsen, Minerals Handbook (Macmillan, 1983)
Table 4

prices to such an extent that the Community frequently has to dump subsidised surpluses in world markets. (Body, 1982, Matthews, 1985)

Trade in primary commodities remains crucial to the prosperity of both rich and poor nations. Even though manufactured exports have grown fast, many, particularly the poorer LDCs, are still very dependent on their earnings from commodity exports. Their growth and their stability are likely to be largely determined by what happens in commodity trade for many years to come. The fall in primary export earnings in real terms which has occurred over the last few years has greatly exacerbated the problem of LDC indebtedness. The obstacles raised by industrialised nations against exports of processed materials from LDCs add to the difficulties of reducing the burden of debt.

Primary commodity trade is still quantitatively important for both exporters and importers, but qualitatively it may be yet more important. Many LDCs regard the attitudes of the North (the industrial nations) to commodity trade policies as a touchstone of their good intentions towards the developing countries. The most carefully worked out ideas for a New International Economic Order lay in the commodity field in the United Nations' proposals for an Integrated Programme for Commodities. These concentrated on the idea of a Common Fund set up to stimulate and provide finance for buffer stocks to be controlled by a series of international commodity agreements, but also concerned Compensatory Financing of commodity export shortfalls in LDCs, access to MDC markets for LDCs' commodity exports and for the development of processing of commodities in the LDCs for export in more advanced forms or even as semi-manufactures. In the remainder of this introductory chapter the main issues of debate in the field of commodity trade are briefly described. Subsequent chapters pick up aspects of these debates and consider the prospects for their resolution by policies currently under consideration in the United Nations Conference for Trade, Aid and Development (UNCTAD) and other organisations.

THE ISSUES OF DEBATE

The relative importance of each issue is a matter of judgement. But judgements can be informed ones based on the potential increase in world income and the effect on its distribution between rich and poor which could result from remedial action. Another criterion would be the likelihood of successful reforms in terms of technical feasibility and ability to gain sufficiently widespread support among the diverse groups of members of the United Nations. We hope to make such assessments in this book but in this Chapter the issues are merely described and the order in which this is done has no special significance. The main issues are agricultural protectionism, discrimination against LDC processing, world food prospects, world supplies of minerals, the division of economic rents between exporting and importing nations, the growth and stability of LDCs' export earnings from commodity exports.

Agricultural Protectionism

The Common Agricultural Policy (CAP) of the EC represents the most formidable obstacle to trade in agricultural products today. The EC forms the largest world market for agricultural products but excludes competition from more cost-efficient producers in both the developed countries of North America and Australasia and from the developing countries. This raises prices for food to Community citizens, damages the interests of food exporting nations and often inflicts serious hurt upon the poorest sections of the population in the rural areas of the developing nations. (Yeats, 1981; Body, 1982; Matthews, 1985; World Bank, 1986)

Apart from reducing the average earnings of food exporting nations the EC also creates greater instability in world markets by dumping surplus sugar, wheat and milk products as subsidised exports in some years while being a net importer in others. The EC's variable import levies also increase the instability of world markets. The levies automatically rise when world prices fall and are reduced when world prices rise. This has the effect of restricting demand when world supplies are abundant and raising demand when world supplies are relatively low. Consequently the swings in world food prices are enhanced. (Bale and Lutz, 1978)

Not only has agricultural protectionism generally been high it has also been growing for most of the industrial nations including the EC and Japan but also Scandinavia and Switzerland. (Matthews, 1985, p. 93) Compared with protection given to manufacturing the levels of protection for agriculture are extremely high.

The effects are damaging to the economies of the protecting nations themselves, to developed agricultural exporting nations such as Australia, Canada, New Zealand and the US, many developing countries and some socialist centrally planned economies.

Within the protecting countries resources which could earn higher returns elsewhere are held in the agricultural sectors. The costs of food and raw materials are pushed far higher than need be, damaging consumers' interests directly and raising the costs of manufactures. Even within agriculture, costs are distorted and resources misallocated. In the UK, for instance, land which is highly suitable for livestock is drawn into grain production while high feed grain prices

5

increase costs of raising livestock. (Body, 1981, p. 4 and Chapters 2-4)

The main arguments put forward in the industrial nations for continuing these protectionist policies are strategic, environmental and social. None are convincing. In an all-out nuclear war the question is clearly irrelevant, but even in some more limited conflict in which international trade in food was interrupted one should remember the very high yields which fallow land produced in the short run in the 1939-45 war. Stocks of essential foods are another way of dealing with this risk.

The environmental arguments could lead to support for a certain amount of aid for farming, but hardly for the planting of large areas of unsuitable land with grain. Encouraging grain production on marginal land is itself probably environmentally damaging because of the highly intensive, chemically-oriented agriculture which results. In so far as society wishes to preserve farming as a contribution to a pleasing countryside environment income transfers to farmers would be a more efficient way of doing it.

The social or income distribution arguments which have been put forward in terms of maintaining incomes for small marginal farmers do not stand up to examination. The main beneficiaries of policies such as the CAP have been the large wealthy farmers and the owners of farmland whose value has increased far faster than almost any other type of investment over the past 15 years. (Howarth, 1985 p. 82) The agro-industries which produce equipment, fertilisers and plant protection chemicals have also gained enormously from the CAP. Relatively, the small farmers have gained much less. Far cheaper and more effective means can be found for giving them direct income support if this is deemed socially desirable. The case for a system of compensatory income transfers to farmers in place of the CAP is put in Dicke and Rodemer (1983).

Analyses of the effects of structural changes in agricultural trade brought about largely by the growth of the EC agricultural protection put the losses to the efficient developed country exporters as high as $4.3 billion in 1979 and $2.9 billion for developing countries with the socialist countries of eastern Europe also losing about $600 million. (Yeats, 1981, Table 7) The employment and income distribution losses in LDCs would also be severe. The most labour intensive activities tend to be in agriculture. The poorest sections of the community normally live in the rural areas and depend on agriculture for their living. Reductions in the value and volume of their outputs and greater instability in their earnings from them must have contributed to worsening rural incomes and immigration to urban areas with all the attendant social problems which have afflicted LDCs in the last ten years. (Valdes and Hayssen 1979; Valdes and Zietz, 1980).

A reduction in agricultural trade barriers of industrial nations would benefit their consumers, produce a slimmed but healthier agricultural sector, bring large gains to both developed and developing country exporters and reduce instability in world prices for agricultural products. However, against the gains to exporters there would be losses for food importing countries. Many LDCs are net importers of grains and dairy products. World prices for their food imports would rise as a result of the increased demand for food imports in Europe and Japan. In Chapter 6 we attempt to assess various attempts to evaluate the overall effects of agricultural protectionism, particularly of the EEC.

Tariff Escalation

The average level of protection against raw or crude forms of food, fibres and minerals is generally less than for processed forms of the same products. This tariff escalation creates severe obstacles to processing within the exporting countries because it raises the level of the effective protection of the processing stage in the importing country. For example, if a quantity of jute yarn valued at $10 in international prices bears a 10 per cent tariff while the jute cloth which could be made from it costs $15 at international prices and has a tariff of 20 per cent then the value added at home prices would be substantially greater than at international prices.

	cif price	Nominal tariff	Cost in Importing Country
jute yarn	$10	10%	$11
jute cloth	$15	20%	$18

Local value added is $ (18−11) = $7

Value added at international prices $ (15−10) = $5

The effective rate of protection = 100 (7/5−1) = 40%

Where the material input is a large proportion of the finished price value added is low, and as the effective tariff varies inversely with value added this can produce some exceptionally high rates of effective protection. For vegetable oils, for example, the effective rate for some countries rises as high as eight times the nominal tariff. (Yeats, 1981, p. 5)

Clearly this denies to LDCs in particular, opportunities for increasing employment and incomes from those agricultural and mineral products where they have a comparative advantage in processing. It is also claimed that freight rates discriminate against processed forms of primary products i.e. transport rates are based more on what the market will bear than on the cubic feet of cargo space and handling costs involved. Recent UNCTAD studies claim that for many commodities LDC producers are at a disadvantage vis a vis the transnational corporations in processing and marketing products because these organisations have certain monopolistic advantages which make it difficult for the LDCs' producers to by-pass the TNCs and develop effective marketing strategies of their own. (UNCTAD, TD 273 and TD/B/C.2/167)

If true, these factors, in common with the undoubted frequency of tariff escalation, make it very difficult for LDCs to set up their own industries to export such products as vegetable oils, milk products or refined metals.

The Problem of Food

Another issue of great significance to the world is the production and availability of food. The production of food for the world as a whole has consistently grown faster than population over the past twenty years. Cereal prices in real terms have been falling for over thirty years. Up to the Ethiopian disaster of 1984 there is evidence of a consistent decline in hunger-related deaths but there remain grounds for grave concern. There has been some slowing down of the rate of growth of output, and actual falls in per capita output, in the poorest regions - low income developing countries generally and more specifically in Africa. (World Bank, 1985, Annex, Table 6)

The effects of continued rapid population growth together with slower growth in food production and a skewed distribution of income have meant that more people are inadequately fed now than ten years ago. 'The absolute numbers of people with food intakes below the minimum critical limit ... is estimated to have been 360 million in the developing countries, excluding Asian Centrally Planned economies, in 1969-71. ... By 1974-76 the number is estimated to have risen to around 415 million.' (FAO, 1979, para.5)

Recent research on diet has shown that past worries about malnourishment, inadequacy of protein particularly, in a diet with adequate calories, were misguided. If the diet supplies enough calories then with a few exceptions it will also supply enough protein. The main problem appears to be one of income and employment. Poor people often do not have the means to obtain enough food even when the national availability of food is sufficient to meet the maximum needs of the whole population. Even in the extreme cases of severe famine there has usually been sufficient food available within the nations affected. The main cause of starvation has been that poor people have neither been able to grow their own food nor had the purchasing power to buy it. Other factors have been war and civil strife which have made distribution of famine relief foods nearly impossible. (FAO, 1979 paras. 8 and 46; Sen, 1982)

The creation of employment through land redistribution and more labour intensive agriculture is one important measure to combat hunger. Better prices for small farmers' typical products and more assistance to them in growing food and cash crops are key policies for governments in creating better food prospects for the rural poor. For the urban poor, better employment opportunities and higher real incomes are the answer. For them lower food prices are an unambiguous benefit. Subsidies for the specific foods of the urban poor, perhaps sold through ration shops, may be the only answer, at least in the short run.

Food Prospects. One recent major study of world food prospects is The Global 2000 Report to the President (Global 2000) commissioned by President Carter and published by Penguin Books (1982). This projects world food production to increase by about 2.2 per cent per year over 1970-2000 (p. 13). This compares with past rates of 2.7 per cent 1960-70 and 2.3 per cent 1970-80. (World Bank, 1982, Table 5.1) On the basis of Global 2000's population projections, average per capita consumption would increase by 15 per cent between 1970 and 2000. But most of the increase would occur in the better-off areas of the world. In the developing countries food output is expected to barely exceed population growth. Over the period 1970-2000 they may achieve together an increase of 9 per cent in per capita food output, but for the huge populations of South Asia little or no improvement is foreseen. The same dismal situation is expected for North Africa and large areas of the Middle-East. In sub-Saharan Africa per capita consumption is actually projected to fall. The major gains are recorded in Latin America and East Asia. For the poor in most of the Third World the outlook continues to be bleak. 'The quantity of food available to the poorest groups of people will simply be insufficient to permit children to reach normal body weight and intelligence and to permit normal activity and good health in adults.' (Global 2000, pp. 17 and 88) Fears are expressed that rising demand from industry for grain, particularly for conversion to alcohol-based fuels plus erosion of land may reduce food below the projected levels.

Trends in Trade in Food. The Global 2000 projections highlight continuing trends towards increasing dependence of most developing countries on food imports, the increased risks of variability in food supply and the growing importance of the decisions on trade and agricultural policy of a few major exporting and importing countries (p. 88).

The first of these is not necessarily detrimental to economic welfare. Generally, it is the relatively better-off developing countries whose food imports are expected to increase. It may reflect their growing comparative advantage in exports of manufactures, energy or raw materials and rising standards of living. The real nutritional problems lie in the poorest countries and the poorer groups within higher-income countries. As indicated earlier most projections show that continued population trends mean that larger absolute numbers of people will suffer from inadequate food than ever before.

But a new study by the UN Population Division provides evidence for the view that while the problem of hunger is still extremely serious, progress in reducing hunger related deaths has been significant. It shows that world wide infant mortality rates have declined from an average 142 per 1,000 in 1950-55 to 89 per 1,000 in 1975-80. (UN, 1982, pp. 31-53) On the basis of this UN data estimates of hunger related deaths have been reduced from a range of '15 to 20 million' to a lower range of '13 to 18 million'. (Prosterman, 1984, p. 9)

The second anticipated problem, increased instability in the supply of food is believed to be due to the need to push back the frontiers of cultivated land into marginal areas with increased susceptibility to weather variations. This makes the maintenance of an open system of trade in food, access to loans for food deficit nations to buy food imports, and food reserves to meet emergencies and to moderate price fluctuations even more important than in the past.

Policy decisions in the Soviet Union, the EC and Japan are likely to have profound effects on both the stability and growth of world production and trade in food. Their heavily protected domestic agriculture throws the costs of instability in their production on to major exporters, lowers incentives to produce food in the lowest cost regions of the world and generally distorts the pattern of consumption and production of food products.

The basic source of the world's food is cereals and starches. These form calorie-efficient diets. They sustain life and health at low cost. But rising incomes and changes in taste tend to shift the pattern of consumption towards meat and other livestock products which are much less calorie-efficient. The land, energy, capital and labour costs of providing the same number of calories by means of livestock rather than a cereal diet are much greater. Cereals are used indirectly to feed animals instead of feeding humans directly. This is a major cause of increased demand for grains. If there should be an unexpectedly large increase in demand for livestock products in, for example, the lower income industrialised nations and the centrally planned economies, this would push up world food prices dramatically.

Food Security. The food crisis of 1972-74, when the world price of wheat and rice approximately trebled from $60 to $200 a ton and from $130 to $500 a ton respectively did arouse the world to take some action to avert a repetition. According to the World Bank's assessment a repeat of that crisis seems unlikely because of the following responses to it:

1. More emphasis by governments on increasing food production.
2. More widely held stocks and improved information.
3. More effective operation of the grain markets and more price responsiveness of demand.
4. Governmental control over grain exports.
5. More international awareness by governments in making policy changes affecting production and acreage.
6. The establishment of an International Food Reserve of 500,000 tons in 1976.
7. A new Food Aid Convention was negotiated in 1980 which raised the minimum annual contribution of food aid from 4.2 to 7.6 million tons.
8. The establishment in 1981 of the IMF Food Facility as an extension of the IMF Compensatory Fund Facility to make financial assistance available to offset fluctuations in a country's food import bills due to higher world prices or a domestic shortfall in production. (World Bank, 1982, p. 55)

Whether these changes are sufficient is still in dispute. The case of food crisis in Ethiopia in October 1984 and followed by further crises in other African countries argues that the problems remain serious at the country level. The problems of chronic hunger and the crises of famines, together with policies to tackle them are considered in Chapter 6.

COMMODITY MARKET INSTABILITY

The experiences of the 1970s highlighted the problems created by sudden changes in commodity prices. The commodity boom of 1972/73 was followed by a slump in the prices of most primary commodity exports in 1974/75. These boom and slump conditions in the main exports of developing countries together with a fourfold rise in the price of oil over 1973-75 created extreme problems for many, but especially for the net oil importing developing countries. It caused a sharp increase in their foreign debt as they borrowed heavily to sustain imports of energy, capital goods, intermediate goods and food

11

necessary to maintain development programmes and current living standards. It added a sense of urgency to the meeting of the United Nations Conference on Trade and Development (UNCTAD) in Nairobi in 1976. That meeting adopted proposals for the 'Integrated Programme for Commodities' which involved inter alia international commodity agreements (ICAs) for up to 18 commodities and a 'Common Fund' whose main function would be to finance buffer stocks held by ICAs.

Chapter 4 deals with these issues in some detail. By way of introduction the main issues are summarised briefly in the following paragraphs.

Instability in prices, quantities traded and earnings from internationally traded commodities must be differentiated from longer term movements which are the result of more fundamental and lasting changes in tastes, technology and resource endowments. Changes in prices which reflect these long term changes are, in a market orientated system, the essential mechanism which leads to the adaptation of consumption, trade and production to new realities.

Even in the shorter term, price changes represent the way in which free markets adapt to scarcities and surpluses in goods. An increase in price is a way of rationing the use of a scarce item so that it is used most efficiently (where it yields the highest utility). It should also lead to sales from private stocks as stockholders take advantage of high prices to realise profits. Equally when prices fall this should lead to new uses for the item with its being substituted for more expensive alternatives. Stocks should rise as speculators see opportunities for profit in buying now for sale later. A free market system which works efficiently should itself yield a near optimum solution, smoothing out price fluctuations as far as the costs of operating stocks will permit. Without some intervention, however, even the most efficient and well-informed privately operated markets cannot achieve a socially optimal situation because private profits cannot always capture all the benefits or costs which accrue to the community as a whole from the price variations. This is a familiar proposition in welfare economics usually illustrated with examples such as a private firm which pollutes a river with its industrial waste and does not have to pay the extra costs of cleaning the river water for domestic use downstream, or of a new toll bridge across a river which is able to extract tolls from users but gains no income from users of older bridges which are now less congested and have fewer traffic delays.

In an analogous way a reduction in price fluctuations may realise benefits which are much greater than those measured by the profits gained by private stockholders. For example it might reduce inflation produced by the ratchet effects in either producing or importing countries which some writers believe are significant factors in causing inflation (Behrman, 1977).

The justification for official intervention exists even if markets were operating as well as they possibly could in an uncertain world, provided that the gains to the community from the intervention exceeded the costs e.g. carrying more stocks than the private sector is willing to do. If the actual markets are for any reason very inefficient the case for intervention to control swings in prices becomes much stronger.

The major risk in intervention to control price movements is that a fundamental realignment of the market may be misinterpreted as a short term change which will be reversed. In that situation price controls merely store up trouble for the future, literally so in the case of a buffer stock which buys up commodities in the expectation of a future rise in demand when the commodity has in fact become obsolescent. The dramatic collapse of the Tin Agreement in October 1985 highlights the risks of attempting to oppose fundamental market forces.

The causes and the consequences of primary product instability are the subject of chapter 4 and the analyses of proposals for dealing with the problem are considered in chapters 5 and 6.

Chapter 2 of this book tries to outline and explain the general current situation of trade in the main commodities. Chapter 3 concentrates on the theoretical and empirical evidence on long term trends in commodity trade and on the general prospects for them as far ahead as the main official projections are prepared to look.

13

Chapter Two

PRIMARY COMMODITY TRADE TODAY

The purpose of this chapter is to survey the current structure in world trade in primary commodities and to explain why
it has developed in this way. The structure includes the
share of the various categories of primary commodities in
world trade, the direction of trade in them and their relative
importance as exports and imports to different regions and
groups of nations. We shall focus on the main trends in
commodity trade over the last twenty years in terms of major
commodities and groups of commodities. The relative importance of specific commodities and commodity groups as exports
and imports for developing countries (LDCs), the industrialised or more developed countries (MDCs) and the centrally
planned economies (CPEs) are shown. Attention is drawn to
the recent growth in trade among LDCs. Some explanations
for the broad trends are sought in terms of economic
variables, natural hazards, and policies followed in both
importing and exporting nations.

THE COMMODITY STRUCTURE OF TRADE: RECENT TRENDS

In the last twenty years trade in primary products (excluding
fuels) has shown: a decline in its share of world trade, a
decline in its share of exports from developing countries; a
decline in developing countries' share of world exports of
primary products and a downward trend in respect of LDCs'
balance of trade surplus in primary products. These are of
course only very broad general trends which conceal within
them a great diversity of experience for particular countries
and particular products. But in this chapter there is neither
time nor space for details save by way of occasional illustration. In sketching out the broad relationships in commodity
trade between the industrialised and developing countries, we
hope that the extremely aggregative nature of the data used
will not distort the picture too much. However, the reader
would do well to bear in mind the over-simplification imposed.

The changing share of primary products in total world trade is shown in Table 2.1. There has been a striking decline in the relative share of non-fuel commodities from 43 per cent of the total in 1960 to 23 per cent in 1980. This continues a long run trend as the importance of manufactured products has grown in world trade, but also reflects, since 1973, the sharp rise in oil prices. Other fundamental causes

Table 2.1: Shares of Major Commodity Groups in World Exports by Value: 1960-80

Product	(percentages)			
	1960	1970	1979	1980
All non-fuel primary products*	43.2	33.3	24.6	23.5
Fuels	9.9	9.2	20.3	23.7
Manufactures	45.7	55.5	53.2	51.3
All Products	100.0	100.0	100.0	100.0
Total value of world exports ($US billion)	127.9	312.1	1,638.4	1,973.0
Excluding fuels				
All food items	21.5	16.2	14.8	14.7
Agricultural raw materials	12.0	6.4	5.3	5.0
Minerals, ores and metals*	14.4	14.1	10.8	11.1
All primary commodities				
Manufactures	50.7	61.1	66.8	67.2
All products excluding fuels	100.0	100.0	100.0	100.0
Total value of world exports excluding fuels ($US billion)	115.2	283.4	1,305.8	1,505.4

* Metals include items which have undergone some elementary manufacturing stages

Note: The above percentages do not add to 100 (totals) because of rounding

Source: UNCTAD Secretariat "World Commodity Trade: Review and Outlook," (TD/B/C.1/236, 4 May 1983) p. 2, Table 1

are the slowing down in the growth of the demand for basic foodstuffs in the richer nations and the tendency for technological change to economise on the need for natural raw materials.

When fuels are excluded, as shown in the lower section of the table, the strong growth in the share of manufactures is clearly evident, as is the steep decline in the share of agricultural raw materials i.e. natural fibres and rubber. Interestingly, within the overall group of primary products the share of trade in food has increased a little while that of agricultural raw materials has declined a lot and ores and metals' share has increased from 26 per cent to 36 per cent. These changes can be seen in Table 2.2 which depicts the shares of major groups of primary commodities within total world trade in non-fuel primary products.

Developing countries are becoming less specialised in non-oil primary products. When oil is excluded, their primary commodity exports declined from 87 per cent to 55 per cent of their total merchandise exports between 1960 and 1979 while their manufactured exports rose from 12 per cent to 44 per cent (UNCTAD, 1983a, Table 2). These changes seem to be evidence of healthy development and diversification, but such a conclusion is subject to the qualification that most LDC manufactured exports are still largely concentrated in a relatively small number of countries in South East Asia plus Brazil, Mexico, India and Pakistan. The large majority of

Table 2.2: Shares of Major Product Groups by Values in World Export of Primary Commodities (ex. fuels)

		1955	1960	1970	1980
1	Food	46.6	44.9	44.2	47.7
2	Agricultural Raw Materials	27.4	25.0	17.5	16.2
3	Ores	7.8	9.0	10.0	8.3
4	Iron and Steel	10.0	12.8	16.5	16.5
5	Non Ferrous Metals	8.2	8.3	11.8	11.2
6	Total of ores and Metals (3) + (4) + (5)	(26.0)	(30.1)	(38.3)	(36.1)
	Total non-fuel commodities	100	100	100	100

Source: UNCTAD, op. cit., p. 19, Table 11

developing countries and especially the low income LDCs still derive most of their foreign exchange earnings from primary exports (UNCTAD, 1983b, Table 6). In a number of cases over 75 per cent of their export earnings come from one or two primary products (Zambia, Uganda, Sudan, Burundi, Ethiopia, Ghana and Fiji for example).

Developing countries' share of world exports of non-fuel primary commodities has also declined from 31 per cent in 1960 to 24 per cent in 1981. Only in ores and minerals have they succeeded in almost maintaining their share. The developed market economies supply over two thirds of world exports of food and non-oil raw materials (see Table 2.3).

An earlier UNCTAD study showed that the overall balance of trade in non-oil primary products of the developing countries had moved from a situation of substantial surplus to near balance between 1955 and 1976 (see Table 2.4).

This trend has probably continued into the 1980s. The share of the MDCs in world imports of non-fuel commodities has fallen from 71 per cent to 66 per cent while for the LDCs over the same period it has risen from 16 per cent to 24 per cent (see Table 2.5).

The general picture which emerges is one of non-oil exporting developing countries having a declining share in a section of world trade which is itself relatively declining. This is partially offset by a rapid growth in their manufactured exports. These are now, as noted previously, over 40% of LDCs' merchandise exports excluding fuel and still growing fairly rapidly, though a mere 10 per cent of world trade in manufactures and concentrated in the exports of a relatively small number of developing countries.

How far is the relative decline in LDCs' shares in commodity exports the result of long term inevitable changes in the world economy and how far the result of policies of both DCs and LDCs?

FACTORS INVOLVED IN THE DECLINING SHARE OF LDCs IN NON-OIL COMMODITY EXPORTS

There are a number of reasons which might explain the downward trend in LDCs' share of world exports of primary commodities. Some of these may be the result of domestic policies and internal developments in their own economies. Others are likely to be the result of changes in tastes and technology in the rest of the world. Some may stem from economic policies followed by the industrial market economies and by the centrally planned economies (CPEs) of East Europe. They may differ from commodity to commodity or for individual countries and any general explanations may have many exceptions. Nevertheless, some generalisations may be worthwhile. In our view it is illuminating to set out a few

17

Table 2.3: Shares of Developed Market Economy Countries, Developing and Socialist Countries in World Exports of Major Commodity Groups

(percentages)

Commodity Group	Developed Market-economy countries				Developing countries				Socialist countries			
	1960	1970	1975	1981	1960	1970	1975	1981	1960	1970	1975	1981
Foods	52.3	59.2	63.1	65.7	37.1	31.8	28.9	27.8	10.6	9.0	8.0	6.5
Agricultural raw materials	52.9	58.5	62.2	59.8	36.2	30.2	25.0	24.0	10.9	11.3	12.8	16.2
Minerals, ores and metals	70.1	70.1	74.2	73.3	17.9	18.7	14.7	17.1	12.0	11.2	11.1	9.6
All non-fuel primary commodities	57.8	63.1	67.1	67.4	31.1	26.7	23.1	23.5	11.2	10.2	9.8	9.1
Fuels	26.5	26.3	17.3	20.1	60.5	63.5	74.1	69.4	12.9	10.2	8.7	10.5
Manufactures	83.6	85.2	84.1	81.5	4.2	5.2	6.7	10.6	12.2	9.7	9.2	8.0
All products	66.7	71.9	66.1	63.0	21.4	17.6	24.2	27.8	11.7	10.5	9.7	9.2

Source: UNCTAD, Handbook of International Trade and Development Statistics, 1984 Supplement (TD/STAT.12.), Table 3.3 (p. 84) and Table A2-A4, A7, A8

Table 2.4: Balance of Trade in Primary Products* between Developed and Developing Countries as % of World Trade

	1955	1970	1976
Developed market economy countries	-9.9	-3.7	-1.7
Developing countries	+9.8	+3.8	+2.1

* Excluding fuels

Source: UNCTAD, "The World Commodity Situation and Outlook", (TD/B/C.1/207, 22 March 1979), p. 37

general hypotheses which seem plausible and to assess their ability to explain the facts. Some of them have been mentioned briefly in earlier sections of this chapter.

HYPOTHESES

1. Developing countries' exports may be concentrated on commodities which on average have lower growth rates than the primary commodities exported by the rest of the world. Their commodity mix may not favour growth.

2. Were they to export commodities, in the same proportions as the MDCs, they may yet fail to achieve as high growth rates as the rest of the world. Such slower growth in exporting could be for any one or more of the following reasons:

   a) their production might be growing more slowly;
   b) the demand for the exportable commodity could be growing more rapidly in their home market than abroad;
   c) world demand for the LDCs' primary commodity exports could be growing more slowly because of increasing levels of protection in MDCs and unfair competition from MDC agricultural exports 'dumped' in world markets with the aid of government subsidies;
   d) LDCs' own policies of protecting manufacturing industries could be drawing resources from primary production or dampening incentives to export commodities. (Export taxes and overvalued exchange rates would be other aspects of an inward looking

19

Table 2.5: Shares of Developed Market Economy Countries, Developing and Socialist Countries in World Imports of Major Commodity Groups

(percentages)

Commodity Group	Developed Market-economy countries				Developing countries				Socialist countries			
	1960	1970	1975	1981	1960	1970	1975	1981	1960	1970	1975	1981
Foods	69.8	72.6	65.8	59.3	20.5	17.2	22.4	26.7	9.2	9.9	11.0	13.1
Agricultural raw materials	73.6	74.2	71.6	66.6	11.5	13.3	15.9	18.6	14.5	12.3	12.2	14.7
Minerals, ores and metals	71.1	76.1	63.5	65.9	13.0	11.7	19.5	21.7	14.5	11.5	16.1	11.4
All non-fuel primary commodities	71.7	74.2	65.8	62.9	16.1	14.7	20.5	24.2	11.1	10.7	13.0	12.9
Fuels	65.6	73.5	75.1	75.7	22.9	15.8	17.3	18.6	8.6	6.4	4.7	4.3
Manufactures	57.0	68.6	62.7	62.1	27.9	20.5	25.7	29.0	12.2	10.3	11.1	8.3
All products	64.7	70.5	65.7	65.2	22.9	18.4	23.0	25.5	11.7	10.4	10.5	8.2

Note: Above percentages do not add to 100 (totals) because of rounding

Source: UNCTAD, Handbook of International Trade and Development Statistics, 1984 Supplement, Table 3.2 (p. 72) and Tables A2-A4, A7, A8

       development strategy stressing import substituting industrialisation)

e) Changes in LDCs' comparative advantages might be shifting resources from their traditional exports towards other products.

A Test of These Hypotheses

We can gain some knowledge of the explanatory value of these hypotheses by the technique of component analysis. The method, the model, the data used and some of the limitations of the technique are given in Appendix A, but a brief outline here may be sufficient to enable some appreciation of the results presented below.

As a group LDCs have a decreasing share of world commodity exports. This reflects slower growth in their commodity export earnings than the rest of the world. The difference between LDCs' export growth and that of the world can be decomposed into a commodity mix component (CMC) and a regional component (RC) where the world is divided into four 'regional groups'. These groups are the more developed countries (MDCs), the LDCs, the centrally planned economies of East Europe (CPE1) and the centrally planned economies of Asia (CPE2).

The regional component, RC, measures the extent to which the deficiency of LDCs' growth of commodity exports is due to factors specific to being in the Third World or being the MDCs or the CPEs of Asia or East Europe. Its effect is isolated by comparing the actual growth of their export earnings with what they would have been if they had the same growth rates as the world. Whereas the commodity mix component, CMC, measures the remaining part of the growth differential which can be attributed to specialisation in slow growing commodities. The CMC is simply the difference between what they would have experienced if their actual exports had grown by the same percentage as the world exports of these groups of commodities and the actual growth of the world export earnings.

As a first approach we have simply broken total commodity exports into two groups: (1) the 18 commodities included in the UNCTAD Integrated Programme for Commodities as being products of special importance to LDCs, and (2) other primary commodity exports. We then show how much of the difference between world commodity export growth and each regional group is due to how their exports are divided between group (1) commodities and group (2) commodities i.e. by their CMC and how much can be attributed to the regional effect (RC). The results for growth over 1971 to 1981 are shown in Table 2.6.

The difference between the actual growth of commodity exports for each region and the growth in the world total of

PRIMARY COMMODITY TRADE TODAY

Table 2.6: Components of Growth Differential (1971–81)

(1) Region	(2) Difference in Growth of Each Region from World Growth(GD)	(3) Commodity-Mix Component (CMC) %	(4) Regional Component (RC) %
MDCs	48.4	16.3	32.1
LDCs	−58.0	−31.9	−26.1
CPE$_1$(Europe)	−127.5	7.7	−135.2
CPE$_2$(Asia)	−1.7	17.6	−19.3

Source: See Table A.1 for data used in calculating these figures

the same exports is shown in column (2). The MDCs' exports grew by 48 per cent more than the world total over this 1971–81 period. LDCs' exports grew by 58 per cent less. In the case of the LDCs 26 per cent of that difference is due to their having lower growth rates of export in both groups of commodities. Had they had the same growth rates as the world their exports would have grown by 26 per cent more. The remaining 32 per cent is due to their being specialised in the 18 IPC commodities which as a group grew more slowly than the group of other primary commodities.

To penetrate further we have to ask why do LDCs have lower growth rates of exports in both groups of commodities and why, even if their exports had the same growth rates as the world, their exports would still have grown 26 per cent less over 1971–81? Part of the answer to the second question lies in climate, geology and history. But before examining the basic causes which underly the CMC and RC factors it may be helpful to repeat the component analysis on a commodity by commodity basis for the 18 IPC commodities for the two regional groups which dominate exports of primary commodities, LDCs and MDCs. The 18 commodities account for over 75 per cent of LDCs primary commodity exports. The details are given in Appendix A Table A.1.

What emerges from components analysis of this group of commodities, of special interest to LDCs, is that growth in LDC exports of these was some 18 per cent less than World growth. The commodity mix (CMC) accounted for about 4 per cent and the regional component for about 14 per cent of this difference in export growth over 1971–81.

The exports of the same group of commodities from the industrially developed nations (MDCs) grew by some 49 per cent more than the average for the world. The commodity mix

22

accounted for 8 per cent and the regional component for 41 per cent of the difference.

When the overall performance of the MDCs and the LDCs are compared the commodity mix factor emerges as much less important than the regional component. Within the CMC most of the difference is due to vegetable oils and bovine meat. They figure relatively prominently in the MDCs' exports but are much smaller shares of the LDCs' exports. As for the regional component which appears to account for so much of the difference in the MDC and LDC performance some qualifications have to be borne in mind.

All of the export data used in this analysis are gross, not net of imports. This seems worrying when one notes that coffee, cocoa and tea are shown as exports from MDCs, but very little, if any, of these crops are grown in MDCs. Most of this is due to re-exports. Some part of the other commodities may also actually be re-exports. MDCs may import in bulk, then package and re-export some of them. However, they have very low weights in their exports and this reduces the likelihood of their affecting the results of the components analysis significantly.

When we look at the commodity mix between IPC and non-IPC commodities the main explanation for the difference in growth lies in the commodity mix component. Within the IPC group, the regional component provides the principal reason. Even if the world were to export the same commodities in the same proportions as the LDCs, the world growth would still be higher than that of the LDCs.

We listed above a number of possible reasons for this. (a) The first was that their production might be growing more slowly so that less would be available for export. The availability of land and exploitable mineral deposits might be decreasing, causing diminishing returns to additional inputs of labour and capital and so slowing the growth of production. This would show up as a fall in the rate of increase in productivity in these crops and minerals compared with MDCs. But it is difficult to see why LDCs should have slower increases in the availability of land and less deposits of minerals than the MDCs which have been more intensively cropped and explored for minerals than most LDCs. (Some Asian LDCs would seem more intensively cropped than many MDCs) Perhaps, differences in the applications of technology could account for lower yields and fear of nationalisation could cause lower extraction rates in LDCs. Actually LDCs' growth rates of production are about the same or greater for most of the 18 commodities and are slower for only cotton, tin and bauxite (See Table 2.7).

(b) The second possible factor was that LDCs' domestic demand for the exportable commodities could be expanding rapidly and thus reducing the supplies available for export. Rising population and incomes could lead directly to increased

23

Table 2.7: World Production and Consumption by Economic Regions: 1980 Volume and Percentage Annual Growth (1970-80)

Commodity Food and Tobacco	WORLD		MDC		LDC		CPE	
	P	C	P	C	P	C	P	C
1 Coffee (GZ)	1.0	0.6	0.0	0.3	1.0	1.3	1.7	2.4
(Vᵃ)	(80.5)	(79.6)	(0.0)	(49.0)	(79.8)	(26.2)	(0.7)	(4.4)
2 Cocoa (GZ)	0.1	-0.2	–	-0.7	0.1	1.7	4.3	0.6
(Vᵇ)	(1557)	(1580)	–	(1038)	(1555)	(169)	(2)	(252)
3 Tea (GZ)	3.8	3.8	0.8	0.3	3.9	5.6	7.4	6.6
(V)	(1.9)	(1.9)	(0.1)	(0.5)	(1.6)	(1.1)	(0.1)	(0.2)
4 Sugar (GZ)	2.3	2.2	2.5	-0.5	2.9	4.0	0.6	1.6
(Vᵃ)	(91.7)	(97.6)	(23.3)	(25.1)	(55.9)	(54.8)	(18.6)	(17.7)
5 Beef & Veal (GZ)	2.2	2.2	1.7	1.2	2.7	3.3	2.6	2.8
(Vᵇ)	(46,698)	(46,555)	(71,009)	(20,628)	(16,449)	(16,474)	(9,240)	(9,454)
6 Rice (GZ)	2.6	2.6	0.9	0.1	2.8	2.8	1.0	0.4
(V)	(259.9)	(260.2)	(13.3)	(9.5)	(233.4)	(236.1)	(13.2)	(14.5)
7 Coarse Grains (GZ)	2.4	2.4	2.7	1.0	2.3	3.2	2.0	3.5
(Vᵃ)	(712.0)	(711.8)	(305.8)	(252.6)	(270.3)	(287.6)	(135.9)	(161.7)
8 Wheat (GZ)	3.2	3.2	4.1	2.6	4.5	4.9	0.7	1.6
(Vᵇ)	(444.5)	(443.7)	(153.4)	(89.3)	(163.4)	(208.5)	(127.7)	(145.9)
9 Oilseeds (GZ)	4.2	4.2	6.0	3.8	4.1	5.0	0.4	2.3
(V)	(45.7)	(45.4)	(13.8)	(13.7)	(27.2)	(26.4)	(4.7)	(5.3)
10 Tobacco (GZ)	2.0	2.0	0.8	1.3	2.7	2.7	1.3	1.3
(Vᵃ)	(5.4)	(5.4)	(1.4)	(1.8)	(3.3)	(2.8)	(0.7)	(0.8)

	1	2	3	4	5	6	7	8
Agricultural Raw Materials								
11 Cotton (GZ)	1.1	1.6	1.2	-1.7	0.5	3.3	3.1	0.8
(V[b]Z)	(14.4)	(14.4)	(2.6)	(3.2)	(8.5)	(8.6)	(3.2)	(2.7)
12 Jute (GZ)	2.0	2.4	0	-5.3	2.0	5.7	0.6	0.5
(V)	(4.0)	(4.1)	(0)	(0.7)	(3.9)	(3.1)	(0.1)	(0.4)
13 Rubber (GZ)	2.8	2.8	–	1.2	2.7	7.7	5.4	-1.0
(V[a])	(3.8)	(3.8)	–	(1.9)	(3.8)	(1.5)	(0.1)	(0.5)
Minerals and Metals								
14 Copper (GZ)	2.2	2.8	-0.8	1.7	4.0	7.1	4.0	4.4
(V[b])	(7.8)	(9.5)	(2.3)	(6.1)	(3.9)	(1.6)	(1.7)	(1.9)
15 Tin (GZ)	0.2	-0.4	1.2	-1.5	-0.2	1.6	4.0	1.7
(V)	(231.2)	(208.5)	(14.2)	(132.6)	(198.9)	(41.2)	(18.1)	(35.7)
16 Bauxite (GZ)	3.9	4.7	6.6	5.2	2.7	4.2	2.1	3.2
(V[a])	(82.6)	(35.0)	(33.9)	(22.1)	(48.6)	(8.1)	(10.1)	(4.7)
17 Iron Ore	1.3	1.4	-0.7	2.9	5.7	2.2	2.2	2.9
(V[b])	(801.9)	(302.0)	(440.4)	(324.7)	(174.2)	(265.1)	(265.0)	(284.0)
18 Manganese (GZ)	2.4	2.1	5.2	-0.6	2.3	7.4	1.9	2.7
(V)	(10.1)	(9.9)	(1.1)	(4.2)	(6.0)	(2.7)	(3.0)	(3.1)
19 Phosphate R (GZ)	5.3	5.3	4.8	3.4	6.7	9.9	3.9	6.0
(V[a])	(135.7)	(135.7)	(53.4)	(68.4)	(55.3)	(35.1)	(27.0)	(32.3)

Note: All volumes are in million tons, except where indicated by (a): 60 kg bags; (b): 1000 tons

P = Production; C = Consumption; V = Volume (1980); G = Growth: % p.a. by least squares

Source: World Bank Report No. 814/82, Price Prospects for Major Commodities, Volumes II-IV

consumption of food and beverages. Increases in manufacturing and processing could reduce the amount of commodities exported in crude form, replacing them with processed versions: instant coffee instead of beans, cotton cloth or shirts instead of cotton etc. The welfare implications for LDCs would be quite different if (b) were a more important factor than (a). As price elasticities of demand in world markets for most of the food and beverage products exported by LDCs are low a slowing of supplies could actually support prices and earnings above what they would have been with faster growth in LDCs' exports of tea, coffee or cocoa. Even where their exports are good substitutes for MDC commodities, where unconstrained price elasticities ought to be high, the artificial barriers to entry into MDC markets due to MDC protectionism would have the same effect of lowering any earnings from increased supplies. So if resources have been switched from supplying foreign markets to supplying home ones, any sacrifice of foreign exchange earnings may have been small compared with the gains from increased consumption and/or from added value in processing. As Table 2.7 makes clear, faster growth of consumption relative to production has been a major factor for most of the 18 commodities.

In fact there were a number of commodities where the quantities exported by LDCs grew less rapidly than for MDCs. The comparisons are available for 1961-1980 in Appendix A, Table A.2. Cereals provide a major example. Not only value but volumes exported of wheat, maize and even rice grew more slowly for LDCs. Rice exports from LDCs actually declined. The probable causes of this include faster population growth in LDCs and a higher income elasticity of demand for basic foodstuffs among people with relatively low incomes. Partly as a result of these two factors LDC food imports have been rising in recent years. As a group their share of imports of food rose from 20 per cent to 26 per cent between 1960 and 1981 (see Table 2.5 above). In addition to the relative demand factor it is also the case that cereal production in LDCs has only just been keeping a little ahead of population growth on average. In a number of African and Asian countries it has fallen behind that minimum. In contrast the high levels of protection and export subsidies given to agriculture in MDCs, together with technological developments, have led to a surge in cereal production which has produced embarrassingly large surpluses of grains.

LDC exporters of grain such as Argentina, Thailand and Burma have suffered by seeing their markets restricted and the international prices of their exports lowered. It is estimated that LDCs' cereal exports would be about 12 per cent higher in quantity and 20 per cent higher in value if the EECs' trade in grain were liberalised (Bale and Koester, 1983, p. 381).

When we turn from food to agricultural raw materials it would seem plausible that increased domestic manufacture of products using natural fibres or minerals as raw materials could explain their relative decline as exports. Unfortunately the evidence does not provide much support for this optimistic interpretation of events. For sisal, jute and wool, at least the growth in quantity of exports in processed forms was also sluggish (UNCTAD, 1979). For cotton, however, it is the case that production of manufactured textiles for both domestic consumption in LDCs and for export has been a significant cause of decline in the quantities of cotton exported. The same may well be true for some of the metals, where there is a clear trend away from exporting ores towards more refined versions of the material. (See Appendix A, Table A.2) The next stage of fabrication into metal products is well-advanced in countries such as India, China, Brazil and Malaysia.

Explanation (c) that protection in MDCs and MDC policies of subsidising agricultural exports are an important factor is supported by a number of empirical studies and statistical estimates of the cost to LDCs of the MDCs agricultural policies (Bale & Koester, Valdes and Zietz, 1980; Sampson and Snape, 1980; Matthews, 1985; World Bank, 1986). LDCs' exports of sugar, grains, meat, fats and oils, fruit and wine are all seriously affected, particularly by the policies of the EEC. As compared with a situation of free trade their exports are lower by many billions of dollars. Precise estimates of the costs to LDCs of the MDCs policies in trade in agricultural products are extremely difficult, particularly if one attempts a full general equilibrium analysis, allowing for repercussions on both exporting and importing LDCs, the resource shifts which would occur in all economies in both the agricultural and the manufacturing sectors as a result of the new structure of prices and opportunities which would result from free trade. Evidence on this question is considered in Chapter 6 below.

It is also difficult to assess the effects of LDCs' own protectionism on their primary commodity exports (d). Most LDCs have overvalued exchange rates, supported by controls on imports of manufactures. They also often have export taxes on commodity exports. The effects are to dampen severely the incentives to produce agricultural exports. As far as producers are concerned the prices of most of the primary goods they export are fixed in world markets in dollars or pounds. An overvalued exchange rate means they get less local currency per ton of jute or rice they export. If there is also an export tax the burden of paying that may fall largely on them. Only if their country is a large enough exporter of their product, or if a number of large exporters have similar export taxes, will the elasticity of demand be less than infinite and enable some part of the export tax to fall on the foreign buyers. But if it is the case that production for export, particularly of food and raw materials, is reduced for most LDCs then their export earnings for some of them may be higher than if they adopted free trade, because the price elasticity of demand facing them, as a group, for products such as coffee, tea and cocoa is likely to be well below unity. Even for others such as sugar, grains, fats and oils and non-ferrous metals, where the MDCs produce substitutes, their barriers to imports may so limit increases in LDC exports that any increase in quantity would result in a more than proportional drop in price; and consequently reduced export earnings. Examination of growth rates for production does not support the view that growth has been slower in LDCs than MDCs for most of the 18 commodities. (Table 2.7)

The final explanation we consider is (e), changes in LDCs' comparative advantage which could lead to a relative decline in their traditional exports. For many, if not most, LDCs this is happening. In terms of Hecksher-Ohlin theory their resource endowment in land and unskilled labour is declining relative to their endowment in physical and human capital as investment, education and transfers of technology take effect. This is most obvious in countries such as Korea, Taiwan, India and Pakistan, but is also true of countries like Brazil, Kenya and Ivory Coast. It is also encouraged by intra-firm trade where MDC transnationals set up subsidiaries to produce components for re-export to USA, Japan or EEC countries. Large retail organisations such as Sears-Roebuck in USA also increase the attractions of manufacturing as they provide technical assistance for production of clothing and sports goods while providing assured markets for finished products of labour intensive manufacturing industries. Their 'know-how' complements the cheap labour of the LDCs and this helps the shift from agriculture to manufacture. We cannot quantify these effects, but that they form part of the explanation for LDCs' declining share of primary commodity exports is sure (Hirsch, 1977, p. 121, Balassa, 1981, pp. 208-9, Helleiner, 1981).

TRADE AMONG DEVELOPING COUNTRIES AND TRADE WITH THE CENTRALLY PLANNED ECONOMIES

Trade among the LDCs is a tiny part of world trade. In 1960 it was 4.8 per cent. By 1970 it had dwindled to a mere 3.5 per cent. But the 1970s saw a sharp rise in its relative share to 7.1 per cent in 1980. In 1970 about 20 per cent of LDCs' exports and imports were to or from other developing countries. By 1980 this had increased to 26 per cent for exports and 30 per cent for imports. When mineral fuels are excluded the picture is modified somewhat. Then LDCs' share in world trade goes from 2.5 per cent in 1970 to 4.2 per cent

in 1980. Exports to other LDCs rise from 19.5 per cent of
LDCs' total exports in 1970 to 30.2 per cent in 1979, but
imports as a share of total non-oil imports only rose from 13.4
per cent to 17.9 per cent (UNCTAD, 1983, Table 28, p. 80).
   For the more recent period 1970-81 the structure of
LDCs' gross exports by the three major non-oil commodity
groups can be seen in Tables 2.8a and 2.8b 'Network of
World Exports'. In 1970 LDCs share of World exports of food
was 30.5 per cent, of which exports to other LDCs was 4.6
per cent, and to MDCs and CPEs was 22.7 per cent and 3.1
per cent respectively. (These numbers do not add precisely
to the total because of rounding.) In 1981 LDCs' share of
world food exports declined to 27.8 per cent with the drop
largely accounted for by exports to MDCs while the share
going to other LDCs and to CPEs both increased to 7.5 per
cent and 4.2 per cent respectively. In raw materials, metals
and ores LDCs' intra-trade rose as a proportion of world
exports but their exports to CPEs fell.
   Recession in the OECD industrial nations plus the growth
in their protectionism must account for much of these
changes, but the adoption of deliberate policies to encourage
intra-LDC trade may have played some part. Numerous regional groupings among LDCs to promote trade were set up in
the 1960s, but the evidence that they had much impact in
promoting interregional trade flows is fairly weak (UNCTAD,
1983 pp. 90-91 and Table 35). Some important causes of the
rise in the share of LDC commodity exports going to other
LDCs are the increased imports of OPEC and other oil-exporting LDCs and the increased demands for raw materials by the
Newly Industrialising Countries (NICs). Given the fall in real
oil prices and reduction in oil exports the first of these may
not provide much further help to LDC exports, but as the
NICs continue to grow and other LDCs move into that category the increased complementarity among LDCs' economies
should foster greater intra-LDC trade. However, recent
studies suggest that the prospects for dramatic increases in
LDC exports either to other LDCs or to CPEs are unlikely
(Bhagwati and Ruggie, 1984).

THE INDUSTRIAL NATIONS AND TRADE IN COMMODITIES

While trade in primary products is crucial to the prosperity of
many LDCs the MDCs are the dominant exporters of food,
agricultural raw materials and metals. This is clear from Table
2.8. They have moved from the position of being net importers of food in 1970 to a situation in 1981 where their net
exports are nearly six times those of the LDCs. The CPEs'
failures in food production are highlighted by the vast increase in their net imports of food from about $950 million to
$14.5 billion. (See Table 2.9 Net Exports and Imports by

Table 2.8a: Network of World Exports by Selected Commodity Groups and Regions of Origin and Destination (millions of dollars, f.o.b.) 1970 and 1981

Destination / Origin		WORLD 1.food	WORLD raw 2.mat.	WORLD metal, 3.ores	MDC 1.food	MDC raw 2.mat.	MDC metal, 3.ores	LDC 1.food	LDC raw 2.mat.	LDC metal, 3.ores	CPE 1.food	CPE raw 2.mat.	CPE metal, 3.ores
WORLD													
1 food	1970	47746			33213			7827			4533		
	81	220777			131003			59052			28915		
2 agricultural raw materials	70		18121			13442			2407			2233	
	81		69343			46170			12931			10160	
3 metal and ores	70			10457			8718			544			1096
	81			38351			28427			4600			4342
MDC													
1 food	1970	27098			20944			4892			1213		
	81	145094			92348			37891			13713		
2 agricultural raw materials	70		10596			8967			1079			515	
	81		41498			31659			6466			3370	
3 metal and ores	70			6084			5590			311			93
	81			21202			17089			2587			567
LDC													
1 food	1970	14557			10820			2187			1499		
	81	61301			34568			16651			9376		
2 agricultural raw materials	70		5468			3448			1170			845	
	81		16615			9689			4833			2019	
3 metal and ores	70			3247			2763			207			270
	81			12866			10272			1745			828

CPE

1 food	1970	4089	1449	797	1820
	81	14432	4087	4509	5826
2 agricultural raw materials	70	2058	1027	158	875
	81	11228	4820	1632	4774
3 metal and ores	70	1126	365	27	734
	81	4235	1067	270	2946

Notes: Commodity Groups: 1 - food: all food items including beverages, tobacco and edible oils and seeds (SITC 0+1+22+4)
2 - raw materials: all agricultural raw materials (SITC 2-(22+27+28)
3 - metal and ores: crude minerals, metallic ferrous ores, metal scrap and crude fertilisers
     (excluding iron and steel (SITC 67) and non-ferrous metals (SITC 68)) (SITC 27+28)

MDC: more developed countries
LDC: less developed countries
CPE: centrally planned economies - including Socialist countries in both Europe and Asia

Source: Handbook of International Trade and Statistics, Tables A2-A4, pp. A6-A14

31

Table 2.8b: Network of World Exports by Selected Commodity Groups and Regions of Origin and Destination (Percentage Shares of World Total for each Commodity Group) 1970 and 1981

Destination Origin			WORLD 1.food	WORLD 2.mat. raw	WORLD 3.ores metal,	MDC 1.food	MDC 2.mat. raw	MDC 3.ores metal,	LDC 1.food	LDC 2.mat. raw	LDC 3.ores metal,	CPE 1.food	CPE 2.mat. raw	CPE 3.ores metal,
WORLD														
1 food	1970		100.0			69.6			16.5			9.5		
	81		100.0			59.3			26.7			13.1		
2 agricultural	70			100.0			74.2			13.3			12.3	
raw materials	81			100.0			66.6			18.6			14.7	
3 metal and ores	70				100.00			83.4			5.2			10.5
	81				100.00			74.1			12.0			11.3
MDC														
1 food	1970		56.3			48.8			10.2			2.5		
	81		65.7			41.8			17.2			6.2		
2 agricultural	70			58.4			49.5			6.0			2.8	
raw materials	81			58.8			45.7			9.3			4.9	
3 metal and ores	70				58.2			53.5			3.0			0.8
	81				55.2			44.6			6.7			1.5
LDC														
1 food	1970		30.5			22.7			4.6			3.1		
	81		27.8			15.7			7.5			4.2		
2 agricultural	70			30.2			18.0			6.4			4.7	
raw materials	81			30.0			13.8			7.0			2.9	
3 metal and ores	70				31.0			26.4			2.0			2.6
	81				33.5			26.8			4.6			2.2

CPE

1 food	1970	8.6	3.3	1.7	3.8
	81	6.5	1.9	2.0	2.6
2 agricultural raw materials	70	11.4	5.7	0.9	4.8
	81	16.2	7.0	2.3	6.9
3 metal and ores	70	10.8	3.5	0.2	7.0
	81	11.2	2.8	0.7	7.7

(LDC's share in World export of food in 1981 was 27.8%, of which, intra-trade accounted for 7.5% and trade with MDC and CPE, 15.7% and 4.2% respectively.)

Note: Figures in columns and rows do not add precisely in totals because of rounding, errors and omissions

Source: The above shares are calculated, using the data given in Table 2.8a (see note at the end of this table)

33

Table 2.9: Net Exports (+) and Imports (–) by Primary Commodity Groups and Regions (millions of dollars, f.o.b.) 1970 and 1981

Destination Origin		WORLD 1.food	WORLD 2.mat. raw mat.	WORLD 3.ores metal,	MDC 1.food	MDC 2.mat. raw mat.	MDC 3.ores metal,	LDC 1.food	LDC 2.mat. raw mat.	LDC 3.ores metal,	CPE 1.food	CPE 2.mat. raw mat.	CPE 3.ores metal,
WORLD													
1 food	1970	–			6115			-6680			944		
	81	–			-14041			-2249			14483		
2 agricultural raw materials	70		–			2846			-3061			175	
	81		–			4672			-3684			-1068	
3 metal and ores	70			–			2634			-2703			-30
	81			–			7225			-8266			-57
MDC													
1 food	1970	-6115			–			-5928			-236		
	81	14041			–			3323			9626		
2 agricultural raw materials	70		-2846			–			-2369			-512	
	81		-4677			–			-3223			-1450	
3 metal and ores	70			-2634			–			-2952			-272
	81			-7225			–			-2685			-500
LDC													
1 food	1970	6680			5928			–			702		
	81	2249			-3323			–			4867		
2 agricultural raw materials	70		3051			2369			–			687	
	81		3684			3223			–			387	
3 metal and ores	70			2703			2452			–			243
	81			8266			7685			–			558

CPE				
1 food	1970	-444	236	-702
	81	-14483	-9626	-4867
2 agricultural raw materials	70	-175	512	-387
	81	1068	1450	-687
3 metal and ores	70	30	272	-241
	81	-57	500	-558

Comments: 1 - MDC was net importer of food in 1970 became net exporter of food in 1981.
MDC imported raw materials and metal and ores from LDC and CPE

2 - LDC, though not exporter of food in both years (1970 and 1981) from the WORLD, was a net food importer from MDC.
For other commodity groups, LDC remained net exporter to MDC and CPE in both years

3 - CPE imported food from both MDC and LDC, exported raw materials and metal and ores to MDC but imported them from
LDC in both 1970 and 1981

This Table gives a better picture of (net) trade flows

Source: The figures for net imports and exports are obtained, using data in Table 2.8a

35

Primary Commodity Groups and Regions.) The developing countries have shifted from net exports to MDCs in 1970 of $5.9 billion to net imports of $3.2 billion in 1981, but have increased their exports to CPEs from $0.7 billion in 1970 to $4.9 billion in 1981.

In agricultural raw materials, metals and ores no such dramatic changes have occurred. The MDCs continue to be the main importers and LDCs the main exporters. (Table 2.9)

The quite dramatic change in the pattern of trade in food products calls for some further comment. We have already dealt with some of the main factors in discussing the reasons for the decline in LDCs' share in world exports of primary commodities. Regarded from the viewpoint of the MDCs the explanations remain much the same. The largest factor has been the faster growth of exports from both the EEC and USA. Table 2.10 shows how the Community's share of world exports of food has risen from 26 per cent in 1970 to 31 per cent in 1981 while for the USA the same statistic rose from 15 per cent to 19 per cent. As far as the EEC is concerned, this is the (unintended) result of the Common Agricultural Policy. European farmers have responded to protection, import levies and export subsidies with huge surpluses in grain, milk products, meat, fruit and wine. While these have brought benefits to some food importing LDCs and CPEs they have probably wrought much greater ill-effects on the majority of LDCs, by damaging their exports, destabilising world food prices and dampening the incentives to produce more food, they have lowered agricultural investment, employment and incomes in many poor countries. They have also inflicted damage upon the efficient agricultural producing nations of Australasia and North America.

Both USA and EEC have also expanded their shares of agricultural raw materials exports for much the same reasons. But the USA's share of mineral exports has fallen while EEC's has risen only slightly.

Table 2.11 shows the converse with USA and EEC food and agricultural raw material imports declining as a proportion of world imports.

CONCLUSION

It is difficult to assess the relative importance of each of these factors in explaining the declining share of developing countries in world exports of agricultural and mineral products (excluding oil). To some extent the change is a natural and beneficial adjustment to changing circumstances. As economies mature they progress from the production of basic foods and raw materials to the production of manufactures. But the fall in LDCs' share in exports of primary products involves other causes. Faster growth in population which

Table 2.10: Shares of USA and EEC in World Exports of Major Commodity Groups

Commodity Groups	USA 1970	1975	1981	EEC 1970	1975	1980
1 All food items	14.9	18.1	18.9	26.1	29.3	31.1
2 Agricultural raw materials	11.5	13.0	14.0	15.1	17.3	16.2
3 Minerals and metals	8.7	7.1	6.5	31.7	35.0	32.7
4 Fuels	5.5	2.6	2.2	14.6	9.3	12.1
5 Manufactures	15.7	14.8	14.7	45.7	45.4	40.0
6 All products	13.7	12.2	11.5	35.9	33.9	30.7

Source: UNCTAD, Handbook of International Trade and Development Statistics 1984 Supplement (TD/Stat.12), Tables 3.2 and 3.4, pp. 73-4 and pp. 84-5

Table 2.11: Shares of USA and EEC in World Imports of Major Commodity Groups

Commodity Groups	USA 1970	USA 1975	USA 1981	EEC 1970	EEC 1975	EEC 1980
1 All food items	13.2	3.7	7.9	49.5	46.4	41.4
2 Agricultural raw materials	9.7	8.8	8.4	48.0	47.5	43.5
3 Minerals and metals*	13.2	10.5	14.5	51.1	43.7	40.0
4 Fuels	11.5	16.1	17.7	46.6	40.8	40.1
5 Manufactures	12.9	9.6	12.2	44.0	42.5	40.1
6 All products	12.5	10.7	13.0	45.9	42.7	40.4

* include iron and steel and non-ferrous metals

Source: as for Table 2.8

reduced surpluses available for export, economic policies which shifted the domestic terms of trade against agriculture, policies in agriculture in some countries which forced farmers into co-operatives or collectives or sought to grow crops and animals on large state-controlled farms, have all had some influence in reducing the rate of growth of exportable crops and increased the need for food imports. In some countries the nationalisation of foreign owned mines and unilateral changes in corporation taxes or on rights to repatriate profits have frightened off foreign investment in the development of mines in LDCs. Some of these can be regarded as self-inflicted wounds upon LDCs' capacity to meet their own needs for food and to generate surpluses of exportable commodities. Many developing countries have learned from their mistakes, changed the emphasis of their policies from an inward-looking to an export-promoting direction, given incentives to their farmers and increased the availability of new technology in the form of new and improved seeds, fertilisers and plant protection. The countries of China, India, Sri Lanka, the Philippines and Ivory Coast are examples of the successes which can be achieved in agriculture by such measures (World Bank, 1986 Annex Table 6). Unfortunately world recession and MDC protectionism are reducing the benefits they would otherwise have received.

Of the various causes of the declining share of LDCs in commodity exports which we have rehearsed above, the best documented and almost certainly the most damaging to LDCs is the agricultural policies of the OECD nations. Their barriers to imports and subsidised exports have inflicted serious losses of foreign exchange and economic welfare upon those developing countries which are net exporters of agricultural products. The policies of the EC, USA and Japan have lowered the quantities of LDC exports which they import, reduced international prices and displaced LDC exports from third markets. The commodities affected include sugar, fats and oils, grains, meat, tobacco, fruit and wines, all of which are important to at least some developing countries. Internal taxes on the beverages, tea and coffee, and taxes on cocoa or chocolate in MDCs also lower LDCs' earnings. Tariff escalation which increases the protection given to processing raw materials in MDCs, denies LDCs' opportunities of raising local value added and increasing employment from the production of fabricated metals and refined and packaged food-products and beverages.

One possible route for LDCs faced by the MDC barriers is to increase trade with other developing countries and with the centrally planned economies. While offering some prospects of beneficial trade growth one cannot be optimistic about this compensating for their declining share vis a vis the MDCs.

The 1970s have seen a remarkable growth in the MDCs' share of world agricultural exports, but this is much more a reflection of deliberate and unintended distortions of incentives, especially in EEC and Japan, than of a change in comparative advantage.

Chapter Three

THE LONG-TERM ISSUES

LONG-TERM TRENDS IN THE TERMS OF TRADE BETWEEN PRIMARY COMMODITIES AND MANUFACTURES:

THEORETICAL CONSIDERATIONS

For long the debates on the trends in the terms of trade between primary commodities and manufactures have been fast and furious. Until 1950, it was generally accepted that diminishing returns in agriculture and mining would cause a tendency for the prices of commodities to rise relative to the prices of manufactures. Then, Raul Prebisch (1950) and Hans Singer (1950) independently launched the hypothesis of secular deterioration in the terms of trade between primary exports of developing countries, the 'periphery', and their manufactured imports from industrialised developed countries, the 'centre'. By focusing attention on this burden to developing countries, they influenced many economists and politicians to advocate protectionist and import substituting policies and countervailing use of market power (e.g. cartels) to improve the LDCs' terms of trade. This has been one of the issues at the centre of international economic diplomacy ever since the first session of the United Nations Conference on Trade and Development (UNCTAD I) in 1961.

The arguments in support of the Prebisch-Singer hypothesis have been challenged by many authors. But before examining these arguments, the concept of the terms of trade and policy implications of changes in them need clarification.

Policy and Welfare Implications

Normally the terms of trade are understood to be the 'commodity' or 'net barter' terms of trade (NBTT) - i.e. the ratio of the price index of primary products (numerator) to that of manufactures (denominator). A deterioration implies that the price index of primary products declines relative to that of manufactures. As defined, these terms of trade have obvious welfare implications which can be conveniently discussed in terms of a simple example. Suppose raw cotton and tractors stand for primary products and manufactures respectively. A deterioration in the commodity terms of trade means an increase in the number of cotton bales that need to be exported to pay for an imported tractor. In the absence of productivity increases, producers of cotton facing a deterioration in the terms of trade would have to devote more resources to cotton production to pay for the same number of tractors and would therefore be worse off. But the deterioration in the terms of trade could be the result of an increase in productivity in cotton. If so, the resources devoted to cotton production in exchange for a tractor may not increase and may even decrease. The NBTT concept is not a sufficient measure of welfare change because it takes no account of changes in productivity.

A more appropriate concept in such a case would be the 'single-factoral' terms of trade (SFTT) which attempts to measure the amount of imports which could be purchased by a unit of factors of production. A deterioration in SFTT suggests an increase in the amount of resources needed in cotton production to pay for a tractor. The SFTT is a good measure of the change in the <u>absolute</u> welfare of cotton producers; but not of their <u>relative</u> welfare - i.e. relative to tractor producers. Productivity may increase in both cotton and tractor production. Consequently the SFTT may improve for both cotton and tractor producers with the improvement being greater for either. Hence, if our interest is in relative welfare, or on the case for or against specialisation on primary commodities, SFTT has an obvious shortcoming. An appropriate concept is one which takes account of productivity changes in both products. This is the 'double-factoral' terms of trade (DFTT) which refers to the ratio of the amount of resources used in producing a tractor to that used to produce the number of cotton bales needed to pay for a tractor. Thus, a deterioration in the DFTT would imply that more resources in primary exporting countries are exchanged for a unit of resources in the manufacture exporting countries.

There is yet another concept involving the terms of trade. Instead of being concerned with the volumes of resources involved in trade, cotton producers may be concerned with the total number of tractors they could obtain in return for the total number of cotton bales they sell - that is to say, the import purchasing power of their export. A concept which measures this directly is the 'income' terms of trade (ITT) which differs from NBTT in that it takes account of the volume of cotton sold. Since in practice it is the ability of developing countries to pay for their imports out of their export earnings that is important in the development context, the ITT is a concept just as useful as the NBTT.

Despite its shortcomings, the NBTT concept dominates in actual conferences and trade dialogues. To some extent, this is because in many low-income countries, productivity increases in commodity production have been relatively slow. For them, even a small annual decrease in the long term trends in their commodity terms of trade would probably reduce their ability to pay for imports and so damage their prospects of growth. Such a burden imposed on the poorest countries would be a serious matter. Another reason for the dominance of the NBTT concept is the sheer difficulty of finding an acceptable measure of productivity change [1].

Reasons for Deteriorating Terms of Trade: Prebisch-Singer Thesis

To provide support for the view, which appears to be held by many spokesmen of developing countries, that the terms of trade of developing countries (being largely primary exporters) are bound to deteriorate, progressively and inexorably, so long as the distribution of economic power remains as it is at present, Prebisch and Singer launched a theory based on relative trade union strength and on differences in the structure of markets for manufactures and for commodities. In view of its dramatic influence on subsequent international debates and policies, a brief outline of this theory is given below.

Prebisch (1949) found that productivity increase was greater in the 'centre' - representing industrialised countries - than in the 'periphery' - representing primary-producing countries - and yet, contrary to the prediction of orthodox economic theory, statistical evidence indicated a long-term trend of the terms of trade against (rather than in favour of) the 'periphery'. To explain these facts, he developed the following argument; in the 'centre' trade unions are more able to secure for themselves the benefits of increased productivity; thus, in the upswing, prices are pushed up by trade union action, while in the downswing they are kept up by union resistance to wage cuts. Singer (1950) put forward a similar argument, that increases in productivity in the industrialised countries accrued to the producers as higher incomes, while in the primary-producing countries such increases in productivity caused a reduction in prices. Therefore, with technological progress and productivity growth, the terms of trade of primary products deteriorated progressively. The industrialised countries had the best of both worlds as producers of manufactures and consumers of primary products, whereas the developing countries had the worst of both worlds as consumers of manufactures and producers of raw materials.

The essence of the Prebisch-Singer explanation lies in an asymmetry in the responses of prices to productivity increases. Thus in the 'periphery', it is assumed that competition between many small producers governs the price of primary products and market clearing mechanisms force the price down when productivity increases, whereas para-market forces (e.g. trade unions or oligopolistic pricing practices) prevent this from happening in the 'centre'. However, the conclusion that the terms of trade move against primary products over time has often been disputed [2]. For example, it can be argued that the cheapening of primary products relative to manufactures would increase demand for primaries – a process which would stop only when the original equilibrium relative price had been restored. To illustrate this point, let us assume that the demands for primary commodities and manufactures grow at the same rate so that the unchanged terms of trade is sustainable. Suppose now the initial price response to the increase in productivity is asymmetrical as argued by Prebisch and Singer e.g. P_m – the price of manufactures – remains constant and P_c – that of primaries – falls. The terms of trade of primaries deteriorate but the market will not be cleared. There will be excess demand for primaries and excess supply of manufactures. If we then assume that the rates of growth of outputs are fixed so that output changes are excluded as a possible adjustment market clearing mechanism, then it follows that P_c must rise above the level at which it fell initially and will go on rising until the initial terms of trade are restored, because only then will the excess demand disappear. Therefore, the asymmetry in the price responses to productivity increase by itself is insufficient to produce the deterioration in the terms of trade.

However, output changes in practice are a possible adjustment mechanism. If we follow classical balance of payment theory to assume that the (export) supplies of primaries and manufactures are perfectly price elastic, then the deterioration in the primary terms of trade along Prebisch-Singer's lines will simply cause an increase in the traded volume of primaries and a decrease in that of manufactures. The price of primaries may then be determined by the level of subsistence wage and productivity and that of manufactures by para-market forces and the resulting price ratio simply determines the ratio of the traded quantities and the trade balance.

Reasons for Deteriorating Terms of Trade: Others
Apart from the asymmetry in price responses to productivity changes, other possible reasons for deterioration in the primary commodity's terms of trade are: first, primary commodities face a downward demand bias because (i) the income elasticity of its demand for them is lower than for manufactures [3] and (ii) technical progress has the effect of con-

tinually increasing the supply of synthetic substitutes for natural products and reducing the raw material content of manufactures and second, they face an upward supply bias because of the existence in the periphery of a reservoir of idle labour which provides an unlimited source of labour supply to the production of primary commodities at some initial real wage. The long-term decline of the terms of trade for primary products can thus be explained in terms of an excess of the growth of supply over demand.

A deterioration in the trends in terms of trade between commodities and manufactures may induce a worsening in those between the less developed countries (LDC) and the more developed countries (MDC), in so far as the former are more dependent on primary exports than the latter. However, these two terms of trade are not the same. The secular terms of trade between LDCs and MDCs have also been found to deteriorate [4] and two of the reasons given are: (i) lack of adaptability and bad luck on the part of LDCs and (ii) low wages in primary production fixed at peasant-earning level in LDCs but not in MDCs [5].

Thus, low income elasticity of demand for commodities, a decreasing material content of industrial production and the improvement of synthetic substitutes combine to slow down the growth in the demand for primaries while the pressure of 'unlimited supply of labour' on the real wage (owing to the existence of a large reservoir of idle or unemployed labour) in developing countries and productivity increase in their exports contribute to the growth in the supply of primaries. Together these factors explain the deterioration in the terms of trade. But movements in the terms of trade affect the balance of payments and cause changes in the exchange rate or in incomes to restore equilibrium to the balance of payments. These in turn affect the terms of trade. In other words, the terms of trade, exchange rate, income and balance of payments are all dependent, yet to our knowledge their interrelationships have not been explained clearly in the literature.

A Simple Model

A simple model of two countries and two products developed by Johnson (1954) to provide a theoretical explanation of chronic balance of payments disequilibria in general and a meaningful concept of 'dollar shortage' prevailing at the time can be extended to explore the arguments more systematically. The mathematical analysis based on the Johnson Model is set out in Appendix B. Here, a brief presentation of the gist of the argument is given.

We assume two countries I and II. Country I exports only commodities and II only manufactures. A 'real' improvement in country I's trade balance occurs when (1) its exchange rate appreciates, (2) the price of its exports rises relative to its imports or (3) the quantity of its exports demanded rises relative to the quantity of imports it demands. An increase in any one of these is sufficient to improve the 'real' trade balance provided the other two remain stationary (or increase).

The quantity of country I's exports is determined by the income in country II and by the relative price of I's export. The quantity of I's imports is determined by its own income and the relative price. There are no supply constraints. Supply elasticities are infinite.

Some Implications of the Model

Let us now examine the contention that the asymmetry in the response of the price of commodities and manufactures to increases in productivity is not, by itself, sufficient to cause deterioration in country I's terms of trade. Let us assume that starting from equilibrium both countries grow at the same rate and that the income elasticity of demand for commodities and manufactures are both equal to unity. That would imply an equal increase in the quantity demanded stemming from the income change. But because productivity increases in commodity production result in a fall in their price while it does not cause a fall in the price of manufactures we have to ask what will be the effect on the terms of trade when all the adjustments which result from this have worked through and equilibrium has been reachieved. It depends on price elasticities and on whether the countries are operating with a fixed exchange rate or a flexible one.

The Flexible Exchange Rate Case. Take first the case of a flexible exchange rate. Then if the 'Marshall-Lerner' conditions are met, that the sum of the price elasticities of demand for exports and imports exceed unity, the relative fall in country I's export price would tend to produce a balance of trade surplus for country I. But, with a flexible exchange rate, the increase in demand for country I's currency would cause it to appreciate until the balance of trade was restored, which would happen when the appreciation in the exchange rate was exactly proportional to the fall in the relative price of the commodity in terms of domestic currency in country I. Consumers in country I would buy more of their exportable commodity at a lower price but the international price would be as it was before the productivity change took place. The terms of trade would be as they were.

Suppose the sum of the elasticities fall short of unity. Then the fall in the relative price of the commodity would worsen the trade balance of country I causing the exchange rate to depreciate which would worsen its trade balance still further. In this perverse case the appropriate response of country I would be to appreciate its exchange rate deliberately to avoid the trade deficit for in this case too the terms of trade would not alter.

The Fixed Exchange Rate Case. Here the asymmetric productivity effect causes the commodity price to fall relative to the manufacture. If the price elasticities sum to more than unity, country I's balance of trade improves and II's worsens. Country II can finance its continued trade deficit with country I to the amount equal to the capital inflow from country I (in the form of repatriation of profits and dividends, etc.). If it does not receive sufficient amounts of capital inflow from country I to maintain a given trade deficit, its income growth may have to be reduced to produce the required reduction in its trade deficit. However, such an income adjustment will affect only the size of the deficit and not the terms of trade.

If the sum of the price elasticities of demand is less than unity the initial change in relative prices worsens country I's trade balance. If a policy of appreciating the exchange rate is ruled out, country I suffers not only a decline in its terms of trade but a worsening balance of trade and possibly reduced income, insofar as it is required to make the adjustments as a deficit country.

Thus, asymmetry of price responses to productivity increases along Prebisch-Singer's line could and would by itself produce a deterioration in the terms of trade under a fixed exchange rate in the context of the Johnson model. There would also be a deterioration or an improvement in the real trade balance depending on whether the sum of price elasticities is less than or greater than unity. In the case of the sum being less than unity, the periphery may find itself having a trade deficit as well as a deterioration in its terms of trade. Moreover, because the burden of adjustment customarily falls on trade deficit countries, the periphery may then have to pursue a deflationary policy to remove the trade deficit and consequently reduce its income growth rate below what it would otherwise be, given the rate of productivity increase. Prebisch-Singer's asymmetry, however, cannot affect the trade balance equilibrium terms of trade, under a flexible exchange rate. Any initial affect on the terms of trade brought about by the asymmetry will be fully offset by the opposite movement in the exchange rate.

The More General Case. To illustrate the sensitivity of the terms of trade to differences in the income elasticity of demand for primary commodities vis-a-vis manufactures, let us assume that country I's income elasticity of demand for manufactures is 1.0 while country II's for commodities is 0.8, the sum of the price elasticities is 1.5 and both countries' rate of growth is 2.5 per cent per annum, the terms of trade of country I would deteriorate at 1 per cent per annum with a flexible exchange rate (see Appendix B p.377). This would be quite sufficient to explain a deterioration of the 1870-1938 order.

In general, the trade balance equilibrium terms of trade would deteriorate if the growth rate in the demand for primary commodities is less than that in the demand for manufactures over time and the sum of price elasticities exceeds unity. The closer the sum is to unity, the greater is the effect of a given difference between the two demand growth rates on the terms of trade. In determining the demand, income elasticities are important. The equilibrium terms of trade could remain constant, even if income in the centre increases twice as fast as that in the periphery, if the income elasticity of the demand for primary commodities is half of that of the demand for manufactures.

While economies of scale, technological progress and capital accumulation - all would contribute to the growth rate of productivity, diminishing returns associated with fixed land resources would reduce it. Hence, the limits to growth argument in favour of an improvement in the primary terms of trade would suggest a lower income growth rate in the periphery. Technological progress in the centre may not only increase its productivity, but also may reduce the income elasticity of its demand for primary commodities if it increases the supply of synthetic substitutes and reduces the material content of manufactures.

Developing Countries' Terms of Trade

As often pointed out, the terms of trade of commodities are not the same as those of developing countries. Many developing countries import considerable amounts of food, oil and other natural raw materials and many others (e.g. India, Taiwan, Korea, Singapore, Hong Kong, etc.) export considerable amounts of manufactures. Similarly, several developed countries (e.g. Canada, Australia, New Zealand) are major exporters of commodities. Indeed the industrially developed nations' share of primary commodity exports, including oil is greater than that of LDCs. (See chapter 2) Furthermore, the terms of trade of different primary commodities exported by developing countries may have experienced widely different long-term trends. As a consequence, the terms of trade of individual developing countries could also differ considerably. If so, the deterioration of the terms of trade of developing countries as a group can to a large extent be attributed to

the fact that the economies of most of them are not sufficiently adaptable or flexible to allow a major switch into the
production of commodities which have more favourable price
trends.

Therefore, while recognising the importance of the
primary commodity terms of trade in the determination of the
terms of trade of developing countries, it is also important to
recognise that the terms of trade of individual developing
countries and those of individual commodities may have widely
different trends. To the extent that this is the case, the
terms of trade of primary commodities as a group and those of
developing countries as a group will lose most of their significance in a discussion of remedial policies or measures. The
correct approach would then be to examine commodity by
commodity and country by country in one's attempt to deal
with problems associated with a secular decline in the terms
of trade.

On the other hand, if asymmetrical price response to
productivity increases along Prebisch-Singer lines generally
exists and plays an important role in determining prices then
one would expect the variation of the trends of terms of trade
within the primary commodities group would be small relative
to the trend of the terms of trade of commodities vis-a-vis
manufactures as a group and the focus of attention on the
trend in the primary terms of trade would therefore be justified.

ANALYSIS OF HISTORICAL TRENDS

In this section, we turn from theory to have a look at the
facts or supposed facts. The questions for discussion are: (i)
Is there a genuine trend in the world-wide commodity terms
of trade over the period 1870s to 1938? (ii) What is the trend
for the seventy-year-period starting from 1900? (iii) Over the
period 1872-1952, do the movements in the price indices vary
among commodity groups and among individual countries? If
they do not, the movements in the world-wide terms of trade
between commodities and manufactures - at an aggregate level
- will not yield useful or meaningful policy implications and
can be positively misleading as a guide to policy if they
display a significant diversity. (iv) Finally, what trends can
be observed in the terms of trade and unit value indices, at
both aggregate and disaggregate levels, for the more recent
period, 1950-1982? Here, we shall consider not only commodity
groups but also individual commodities of importance to international trade. The period 1870s-1938 is chosen because it
was used in Prebisch (1950) and on it much of the debate
centres. The period 1900-1970 is chosen because it has the
same length and conveniently excludes the first oil shock
(1973-4).

The Net Barter Terms of Trade between Primary Commodities and Manufactures for 1870s - 1938 Period

The international interest in the terms of trade issues renewed by the Prebisch-Singer thesis led naturally to controversy over the validity of its statistical base. Prebisch (1950) relied on the evidence from the net barter terms of trade (NBTT) of the United Kingdom for the whole of its merchandise trade. Using two partially overlapping series (those of Schlote and the Board of Trade) [6], he produced an index for the period 1876-80 to 1938 which showed a clear secular improvement in the United Kingdom terms of trade. He inferred from this that there was a world-wide secular deterioration in the NBTT of traded primary products as Britain was the most important exporter of manufactures and importer of primary products for a large part of this period.

Prebisch's inference from this data was subject to several criticisms: (i) the United Kingdom NBTT were not representative of the industrial countries as a whole and hence its inverse could hardly be used as a proxy for the terms of trade [7]. (ii) primary products imported by industrialised countries included commodities predominantly produced and exported by developed countries. (iii) exports were valued f.o.b. whereas imports were valued c.i.f. and so the improvement in the United Kingdom's NBTT could be due partly or even wholly to a reduction in transport or insurance costs and not to a relative fall in the prices received by primary producers [8]. (iv) as the improvements in the quality of manufactures and the introduction of new ones are not adequately taken into account, the price index of manufactures is biased upwards and thereby contributes wholly or partly to a deterioration in the NBTT of primaries [9].

Although plausible these criticisms may not be significant in practice. Are they sufficiently supported by empirical evidence to amount to a refutation of the statistical inference of deterioration? Spraos (1980) attempted to resolve this question. His short answer was that 'a deteriorating trend is detectable in the data, but its magnitude is smaller than suggested by Prebisch's choice of series' [10]. His penetrating assessment of the empirical significance of the criticisms is summarised below.

Is the evidence drawn from the United Kingdom misleading? A combined NBTT of the industrialised countries of Europe (starting in the 1870s) with United Kingdom netted out - produced by Kindleberger (1956) showed that unlike the United Kingdom, other European countries experienced no significant trend in their NBTT up to the Second World War. Lipsey (1963, pp. 451-2) produced a NBTT between United States' imported primaries and exported manufactures which appears to have no trend. The terms of trade of primaries vis-à-vis manufactures of seven European countries - produced by Morgan (1959-60) moved so differently that no generalisation could be made. It appears therefore that United Kingdom evidence was unrepresentative of developed countries as a whole.

Three more representative series are (i) the League's series (ii) Lewis series and (iii) UN series (see Table 3.1). Although the League's series was also based on British data up to 1929, there were several differences: (i) the price index of manufactures was based on both British exports and British imports of manufactures, the latter included as a proxy for manufactures of non-British origin and (ii) for 1929 and later years the coverage was extended further by using world trade data compiled by the League of Nations. Since the League series suggests an annual rate of decrease of 0.9 per cent, it seems that Prebisch exaggerated the downward trend for primary products but the downward trend nevertheless appears to be confirmed.

Lewis (1952) tried to improve on the League series by incorporating the prices of imports and exports of manufactures of the United States and in other ways. His series turns out to correlate highly with the League series but suggests a slightly lower annual decline rate of 0.5 per cent. The UN Secretariat subsequently produced a more systematic and conceptually homogeneous series. The UN series measures the unit value of worldwide exports of SITC classes 5-8. This SITC dichotomy approximates better, but still not very accurately, the commodities/manufactures distinction. The UN series shows greater variation and suggests an annual rate of decrease of 0.7 per cent for 1900-38 period. Thus the leap from the evidence of United Kingdom NBTT to an inference about the world-wide terms of trade between primaries and manufactures was not misleading as to direction but did give an exaggerated impression of the magnitude of the deterioration.

Available evidence does not suggest a lower rate of deterioration of the NBTT for the narrower range of primaries originating predominantly in developing countries. The data for the unit value of US agricultural exports and imports assembled by Lipsey (1963, pp. 151-2) reveal a rate of increase for exports and a rate of decrease for imports. This suggests that the worldwide NBTT for primary commodities would deteriorate more rather than less if the primary commodities important in U.S. agricultural exports are excluded. The unit value index for industrial Europe's combined exports and imports of primaries and the unit value index for industrial Europe's imports of primaries from 'other' groups of countries, constructed by Kindleberger (1956, p. 265), show a cumulative decrease rate of 22 per cent and 38 per cent respectively for the period 1872-1938, and hence suggest that

51

Table 3.1: Approximations to Net Barter Terms of Trade between Primary Products and Manufactures up to 1938 (price or unit value of primary products – price or unit value of manufactures: 1913 = 100)

Year	Prebisch (1)	League (2)	Lewis (3)	UN (4)	Year	Prebisch (1)	League (2)	Lewis (3)	UN (4)
1871			103.0		1901			96.1	85
1872			105.2		1902			96.1	88
1873			106.7		1903	101	96	96.0	90
1874			105.5		1904			94.1	90
1875			103.2		1905			92.9	93
1876			103.2		1906			97.1	90
1877	119	107	105.9		1907			98.3	88
1878			102.8		1908	102	97	93.5	93
1879			99.8		1909			95.0	96
1880			100.0		1910			96.0	100
1881			101.6		1911			98.2	103
1882	122	106	103.6		1912	101	100	100.3	100
1883			100.5		1913			100.0	100
1884			97.8						
1885			96.0						
1886			92.6		1921	71	69	70.5	65
1887	115	100	94.5		1922	76	75	75.9	76
1888			95.9		1923	78	83	90.6	87
1889			97.6		1924	82	88	92.4	88
1890			95.6		1925	84	90	93.7	98

Year	(1)	(2)	(3)	(4)
1891	95.5			
1892	93.4			
1893	95.5	97		107
1894	92.8			
1895	89.2			
1896	90.1			
1897	92.3	99		104
1898	93.5			
1899	94.8			
1900	98.0		80	
1926	95.5	91.2	88	82	91
1927	93.4	93.0	91	82	93
1928		89.2	88	84	93
1929		88.9	86	84	91
1930		78.6	77	76	72
1931		70.5	68	69	64
1932		65.1	65	69	60
1933		66.5	65	67	61
1934		72.1	70	69	68
1935		73.2	72	70	70
1936		77.1	74	72	76
1937		81.4	79	76	82
1938		74.7	73	70	68

Sources: Column (1). United Nations, Economic and Social Council, Post War Price Relations in Trade between Under-Developed and Industrialised Countries (New York, 1949) (mimeo), later published as Relative Price of Exports and Imports of Underdeveloped Countries (Lake Success, New York, 1949)
Column (2). As for column (1). Based on League of Nations, Industrialisation and Foreign Trade (Geneva, 1945)
Column (3). W.A. Lewis, 'World production, prices and trade, 1870-1960', Manchester School of Economic and Social Studies (1952), vol. 20, pp. 105-38
Column (4). United Nations, Statistical Yearbook 1969
(Reproduced from Spraos (1980), Table 1))

the primary goods exported mainly by developing countries have experienced a bigger fall.

Since the NBTT of primaries are apparently defined to be the c.i.f. import price of primaries divided by the f.o.b. export price of manufactures, it appears that a fall in freight costs would affect the c.i.f. price and hence the terms of trade. Indeed, Ellsworth (1956) produced evidence showing a sharp decline in freight costs brought about by the advent of the steamship in the last quarter of the nineteenth century and argued that the whole of the apparent deterioration of the NBTT of primaries in the period 1871-1905 could be explained by this factor. However, a decrease in the freight costs would not necessarily cause a deterioration in the terms of trade of commodities [11]. A decrease in freight costs which is proportionally not greater than the decrease in the f.o.b. price would not cause the c.i.f. price to fall at a greater rate than the f.o.b. price. Since the Sauerbeck price index and the Isserlis (1938) freights index tread a parallel course on the graph, Spraos (1980, p. 116) was right to conclude that there would be no valuation bias, in the sense that an f.o.b. and a c.i.f. index would not behave differently. The charge of a valuation bias for the relevant period as a whole appears to be also refuted because a bias in the middle of the period is cancelled in later years.

It has often been asserted but with little or no factual demonstration that quality improvements were greater for manufactures than for primaries. But quality improvements can take the form of changes in the proportion of high grades as well as in improving physical properties resulting from technical progress. For example, the proportion of Kenyan coffee beans of highest quality (AA) harvested was 0.2 per cent in 1957-8 and 16.3 per cent in 1964-5 (Krug and Poerch, 1968, p. 133). The proportion of Greek cotton output with a staple length of 28 mm or more was only 11.3 per cent in 1954 and became as much as 97.3 per cent in 1970 (US Department of Agriculture, 1971). Because of this quality improvements in commodities can be underestimated. If quality improvements are liable to be under-allowed for on both sides, no presumption can be made a priori concerning a bias in the terms of trade from this source.

It can be shown that by ignoring the change in the grade composition of each commodity in a construction of its unit value index, the rate of commodity price increase is overstated or that price decrease is understated [12]. Similarly, it can be shown that ignoring quality improvements in manufactures overstates their price increases. Thus, whether there was quality bias in the NBTT series is not self-evident but remains an issue for research.

The Terms of Trade for 1900-7 Period

Apparently, the only series which covers this period, including decades on either side of World War II, is that published by the United Nations. Spraos fitted a trend to this series over the entire period and found a positive growth rate which is statistically insignificant. Believing that this is not the best series available for after the Second World War years, Spraos resorted to splicing the UN series for pre-war and the World Bank series for post-war and found that the hybrid series for the period 1900-70 yields a negative but statistically non-significant growth rate, even if the link year most favourable to the deteriorating hypothesis (1956) was chosen. Thus, the primary terms of trade appeared to be constant over the 1900-70 period [13]. Sapsford (1985), however, obtained statistically significant negative growth rates for the two sub-periods 1900-38 and 1950-70. These results can be reconciled with that for the 1900-70 period by the observation that there was a substantial upward shift in the intercept during the 1939-49 period. The new results could be considered to support the deterioration hypothesis for the period 1900-70 if events in the 1940s could be considered 'unique' rather than 'recurring', say, every 40-50 years.

Conclusion on the Long-term Trend in the Primary Terms of Trade

Over the seventy years period up to the Second World War, the evidence indicates a deteriorating trend in the primary terms of trade. The various criticisms often raised against the deterioration hypothesis though plausible are themselves unsupported by such data as have been analysed. However, over the seventy year period, starting from 1900, the evidence points to a trendless primary terms of trade, although statistical arguments for deterioration could still be made.

Divergences Among the Unit Value Indices of Commodity Groups

Table 3.2 below presents the export and import unit value indices of industrial Europe [14] by commodity groups for selected years. There is a bigger difference between the indices of the two primary commodity groups - food [15] and raw materials - for industrial Europe's exports than for its imports. With 1913 as base, the indices for 1952 food and raw materials are respectively 244 and 324 for exports and 260 and 231 for imports. Thus, it appears that over the 1913-52 period the prices of raw materials rose far more for the industrial European exports than for their imports but the prices of food exported and imported by it rose about the same.

Table 3.2: Export and Import Unit-value Indexes of Industrial Europe by Commodity Groups, Selected Years, 1872-1952 (Dollar relatives)

	Food, drink, and tobacco	Raw materials	Metal manufactures	Machinery	Vehicles	Chemicals	Textiles	Other manufactures	Total
Exports: (End-year weights; beginning year = 100)									
1900-1872[a]	(71)[a]	(81)[a]	(85)[a]	(107)[a]	(..)	(71)[a]	(51)[a]	(74)[a]	(70)[a]
1900-1872	58	79	71	112	47[b]	38	59	55	64
1913-1900	114	100	118	119	76	59	118	101	106
1928-1913	149	130	122	165	68	128	158	114	135
1938-1928	74	92	135	129	92	104	66	91	96
1952-1938	222	270	237	193	161	184	273	221	218
Imports:									
1900-1872	68	70	74	103	..	57	66	44	70
1913-1900	119	117	106	104	157	85	115	95	115
1928-1913	145	126	112	221	72	109	158	131	132
1938-1928	71	70	85	126	80	102	66	75	73
1952-1938	252	263	264	214	196	163	194	185	250
Exports: (1913 = 100)									
1872[a]	(124)[a]	(124)[a]	(100)[a]	(79)[a]	(..)[a]	(238)[a]	(167)[a]	(134)[a]	(134)[a]
1972	151	127	119	75	281	446	144	180	149
1900	88	100	85	84	132	169	85	99	94
1913	100	100	100	100	100	100	100	100	100
1928	149	130	122	165	68	128	158	114	135
1938	110	120	165	213	63	133	104	104	130
1952	244	324	391	411	101	245	283	230	283

Imports:

	1872	1900	1913	1928	1938	1952
	124	87	100	132	96	240
	239	105	100	131	98	181
	132	87	100	158	104	202
	207	118	100	109	111	181
	..	64	100	72	58	114
	93	96	100	221	256	548
	127	94	100	112	95	251
	122	85	100	126	88	231
	123	84	100	145	103	260

a Except Germany

b Based on trade of less than $10 million

Source: Kindleberger (1956, Table 5, p. 78)

By looking at the year 1952 with 1913 as base, we can observe the wide divergences among the indices of manufactured commodity groups, ranging from 101 for vehicles exported to 548 for machinery imported (or 411 for machinery exported), with the indices for chemicals, textiles and other manufactures varying with the 181-283 range.

Thus, in view of the small divergences in the price movements of different primary commodity groups but large divergences in those of different manufactured commodity groups, it is perhaps more meaningful to speak of a world price index for primaries than for manufactures.

Divergences Among the Primary Terms of Trade of Individual Industrial European Countries

Since the prices of different manufactures behaved so differently over the relevant period, we should expect that the terms of trade between primary commodities and manufactures would also be widely different for different European countries in so far as the structures or compositions of their manufactured exports were different. Thus, Table 3.3 gives the terms of trade between manufactures and primary products for industrial European exports by countries and for industrial European imports by areas. The terms of trade based on 1913 show ranges of 70-134 and 49-173 for 1900 and 1952 respectively. The differences among the primary terms of trade of individual countries are sufficiently large to warrant doubt about the usefulness of generalisations based on worldwide terms of trade between primary products and manufactures. Indeed, Kindleberger (1956, p. 72) summed up by saying: 'few generalisations of the terms of trade between world manufactures and world primary products are valid but that they tend to turn against underdeveloped countries and in favour of developed countries' [16].

Real Commodity Prices for the 1950-82 Period
Commodity Groups

The annual growth rates of the real prices for (1) 33 commodities of importance to world trade, (2) total agriculture, (3) timber and (4) metals/minerals, together with sub-groups of food categories and a sub-food agricultural commodities category are presented in Table 3.4 for the 1950-82 period and various sub-periods. These real prices are obtained by dividing the actual nominal prices by the index of CIF US dollar prices of industrialised countries exports' to developing countries. These real prices can be conceived as the terms of trade of the commodities or commodity groups concerned.

Over the 1950-82 period, the real price of 33 commodities of importance to developing countries decreased at an annual rate of 1.1 per cent. Those of total agriculture and metals/minerals decreased at annual rates of 1.2 per cent and 1.1

Table 3.3: The Terms of Trade between Manufactures and Primary Products, Selected Years, 1872-1952

Total exports based on the export indexes of

	United Kingdom	Germany	France	Italy	Netherlands	Belgium	Sweden	Switzerland	Industrial Europe
1872	116	103	115	149		121	113	115	112 *
1900	70	108	99	105		134	127		96
1913	100	100	100	100	100	100	100	100	100
1928	126	105	75	93	96	75		116	101
1938	136	123	77	127	104	86	116	172	112
1952	117	67	68	124	101	138	64	173	93

Total imports based on industrial European imports from

	Industrial Europe	Other Europe	Total Europe	United States	Areas of recent settlement	All other	World
1872	124	138	114	102		137	111
1900	112	115	99	123	119	100	118
1913	100	100	100	100	100	100	100
1928	106	72	105	79	87	91	94
1938	113	118	117	134	83	182	118
1952	94	89	94	69	49	172	202

* Excluding Germany, 118

Source: Kindleberger (1956, p. 79, Table 6)

Table 3.4: Annual Growth Rates (%) of Commodity Prices (Constant US Dollars)

	33 Commodities Total	Agriculture Total	Food Beverages	Cereals	Fats/Oils	Other	Non-food	Timber	Metals & Minerals
50-59	-2.61**	-3.03**	-1.67	-4.31**	-4.31**	-2.65	-4.69**	-2.86	-0.19
60-69	0.89*	-0.34	-0.20	2.62**	0.26	-0.70	-2.10*	1.79	3.57**
70-79	-1.28	0.22	5.77	-3.04*	-2.40	-4.24	-1.51	2.20	-4.64**
80-89	-11.44**	-13.40**	-7.18**	-8.45	-7.04	-24.35**	-11.09**	-11.72	-6.33**
70-82	-1.82	-1.76	0.86	-3.32	-3.98**	-2.55	-1.96*	3.10*	-3.81**
60-82	-0.83*	0.06	0.28	-1.28	-1.25*	0.65	-2.00**	1.62**	-1.86**
50-82	-1.23**	-0.86**	-1.35**	-1.26**	-1.25**	0.12	-2.35**	1.31**	-1.12**
50-79	-1.10**	-0.68*	-1.25**	-1.04**	-0.87***	-0.08	-2.40**	1.01**	-0.85**

Note: 1. The annual growth rate is obtained in two steps as follows:

First Step: Obtain the following estimated regression equation, using ordinary least squares method. $\log P_t = a + bt + u_t$, where P_t is price in period t and b is the least-squares estimate of the exponential growth rate.

Second Step: Obtain the annual growth rate g, using the following equation: $g = e^b - 1$

2. * and ** indicate that the exponential growth rate (b) from which the annual growth rate (g) is obtained is significant at 5% and 1% respectively.

3. The commodities included in each group are: beverages etc. (see Table 3.5, p.63).

Source: Calculations, using data from Commodity Trade and Price Trends, World Bank/The Johns Hopkins University Press, August 1982.

per cent respectively. Of the agricultural commodities, the real price of food decreased at a smaller annual rate (0.9 per cent) than that of non-food (2.4 per cent). Of the food items, the real prices of beverages, cereals and fats/oils decreased at annual rates 1.4 per cent, 1.3 per cent and 1.3 per cent respectively, while that of 'other food' (consisting of remaining food items) remained approximately constant.

Comparing the annual growth rates of real prices over the three decades, 50s, 60s and 70s, one can observe the tendencies for commodities prices to do well in the 60s and to do worst in the 50s. Thus the real price of 33 commodities decreased at 2.6 per cent per annum in the 50s, increased at 0.9 per cent per annum in the 60s and decreased at 1.3 per cent per annum in the 70s. However, metals/minerals did worst in the 70s - its real price decreased at 4.6 per cent per annum in the 70s but increased at 3.6 per cent in the 60s and remained about constant in the 50s. Examining the various sub-groups of food, we can observe large differences in the growth pattern of the real prices of beverages, cereals and fats/oils. Thus, while in the 70s, the real price of beverages increased at 5.8 per cent per annum, those of cereals and fats/oils decreased at 3.0 per cent per annum and 2.4 per cent per annum respectively and that of remaining food items also decreased at 4.2 per cent per annum. On the other hand, in the 60s, the real price of cereals increased at 2.6 per cent per annum while those of all other sub-groups of food remained about constant; in the 50s cereals' price fell the most at 4.7 per cent per annum, followed by that of fats/oils at 4.3 per cent per annum, while beverages and other food fell considerably less at 1.7 per cent per annum and 2.7 per cent per annum respectively.

The real prices of all groups of commodities fell very sharply over the last three years of the sample (1980-82). The real prices of 33 commodities, total agriculture and metals/minerals decreased at annual rates of 11.4 per cent, 13.1 per cent and 6.32 per cent respectively. Of agricultural commodities, those of food decreased at 13.4 per cent per annum (with beverages, cereals and fats/oils decreased at annual rates 7.2 per cent, 8.5 per cent and 7.0 per cent respectively) and non-food, at 11.1 per cent. Hence, excluding these last 3 years would reduce somewhat the annual decrease rates of the real prices of all groups apart from non-food and sub-groups. Thus for the period 1950-79, the annual decrease rate of 33 commodities, total agriculture and metals/minerals were 1.0 per cent, 1.1 per cent and 0.9 per cent respectively.

Twelve Major Commodities
The annual growth rates of the 12 agricultural commodities of importance to world trade - coffee, cocoa, tea, sugar,

61

bananas, rice, wheat, maize, cotton, jute, sisal and rubber - are given in Table 3.5 for the period 1950-81 and various sub-periods. It can be seen that within each sub-group of beverages, cereals and agricultural raw materials (i.e. 'non-food' groups), there is great diversity in growth performance in the period 1950-81 and in each sub-period.

Of the beverages, cocoa prices showed the highest growth in the last two decades with annual growth rates of real price at 4.1 per cent and 5.0 per cent in the periods 60-69 and 70-81 respectively, whereas coffee's real price increased at 3.4 per cent per annum and decreased at 4.1 per cent per annum and tea's real price decreased at 3.9 per cent per annum, and 2.9 per cent in those two periods. Over the whole period 1950-81, tea did the worst with an annual rate of decrease of 3.1 per cent, followed by coffee with an annual rate of decrease of 1.3 per cent, while the real price of cocoa remained about constant.

Similarly, individual cereals also had divergent fortunes concerning real price trends. In the 50s, the real price of maize grew at an annual rate of 6.7 per cent, whereas those of rice and wheat decreased respectively at 2.9 per cent and 4.5 per cent. In the 60s, the real price of maize increased at a much lower annual rate of 1.1 per cent, whereas that of rice increased at a really high rate of 4.6 per cent while wheat's real price remained constant. In the 1970-81 period, all three had negative price trends, with maize doing worst with an annual rate of decrease of 4.3 per cent, wheat at 2.2 per cent and rice at 1.7 per cent. Over the whole 1950-81 period, while the real price of rice grew slightly at 0.7 per cent per annum, those of wheat and maize decreased at 1.1 per cent per annum and 1.6 per cent per annum respectively.

Finally, the four agricultural raw materials can also be seen to have widely different price trends in each sub-period as well as in the whole sample period. In the 50s, sisal had a dramatic fall in real price at 11.2 per cent per annum, followed by cotton at 5.1 per cent per annum and rubber at 4.8 per cent per annum, whereas jute's real price increased at 2.4 per cent per annum. In the 60s sisal continued to do badly at a rate of decrease of 6.5 per cent per annum, with cotton and rubber also doing badly at rates of decrease of 0.6 per cent per annum and 5.4 per cent per annum respectively and jute continued to do well at a growth rate of 1.9 per cent per annum. However, in the period 1970-81, the fortunes were reversed, when the real price of jute fell substantially at an annual rate of 9.5 per cent, followed by cotton at 2.1 per cent and rubber at 0.4 per cent while sisal's real price recovered slightly at a growth rate of 0.8 per cent. Over the entire 1950-81 period, the real prices of all four had sizeable annual decrease rates at 1.6 per cent, 2.5 per cent, 1.7 per cent and 3.5 per cent for cotton, jute, sisal and rubber respectively.

Table 3.5: Annual Growth Rates (%) 12 Major Commodities (Constant US Dollars)

	Coffee	Cocoa	Tea	Sugar	Bananas	Rice	Wheat	Maize	Cotton	Jute	Sisal	Rubber
50-59	-1.12	-0.89	3.04	-5.82*	-1.98*	-2.90**	-4.51**	6.67**	-5.09**	2.44	-11.19**	-4.78
60-69	3.44**	4.11	-3.93**	-6.19	0.87	4.63**	0.02	1.07	-0.59	1.93	-6.47**	-5.41**
70-81	-4.14*	5.04	-2.90*	0.89	-1.74*	1.67	-2.23	-4.34**	-2.14	-9.54	0.77	-0.42
60-81	-2.10**	3.30**	-4.27**	-2.97	-2.31**	0.74	-0.85	-1.44**	-0.55	-4.70**	-0.95	-3.16**
50-81	-1.31**	0.18	-3.09**	0.50	-2.13**	0.71	-1.08**	-1.63**	-1.56**	-2.46**	-1.74**	-3.54**

Note: 1. See footnote (1) and (4) under Table 3.4 for the method of calculating annual growth rates and sources respectively

2. (a) Cocoa: New York plus London ICCO price
   (b) Coffee: Brazilian Santoo 4 - after 1973; Unwashed Arabica
   (c) Tea: Average all tea
   (d) Sugar: International Sugar Council 'World' daily price
   (e) Bananas: Any origin
   (f) Rice: Thai FoB Bangkok
   (g) Wheat: Canadian 1972-81 No. 1 Western Red Spiny; 1950-71: Manitoba
   (h) Maize: United States FoB Gulf Ports
   (i) Cotton: Mexican
   (j) Jute: 1964-81 only; Bangladesh White D
   (k) Sisal: Kenyan/Tanzanian No. 3
   (l) Rubber: London Market

63

One fact which emerges from the above examination of price trends is the wide dispersion of growth rates of individual commodities within each sub-group and of sub-groups for each sub-period as well as for the entire sample period. This makes it difficult to draw useful conclusions about individual commodities from the price trends of the groups or sub-groups to which they belong. Thus, over the period 1950-81, the real price or terms of trade of primary commodities (represented by 33 commodities of importance to world trade) appeared to deteriorate at the (statistically significant) rate of over one per cent per annum. But this rate of decrease concealed a wide diversity of growth trends of different commodity groups and sub-groups and individual commodities. However, one generalisation can still usefully be made - that is that the terms of trade of all commodity groups and sub-groups deteriorated over the period 1950-81.

Estimation of Trend Price and Price Fluctuation
The greater is the instability of price, the more difficult it is to estimate the price trend. Thus, in statistics, the reliability of an estimate is defined to vary positively with its variance. Since the variance of the estimate (or its root) of the price trend has also been used as an indication of the average degree of price fluctuation, this means that for commodities or commodity groups with large price fluctuations, estimates of price trends or annual growth rates become unreliable - such estimates could be regarded as crude guesses of the true magnitudes (assuming that these could be defined), particularly if the price series also display some cyclical patterns [17].

REVIEW OF COMMODITY PROJECTIONS

To derive welfare implications from movements in the terms of trade is certainly difficult, as shown above. But a decline in the growth of demand for primaries, stemming from low income elasticity, low growth rates of population, industrial production or low income growth in the industrial countries does justify concern. Such reasons for declining terms of trade sustained for the next decade or so, could mean that countries dependent on primary product exports would find that their export earnings would fail to keep pace with growing import needs. Some might maintain exports by diversifying into manufactures, but low-income LDCs which tend to depend on primary exports, may find this difficult and will either have to reduce their economic growth or incur persistent deficits, unless their needs are met by foreign borrowing or official aid.

In the long-run, a decline in the commodity terms of trade necessarily reflects an excess of the growth rate of supply over demand (associated with a constant terms of trade), as in the long run stocks become less important as determinants of prices. Such a decline would inevitably benefit countries which are predominantly importers of primary commodities.

But the proportional effects would be much greater on the exporters than on the importers. This is because while many low-income countries depend heavily on the export of a few commodities the major importers are rich industrial countries where primary commodities contribute a small and decreasing fraction of total imports. A decline in the terms of trade would damage the economic development of the many developing countries involved but would confer relatively minor benefits on the industrial nations [18]. Yet, industrial countries, as revealed in their government's reaction, appear to be almost as sensitive to any attempt to use policy intervention to enhance the real prices of primary commodities as are developing countries to the effects of declining commodity prices on them.

As a group, developing countries cannot improve the trend in their export earnings by expanding production and export volume, because the price elasticities of the demands for almost all primary commodities are less than unity, even in the long run. If econometric estimates of their price elasticities are to be believed, their export earnings can be raised only by reducing supply and/or increasing export demand. Supply could be reduced either by cutting production or by raising domestic demand. Increased demand could be stimulated by discovering new uses, removal of barriers on primary imports in industrial countries or both. Increased productivity in primary production may not be an unmixed blessing for while it may reduce the effort required to produce each ton of, say coffee, it is likely at the same time to reduce total coffee export revenues.

Given continuing concern over the future movements of the terms of trade, this section reviews the following major official and unofficial projections which bear on this issue:- (1) the reports by the World Bank, Price Prospects for Major Primary Commodities (Reports No 814/82 and 814/84, (2) the report by F.A.O. Agriculture:Towards 2000 (1981) and (3) the report by the U.S. Council on Environmental Quality and the Department of State, The Global 2000 Report to the President (which was commissioned by President Carter but disregarded by Reagan). (Three other influential reports with relevant but now largely outdated projections are: the first and second reports of the Club of Rome, Limits to Growth (1972) and Mankind at the Turning Point (1975) and the report of the Hudson Institute, The Next 200 Years (1977) are reviewed in Appendix C. Such long-term projections should obviously be considered tentative in nature.) By far the most useful projections for our purposes in terms of coverage, analysis and detail are those by the World Bank, which include explicit price projections not only for commodity groups but also for most commodities of importance to world trade. According to the World Bank approach, a deterioration in the terms of trade of a commodity usually simply reflects an excess of the growth rate of world supply over that of world demand. The Bank projections take only an indirect and limited account of the effects of resource cost limits – in the form of diminishing returns associated with the limits of the world land areas and minerals – which feature prominently in all other studies.

The World Bank Projections

The World Bank has produced forecasts to the year 1995 not only for the primary commodity terms of trade of developing countries but also for the real and nominal price indices of individual commodities and commodity groups of importance to world trade. These price forecasts are produced mainly for use in forecasting the balance of payments of countries to which the World Bank lends in appraising investment projects that include these commodities as inputs or outputs.

There are basically three methods used by the World Bank to make long-term projections of prices. One uses formal models based on the underlying structure of the industry, estimating supply and demand equations by country and/or region. Most of the models are econometric in nature, usually estimated by simple ordinary least-squares procedures, and built around a common structure of a supply block, a demand block, and an inventory demand equation normalised on price. A world market price links the equations which are solved simultaneously to give production, consumption and implied trade flows for each country or region. Thus, models are as large as 150 equations and may be specified in such a way that price cycles can be modelled and projected. Examples of formal econometric models used are: tin, rubber, coffee, cocoa, fats and oils and petroleum.

The second method involves the notion of a simple comparative-static equilibrium model of production and consumption disaggregated by region, where price is used to achieve a unique equilibrium in each year. Thus, consumption projections are made by applying exogenously determined income elasticities of demand by region to projected GNP and population and production projections are made by using projected productivity growth rates or extrapolating past trends modified to incorporate other sources of information. Then, through successive interactions using econometrically estimated price elasticities of consumption and production, prices are parametrically changed until global production and consumption converge to equilibrium.

The third method involves the use of less formal long-run marginal (or average) cost models. These models which are mostly used to project (or to validate other projections of) long run mineral-metal prices, may incorporate great details for the underlying industry structure, including such variables as capacity utilisation, various measures of industrial activity and strategic (government) stock piling. Trade projections by region are implied from the deficit or surplus of production. Since the model is a long-run one, stock levels are not important. This method is used for commodities such as wheat, rice, maize, cotton, fertilisers, citrus fruit, bananas and timber.

The World Bank models are rather simple and relatively small in size but have the advantage of being easily and cheaply manageable and easily updated. Although they may be useful as operational tools for their projection purposes they are inadequate as tools for producing conditional projections for alternative policy scenarios, e.g. the effects of various commodity agreements, without considerable modification [19]. Despite the various shortcomings of the models used, the World Bank projections are now more widely accepted by economists and politicians than any other projections.

It should be noted that the forecasts for 1985 onwards indicate only general trends and hence actual prices in any particular year may differ substantially from the World Bank long-term forecasts, in so far as the cyclical and random components of price movements are large. Furthermore, the long-term projections of commodity prices assume a macroeconomic scenario for the period 1995 that is meant to capture the basic trends in the world economy. This scenario involves assumptions relating to the projected growth rates of GDP, population, international price level and petroleum price. It is important to note these assumed growth rates before discussing the implications of the projections, because any change in any one of these projected growth rates could substantially alter the World Bank price projections.

Assumptions Underlying Price Projections

Real GDP growth projections for developing countries and industrial countries from 1985 to 1995 are assumed to be the mid-point of the High and Low scenarios described in the World Development Report, 1981, whereas those for the centrally planned economies are based on the latest 'Project Link' information. The overall real annual GDP growth for the world economy is, therefore, taken to be 3.9 per cent up to 1990 and 3.8 per cent between 1990 and 1995. The population projections used are also those of the World Development Report, 1981. Thus, the annual growth rate of world population is taken to be 1.7 per cent and 1.6 per cent for the 1985-1990 and 1990-1995 periods respectively [20]. The long-term international inflation rate is taken to be the annual growth rate of the unit value index of manufactured exports (SITC 5-8) from industrial to developing countries on a c.i.f. basis. For 1983-90, the inflation rate is assumed to equal the growth rate of the US deflator for OECD North at 6 per cent per annum. The World Bank assumes that this rate will continue for the 1990-1995 period. This projected inflation rate is in line with those available from other major forecasting organisations which range between 6 per cent and 7 per cent per annum. Finally, the annual growth rate of petroleum prices (in real terms) is projected to be about 2.5 per cent for the period 1985-95 as a whole. This projection of the growth rate of the petroleum price in real terms was based on a detailed analysis of the world energy situation, the demand for OPEC oil and the relationship between this demand and OPEC production capacity. It is in line, with the expected cost-price structure of petroleum substitutes [21].

Price Projections

The projected real price indexes (using developing countries exports as weights) for various-commodity groups and their growth rates for the periods 1980-85, 1985-90, 1990-95 and 1985-95 are given in Table 3.6. Thus after recovering in 1983-85, as the cycle in world economic activity turns upwards, non-fuel commodity prices in constant dollar terms are projected to increase only slowly until 1990. Relative to the magnitude of the 1981-82 price trough, the expected 1983-85 recovery is rather weak and the trend price increase from 1985 to 1995 appears to be only just enough to restore the prices of non-fuel commodities in real terms to their 1979-80 levels - a level which appears to have been below the long-term trend. Thus, the overall outlook for non-fuel commodity prices relative to those of manufactured goods does not look very promising. We can see from Table 3.6 that the 'real' price indices of all non-fuel commodities other than non-food (which consists of cotton, jute, rubber and tobacco) are projected to be lower in 1995 than they were in 1980.

The price prospects vary considerably across commodity groups. Fats and oils followed by tropical timber face declining real prices while for beverages real prices remain about constant over the 1985-95 period. A chronic over supply situation is expected in both coffee and cocoa until 1990 and their real prices are not expected to recover much by 1995.

Similarly, despite the increasing scarcity of easily accessible forest products, supply appears to more than keep pace with a slow growth in world demand and hence produces a downward pressure on real timber prices. The cereals' prices in real terms are projected to increase very slowly

Table 3.6: Weighted Index of Commodity Prices (Constant US Dollars, 1977-79 = 100)

Commodity Groups 21	Estimated 1980	Projected 1985	Projected 1990	Projected 1995	Annual Growth Rates (%) 1980-5	1985-90	1990-5	1985-95
Petroleum	160	158	180	220	-0.3	2.6	4.1	3.4
33 commodities	104	82	93	95	-4.6	2.5	0.4	1.5
Agriculture	101	77	91	92	-5.3	3.4	0.2	1.8
Food	101	73	88	90	-6.3	2.8	0.5	2.1
Beverages	69	65	61	66	-1.2	-1.3	1.0	0.2
Cereals	108	88	97	94	-4.0	2.0	-0.6	0.7
Fats and oils	89	84	80	79	-1.1	-1.0	-0.3	-0.6
Other	159	72	134	134	-14.7	13.2	0.0	6.4
Non-food	103	97	102	104	-1.2	1.0	0.4	0.7
Timber	124	120	111	118	-0.7	-1.6	1.2	-0.2
Minerals-metals	105	91	96	99	-2.8	1.1	0.6	0.9

Note: 1. Computed from unrounded data and deflated by the unit value index of manufactured exports (SITC 5-8) from industrial to developing countries (i.e. the unit value index of a c.i.f. basis. The weights used are the 1977-79 developing countries' export values

2. The commodities included in each group: Beverages: cocoa, coffee, tea; Cereals: maize, rice, wheat, grain; Fats and Oils: palm oil, coconut oil, groundnut oil, soy beans, copra, groundnut meal, soybean meal; Other Foods: sugar, beef, bananas, oranges; Non-food: cotton, jute, rubber, tobacco; Timber: logs; Mineral-metals: copper, tin, nickel, bauxite, aluminium, iron ore, manganese ore, lead, zinc, phosphate rock

3. 3-year moving average centred on 1980; i.e. the average of 1979-81 to represent a trend value for 1980

4. Calculated on the basis of the estimates of 1980 trend values and the 1985 projected value

Source: World Bank, Economic Analysis and Projections Department, Commodity Studies and Projections Division. Table 3, Report 814/84

between 1985-95 and are lower in 1995 than in 1980. Apparently, growing needs of rapidly increasing population in the developing countries are not expected to be translated into effective demand for cereals and so raise their real prices. This contrasts with projections in all the other reports.

The prices of non-food agricultural commodities are projected to grow slowly in real terms in the 1985-95 period despite pressure of rising petroleum prices on the price of their (petroleum - based) synthetic substitutes. While natural rubber has a reasonably favourable price prospect in real terms with real prices growing at an annual rate of just over 2 per cent over the 1985-95 period, jute will continue to have a poor price prospect because of increasing price competition from synthetic substitutes and cotton barely maintains its real price over this same period.

Mineral-metal prices in constant dollar terms are projected to increase again quite slowly from 1985 onwards when new investments are required to expand capacity to meet market demand. These forecasts are based on the assumption of normal investment conditions which would stimulate an efficient exploitation of world mineral resources. Mineral-metal prices in real terms would increase a great deal more if national investments do not continue to be supplemented by international capital. Policy actions by producers and changes in the risk perceptions of international investors could deter investment and lead to sub-optimal exploitation of world mineral resources.

Implications of World Bank Price Projections

In this section, to avoid possible confusion and misunderstanding, we shall use the World Bank's terminology concerning country groups, i.e. developing countries and industrial countries instead of less developed countries and more developed countries.

The weighted index of constant dollar prices of 33 non-fuel commodities for developing countries (in regional groups), industrial countries and the world are given for selected years, together with the growth rates for various periods are given in Table 3.7. It can be seen that this index shows a rate of growth over the 1985-95 period highest for developing countries in Latin America at 2.6 per cent per annum and a rather low rate of increase of about 1.0 per cent for those in Africa and Asia, with a rate of 1.5 per cent for developing countries as a whole. At this rate of increase, none of the LDC regions would recover the 'trend' levels of real prices prevailing in 1980. Although commodity prices for Latin America grow faster than those for other regions, they also suffered greater fall between 1980 and 1985. Comparing the indexes for the two years 1980 and 1995, the prices of the non-fuel commodities in real terms can be seen to be 7.0 per cent (Africa), and 10.1 per cent (Latin America) and 8.4 per cent (Asia) lower in 1995 than they were in 1980. For developing countries as a whole, industrial countries and the world, the non-fuel commodities prices in real terms are respectively 8.7 per cent, 6.5 per cent and 7.0 per cent lower in 1995 than they were 1980. Thus, although non-fuel commodity prices are projected to increase over the 1985-95 period, they do not recover the ground lost in 1980-85 (particularly the losses occurring in 1981-82). Despite a lower projected rate of growth 1985-95 (0.5 per cent per annum), the price index of non-fuel commodities exported by the industrial countries is higher relative to its level in 1980, than the price index of non-fuel commodity exported by developing countries. Looking at the period 1980-95 as a whole, it appears that commodities exported by industrial countries fare better than those exported by developing countries.

The projected improvement in the price of non-fuel primary commodities, relative to those of manufactured products, simply indicate a tendency in the purchasing power of the former to recover slowly over time and to recoup partially the losses incurred in 1981-83.

While for developing countries as a whole, the share of non-fuel primary commodities in total exports declined from 68 per cent in 1960 to 35 per cent in 1979, for low income and middle-income oil-importing developing countries these shares were 49 per cent and 42 per cent respectively in 1979. In the 1960s, the real export earnings of developing countries grew at 3.6 per cent per annum with annual growth rates in volume and price being about 3.0 per cent and 0.6 per cent respectively. In the 1970s their real export earnings grew at a much lower rate of 1 per cent per annum both because of the lower growth rate of volume at 1.5 per cent per annum and a decline in real price at 0.5 per cent per annum. Over the 1980-85 period, while price is estimated to decline at 4.6 per cent per annum, on the basis of the latest available estimate of World Bank [22], volume is shown to increase by 2.8 per cent per annum, hence real export earnings of developing countries appear to have decreased at 1.8 per cent per annum. Some recovery of export earnings is projected for the 1985-95 period, with real price projected to increase at 1.5 per cent per annum and volume to increase at 2.5 per cent per annum, giving an increase in real export earnings of 4 per cent per annum. On the basis of these growth rates, real export earnings of developing countries will be 17 per cent higher in 1995 than they were in 1980, representing an annual growth rate of 1 per cent for 1980-95 period as a whole, i.e. the same as the rate prevailing in the 1970s. Thus starting from the trough in 1980-85 period, the pro-

Table 3.7: Weighted Index of 33 Commodities (Excluding Energy)
(Constant US dollars: 1977-79 = 100)

| | Estimated | Projected | | | Annual Growth Rate (%) | | | |
	1980	1985	1990	1995	1980-5	1985-90	1990-5	1985-95
Developing Countries	104.0	82.0	93.0	95.0	-4.6	2.5	0.4	1.5
Africa	91.8	77.1	81.1	85.4	-3.4	1.0	1.0	1.0
Latin America	109.0	75.9	95.9	98.0	-7.0	4.8	0.4	2.6
Asia	104.4	85.6	94.3	95.6	-3.9	2.0	0.3	1.1
Industrial Countries	106.3	94.9	98.7	99.4	-2.2	0.8	0.1	0.5
World	104.8	88.6	96.0	97.5	-3.3	1.6	0.3	1.0

A 3-year moving-average centre on 1980 to represent an estimate of the trend value for that year

Source: World Bank Report No. 814/84, op. cit., Table 7

jected real export earnings in 1995 can be seen once again largely as a recoup of the lost grounds, with the underlying trend growth rate remaining as low as that prevails in the 1970s.

The overall implications of World Bank projections do not appear therefore to be encouraging for developing countries. It appears that the growth in the purchasing power of their export non-fuel commodities will be insufficient to enable them to achieve even modest development targets. The implications are even less encouraging for low-income oil-importing countries which are more dependent on them. For many of these countries the exports of a few commodities contribute a very large proportion of their total export earnings. Thus, in 1976-78, for example, over 25 countries obtained over 70 per cent of their export earnings from no more than four commodities. Most of these are low-income African and Asian countries and a few are Latin American countries.

Among the commodities of major importance to the export earnings of low-income developing countries are the following four: coffee, cocoa, sugar and cotton. Coffee contributes over 20 per cent of the total export earnings of 19 countries, whereas cocoa, sugar and cotton contribute over 20 per cent of the total export earnings of 6, 8 and 5 countries respectively [24]. The prices of these commodities in real terms, together with their growth rates over various periods are given in Table 3.8. It can be seen from Table 3.8 that sugar had the largest percentage price fall in the 1980-85 period and also has the largest projected price increase in the 1985-90 period. While real price of cotton recovers very little over this same period, the real prices of both coffee and cocoa are projected to fall further. In the 1990-95 period, the real prices of sugar and cotton are projected to remain constant, those of coffee and cocoa recover somewhat. Taking the longer 1980-95 period as a whole, while the real price of coffee and cotton remain about constant, those of cocoa and sugar decline at annual rates of 1.7 per cent and 1.3 per cent respectively. Thus, the price forecasts of these commodities are again quite discouraging for countries heavily dependent on them.

Given the trends in world consumption and demand for non-fuel commodities, an attempt to increase export earnings from them by increasing their volumes would cause export earnings to decline even further, because of low price elasticities of the demands for these commodities. For example, the price elasticities of world demand of coffee, cocoa, sugar and cotton are estimated to be around -0.27, -0.41, -0.07, and -0.22 respectively [25]. This means that other things being equal, i.e. given the growth rate of demand, an increase in the annual growth rate of the volume supplied by 1 per cent would reduce the total export earnings from coffee, cocoa, sugar and cotton by 2.7 per cent, 1.4 per cent, 13.3

73

Table 3.8: Coffee, Cocoa, Sugar, Cotton Prices and Growth Rates in Constant 1983 US Dollars

Commodity	Estimated[a] 1980	Projected 1985	Projected 1990	Projected 1995	Annual Growth Rate (%) 1980–5	1985–90	1990–5	1985–95	1980–95
Coffee (c/kg)	320	295	291	312	-1.6	-0.3	1.4	0.6	-0.2
Cocoa (c/kg)	254	204	169	195	-4.3	-3.7	2.9	-0.5	-1.7
Sugar (s/MT)	382	125	315	315	-20.0	20.3	0.0	9.7	-1.3
Cotton (c/kg)	177	170	173	175	-0.3	0.4	0.2	0.3	-0.1

[a] A 3-year moving-average centres on 1980 as an estimate of 1980 trend value

Source: World Bank Report, September 1984, Table 1

per cent and 4.5 per cent respectively. Of course, small individual countries can raise their export earnings from each commodity by expanding their supplies. However, in doing so they raise their export earnings only at the expense of other exporters. To raise the export earnings of developed countries from commodities with inelastic demands requires policy measures to reduce rather than to increase production. The problem of getting small countries to agree to participate in schemes of export and production control will be discussed in later chapters.

Industrial countries which derive sizeable proportion of their export earnings from non-fuel commodities such as Australia, New Zealand and Canada may also be concerned about the relatively poor prospects for their commodity exports implied by the World Bank price projections. Although an inadequate growth in the export earnings of primary commodities may not present them with serious balance of payments problems, the average incomes in their agricultural sectors will adversely be affected and hence their farmers may require state assistance to maintain their real income or to diversify. To maintain the standard of living in the agricultural sectors, labour productivity may need to be raised and rural population reduced.

As far as other primary-importing industrial countries are concerned, the World Bank price projections suggest for the future 1985-95 period relatively abundant supplies of non-fuel commodities at prices in real terms below the 1980 levels. At these low real prices, there appear to be no need for further substitution against natural products. Instead, to benefit themselves as well as the low-income developing countries, they can steadily dismantle trade barriers against imports of non-fuel commodities and perhaps participate in research to find new uses for these commodities and to improve their quality.

Limitations of World Bank Price Projections

The World Bank are well aware of the sensitivity of their price forecasts to changes in the underlying assumptions concern economic growth and inflation. Since 1980, income and inflation have fluctuated considerably more, making long-term projections of their trends more difficult. The price projections are based on what the World Bank assume to be most likely to occur concerning government policies affecting production and trade of primary commodities, market structures and market conditions. Since what are likely to occur are not necessarily what are desirable, the World Bank projections can be considered to be 'positive' rather than 'normative'. Furthermore, as mentioned earlier, the World Bank projections for 1990 and 1995 represent the projected trend levels for these years. Future actual prices may differ significantly from those projected prices, even if all World Bank assumptions hold true and their models are proved to be accurate because of the possible large random and cyclical components which may occur in these years.

Owing to the increased uncertainties concerning inflation and GDP, the World Bank has attempted to review their price projections every two years. It is disturbing, however, to see that price projections for the same commodities over the same periods can vary so much between reports published at different dates. For example, the projected price indexes for 33 commodities in real terms for 1985 and 1995 are 92 and 101 respectively in the 1982 report, and become 82 and 95 in the 1984 Report [26]. The implied annual growth rate is 0.9 per cent in the earlier report and 1.5 per cent in the later one. The difference between these two implied growth rates is quite significant. The differences are even greater for some commodity groups. For example, the indexes of the real prices of timber products for these two years in the 1982 Report are 109 and 139 respectively and in the 1984 Report become 120 and 118. The annual growth rates of timber products in the two reports over 1985-95 period are 2.5 per cent and -0.2 per cent respectively. The annual growth rate of real prices projected for 'other' food categories is -0.2 per cent in the 1982 Report and becomes 6.4 per cent in the 1984 Report. Although at the time of writing we have received summary tables of projections to be published in the 1984 Report, we have not yet had the 1984 Report. Hence, explanations by the World Bank for the drastic revisions of some prices are not available to us at the time of writing. However, in the 1982 Report, the World Bank does give some explanation for revising price projections presented earlier in the 1980 Report [27].

The 1982 Report revises downward all price forecasts to 1990 given in the 1980 Report, suggesting a considerable deterioration in the long-term price prospects for non-fuel commodities since the preparation of the earlier report. One reason given is the substantial downward revision of long-term economic growth expectations in both industrial countries and centrally planned economies and another is the assessment of supply prospects of key tree crops and cereals which involves an upward revision of the projected production of perennial crops and a downward revision of the important demand of key-cereal importing countries because of greater progress towards cereal self-sufficiency there. There is no doubt that plausible explanations will be given for the revision made to price forecasts in the 1984 Report. However, large revisions of price forecasts do reduce confidence in them and increase uncertainties concerning the prospects for commodities.

The use of projections of real GDP growth rates and international inflation rates as though they are exogenously given factors is itself questionable. It is difficult to see, for example, how future GDP growth rates of developing countries can be independent of the price trends of the 33 commodities included in the Study. Ideally, projections of the price of the 33 commodities, real GDP growth rates of countries and the price index of manufactures should be produced together in an integrated approach.

Price projections are still recognised by countries in making their future production plans for commodities. Decisions once made and actions once taken may be costly to alter. Therefore, in so far as price projections can be made more reliable by further expenditure on manpower, data collection or computer software, etc., [28] such additional expenditure may prove to be very small relative to the costs resulting from taking wrong decisions because of the large inaccuracies of the forecasts.

Other Projections

The studies which produce other projections are all concerned with the question relating to the future trends of world population, agricultural production, resources and environment. All suggest increase in the real prices of land-intensive commodities as a consequence of population pressure on the fixed world land area. Resource inputs - including land, water, minerals, energy and renewable biological resources - could be locally, if not globally, limiting. How binding are such resource constraints depends on the type of substitutions that can be made, the degree of success of technological innovation in overcoming them, and the extent to which the production/consumption pattern would move away from resource-intensive products. Thus, projections of different studies will differ according to the assumption made concerning the resource constraints and the effects of the diminishing returns associated with them. For example, the main conclusions of the Global 2000 Report are:

> If present trend continues, the world in 2000 will be more crowded, more polluted, less stable ecologically and more vulnerable to disruption. Despite greater material output, the world's people will be poorer in many ways than they are today. For hundreds of millions of people, the outlook for food and other basic necessities will be no better and for many it will be worse. (p. 1)

These conclusions are not as pessimistic as those by the Club of Rome, which projects severe world food shortages, severalfold increases in world food prices and mass starvation - but are more pessimistic than those by the Hudson Institute which looks further into the future. Among its rather optimistic conclusions is the following:-

> ... 200 years ago almost everywhere human beings were comparatively few, poor and at the mercy of the forces of nature, and 200 years from now, we expect, almost everywhere they will be numerous, rich and in control of the forces of nature ... Almost all countries eventually will develop the characteristics of super- and post-industrial societies. (p.1)

All these conclusions are important and warrant serious attention from the world governments. Apart from the Hudson Institute, all other studies focus attention on the concept of 'carrying capacity' of the earth and the potential harms resulting from 'overshooting' it. In so far as a population requires resource in proportion to its numbers, then the population cannot grow beyond the size established by the resource limits, if these exist. While economists refer to this 'carrying capacity' as Malthusian logic, biologists think of it as simple commonsense. Those who believe (as the report of the Club of Rome) that overshooting the earth's carrying capacity would irrevocably reduce it, tend to produce more gloomy forecasts and press for urgent actions to curtail population growth and economic growth. At the other extreme, those who believe (as the Hudson Institute) that resource limits are flexible and can be extended by human ingenuity would tend to give optimistic forecasts and stress instead the dangers of handicapping the progress of science in extending those limits, if economic growth is reduced.

Agriculture: Toward 2000

The FAO Study (AT 2000) does not attempt to forecast what will actually happen up to the end of the century but to discuss the implications for agriculture of three scenarios for 90 developing countries:- a Trend Scenario, Scenario B and Scenario A - each of which is successively more satisfactory in providing the required nutrients to the third world population than the previous one and is therefore more ambitious in terms of increase in inputs requirements, land utilisation, cropping intensity and yields per unit land area. The Trend Scenario is based mainly on an extrapolation of past trends in production and consumption of agricultural products. It can however still be considered optimistic because it is assumed that no further declines in per capita calorie supplies would occur in the poorest countries where such declines have taken place and that all food deficits - could be covered through imports [29]. Scenario B assumes the achievement of modest growth rates in both agriculture, and the overall economy of developing countries (about 5.7 per cent per annum). Finally, Scenario A assumes the achievement by developing countries of the overall economic growth objectives of the new UN International Development Strategy (IDS) and substantially

78

improved agriculture (7.0 per cent for the developing countries as a whole) [30].

According to the Trend Scenario, despite the rather optimistic assumption of no further declines in per capita calorie supplies anywhere, per capita calorie supplies continued to fall short of national average requirements in 34 countries which accounted for about half of the total population of the 90 developing countries under study. This should be cause for greater concern than might appear at first since to ensure adequate supplies to everyone, a substantial margin above 100 per cent national average requirements is needed. For developing countries as a whole, while there will be very limited gains in per capita calorie supplies, there will be large increases in the numbers of the undernourished and people at risk of famine. Cereal import requirements will also increase substantially and the agricultural surplus will almost disappear [31].

As far as Scenario B is concerned, most countries in the Far East, the Near East and Latin America will only just keep their past record but those in Africa will have to almost double their annual production growth rate to 3.4 per cent. Yet even this would raise per capita production in Africa only by less than 0.5 per cent per annum because of a high rate of population growth there. To meet demand growing at 3.6 per cent per annum under this scenario many problems have to be faced to raise agricultural production. Expansion of arable land provides 26 per cent of the additional crop production, increased cropping intensity 14 per cent and yield, 60 per cent. Land suitable for adding to cultivated area inevitably becomes more scarce. For the 90 countries as a whole, 40 per cent of total arable land potentially available was already under cultivation by the mid-1970s. By the end of the century, the Far East would be using 87 per cent of its arable area, the Near east, 67 per cent and Africa and Latin America, 39 per cent. The low-income developing countries are faced with a tremendous task both in agriculture and in the non-agriculture sectors. The process of industrialisation will prove more difficult for them than in the past under increasingly tight balance of payments conditions. Per capita incomes earned in agriculture in the developing countries would fall behind those earned in non-agricultural sectors. Leaving aside 20 developing countries with less than 15 per cent of the GDP accounted for by agriculture, the ratio of per capita agricultural to non-agricultural incomes, was about 1 to 4 in the mid-1970s, would be projected to fall to 1 to 6 by year 2000, despite an absolute rise in real terms of per capita incomes earned in agriculture in these countries of almost 50 per cent by 2000.

The tasks facing developing countries in meeting the more optimistic and ambitious targets concerning agricultural supplies under Scenario A would be even more formidable in

79

terms of increased input requirements. However, meeting the more desirable agricultural targets under Scenario A is considered feasible, provided both developing and developed countries take actions now, as many of the most effective means of increasing agricultural supplies take quite a long time to produce results, e.g. major land development schemes may require up to 20 years and plant breeding involves at least 10 years of research and testing.

Thus, by the year 2000 a projected world population of over 6 billion will require an agricultural output about 60 per cent greater than in 1980. Demand for food and agricultural products in developing countries will double. The results of the FAO AT 2000 study clearly suggest that many of the decisions affecting the world food situation in 1990 and 2000 should be made within the next few years. Furthermore, these results reinforce the view that increase in food production would improve the nutrition of most of the people but would not, in itself, end the scourge of hunger. The eradication of hunger and undernourishment requires not only increased food production but also better distribution of the produce.

It is surprising that results associated with different projections of world population (i.e. different variants) are not produced. The required increase in food production would be lower with lower population projections and it is difficult to see how food production can be made to keep up with the fast growing population in the Third World in the future without a reduction in the actual rates of population growth in the developing countries.

Global 2000 Report
The Global 2000 Study projects a world population of 6.3 billion by the year 2000, with 5.0 billion being accounted for by developing countries and projects world food production to grow at an average annual rate of about 2.2 per cent over the 1970-2000 period. At this growth rate, food production will be 90 per cent and 55 per cent higher in 2000 than in 1970 and 1980 respectively. Its projections also indicate that most of the increase in food production will come from more intensive use of yields - enhancing, energy-intensive inputs and technologies such as fertiliser, pesticides, and irrigations - in many cases with diminishing returns. Land under cultivation is projected to increase only by 4 per cent by 2000 because most good land is already being cultivated. While one hectare of arable land supported an average of 2.6 persons, by 2000 it will have to support 4 persons. For food production to keep pace with rising world demands, world agriculture will have to depend more and more on petroleum and petroleum-related inputs. As a result of this increased petroleum dependence, the real price of food is projected to

increase 95 per cent over the 1970-2000 period. A faster rise in energy prices will also be reflected in a faster rise in food prices. On the average, world food production is projected to grow at slightly faster rate than population with the result that per capita food consumption being about 15 per cent higher in 2000 than it was in 1970. For developing countries as a whole, per capita consumption would be only 9 per cent higher in 2000 than in 1970 but with substantial variations among regions and countries.

Income and food distribution within individual developing countries is so skewed that national average per capita calorie supply is reckoned to have to be 10-20 per cent above minimum levels before the poorest are likely to be able to afford a diet that meets the FAO minimum standard. Latin America is the only region where average per capita calorie supply is projected to be 20 per cent or more above the FAO minimum standard in the year 2000. In the other regions of developing countries - South, East, and South-East Africa, poor areas of North Africa, a disastrous fall in food supply per capita is projected. Assuming no recurrence of severe drought, per capita food supply in developing countries in central Africa is projected to be over 20 per cent below the FAO minimum standard.

The Global 2000 Study's conclusions are based on several non-integrated models. They are broadly consistent with those of other global studies considered, apart from those of the Hudson Institute, despite considerable differences in models and assumptions. Their main strength lies in the richness of detail (for individual sectors - food and agriculture, forests, water, energy, etc.,) they cover and their main serious weakness is the lack of linkages among the sectors. This is responsible for many of the Study's apparent inconsistency and contradiction. Simulations carried out by the Study on other models (World 3 and the World Integrated Model) with linkages removed have produced more favourable outcome. On the basis of this, the Study speculates that the omission of linkages in its models imparts an optimistic bias to its conclusions, especially concerning GNP for year 2000.

CONCLUSION

Available evidence suggests that the net barter terms of trade of primary commodities vis-a-vis manufactures deteriorated over the seventy years period starting from 1868 but remained constant over the seventy years period, from 1900. Although it is difficult to derive clear welfare implications from movements in these terms of trade, the effects of their decline on low-income LDCs specialising in primary exports does justify concern. Theoretical considerations do not lead to any clear indication of the direction in the secular trend in these terms of trade. On the one hand, low income elasticities (resulting from the operation of Engels' law), low population growth in the MDCs, technological progress in the production of substitutes for natural raw materials and in the reduction of material contents of final products appear to suggest a sluggish growth in world demand for primary exports. On the other hand, continued high rates of population growth and economic development in LDCs combined with diminishing returns associated with the world fixed land resources together suggest a sluggish growth in the world supply of primary exports. Hence, on balance, one cannot infer much about the direction of the future terms of trade of primary products on a priori grounds.

Forecasts of their future trends require not only the estimation of many co-efficients (e.g. price and income elasticities) but also the projection of many variables, including future growth rates of income, population and inflation not only at the world level but also at regional levels. Strictly speaking, these variables and the terms of trade are interdependent and are jointly determined by exogenous forces, such as technical progress, changes in tastes, social values and attitudes, etc. (Even these variables may not entirely be independent of income or terms of trade movements).

World Bank forecasts are not encouraging for developing countries. The prices of the non-fuel commodities are projected to be lower in real terms in 1995 than they were in 1980. Their apparent improvements over the year 1983 only indicate a slow and incomplete recovery of the ground lost in the 1981-83 period. The projected real export earnings in 1995 can largely be seen as a recovery from the trough in 1980-85 period, with the underlying trend growth rate (about 1 per cent per annum) remaining as low as that in the 1970s.

However, the World Bank forecasts are sensitive to the underlying projections of economic growth and world inflation and these have become quite unstable since 1980 and thereby making long-term projections more hazardous. The forecasts are also based on what the Bank assume to be the most likely policies pursued by governments. These policies can suddenly be reversed with the election of new governments with different political beliefs and the later forecasts could become quite different. This however does not mean that the World Bank forecasts should not be taken seriously and should not cause some concern to all governments interested in harmonious international relations. The prospects for commodities might turn out to be brighter, but could also be even gloomier than those suggested by the present World Bank forecasts if no new policies are implemented.

Forecasts for years further into the future, i.e. the year 2000 and beyond, suggest an increase in the terms of trade of land intensive commodities as a consequence of population pressure on the resources of the world which are relatively fixed. Projections of different major studies differ according to the assumption made concerning the extent to which resource constraints can be pushed back by the substitution process in both production and consumption away from the land intensive commodities and technological innovation.

Although the 'limits-to-growth' conclusions might appear too pessimistic and are questionable because of the controversial assumptions on which they are based (e.g. the strict binding of the natural limits) they should serve as important warnings to all governments about the need to look far ahead into the future, beyond the period they expect to remain in office. Attention to long-term future problems does not necessarily mean a curtailment of economic growth, as proposed by the Club of Rome. Economic growth is desirable in itself and should be curtailed only if all else fails. Curtailment of economic growth could easily produce its own problems as the Hudson Institute rightly stresses. Since effective solutions to long-term problems may take years or decades to take effect, the governments should pool their knowledge and resources now to find them. In practice, this is unlikely to occur because of the pre-occupation of governments with short-term and medium-term problems and objectives, their lack of confidence in distant projections and the cold war atmosphere which inhibits mutual trust.

NOTES

1. In symbols, let P_c and P_m be the price indices of primary commodities and manufactures respectively, A_c and A_m, the productivity indices of primary exporter (periphery) and manufacturers exporter (centre) respectively and Qc the volume index of primary export, then (for the periphery) we have the following definitions of various terms of trade:

$$\text{NBTT} = P_c/P_m; \text{SFTT} = P_c A_c/Pm; \text{DFTT} = P_c A_c/P_m A_m$$
$$\text{and ITT} = P_c Q_c/P_m.$$

2. See Haberler 1959, 1961, 1964, Meier 1963, pp. 60-81, Flanders 1964, Johnson 1967, p. 250, Pincus 1967, pp. 131-32, Spraos 1979, pp. 17-21.

3. The importance of low income elasticity of demand for primaries as a cause of the deterioration in its terms of trade has also been recognised by other authors in various ways. In explaining the decline in the primary terms of trade, Singer discussed the role of income-inelastic demand right from the beginning, Bernstein (1960, pp. 50-1) focused attention on the decline in the proportion of income spent on food as well as on the decrease in the material content of manufactures and Kindleberger (1943, p. 349) considered the operation of Engels' law of consumption.

4. Kindelberger (1956, p. 306) and Myrdal (1956, p. 230-1.
5. Lewis (1955, 1969, 1972).
6. These series are given in United Nations (1949), table 5.
7. See for example, Kindleberger (1956, pp. 261-3), Meir and Baldwin (1957, p. 234), Haberler (1959, p. 20), Meier (1963, p. 59), Lipsey (1963, p. 17), Johnson (1967, p. 249), Bairoch (1975, pp. 114-5).
8. See for example, Viner (1953, p. 114), Ellsworth (1956), Meir and Baldwin (1957, p. 236), Haberler (1959, p. 20), Bairoch (1975, pp. 115-9).
9. See for example, Viner (1953, p. 114), Meier and Baldwin (1951, p. 236), Streeten (1974), Schloss (1977).
10. See Spraos, (1980, p. 109).
11. Thus, let P_f, P_c and F represent f.o.b., c.i.f. prices and freight costs respectively then

$$P_c = P_f + F$$

and in terms of growth rates:

$$\dot{P}_c = a\dot{P}_f + (1-a)\,\dot{F}$$

where $\dot{P}_c$, $\dot{P}_f$ and $\dot{F}$ are proportional growth rates of P_c, P_f and F respectively and $a = P_f/P_c$.

If $\dot{P}_f = \dot{F}$, then $P_c = P_f$ and there is no valuation bias even if $F<0$.

12. Let a commodity have two grades 1 and 2, whose prices per ton are respectively P_{1t} and P_{2t} and whose quantities in tons are Q_{1t} and Q_{2t} respectively. Suppose P_{1t}, P_{2t}, Q_{1t} and Q_{2t} take respectively the following values $100, $200, 80 tons and 20 tons in 1 year t=1 and $100, $200, 20 tons and 80 tons in year t=2. The price of each grade remains constant and the Laspeyres index for the two grades also remains constant but the price per ton - if the difference in grades is ignored - increases from $120 to $180.
13. Spraos (1980) gave a number of arguments to support the deterioration case for this period. However, as he himself admitted, it is difficult and perhaps impossible to assess the combined weights of these arguments. In assessing the trend of primary terms of trade for the period including the 1970s, there is also a case for excluding petroleum.
14. Industrial Europe was defined as eight countries: the United Kingdom, Germany, France, Italy, the Netherlands, the Belgium-Luxemburg Economic Union, Sweden and Switzerland.

15. Food includes drink and tobacco.

16. Kindleberger (1956, p. 81) found that within Europe, the terms of trade had improved most (on the 1913 base) for the small developed countries, and behaved worst for France and Italy which are the least developed countries of the group. The inversion of the terms of trade of Europe with other areas show US has had the most favourable terms of trade with Europe and all other countries - mainly under-developed countries, the worst.

17. Given the following regression model:

$\log P_t = a + bt + U_t$, when P_t = price in period t, b is the exponential growth rate estimated by ordinary least squares and U_t is the estimated residual. The variance of b is given by: Var b = Var $U / \Sigma (t-\bar{t})^2$ where Var $U = \Sigma U^2 / (n-2)$, $t = t/n$ and n = sample size. It can be seen that the larger is Var U (or the degree of price fluctuation), the larger is Var b and hence the more unreliable the estimate, following the definition of reliability in statistics. The 95 per cent confidence intervals for b for $n - 2 = 31$ is:

$$b \pm 2.04\sqrt{\text{Var } b}$$

Hence, the larger is Var U, the larger is Var b, the wider is the confidence intervals for b.

Note that if successive values of U_t are correlated, sugges-ting the correlation of successive values of the true residuals, it can be shown that the above formula for Var b under-estimates its 'true magnitude' so that on the basis of this formula, b appears to be more reliable than it really is. Since price series tend to have cycles, autocorrelation of the residuals would normally be expected.

18. Inclusions of some food items such as wheat and beef would of course raise the benefits of declining primary terms of trade to industrial nations. A decline in the primary terms of trade would also have important effects on developed countries such as Australia, New Zealand and Canada.

19. However, in deriving price projections, the World Bank did attempt to use exogenous information, e.g. on developments in key countries or likely changes on the market structure within the model or to modify model results.

20. Annual growth rates of GDP for the periods 1983-1990 and 1990-95 are respectively 3.7 per cent and 3.5 per cent for industrial countries, 4.9 per cent and 5.3 per cent for developing countries and 3.5 per cent and 3.5 per cent for centrally planned economies. Annual growth rates of population for these two periods are respectively 0.5 per cent and 0.5 per cent for industrial countries, 2.0 per cent and 1.9 per cent for developing countries and 1.1 per cent and 1.0 per cent for centrally planned economies. (See World

85

Bank Report, op. cit., Tables 11, 12 and Annex C).

21. Changes in petroleum prices will affect not only the prices of primary commodities facing petroleum-based substitutes but also the long-term average marginal costs of those primary commodities (e.g. minerals and metals) for which energy costs represent a substantial component of the total. While shares of industrial countries in world total energy consumption is projected to decline from 53.0 per cent in 1980 to 47.9 per cent in 1990 and 45.0 per cent in 1995, that of the developing countries is projected to increase from 22.8 per cent in 1980 to 28.1 per cent in 1990 and 31.4 per cent in 1995. Natural gas and primary electricity shares in total energy consumption increase at the expense of liquid fuels, whose share declines from 44.6 per cent in 1980 to 37.5 per cent in 1990 and 34.3 per cent in 1995. See World Bank Report, No. 814/812.

22. Since in an office memorandum received in October 1984, only new prices forecasts, (intended for publication in Report No. 814/84) are given, we have to rely on the earlier projections of volumes given in World Bank Report No 814/82.

23. See footnote 22 above for source of volume projections. In the earlier report, i.e. No 814/82, projected annual growth rate of price in 1985-95 is 0.9 per cent rather than 1.5 per cent. This new rate of price increase is consistent with the previous projected rate of volume increase if the increase in the growth rate of price is brought about by an upward revision in the growth rate of demand.

24. World Bank Report, No. 814/82, Table 27, p. 70.

25. These are the average of the lower and upper bounds of price elasticities given in World Bank Report No. 814/82, Table 29, p. 76.

26. The projections to be published in the 1984 Report were made available to us earlier in an official memorandum. The figures referred to as given in 1984 Report are in fact from tables received earlier.

27. See World Bank Report No. 814/82, p. 41-44.

28. Forecast errors can be reduced by improved specification and estimation of the commodity models, e.g. using more sophisticated mixed estimation methods to incorporate extraneous information and better quality data. With more personnel, the World Bank could take the initiative of sending out questionnaires to countries to obtain data more appropriate to their needs. Since future projections are sensitive to GDP projections, special attention should be devoted to the production of the latter.

29. Perhaps it would be better to relax this assumption to show what could happen to the nutrients standard in the poorest regions if further declines in per capita calorie supplies are allowed to persist!

30. The Medium variant of UN population projections is assumed in all these scenarios. For each country, the analysis

covers 28 crops, 6 livestock products, 6 classes of rainfed and irrigated land, 9 current inputs and 26 investment items. These differences between the scenarios are larger for individual countries than for the aggregate of 90 countries.

31. Raising global agricultural output may do little to reduce the risk of famine, which has occurred even in areas with adequate food supplies at national or regional levels:- the groups affected by famine are just too poor or too weak politically to obtain a fair share of the available food or society is unwilling or unable to help. Often, the lack of transport to bring food to remote areas is the actual breakdown.

Chapter Four

COMMODITY MARKET INSTABILITY

The instability of commodity prices has long attracted attention. Attempts to deal with it by price stabilising international commodity agreements (ICAs) go back to the early 1930s and a set of proposals incorporated in the Havana Charter in 1948. Since then, ICAs for various commodities have been attempted or at least considered. The sharp fall in commodity prices after the 1972-74 boom revised interest in such measures. Proposals for stabilising commodity markets were debated in the meeting of Commonwealth Heads of Governments at Kingston, Jamaica, in May 1973 and proposals for an Integrated Programme for commodities (IPC) (which includes a Common Fund to finance international butter stocks) were put forward in the fourth meeting of the United Nations Conference on Trade and Development (UNCTAD IV) in Nairobi in May 1976.

Price instability is believed to be harmful not only because it increases risks to importers, exporters, producers and consumers but because it destabilises export earnings, imports, investment, employment, government expenditures and may retard economic growth. These effects may occur both within a sector of the economy and in the economy as a whole. In the 1950s and 1960s the need to stabilise the export earnings of primary producing countries, because of the importance of exports for meeting the financial development needs of these countries, was emphasised. At the same time, many people realised that ICAs were difficult to negotiate, suitable for only a small number of commodities and often ineffective in stabilising prices and/or export earnings of primary producing countries. As a result, the idea of compensatory financing was conceived and shared the focus of attention.

Both approaches are discussed in Chapter 5. This chapter concentrates on the theoretical arguments and the statistical evidence on the magnitudes, causes and consequences of commodity price and earnings instability.

The concept of instability and the problems of measuring it need to be considered. In a market system some changes in price are necessary to induce supply to adjust to demand in the long run. In the short run - when the supply is fixed or inelastic - price changes are a useful mechanism for rationing out scarce goods among competing consumers, according to their willingness and ability to pay. If prices are stabilised it may reduce their effectiveness as 'signals' to producers and consumers to take actions to eliminate or reduce future short-ages and surpluses. Price fluctuations are a 'problem' only if they are excessive and/or produce misleading signals to economic agents - causing them to make wrong decisions which may lead to unnecessary swings in supply and demand, especially when production and/or consumption levels lag behind the decisions to alter them. In other words, some but not all price movements can be regarded as harmful. But if we use the term instability to refer to the parts of price changes which are undesirable, then some way must be found to distinguish between the acceptable and unacceptable components of price fluctuations. It is now commonly accepted that price instability should be measured as some average of the deviations of price around a trend to be determined according to some criteria. This is based on the implicit assumption that price which moves along a steady state growth path reflecting the equilibrium between the growth of supply and demand may be regarded as ideal and the nearest export approximation to this is a trend line fitted to actual prices. A smooth trend line for prices may be regarded as ideal from the efficiency point of view in the sense that price stabilisation on it (assuming feasible and cost-less) would increase world welfare. The three sources of welfare gains of price stabilisation are: (a) efficiency benefits (in terms of consumers' and producers' surpluses); (b) reduction of risk to consumers and producers; and (c) favourable macro impacts on aggregate investment, employment and income. According to Newberry and Stiglitz (1981, p. 26), source (b) might be less than has previously been thought and that producers could actually be made worse off.

THE MEASUREMENT OF INSTABILITY

The prices of different commodities generally have different patterns over time. Some commodities apparently display large cyclical swings. Others show large year-to-year changes, with sharp rises followed quickly by sharp falls. Yet others are stable for most years with occasional large swings. It is difficult therefore to judge which series is more unstable without a clear definition of instability.

If instability is to be measured as the <u>average deviation</u> from <u>a trend</u>, this involves not only the choice of a trend but also the choice of a measure of average deviation. In choosing a trend, one should consider whether to specify it over the medium-term of say, five years or over the longer-term of ten or more years. Results may vary significantly when different time horizons are considered. This is particularly true if the sample period includes the last decade when large swings in exogenous factors and rapid transformation of the economies of many countries have taken place. Clearly, the purpose of the analysis and the pattern of the time series should be crucial in determining the choice of the time horizon and trend. For example, a medium-term trend taking account of a full cycle may be relevant if the problem at hand is concerned with short-run financial needs caused by export earnings instability. A long-term trend may be relevant if the objective is to find policy measures to alter the longer-run character-istics of the countries' export performance.

The Choice of an Average Deviation
There are two alternative ways of measuring the average deviation around a trend. The deviation from trend can be positive (an average) or negative (a shortfall). One can either: (i) ignore the difference in signs and take the average of all the percentage deviations in absolute values or (ii) square all the deviations first and then take the square root of the average of the squared percentage deviations [1], in producing an index of instability. The latter gives pro-gressively greater weights to larger deviations than the former and is more relevant if occasional or sporadic fluc-tuations cause proportionally greater problems than small ones. Let us name the former the mean absolute deviation index (MAD) and the latter the root mean squared deviation index (RMSD). The RMSD index invariably produces a higher measure of instability than the MAD index and the difference between the two indices is larger for those time series which are dominated by large changes. A possible objection to the RMSD index is that a time series may be considered relatively unstable (on its basis) largely on account of a few extreme observations, which may be due to abnormal circumstances which are unlikely to recur in the future. However, insofar as a quadratic loss function is preferred to a linear one on a priori and/or practical grounds (e.g. when the marginal adjustment cost associated with a shortfall rises with the increase in the size of the shortfall) the RMSD should be favoured, and probably the better way of dealing with the cases just mentioned is to omit these abnormal years in the calculation of the trend and average deviation.

The Choice of a Trend

The two most popular methods for estimating a trend are the moving average method and the ordinary least-squares method. The moving average method gives a trend value for a year j as an average of the observations on m (usually 3, 5 or 7) years centring on the year j [2]. For example, suppose the values for the three years 1970, 1971 and 1972 are 180, 80 and 145 respectively, then the trend-value for 1971 by a 3-year moving average is 102. A moving-average trend normally gives a smaller instability index (MAD or RMSD) than a trend estimated by least-squares, mainly because the latter uses all the observations of the sample period to produce the trend value for each year, whereas the moving average uses only a small sub-set of these observations. In other words, the least-squares trend is either a straight line or a smooth curve whereas the moving-average trend still shows up and down movements in response to actual observations. Although the moving average would provide a better fit to the data than the least-squares trend, it may not be indicative of long-run behaviour.

It is possible to have a trend estimated by what may be called an adaptive least-squares method. For example, the observations on the 1971-80 period may be used to produce a least-squares estimate for the trend value of 1980 and the observations on the 1972-81 period may be used to produce an estimate for the trend value of 1981 and so on. This should produce an implicit 10-year trend which will in general move up and down, like a moving average, to take account of the latest change in the observations. The trend values of the first nine years, however, cannot be obtained using this method. If the sample period is say 40 years but the relevant period for trend specification is say only 10 years, then this method may be used in preference to the smooth least-squares trend produced by using all 40 observations, as the latter represents in effect a long-term 40-year trend. By using such a long-term trend, when the purpose of analysis requires a medium-term trend, instability may be greatly exaggerated.

The Choice between Linear and Exponential Trends

As economic variables (e.g. population, income, output, etc.) tend to grow exponentially, a priori considerations suggest an exponential trend. However, in many actual cases, the linear trends produce better fits in the sense of having smaller average deviations than the exponential ones. Does this necessarily mean that for such cases the true trends are linear? The answer is no. For example, if the deviation from the linear trend in absolute value tends to increase or decline over time or if it is correlated with those in the previous years [3], then the least-squares estimate of the trend will be more unreliable [4] than some alternative method of trend estimation (e.g. a weighted or generalised least-squares method) and the usual least-squares formula for the variance of the trend estimate could produce a very misleading indication of its reliability [5]. This suggests that the trend should be so chosen that the deviation around it should be 'well-behaved' in the sense of being trendless, and independent between successive values. When well-behaved deviations are insisted upon in the choice of a trend and appropriate estimating methods are used to produce them, exponential trends may often be preferred even though linear trends may produce better fits to the data.

However, it is still not clear that for the problems at hand, one is in fact interested in the deviations around the 'true' trend rather than some observed trend. If one is interested in forecasting the financial needs associated with possible future instability and if it is believed that the underlying 'true' trend will continue, then the average deviation around the 'true' trend in the past would provide a better guide to what it will be in the future - than the average deviation around the 'observed' trend. In such a case, one should use the most efficient estimate of the 'true' trend in measuring instability. A linear least-squares trend would be such a trend only if the deviation from it is well-behaved in the sense discussed above. In practice, the exponential and linear trends appear to be almost equally good in most cases, on the basis of econometric criteria. So to facilitate comparison it is best to stick to a single trend and of the two methods the exponential trend is preferable on a priori grounds.

A Problem Associated with the Exponential Trend

Let w_t be the percentage deviation from an exponential trend and u_t be the deviation of the logarithm of the actual value from that of the exponential trend (which becomes a linear function of time), then even if u_t has a normal distribution with zero mean and constant variance, w_t would have a mean which is not zero as required but is positive and varies positively with the variance of u_t. In other words, reducing the variance of u_t (e.g. by adopting a stabilising measure) would also reduce the mean of w_t [6]. Hence the square root of the RMSD index would be an estimate not of the variance of w_t but a combination of the variance and the square of the mean of w_t. Insofar as our purpose is to estimate the 'true' variance of w_t, then the index used should be the root of the average of squared deviations of w_t from its arithmetic mean $(\bar{w})$, with the average being obtained as the sum divided by the number of degrees of freedom [7] (which is in this case the number of observations, minus the two degrees lost due to the need for estimating the intercept and the slope of the time trend) rather than the number of observations itself. However, the RMSD index may as well be used because of its simplicity and widespread use.

The Change in Trend

Suppose in a sample period of 20 years, one observes a change in trend in the middle of this period. The question is whether instability should be measured around two different trends or around a single trend for the whole period. An index which is based on a single trend would in this case appear to overestimate the degree of instability. On the other hand, an index which is based on two different trends may underestimate the extent of instability in the sense that the shift in the trend itself is not regarded as a fluctuation. Large and sporadic shifts in trends may cause just as much problems to planning and investment as regular fluctuations. Moreover, in practice, it may often be difficult to distinguish between shifts in the trend and the movements along some longer term cycles. It is difficult to say whether a shift in a short-term trend in one direction will not reverse itself later when a longer period is considered.

Predictable vs Unpredictable Changes

It has been argued that only unpredictable fluctuations should be included in a measure of instability. On the basis of this argument, the average of deviations around some predicted values (e.g. produced by the Box-Jenkin ARIMA method) has been proposed as an instability index. Since each predicted value may involve not only a trend value but also a deviation from trend, such an index implies that fluctuations which are predictable cause no problems to planners. This is in general not true. While it may be easier to deal with predictable than unpredictable changes because one has more time to take corrective actions, the problem of making the necessary adjustments still exists and hence changes which are predictable are still a nuisance, cause costs and should therefore be included in a measure of instability. Since it is difficult to determine the relative weights associated with each type of change (predictable and unpredictable) because no general loss-function exists, it may be useful for some purposes, to give separately two indices, one which includes all changes and the other, only unpredictable changes.

The distinction between predictable and unpredictable fluctuations has also been debated in different forms. For example, Michaely (1982) distinguished between regularly reversing fluctuations and sporadic fluctuations and suggested that the latter cause more problems. Massell (1969, p. 404) distinguished between the stability and certainty of income. He drew attention to the fact that it is in principle possible for income to fluctuate over time and yet be known in advance with certainty, e.g. fairly regular seasonal fluctuations are quite common. This should make it easier for the government to time stabilisation policies to reduce the effects. Furthermore, most stabilisation programmes require reserves and their required size would be smaller if fluctuations of similar magnitudes are of the regularly reversed type than if they are sporadic. Hence from both the viewpoints of the requirement for reserves and predictability, it is useful to distinguish between these two types of fluctuations. Homi Katrak (1973) suggested that the magnitude of fluctuations (as measured by the mean of the percentage absolute deviation figures) and the variance of fluctuations (i.e. the variance of the percentage absolute deviation around its mean) should be used as measures of the regularly reversing fluctuations and sporadic fluctuations respectively. As it turns out, our MAD index is in fact the mean fluctuation referred to by Katrak and the difference between the square of our RMSD and that of MAD is the variance of this fluctuation [8]. Hence, the root of this difference provides us with a measure of the extent of sporadicity in the fluctuations, whereas the MAD continues to measure the average magnitude (or amplitude) of fluctuations.

However, the above measures of mean and variance of fluctuations have not quite removed all the problems. It is possible for two time series to have the same MAD and RMSD, i.e. the same mean and variance of fluctuations, and yet one be regularly reversing, the other not. For example, consider the following two series:

```
Series A: -1   1  -1   1  -1  1  -1  1  -1   1  -1  1
Series B: -1  -1  -1  -1   1  1   1  1  -1  -1   1  1
```

Series A is perfectly regularly reversing, whereas series B is not. It is clear that series A is easier to predict and requires less reserves for stabilisation than series B and yet both series should have the same MAD and RMSD, with MAD = RMSD, i.e. zero sporadicity. Hence the difference between MAD and RMSD on the variance of fluctuation provides a very crude indication of predictability or reserves requirement.

Furthermore it is important to recognise that predictability and reserves requirement need not be inversely related. It is possible for a more predictable series to require greater reserves. For example, consider:

```
Series C: -1   1   1  -1  1  -1  -1  -1   1  -1  1  1
Series D: -1  -1  -1   1  1   1  -1  -1  -1   1  1  1
```

It can be seen that series D is perfectly predictable with a regular cycle, i.e. 3 years up and 3 years down, whereas series C is largely random in its ups and downs. It is worthwhile to hold reserves up to the level at which the cost of holding the last unit equals the adjustment cost saved by it multiplied by the probability that it would in fact be used. Let us assume that the marginal adjustment cost exceeds the marginal cost of reserves - this is a necessary condition for reserves to be held at all. Examination of series D suggests that the optimal level of reserves should be 3, since it is a certainty that the third unit of reserves is needed. Suppose we make the plausible assumption that series C is generated by a binomial distribution in which there is an even chance for either -1 or +1 to occur, then the optimal level of reserves associated with it would be less than 3, if the marginal adjustment cost is less than eight times the marginal cost of holding reserves (since the probability of the third unit of reserves being used, i.e. probability of more than three consecutive negative values, is one-eighth). Hence, provided that the ratio of adjustment cost to reserve holding cost is less than eight, series C would require less reserves for stabilising purpose than series D.

COMMODITY INSTABILITY: HISTORICAL EVIDENCE

In this section we attempt to consider the following factual questions:

(a) Which are the most unstable commodities?
(b) Are commodities' prices more unstable than those of manufactured products?
(c) Do LDCs on average have more unstable export proceeds than MDCs?

The next section will attempt to evaluate explanations for these facts.

Our index of instability has been defined as an average of the percentage deviations around a trend. To facilitate comparison, a common trend will be chosen throughout and the exponential trend is chosen in preference to the linear trend because the former appears to be more suitable for the following reasons: (i) economic variables affecting demands, supplies and prices of commodities are more likely to have exponential trends; and (ii) the demand and supply functions are more likely to have a log-linear rather than a linear form. In any case, as mentioned earlier, there is (with few exceptions) little difference in practice between the goodness of fit of the exponential trend and the linear trend. To illustrate the difference between the measured magnitudes of instability produced by two different methods of obtaining the average deviation (i.e. the RMSD and MAD) the results for both of these are presented in the first two Tables. Subsequently only the results for the one which is the more appropriate method to be used in each case are presented.

COMMODITY MARKET INSTABILITY

Commodities Suffering the Most Unstable Prices

It is useful to identify at an international level those commodities which have the most volatile prices and export earnings, since it is likely that those commodities should, prima facie, derive highest potential benefits from stabilisation measures and so should merit the most attention in any international stabilisation programmes, other things (e.g. storage costs) being equal. However, often it is at the individual country level that adverse consequences of commodity instability have to be considered. Some countries may have relatively stable prices and proceeds for commodities whose prices and proceeds may be unstable at world level. On the other hand, for commodities stable at world level, many countries may have unstable prices and proceeds. Insofar as the export earnings of the major exporters of a commodity are significantly offsetting, it is possible for the world total export earnings to be considerably more stable than those of most individual exporters. The world price of a commodity quoted in the commodity exchanges in London or in New York may show a high degree of stability and yet it is entirely possible for the prices actually received by most of its exporters to be unstable, because the quoted world price may be unrepresentative of the prices they actually received. In fact, each country's export unit value would be a better indicator of the price received for the commodity than the world market price. It will be shown that the instability of price and proceeds for every commodity facing the individual exporting countries varies a great deal across these countries and is on average larger than for those at world level. In view of the differences of instability at country and world level, it is useful to evaluate commodity instability at both levels.

Instability at World Level

In considering which commodities suffer the most price instability, one immediately faces the problem of choosing between the nominal (or current dollar) world prices and the real (or constant 1980 dollar) world prices. Insofar as one is concerned with the import purchasing power of commodity exports the 'real' market prices are the more fundamental and should be preferred. To obtain the real prices, this study will follow the World Bank practice in deflating the nominal prices by an index of the prices of manufactures exported by the MDCs. But, as many financial transactions are still assessed in nominal rather than real terms, we show both.

The rankings of commodities on the basis of price instability are sensitive not only to the choice of nominal or real terms but also to the choice of trend and period.

Instability in Nominal Terms

Table 4.1 ranks the major commodities in terms of the instability of nominal world prices for the period 1951-80, on the
basis of the RMSD index (column 1). The five commodities
with the most volatile prices are sugar (81.2), sisal (60.2),
coffee (59.5), cocoa (56.5) and zinc (50.0) and the five with
the least unstable prices are tobacco (17.0), bananas (19.8),
copper (23.4), tea (23.7) and jute (26.3). All the ranks are
given in the brackets next to the figures for the instability
index. The MAD indexes in column 2 are of course smaller
than the corresponding RMSD indexes in column 1 and the
association between their rankings is as expected, very high.
(The rank correlation is 0.94.)

Instability in Real Terms

The various price instability indexes in real terms are given
in columns 1-4 in Table 4.2, again with their associated ranks
in the brackets. The results change quite dramatically.
Copper and jute, which are two of the five commodities with
the lowest price instability in nominal terms, are now among
the top five commodities with the highest price instability in
real terms, their instability indexes actually increase from
23.4 and 26.3 to 35.7 and 38.4 respectively. The reason why
instability is higher in real terms than in nominal terms is the
high negative correlation between the deviations of the
nominal commodity price and those of the deflator (i.e. the
index of manufactures' prices). In general, however, we
should expect the deviation from trend of the nominal prices
of most commodities to vary positively with those of the
deflator, causing the price instability indexes to be lower in
real terms than in nominal terms. The results on the whole
confirm this expectation. For example, the instability indexes
of sugar, sisal, coffee, cocoa and zinc (i.e. the five commodities with the most unstable nominal prices) fall from 81.2,
60.2, 59.5, 56.5 and 50.0 in nominal terms respectively to
66.4, 43.5, 39.7, 38.4 and 38.2 in real terms respectively. In
particular, tin, which has a nominal price instability index of
34.7 becomes one of the five commodities with the least
unstable price instability in real terms at 16.3. The
association between the instability indexes in real and nominal
terms is as expected, positive but relatively low. (The rank
correlation is 0.70.)

Sensitivity of the Length of the Trend

It has been pointed out that on the basis of a single trend
over the whole period, the magnitude of measured instability
increases as the length of the period increases but the extent
of the increase could vary considerably across commodities,
depending on the time pattern of individual price series. A

Table 4.1: Instability Indices of Nominal Term World Prices of 18 Major Commodities

	1951-80				1951-60		1961-70		1971-80	
	RMSD (1)	MAD (2)	RMSD1 (3)	MAD1 (4)	RMSD (5)	MAD (6)	RMSD (7)	MAD (8)	RMSD (9)	MAD (10)
Sugar	81.2 (1)	53.9 (1)	57.4 (1)	38.6 (1)	20.0 (6)	14.4 (6)	60.9 (1)	48.0 (1)	76.0 (1)	53.4 (1)
Sisal	60.2 (2)	41.4 (4)	36.9 (2)	25.0 (2)	29.8 (1)	25.9 (1)	19.2 (2)	13.6 (3)	53.3 (2)	35.5 (2)
Coffee	59.5 (3)	44.9 (2)	25.5 (6)	15.8 (6)	17.1 (9)	14.0 (7)	11.8 (8)	10.1 (7)	38.9 (6)	23.4 (8)
Cocoa	56.5 (4)	44.4 (3)	23.4 (7)	17.9 (4)	22.3 (4)	16.8 (5)	16.7 (4)	12.6 (4)	29.5 (9)	24.2 (7)
Zinc	50.0 (5)	32.7 (5)	28.9 (3)	20.0 (3)	22.2 (5)	19.0 (4)	14.2 (5)	10.7 (5)	42.5 (5)	30.4 (5)
Rubber	39.0 (6)	29.3 (6)	19.6 (11)	13.0 (11)	27.9 (2)	20.6 (3)	8.7 (11)	6.1 (11)	17.3 (12)	12.3 (13)
Copra	37.0 (7)	26.4 (8)	28.7 (4)	16.4 (5)	15.2 (10)	12.5 (10)	6.7 (14)	5.0 (14)	46.9 (3)	31.6 (3)
Tin	34.7 (8)	25.7 (9)	12.0 (15)	9.3 (14)	10.8 (12)	9.1 (12)	11.7 (9)	9.8 (8)	13.4 (15)	9.0 (16)
Wool	34.4 (9)	24.9 (11)	22.5 (8)	13.5 (10)	18.0 (7)	12.7 (9)	10.4 (10)	8.6 (10)	33.0 (8)	19.3 (10)
Rice	31.9 (10)	23.0 (12)	26.6 (5)	15.6 (7)	6.5 (14)	4.8 (15)	13.3 (6)	10.7 (6)	43.6 (4)	31.1 (4)
Wheat	31.8 (11)	25.3 (10)	20.1 (9)	11.8 (12)	5.7 (15)	5.1 (14)	4.0 (17)	3.4 (17)	34.2 (7)	27.0 (6)
Cotton	30.0 (12)	26.9 (7)	9.4 (16)	6.7 (16)	3.7 (18)	3.6 (17)	3.5 (18)	3.5 (18)	15.5 (14)	13.3 (12)
Maize	26.7 (13)	22.1 (13)	14.2 (13)	9.5 (13)	4.5 (17)	3.5 (18)	6.8 (13)	5.8 (12)	23.1 (10)	19.3 (11)
Jute	26.3 (14)	19.1 (15)	18.3 (12)	14.0 (9)	27.4 (3)	22.9 (2)	12.0 (7)	9.8 (9)	10.4 (16)	9.5 (15)
Tea	23.7 (15)	18.1 (16)	12.8 (14)	8.9 (15)	13.5 (11)	10.3 (11)	5.7 (16)	4.8 (15)	16.5 (13)	11.5 (14)
Copper	23.4 (16)	20.3 (14)	20.0 (10)	15.5 (8)	18.0 (8)	12.7 (8)	18.5 (3)	14.1 (2)	23.1 (11)	19.7 (9)
Bananas	19.8 (17)	17.3 (17)	5.9 (18)	4.6 (18)	5.2 (16)	4.4 (16)	6.4 (15)	4.7 (16)	5.9 (18)	4.7 (18)
Tobacco	17.0 (18)	13.7 (18)	7.6 (17)	6.4 (17)	7.8 (13)	7.2 (13)	7.5 (12)	5.6 (13)	7.4 (17)	6.2 (17)

Sources and Definitions: see at the end of Table 4.2

Rank correlation

	Col 2	Col 3	Col 5	Col 7	Col 9	Col 1 of Table 4.2
Col 1	0.94	0.8	0.54	0.69	0.75	0.70
Col 5				0.72	0.18	
Col 7					0.48	

single long-term trend, say of 30 years, may however produce an exaggerated impression of price instability for some commodities, for which shifts in medium-term (say 10 year) trends occurred. For these commodities, the average true instability indexes for the sub-periods may be much lower than for the total period (covering the sub-periods).

To take account of possible shifts in the medium-term trends, three exponential trends are estimated for the three decades 1951-60, 1961-70 and 1971-80 and the deviations from these three trends are pooled to produce a single index (RMSD1 or MAD1). The results are given in columns 3 and 4 respectively in Table 4.1 for nominal prices and in Table 4.2 for real prices. As expected the instability index is lower for every commodity, with the reduction being greatest for bananas, cotton and tin (about two-thirds) and least for copper (less than one-fifth), with cocoa and coffee (about a half) somewhere in between. Table 4.2 shows similar results when instabilities are compared in real terms. Thus, the results clearly confirm the view that the use of a single long-term trend over a long-period (say 30 years) would greatly increase the index of instability of many commodities. If for most predictive purposes, a period of ten years is considered long enough for a trend, the RMSD1 index (based on several trends) is arguably a better measure of instability than the RMSD index (based on a single trend) when the period under study extends into several decades. Although the reduction in instability (when RMSD1 is used instead of RMSD) is greater for some commodities than for others, this is not sufficient to produce a poor association between the two indexes. (The rank correlation coefficient is 0.80.)

Sensitivity to the Choice of Period

The columns 5-10 of Table 4.1 show the magnitudes of nominal price instability for the 18 major commodities for the three decades 1951-60, 1961-70 and 1971-80. The ranking can be seen to change dramatically from one decade to the next. Commodities which appeared to be the most unstable in one decade became relatively stable in the next. For example, over 1951-60 jute and rubber are two of the three most unstable commodities with indexes of 27.4 and 27.9 respectively. In the 1961-70 decade, their indexes fall to 12.0 and 8.7 respectively and their ranks in descending order of instability become seventh and eleventh respectively. On the other hand, the instability indexes of sugar and rice increase from 20.0 (rank 6), to 6.5 (rank 14) respectively in 1951-60 to 60.9 (rank 1) and 10.4 (rank 6) respectively in 1961-70. The differences between the rankings for the 1961-70 and 1971-80 decades are even more marked. (The rank correlation coefficient of the indexes for the last two decades is only 0.48 as compared with 0.72 for the first two decades. The

Table 4.2: Instability Indices of Real Term World Prices of Major Commodities

	1951-80 RMSD (1)	1951-80 MAD (2)	1951-80 RMSD1 (3)	1951-80 MAD1 (4)	1951-60 RMSD (5)	1951-60 MAD (6)	1961-70 RMSD (7)	1961-70 MAD (8)	1971-80 RMSD (9)	1971-80 MAD (10)
Sugar	66.4 (1)	44.2 (1)	54.1 (1)	36.8 (1)	18.5 (8)	13.0 (8)	62.0 (1)	48.6 (1)	67.7 (1)	48.7 (1)
Sisal	43.5 (2)	29.1 (4)	33.1 (2)	23.4 (2)	28.2 (2)	24.6 (2)	20.2 (2)	14.9 (2)	45.6 (2)	30.5 (2)
Coffee	39.7 (3)	26.3 (6)	27.2 (3)	16.4 (5)	19.4 (7)	15.5 (6)	10.8 (9)	9.1 (9)	41.6 (3)	24.5 (6)
Jute	38.4 (4)	31.8 (2)	19.2 (10)	13.6 (9)	30.5 (1)	25.2 (1)	10.9 (8)	9.2 (8)	7.8 (16)	6.3 (16)
Zinc	38.2 (5)	24.3 (7)	25.8 (4)	18.3 (4)	21.1 (5)	18.4 (4)	14.2 (5)	10.5 (6)	36.8 (6)	25.9 (5)
Cocoa	37.0 (6)	27.3 (5)	24.4 (6)	18.5 (3)	23.7 (4)	17.6 (5)	18.5 (3)	14.7 (3)	29.8 (8)	23.3 (7)
Copper	35.7 (7)	29.9 (3)	20.0 (9)	15.8 (7)	20.6 (6)	14.5 (7)	17.9 (4)	14.2 (4)	21.2 (10)	18.8 (9)
Rice	26.4 (8)	18.2 (8)	23.5 (7)	14.6 (8)	7.5 (13)	5.3 (15)	14.1 (6)	11.5 (5)	37.4 (5)	27.0 (4)
Copra	25.8 (9)	17.7 (9)	25.7 (5)	16.0 (6)	14.7 (11)	12.1 (11)	8.0 (12)	6.6 (12)	41.3 (4)	29.3 (3)
Wool	25.4 (10)	15.0 (11)	22.4 (8)	12.9 (11)	17.7 (9)	12.2 (10)	10.4 (10)	8.2 (10)	33.0 (7)	18.4 (10)
Rubber	21.1 (11)	16.2 (10)	19.2 (11)	13.2 (10)	27.2 (3)	21.6 (3)	10.0 (11)	6.8 (11)	16.3 (13)	11.2 (14)
Wheat	20.2 (12)	12.9 (15)	16.7 (12)	10.2 (12)	4.7 (16)	4.3 (16)	4.3 (16)	3.5 (16)	28.3 (9)	22.8 (8)
Tea	17.2 (13)	14.2 (12)	14.4 (13)	9.5 (13)	16.3 (10)	12.8 (9)	3.7 (18)	3.1 (17)	18.5 (11)	12.7 (12)
Maize	16.4 (14)	13.1 (13)	11.2 (14)	8.3 (15)	4.5 (17)	4.2 (17)	6.5 (15)	5.5 (15)	17.8 (12)	15.1 (11)
Tin	16.3 (15)	13.1 (14)	10.5 (15)	8.6 (14)	9.3 (12)	8.2 (12)	11.4 (7)	9.4 (7)	10.5 (15)	8.1 (15)
Cotton	13.9 (16)	11.1 (16)	9.0 (16)	6.3 (17)	4.4 (18)	3.6 (18)	4.0 (17)	2.6 (18)	14.3 (14)	12.6 (13)
Tobacco	12.6 (17)	10.1 (17)	7.4 (17)	6.4 (16)	7.3 (14)	6.4 (13)	8.0 (13)	6.5 (13)	7.0 (17)	6.2 (17)
Bananas	10.0 (18)	8.4 (18)	6.7 (18)	5.7 (18)	6.4 (15)	5.8 (14)	6.9 (14)	5.5 (14)	6.7 (18)	5.8 (18)

Notes: 1. Exponential trend is used throughout

2. RMSD = Root Mean Square Deviation Instability Index $= \sqrt{\frac{1}{n} \Sigma [(X_i - \hat{X}_i)/\hat{X}_i]^2}$

Where X and $\hat{X}$ are the actual and trend values in period i.

COMMODITY MARKET INSTABILITY

MAD = Mean Absolute Deviation Instability Index = $\frac{1}{n}\Sigma|X_i - \hat{X}_i|/\hat{X}_i$

RMSD1 = The RMSD index for 1951–80 period, basing on three separate trends for the three periods 1951–60, 1961–70 and 1971–80. It is estimated as the root of the mean of the squares of the RMSDs for the three sub-periods, i.e.

$$RMSD1 = \sqrt{\frac{1}{3}\sum_{i=1}^{3} RMSD_i^2}$$ where $RMSD_1$, $RMSD_2$ and $RMSD_3$ refer to the above three sub-periods respectively

MAD1 = The MAD index for 1951–80 period, basing on three separate trends

$$MAD1 = \frac{1}{3}\sum MAD_i$$ where MAD_i is the MAD for period i = 1, 2, 3

Source: Data supplied from UNCTAD Secretariat. These data can also be found in World Bank Report No. 814/82.

rank correlation coefficient for 1951-60 and 1971-80 is even lower at 0.18.) The association is even poorer between the magnitudes of the indexes than between their ranks. This is because even when the ranks of some commodities stay the same the magnitudes of their indexes may change at very different rates. For example, although the rank of sugar and sisal remain first and second respectively in the 1960s and 1970s, the index of sugar increased only modestly from 60.9 to 76, whereas that of sisal increased sharply from 19.2 to 53.3 over the same two decades.

These inter-period changes in their ranking appear to support the view that random factors rather than basic characteristics of particular commodities play the more important role in their price instability. If stable, systematic factors, such as relatively low price elasticities of supply and demand, low/high income elasticities of demand, or specific characteristics of supply are the main determinants of the degree of price volatility, then the commodities which are relatively unstable in one period should also be relatively unstable in another. Since the rankings vary so much from one period to the next, it is difficult to identify un-ambiguously those commodities which are most prone to price instability for policy or other purposes. However, on balance from the results over the three decades it appears that the five most unstable commodities are sugar, sisal, cocoa, zinc and coffee.

Objections to the Use of the World Prices
The price series used are the annual average prices recorded in the commodity market centres (mainly London and New York). To rank the commodities in terms of the instability indexes of these price series may be open to a number of objections. First, the movements may provide a poor guide to the changes in the prices received by exporting nations because: (i) only a small proportion of the volume of the commodity may be traded in the commodity exchanges at these prices; (ii) for some commodities (e.g. sugar) a large proportion of exports is under special arrangements with prices and quantities fixed in advance for particular periods; and (iii) for others, exports are conducted under bilateral contract deals with the CPEs. One example is aluminium where the amount of spot metal passing through the free market is small compared with that under fixed price contracts [9].

Second, the annual prices quoted are the unweighted arithmetic averages of the reported daily prices on the commodity exchanges, even though the quantities traded at different prices may vary a great deal. If the quantities sold at extremely high or low prices are relatively small, an un-weighted average of daily prices would exaggerate their volatility.

Thirdly, most countries export more than one type and grade of most agricultural commodities but the composition of their exports can vary from year to year. As the prices quoted on the commodity exchanges are only for specific types and grades of a commodity this may give a misleading picture of the average prices fixed by the country. Table 4.3 shows that different grades and types of coffee and cotton have different growth rates and instability indices over 1960-69, 1970-79 and 1960-82 periods. It can be seen that the instability index for different grades of coffee varies from 40 to 73 for 1960-69 period and from 24 to 36 for the 1970-79 period. The instability index for cotton also shows considerable variation across grades from a low of 23 to a high of 46 for the 1960-69 period and 11 to 21 for the 1970-79 period. This is an argument for using export unit values rather than market prices.

Instability of World Export Unit Value (EUV)

Table 4.4 shows that the world export unit value is more stable than the world market price quoted in the commodity exchanges for every one of the ten core commodities, except jute. The differences between the magnitudes of the indexes of EUVs and prices instability are large for only four out of the five most unstable commodities, sugar, hard fibres (sisal), coffee and cocoa, and are quite small for the remaining six. Nevertheless, market prices greatly exaggerate the price instability facing exporters of some commodities. The fact that EUVs are generally more stable than prices suggests that the prices received by exporters for quantities traded outside the commodity markets are more stable than the quoted prices. This is particularly true for sugar where the EUV is about half as unstable as price. Although market prices exaggerate the degree of instability more for some commodities than for others, this is unsufficient to affect the ranking of commodities in terms of instability. The rank correlation between the instability indexes for market prices and those for EUVs is very high indeed, at 0.98 (RMSD) and 0.93 (MAD).

Earlier, we contended that the export unit value (EUV) for a commodity would reflect more accurately the price each exporting country receives than the world market price quoted in the commodity exchanges. Tables 4.5 and 4.6 present RMSD and MAD instability indexes respectively of value, volume and unit value for each of the ten core commodities exported by the ten most important exporting countries in terms of shares in world export values (which are also given). But let us limit discussion to the RMSD index. For a number of commodities such as sugar, hard fibres, cotton, jute and tea the variation in the degree of EUV instability experienced by different exporting countries

COMMODITY MARKET INSTABILITY

Table 4.3: Different Grades of Quoted Prices of Coffee and
Cotton: Growth Rates (%) and Instability
Indices (%) (Growth rates are given in brackets
below the figures for instability)

	1960–69	Periods 1970–79	1960–68
Coffee			
Columbian mild Arabicas	40.1 (-6.1)	23.6 (17.9)	65.9 (6.6)
Brazilian and other Arabicas	43.2 (-5.8)	28.3 (18.2)	69.0 (6.5)
Other mild Arabicas	49.9 (-6.1)	35.8 (18.7)	82.6 (7.5)
Robustas	73.1 (-3.1)	28.7 (19.4)	92.9 (7.8)
Composite indicator price	54.3 (-4.8)	28.4 (18.9)	78.4 (7.1)
Cotton			
(Extra Long) Egypt	46.2 (-2.3)	20.5 (11.2)	50.0 (5.7)
(Long) Sudan	23.1 (-4.5)	20.7 (12.3)	36.9 (4.9)
(Medium) Mexico	34.6 (-5.8)	13.4 (10.9)	47.7 (5.0)
(Medium) Nicaragua	33.7 (-6.4)	15.8 (10.8)	48.5 (4.9)
(Short) US	29.6 (-6.2)	16.8 (10.1)	43.6 (4.9)

Source: Calculations on the basis of data supplied from the
UNCTAD Secretariat. These data can also be found in UNCTAD,
Handbook of International Trade and Development Statistics,
Supplement '84, Instability Index: RMSD

Table 4.4: Instability Indices of World Export Unit Values and Market Prices (Current Dollars) for Ten Core Commodities 1971-80

| | Export unit values | | Market price | |
	RMSD	MAD	RMSD	MAD
Sugar	39.5	29.7	76.0	53.4
Hard Fibres	34.1	23.3	53.3	35.5
Coffee	27.3	17.8	38.9	23.4
Copper	20.6	17.1	23.1	19.7
Cocoa	19.7	16.1	29.5	24.2
Rubber	15.5	11.1	17.3	12.3
Tea	14.3	11.1	16.5	11.5
Cotton	11.9	9.0	15.5	13.3
Jute	11.4	9.0	10.4	9.5
Tin	10.7	8.5	13.4	9.0

Source: Data used to produce the first two columns are supplied from the UNCTAD secretariat. The last two columns are from Table 4.2

is particularly large. Thus, the range is 7.4 (India) to 64.4 (Brazil) for hard fibres, 6.3 (USSR) to 28.9 (India) for cotton, 6.7 (Belgium) to 23.1 (UK) for jute and 21.6 (USA) and 72.7 (Brazil) for sugar and 9.1 (UK) and 23.6 (Argentina) for tea. For other commodities, differences across countries concerning EUV unstability remain quite considerable.

Apart from two commodities - sugar, in which only four countries have EUVs more stable than the world's, and cotton, in which nine countries have EUVs more stable than the world's - in all others, between five and seven countries have more stable EUVs than those of the world (i.e. for these commodities, the EUVs of the world are only slightly higher than the average for the countries). Thus, on average, the world's EUV for each commodity does not tend to exaggerate the instability of the price received by the individual major exporters. Furthermore, examination of the figures in the last two columns for each commodity representing instability indexes of EUV and shares, reveals little association between them. This suggests that larger exporting nations do not tend to have either more or less stable prices than smaller ones. This may not be surprising because there are no clear a priori reasons for expecting either a positive or negative association between the size of market share and the degree of price instability.

Table 4.5: Instability Indices (RMSD) of Value, Volume and Unit Value and Share (1971-80)

	Val.	Vol.	UV	Share
Sugar				
World	35.1	5.6	39.5	100.0
Cuba	33.9	9.8	31.4	31.5
Brazil	82.6	27.5	72.7	7.6
France	21.0	18.6	31.9	7.3
Australia	40.3	11.7	89.0	6.8
Philippines	54.8	27.3	59.8	4.7
Dominican Republic	53.6	7.4	57.4	3.1
Germany Fed. Rep. of	45.5	39.2	27.1	2.4
Thailand	73.7	51.9	50.6	2.4
Belgium-Luxembourg	16.4	25.6	22.2	1.9
United States	636.2	487.1	21.6	1.1
Cotton and Cotton Yarn				
World	8.3	6.8	11.9	100.0
United States	18.4	20.8	12.8	21.3
USSR	13.5	9.7	6.3	14.4
Egypt	18.8	12.0	24.0	8.7
Turkey	23.1	28.6	22.3	5.7
Pakistan	39.7	49.6	23.2	4.5
Mexico	14.0	13.2	17.0	3.6
Greece	15.4	15.7	18.3	2.5
Brazil	26.2	34.7	14.9	2.5
Republic of Korea	20.2	20.8	17.1	1.7
India	46.1	68.9	28.9	1.1
Coffee				
World	19.4	7.1	27.3	100.0
Brazil	24.0	17.3	31.5	20.3
Colombia	12.2	16.7	29.5	15.4
Ivory Coast	26.1	16.4	23.8	5.8
El Salvador	22.3	12.4	26.9	4.6
Indonesia	33.5	8.4	36.5	4.0
Mexico	24.9	17.2	27.4	4.0
Uganda	26.2	12.9	32.0	3.7
Guatemala	24.1	6.2	23.4	3.7
United States	45.0	33.7	18.5	2.5
Costa Rica	26.5	12.8	30.6	2.5
Copper				
World	25.4	5.0	20.6	100.0
Chile	23.9	7.5	22.1	18.1
Zambia	23.2	6.2	21.8	13.5
Canada	26.1	9.1	19.9	11.1
Zaire	28.4	8.8	22.6	8.5

Table 4.5: (continued)

	Val.	Vol.	UV	Share
Belgium-Luxembourg	27.1	6.9	23.3	6.7
Peru	27.2	17.4	24.0	5.2
Philippines	33.9	3.9	33.1	4.3
Papua New Guinea	28.9	19.7	19.5	3.5
United States	25.7	15.2	20.1	3.1
Poland	10.6	14.6	17.1	2.2
Tin				
World	12.7	3.7	10.7	100.0
Malaysia	12.0	4.3	10.5	36.4
Thailand	17.3	14.9	11.0	13.1
Bolivia	16.0	8.2	12.5	12.8
Indonesia	18.2	8.2	11.8	12.2
United Kingdom	19.5	17.6	17.1	5.1
Australia	17.0	13.8	9.0	3.5
China	41.9	38.9	18.3	2.7
Singapore	35.7	44.1	16.5	2.4
Germany Fed. Rep. of	31.7	28.2	9.8	1.6
Brazil	48.0	34.2	15.4	1.2
Cocoa Beans				
World	17.2	5.1	19.7	100.0
Ghana	12.5	12.0	15.7	23.1
Ivory Coast	20.5	15.5	16.4	19.5
Nigeria	32.1	11.9	26.5	16.7
Brazil	33.0	19.3	35.3	12.6
Cameroon	19.0	13.9	21.1	6.4
Papua New Guinea	30.6	11.0	25.8	2.4
Dominican Republic	35.6	9.0	33.7	2.2
Ecuador	62.7	32.1	31.4	2.2
Malaysia	39.7	15.2	27.2	1.8
Netherlands	77.5	79.9	17.4	1.4
Tea				
World	15.2	1.5	14.3	100.0
India	20.9	8.5	18.7	27.2
Sri Lanka	12.9	9.0	14.4	21.9
China	20.3	7.5	15.7	8.6
Kenya	22.6	10.0	18.3	8.2
United Kingdom	14.7	13.5	9.1	7.1
Indonesia	22.3	9.5	23.5	5.1
Malawi	17.2	6.1	14.6	2.1
Netherlands	15.5	18.4	13.5	2.0
Bangladesh	21.1	19.5	20.8	1.7
Argentina	24.5	12.6	23.6	1.5

Table 4.5: (continued)

	Val.	Vol.	UV	Share
Jute & Manufactures				
World	13.8	6.7	11.4	100.1
Bangladesh	12.9	11.5	13.7	36.2
India	24.0	10.5	16.5	34.2
Thailand	18.1	18.8	8.8	7.2
Belgium–Luxembourg	16.9	15.1	6.7	5.5
USSR	25.6	18.9	9.9	3.3
Netherlands	35.2	27.0	8.7	1.7
China	152.3	179.3	21.3	1.6
Nepal	21.8	28.8	18.1	1.5
United Kingdom	14.9	19.8	23.1	1.4
Germany Fed. Rep. of	11.4	12.4	8.9	1.1
Rubber				
World	19.3	4.2	15.5	100.0
Malaysia	20.8	5.7	16.1	50.6
Indonesia	16.9	4.3	14.5	23.4
Thailand	23.7	7.7	17.6	12.7
Sri Lanka	18.0	9.0	18.1	4.4
Liberia	16.0	4.8	12.6	2.4
United States	18.9	13.8	8.0	1.0
Nigeria	53.7	22.3	31.4	0.9
Viet Nam	33.2	34.5	19.8	0.7
Zaire	19.0	7.1	17.4	0.6
Ivory Coast	21.2	4.9	18.0	0.5
Hard Fibres & Products				
World	37.5	10.0	34.1	100.1
Brazil	67.1	20.5	64.4	18.9
Unit. Rep. of Tanzania	39.7	7.3	49.0	10.9
Philippines	32.5	12.7	28.1	9.8
Mexico	35.4	25.4	51.4	8.9
India	10.0	9.0	2.4	6.3
Portugal	47.8	21.6	34.9	6.2
Belgium–Luxembourg	38.0	15.2	23.8	5.9
Kenya	98.3	32.4	41.3	4.2
Sri Lanka	14.0	10.6	11.0	3.6
Germany Fed. Rep. of	38.9	30.5	14.7	2.6

Source: Calculations using data supplied from the UNCTAD
Secretariat

Table 4.6: Instability Indices (MAD) of Value, Volume and
          Unit Value and Share (1971-80)

	Val.	Vol.	UV	Share
Sugar				
World	26.0	3.5	29.7	100.0
Cuba	25.8	8.0	25.1	31.5
Brazil	63.5	24.4	53.1	7.6
France	17.5	16.2	25.6	7.3
Australia	29.0	9.9	26.4	6.8
Philippines	46.3	19.9	44.7	4.7
Dominican Republic	34.4	5.7	38.3	3.1
Germany Fed. Rep. of	32.7	33.0	22.3	2.4
Thailand	61.8	39.2	37.5	2.4
Belgium-Luxembourg	13.1	17.5	17.3	1.9
United States	348.8	279.8	18.7	1.1
Cotton & Cotton Yarn				
World	6.6	5.3	9.0	100.0
United States	13.6	18.9	12.0	21.3
USSR	11.1	7.9	5.0	14.4
Egypt	13.3	10.6	19.7	8.7
Turkey	18.1	21.2	13.9	5.7
Pakistan	31.9	38.0	18.4	4.5
Mexico	12.1	10.9	11.3	3.6
Greece	11.4	13.9	12.3	2.5
Brazil	18.5	28.8	11.8	7.5
Republic of Korea	16.7	15.7	12.5	1.7
India	37.8	54.6	21.9	1.1
Coffee				
World	14.1	5.6	17.8	100.0
Brazil	18.9	13.5	20.3	20.3
Columbia	10.3	13.0	19.9	15.4
Ivory Coast	18.6	12.9	15.1	5.8
El Salvador	14.6	10.6	19.9	4.6
Indonesia	23.5	6.3	23.0	4.0
Mexico	21.0	15.4	17.8	4.0
Uganda	16.7	11.5	19.7	3.7
Guatemala	16.0	5.0	16.8	3.7
United States	34.4	28.1	14.1	2.5
Costa Rica	17.6	11.5	21.1	2.5
Copper				
World	19.5	3.9	17.1	100.0
Chile	17.4	6.7	18.1	18.1
Zambia	19.0	4.9	18.1	13.5
Canada	20.8	8.1	16.9	11.1
Zaire	18.4	7.7	13.9	8.5

Table 4.6: (continued)

	Val.	Vol.	UV	Share
Belgium-Luxembourg	21.2	5.0	18.8	6.7
Peru	21.3	15.1	20.2	5.2
Philippines	28.4	3.1	27.2	4.3
Papua New Guinea	21.4	11.3	15.3	3.5
United States	21.1	13.3	15.0	3.1
Colombo	7.6	13.1	13.7	2.2
Tin				
World	8.4	2.8	8.5	100.0
Malaysia	7.4	3.8	7.4	36.4
Thailand	14.6	13.2	7.5	13.1
Bolivia	13.5	5.9	8.3	12.8
Indonesia	11.8	6.6	7.9	12.2
United Kingdom	15.7	13.6	12.5	5.1
Australia	13.2	10.6	6.8	3.5
China	36.0	32.9	14.7	2.7
Singapore	26.2	34.3	14.8	2.4
Germany Fed. Rep. of	28.8	24.0	7.4	1.6
Brazil	36.6	28.5	13.0	1.2
Cocoa Beans				
World	14.4	4.4	16.1	100.0
Ghana	10.7	10.3	14.9	23.1
Ivory Coast	16.2	13.0	13.9	19.5
Nigeria	25.6	10.4	21.8	16.7
Brazil	27.6	14.8	27.0	12.6
Cameroon	15.1	10.4	17.3	6.4
Papua New Guinea	26.7	7.2	23.6	2.4
Dominican Republic	23.7	7.2	23.1	2.2
Ecuador	39.3	20.9	24.1	2.2
Malaysia	24.8	13.1	21.2	1.8
Netherlands	64.5	66.3	14.0	1.4
Tea				
World	11.5	1.2	11.1	100.0
India	13.2	6.7	14.7	27.3
Sri Lanka	11.5	3.7	10.8	21.9
China	17.7	5.7	13.5	8.6
Kenya	18.1	9.8	13.0	8.2
United Kingdom	10.6	9.8	7.8	7.1
Indonesia	15.5	7.6	14.0	5.1
Malawi	10.5	5.3	9.7	2.1
Netherlands	11.3	14.2	11.3	2.0
Bangladesh	15.3	16.2	18.8	1.7
Argentina	16.3	9.3	15.7	1.5

Table 4.6: (continued)

	Val.	Vol.	UV	Share
Jute and Manufactures				
World	11.7	5.2	9.0	100.1
Bangladesh	11.8	9.4	11.9	36.2
India	17.9	9.2	13.3	34.2
Thailand	15.3	15.4	6.5	7.2
Belgium-Luxembourg	14.6	13.2	6.3	5.5
USSR	21.3	15.7	8.3	3.3
Netherlands	30.0	22.4	7.5	1.7
China	74.7	85.4	16.1	1.6
Nepal	22.4	23.3	14.5	1.5
United Kingdom	12.1	18.4	18.9	1.4
Germany Fed. Rep. of	10.6	9.4	7.4	1.1
Rubber				
World	14.2	3.2	11.1	100.0
Malaysia	15.5	5.1	11.8	50.6
Indonesia	13.0	3.4	10.8	23.4
Thailand	18.5	5.8	12.8	12.7
Sri Lanka	13.0	7.3	12.2	4.4
Liberia	11.8	4.2	8.1	2.4
United States	17.0	11.8	6.4	1.0
Nigeria	36.8	20.8	25.2	0.9
Viet Nam	27.3	24.9	14.3	0.7
Zaire	14.3	6.1	11.7	0.6
Ivory Coast	16.3	4.0	14.1	0.5
Hard Fibres & Products				
World	22.9	7.5	23.3	100.1
Brazil	38.1	14.4	44.3	18.9
Unit. Rep. of Tanzania	26.3	6.7	32.4	10.9
Philippines	21.5	9.4	22.6	9.8
Mexico	24.2	19.2	34.6	8.9
India	8.6	6.8	6.6	6.3
Portugal	28.0	18.8	24.3	6.2
Belgium-Luxembourg	28.1	12.1	17.0	5.9
Kenya	60.4	25.1	27.9	4.2
Sri Lanka	10.1	7.1	9.1	3.6
Germany Fed. Rep. of	25.1	20.7	9.2	2.6

Source: Calculations using data supplied from the UNCTAD
Secretariat

Instability of Export Earnings

On the other hand, there are good a priori reasons for expecting that the larger exporters have more stable earnings than smaller ones. Large exporters tend to export to more markets (hence lower geographical concentration), have lower supply fluctuations (because of having a larger number of producers, possibly spreading over a wider land area) and have price movements offsetting quantity movements more often, by virtue of their larger shares in world volume. However, although the association between the degree of earnings instability and market shares appears to have the expected negative sign it is weak for all commodities. It appears that other factors are more important than market shares in the determination of earnings instability.

The first column of Table 4.5 shows for each commodity that earnings are considerably more stable at world level than at individual exporting countries' levels. Thus in six commodities, there are at least eight countries with more unstable earnings than those of the world and in the remaining four, at least six countries display greater fluctuations. Moreover, there is a large variation in the degree of earnings instability across the exporters. For sugar the range of the earnings instability for individual countries is 16.6 (Belgium) to 82.6 (Brazil) (with USA having 636.2); cotton 13.5 (USSR) to 39.7 (Pakistan); coffee 12.2 (Colombia) to 45 (USA); copper 10.6 (Poland) to 33.9 (Philippines); tin 12.0 (Malaysia) to 48.0 (Brazil); cocoa 12.5 (Ghana) to 62.7 (Ecuador); tea 13.9 (Sri Lanka) to 23.2 (Indonesia); jute 11.4 (Germany) and 12.9 (Bangladesh) to 35.2 (Netherlands) and 152.3 (China); rubber 16.0 (Liberia) to 53.7 (Nigeria) and hard fibres 10.0 (India) to 67.1 (Brazil).

The differences in volume instability across countries are generally even more pronounced than the differences in earnings instability and in most cases are their main cause. Thus relative stability of earnings and volume at world level conceal serious earnings instability problems facing many individual countries and reflect offsetting movements of earnings and volumes of the major exporters.

The most remarkable fact which emerges from Table 4.5 is that at the world level, volume is much more stable than price for all commodities. The ratio of the instability of volume to that of price ranges from 10 per cent and 14 per cent for tea and sugar respectively to 57 per cent and 58 per cent for cotton and jute respectively. This largely reflects the very low price elasticities of world supply and demand. It is dangerous to infer more from this about the dominant source of variation, since this fact alone does not reveal whether supply fluctuations or demand fluctuations are largely responsible for market instability. All we can say in the context of a static model is that demand (supply) shifts are

Table 4.7: Price Instability Indices of Manufactures Exported by Four Major Industrial Countries, 1971–80 (percentages)

Manufactured Products	Federal Republic of Germany		Japan		United Kingdom		United States of America	
	RMSD	MAD	RMSD	MAD	RMSD	MAD	RMSD	MAD
Chemicals								
Organic chemicals	17.7	12.4	14.8	12.2	11.4	10.6	15.1	12.3
Fertilisers	33.2	23.2	35.2	23.7	-	-	12.5	10.0
Plastic materials	13.9	10.0	24.6	16.4	9.6	8.9	12.1	10.1
Goods-bymaterials								
Rubber goods	5.4	4.5	11.2	9.2	9.4	7.9	4.4	13.5
Paper goods	6.7	5.2	-	-	8.8	7.1	4.8	3.9
Iron and steel bars, rods, etc.	13.5	9.8	18.9	13.4	-	-	3.9	2.9
I & S plates, sheets	16.1	11.3	12.9	7.4	5.0	4.4	4.0	2.7
I & S wire	12.3	9.2	17.2	11.9	-	-	7.5	6.3
I & S tubes, pipes and ft.	13.7	11.2	20.8	14.9	6.2	5.0	4.9	3.9
Tools	5.4	4.7	10.1	8.3	9.1	7.6	3.9	2.9
Metal goods	4.5	4.0	18.0	11.5	-	-	3.9	3.4
Machinery & Equipment								
Power generating Machinery	4.7	4.1	4.5	4.0	-	-	3.7	2.8
Agriculture Machinery	4.6	4.1	6.3	5.1	8.4	6.7	2.8	2.0
Office Machines	5.0	4.7	14.9	12.5	-	-	4.2	3.6
Metalworking Machinery	5.1	4.7	11.8	9.0	8.4	7.2	3.4	2.8
Textiles & Leather Machinery	4.7	4.4	16.7	12.7	-	-	1.7	1.3
Sp. industries' machines	5.2	4.6	4.4	3.5	7.9	6.5	3.3	2.4
Machinery and appliances	5.0	4.6	5.2	4.6	-	-	3.7	2.9

Electric machinery	5.0	4.4	5.9	4.9	–	–	2.7	2.1
Telecommunications	4.9	4.5	5.3	4.5	8.1	6.6	1.9	1.6
Domestic electrical appliances	4.8	4.3	6.9	6.4	11.1	9.1	3.4	2.7
Other electrical equipment	4.5	3.8	6.4	5.6	–	–	8.1	6.7
Road Motor vehicles	4.4	4.1	4.5	4.0	–	–	4.8	3.5
Clothing	5.3	4.8	6.9	5.3	–	–	1.9	1.5
Scientific, medical equipment	4.9	4.6	6.2	4.0	–	–	2.9	2.4
Watches and clocks	6.2	5.6	9.3	6.8	–	–	3.2	2.8

Source of data used: UNCTAD, Handbook, op. cit., pp. 52-5

the main cause if the price elasticity of demand is greater (smaller) than that of supply [10]. Unfortunately it is difficult, if not impossible, to say whether price elasticity of demand is greater or smaller than that of supply on a priori grounds.

Instability: Commodities vs Manufactures

It has been asserted that commodity prices are more unstable than the prices of manufactures because of lower price elasticities, more vulnerability to vagaries of weather, and the freely competitive rather than the oligopolistic pricing more common with manufactures. But the evidence on this is scanty. Results from aggregate price indexes of groups of commodities and manufactures may be misleading since they conceal offsetting changes and large variations in the experiences of individual goods. To get a clearer idea of the differences between the degrees of price instability experienced by commodities and manufactures, it is necessary to compare their indexes at disaggregated levels.

Table 4.7 shows the instability indexes (RMSD) of the price of 26 groups of manufactures exported by UK, USA, Japan and the Federal Republic of Germany (FRG). Of the three groups of manufactures, chemicals appear to be the least and machinery the most stable. In fact, of the 15 indexes of goods under the heading of machinery and equipment exported by FRG only watches and clocks have an index of 6 whereas all the rest have indexes under 6. As far as USA is concerned, apart from chemicals and goods under the headings of other electrical equipment and iron and steel wire, all products have indexes under 5. USA tends to have lower indexes for all manufactures. For all commodities, chemicals are considerably more unstable than the other manufactured goods. In particular, the prices of Germany and Japan's fertilisers and Japan's plastic materials, with indexes of 33.2, 35.2 and 24.6 respectively, are more unstable than some commodities' prices.

Compare these price indexes with the commodity price indexes given in column 9 in Table 4.1 for the 1971-80 period. The evidence at this level of disaggregation clearly supports the view that commodity export prices are considerably more unstable than those of manufactured exports, since of the eighteen IPC commodities nine have indexes over 30, six have indexes over 15 and the remaining three have indexes between 6 and 10. In fact the indexes of sugar and sisal are as high as 76 and 53.3 respectively. The relevant statistical test [11] shows that the difference between the rankings of manufactures and commodities is highly significant.

COMMODITY MARKET INSTABILITY

Instability: Developing Countries vs Industrial Countries

Export proceeds from LDCs are likely to be more unstable than for MDCs and this is borne out by the data set out in Table 4.8. The means of the indexes for 90 developing countries (excluding 3 capital surplus countries - Saudi Arabia, Kuwait and Libya) for the three decades 1950-60, 1960-70 and 1970-80 are 12, 11.4 and 15.6 respectively whereas those for 19 industrial countries for the same three decades are 6.9, 4.0 and 6.6. The mean of MDCs' indexes is about three-fifths of that of LDCs' indexes in the first decade, just over a third in the second decade and two-fifths in the last decade. This clearly shows that LDCs' export proceeds are considerably more unstable than those of MDCs in all three decades. The differences between the LDCs' indexes and MDCs' indexes are significant at the 0.1 level in all three decades [12].

The large standard deviations for the LDCs' indexes in Table 4.8 indicate considerable variations in the instability indexes of individual countries. Nevertheless, out of 89 LDCs only 13, 9 and 8 have indexes lower than the mean instability for MDCs for the three decades 1950-60, 1960-70 and 1970-80 respectively.

When the groups of LDCs are separated into two groups: low-income and medium-income groups, the low-income LDCs, on average, are more unstable than medium-income LDCs. This difference is statistically significant at the 1 per cent level as is the difference between medium-income LDCs and MDCs.

The relative stability of individual MDCs can be illustrated in another way. Of the 22 most stable countries, 16 are MDCs and only 3 are low-income LDCs (India, Sri Lanka and Malawi). The 3 MDCs which are not in the list of the most stable 22 countries are Australia, Finland and Spain whose ranks in descending order of stability are 27, 30 and 37 (the most stable country has rank 1). Apart from Canada, with rank 5, all major commodity exporting MDCs are more unstable than the majority of MDCs. Thus, USA, New Zealand and Australia have ranks, 20, 21 and 27 respectively.

COMMODITY INSTABILITY: CAUSES

Although price and earnings fluctuations may share common causes and are interrelated, some gain in clarity can be achieved by considering their causes and effects separately. With unitary demand elasticity, supply shifts will affect price but not earnings. Furthermore, because supply shifts cause opposite movements in price and quantity, in markets in which supply shifts are the predominant source of fluctu-

116

Table 4.8:   Instability Index (MAD) of Individual MDC and
             LDCS

Country	1950–80		1950–60		1960–70		1970–80	
£Nepal	42.2	(1)	63.6	(1)	51.6	(3)	11.9	(53)
£Dem. Kampuchea	41.1	(2)	11.8	(33)	22.1	(9)	89.3	(1)
Mauritania	35.3	(3)	17.6	(10)	70.1	(1)	18.2	(26)
Congo	31.3	(4)	42.2	(2)	23.4	(8)	28.2	(6)
Iran	31.3	(5)	39.0	(3)	8.2	(46)	46.6	(2)
£Rwanda	30.7	(6)	12.3	(25)	59.3	(2)	20.5	(15)
£Lao, PDR	26.2	(7)	12.5	(24)	34.2	(6)	31.8	(5)
Lebanon	21.5	(8)	12.2	(26)	5.7	(72)	46.6	(3)
£Burundi	20.7	(9)	6.2	(89)	36.3	(4)	19.7	(19)
£Mali	19.8	(10)	12.1	(27)	35.8	(5)	11.5	(56)
£Togo	18.1	(11)	22.3	(6)	9.2	(39)	22.9	(11)
Yemen PDR	17.6	(12)	8.8	(64)	11.5	(28)	32.5	(4)
Iraq	16.9	(13)	19.3	(9)	5.3	(79)	26.2	(7)
Zambia	16.7	(14)	17.3	(11)	12.7	(22)	20.1	(17)
£Niger	16.2	(15)	25.6	(5)	14.7	(17)	8.3	(76)
Korea Rep. of	15.7	(16)	26.7	(4)	4.2	(90)	16.3	(32)
£Benin	15.7	(17)	10.8	(38)	24.2	(7)	12.2	(51)
£Upper Volta	15.5	(18)	13.8	(19)	19.7	(10)	12.9	(44)
Yemen Arab Rep.	15.3	(19)	4.6	(100)	15.2	(16)	26.2	(8)
Algeria	15.1	(20)	7.9	(69)	17.7	(13)	19.6	(20)
£Zaire	14.9	(21)	9.3	(59)	18.9	(11)	16.5	(31)
Syria Arab Rep.	14.9	(22)	16.1	(13)	10.8	(31)	17.7	(29)
Senegal	14.6	(23)	15.3	(14)	4.7	(86)	23.8	(10)
Jordan	14.4	(24)	20.5	(7)	8.7	(42)	13.9	(41)
£Guinea	14.4	(25)	16.3	(12)	10.7	(32)	16.1	(34)
£Burma	14.3	(26)	12.0	(28)	16.5	(14)	14.3	(40)
£Pakistan	14.2	(27)	14.2	(18)	16.0	(15)	12.3	(50)
Indonesia	14.1	(28)	9.3	(58)	11.6	(27)	21.4	(14)
Zimbabwe	13.7	(29)	9.7	(46)	18.3	(12)	13.0	(43)
Cuba	13.6	(30)	9.5	(49)	11.9	(25)	19.5	(21)
Dominican Rep.	13.6	(31)	9.7	(45)	13.1	(20)	18.0	(28)
Nigeria	13.6	(32)	7.8	(70)	11.3	(29)	21.6	(13)
Papua New Guinea	13.6	(33)	8.2	(68)	6.6	(64)	25.9	(9)
Liberia	12.8	(34)	19.4	(8)	11.6	(26)	7.4	(83)
Chile	12.0	(35)	9.4	(53)	6.7	(62)	19.7	(18)
Nicaragua	11.9	(36)	10.0	(44)	10.0	(35)	15.7	(35)
£Chad	11.7	(37)	12.3	(23)	12.1	(24)	10.4	(62)
Ecuador	11.6	(38)	7.0	(79)	8.4	(45)	19.3	(22)
£Bangladesh	11.3	(39)	11.2	(37)	4.4	(88)	18.4	(24)
£Sierre Leone	11.2	(40)	11.7	(34)	10.6	(33)	11.4	(57)
Panama	11.2	(41)	8.5	(66)	13.4	(18)	11.7	(54)
Paraguay	11.2	(42)	10.2	(41)	10.9	(30)	12.4	(49)
Malaysia	11.2	(43)	15.2	(15)	6.8	(60)	11.0	(60)
Bolivia	11.0	(44)	11.4	(36)	6.9	(58)	14.7	(37)
£Sudan	10.9	(45)	15.0	(16)	7.6	(52)	10.0	(65)

Table 4.8: (continued)

Country	1950–80	1950–60	1960–70	1970–80
£Uganda	10.8 (46)	11.9 (30)	7.6 (53)	12.8 (46)
£Haiti	10.6 (47)	13.2 (21)	8.5 (44)	10.2 (64)
Lesotho	10.6 (48)	8.8 (65)	8.7 (43)	14.3 (39)
Peru	10.5 (49)	9.6 (48)	3.9 (94)	18.1 (27)
Kenya	10.4 (50)	9.2 (62)	12.4 (23)	9.7 (69)
Singapore	10.1 (51)	10.6 (40)	10.3 (34)	9.4 (71)
£Somalia	10.1 (52)	9.4 (55)	9.5 (36)	11.3 (58)
Angola	9.9 (53)	7.8 (71)	5.3 (80)	16.7 (30)
Cameroon	9.9 (54)	11.6 (35)	6.2 (68)	12.0 (52)
£Mozambique	9.9 (55)	5.3 (96)	4.2 (91)	20.3 (16)
Uraguay	9.8 (56)	13.3 (20)	7.6 (50)	8.6 (75)
Trinidad & Tobago	9.6 (57)	3.6(105)	3.3(102)	22.0 (12)
Morocco	9.6 (58)	7.3 (75)	3.2(103)	18.3 (25)
£Central Afr. Rep.	9.6 (59)	7.3 (76)	13.2 (19)	8.3 (77)
Argentina	9.6 (60)	9.4 (52)	6.8 (59)	12.5 (48)
£Ethiopia	9.6 (61)	11.9 (31)	6.5 (66)	10.3 (63)
£Tanzania	9.4 (62)	11.8 (37)	9.0 (41)	7.5 (82)
Tunisia	9.4 (63)	8.5 (67)	3.6 (96)	16.1 (33)
Egypt	9.4 (64)	10.7 (39)	7.6 (51)	9.8 (68)
Venezuela	9.1 (65)	6.9 (82)	1.6(107)	18.7 (23)
Greece	8.6 (66)	9.6 (47)	3.5 (98)	12.8 (45)
Hong Kong	8.5 (67)	14.8 (17)	4.6 (87)	6.1 (93)
Colombia	8.5 (68)	11.9 (29)	6.3 (67)	7.2 (84)
Mexico	8.4 (69)	6.9 (83)	3.6 (95)	14.7 (36)
Turkey	8.3 (70)	10.0 (43)	3.5(100)	11.5 (55)
*Spain	8.3 (71)	9.1 (98)	9.2 (83)	6.6(100)
Brazil	8.3 (72)	5.9 (94)	7.9 (48)	11.0 (59)
Jamaica	8.2 (73)	9.3 (57)	5.5 (73)	9.8 (66)
Ivory Coast	8.2 (74)	9.5 (50)	5.4 (76)	9.6 (70)
Portugal	8.1 (75)	6.5 (86)	3.5 (99)	14.3 (38)
£Afghanistan	7.9 (76)	10.2 (42)	5.5 (75)	8.1 (80)
Philippines	7.9 (77)	6.1 (90)	7.0 (56)	10.5 (61)
*Finland	7.6 (78)	12.7 (84)	4.1 (63)	6.0 (90)
El Salvador	7.5 (79)	7.4 (74)	5.4 (77)	9.8 (67)
Honduras	7.4 (80)	9.2 (61)	7.1 (55)	6.0 (95)
*Australia	7.3 (81)	7.7 (81)	4.5 (57)	9.7 (86)
Thailand	7.2 (82)	7.5 (73)	6.0 (70)	8.1 (79)
£Madagascar	7.2 (83)	9.5 (51)	5.4 (78)	6.7 (89)
Guatemala	7.0 (84)	6.2 (88)	6.8 (61)	8.1 (78)
Ghana	7.0 (85)	6.6 (85)	8.1 (47)	6.3 (92)
Costa Rica	6.9 (86)	9.4 (54)	4.9 (82)	6.5 (91)
*New Zealand	6.7 (87)	5.0 (63)	5.7 (40)	9.3 (74)
*United States	6.6 (88)	9.0 (95)	2.7 (71)	8.2 (97)
*Germany, FR	6.5 (89)	9.1 (93)	3.6 (69)	6.8 (94)
*Norway	6.5 (90)	8.9 (99)	2.5 (85)	8.1(101)
£India	6.5 (91)	7.0 (80)	5.5 (74)	6.9 (88)

Table 4.8: (continued)

Country	1950–80	1950–60	1960–70	1970–80
*Sweden	6.4 (92)	7.7(103)	2.9 (92)	8.6(103)
S. Africa	6.3 (93)	4.3(102)	1.5(108)	13.1 (42)
Yugoslavia	6.3 (94)	7.1 (78)	4.8 (84)	6.9 (87)
*Belgium	6.3 (95)	8.7(107)	4.0(104)	6.1(106)
*Japan	6.2 (96)	7.6(100)	4.5(106)	6.6(100)
£Malawi	6.1 (97)	6.1 (92)	6.6 (65)	5.7 (98)
*Austria	5.8 (98)	6.8 (97)	5.1 (81)	5.6 (99)
*France	5.7 (99)	6.3(106)	4.2 (97)	6.5(105)
*Netherlands	5.6(100)	4.1 (56)	4.0 (37)	8.7 (72)
*Ireland	5.3(101)	7.1 (77)	4.8 (54)	4.0 (85)
£Sri Lanka	5.1(102)	6.1 (91)	3.5(101)	5.8 (96)
*Canada	4.8(103)	5.8(101)	4.7 (89)	3.9(102)
*Italy	4.4(104)	6.9(104)	1.9 (93)	4.3(104)
*Denmark	4.1(105)	2.3 (22)	3.0 (21)	6.9 (47)
Israel	3.8(106)	6.3 (87)	2.5(105)	2.5(107)
*United Kingdom	3.6(107)	3.5 (60)	2.6 (38)	4.7 (73)
*Switzerland	3.4(108)	2.9 (72)	2.1 (49)	5.2 (81)
Mean:				
MDC	5.8(2.1)	6.9(2.6)	4.0(1.7)	6.6(1.8)
SD† Low income LDC	15.1(13.9)	13.4(10.8)	16.3(14.1)	15.5(15.1)
Med income LDC	12.0(8.3)	11.3(7.0)	8.9(5.2)	15.7(8.6)

Source: Cols. 2–4 World Bank Report No. 814/82, Table 45, p. 107. Col. 1 = (Col. 2 + Col. 3 + Col. 4)/3. SD† – Standard Deviation in brackets. * – AIDC; £ – Low-income LDC; Medium-income LDC, otherwise. Instability Index: Mean absolute deviation

ations, price instability tends to exceed earnings instability. Demand shifts, on the other hand, cause shifts in both price and quantity in the same direction and hence earnings instability tends to exceed price instability. However, this does not mean that the excess of earnings instability over price instability implies that demand shifts are the main source of fluctuation. Although large shifts in supply and demand, and low price elasticities of supply and demand are responsible for price instability, large shifts in supply and low price elasticity of supply contribute to earnings instability only to the extent that the price elasticity of demand falls short of unity. Supply shifts and supply price elasticity play no role in determining earnings instability if demand has a unitary price elasticity. Moreover, the influence of supply on

119

earnings instability depends on the difference between the price elasticity of demand and unity, irrespective of the sign of this difference, i.e. irrespective of whether demand is inelastic or elastic.

The above conclusions can be demonstrated with the help of a model in which both demand and supply are related to that of current price. However, while it may still be plausible for demand to be related to current price, it is more plausible for supply to be related to last year's price as in the case of annual crops or to the price prevailing three to eight years before, in the case of tree crops. These cases give rise to what is usually known as a cobweb model whose stability requires that the price elasticity of demand (ignoring sign) exceeds that of supply. Comparing the variances of earnings produced by the cobweb model and the conventional market model, even with the same variances of supply and demand shifts and price elasticities, earnings are more unstable when supply responds with a lag to an earlier price than when it responds to the current price. Furthermore, any reduction in the price elasticity of a lagged supply can be seen to stabilise earnings, irrespective of the magnitudes of the other factors involved. Both price and quantity are also more unstable in the cobweb model than in the conventional one.

It is also unrealistic to relate demand to current price for commodities such as natural rubber, jute, sisal, cotton and minerals. The demands for these commodities are derived demand and changes in them may require lumpy investment in plants which last many years ahead and require time to establish. Demands for them are more plausibly dependent on what firms consider to be the long-term prices. Year-to-year changes in the price levels would affect demands only insofar as they affect the long-term prices expected by firms. How price expectations are actually formed may vary a lot from firm to firm. But a reasonable and simple proxy could be a weighted average of all past prices with the weights declining geometrically, so that the earlier the actual prices, the lower are their weights in determining the expected prices. Such price expectation formulation leads to a demand function which relates demand in the current year to price in the same year and demand in the previous year.

As an increase in the supply of a commodity requires expenditure on inputs which have effects on yields beyond a single year, it is also plausible for supply to be related to some expected longer term price and similar arguments to the above would lead to the specification of supply as being related to current or last year's price and last year's supply. The derivation of the equations for the variances of price, quantity and earnings for the model in which both supply and demand are related to last year's price, supply and demand respectively are given in Appendix E. For convenience let us call this last model the 'adjustment-lag' model. The presence of lagged demand and supply in the equations increases the instability of price, quantity and earnings, and the larger are the lagged coefficients, the more unstable are these variables.

The importance of price elasticities can be illustrated with the help of some simple numerical examples, using in turn the three models just discussed. It can be seen from Table 4.9 that lags in either form greatly increase the instability of price and earnings, leaving quantity relatively stable. Quantity is more stable than price throughout because price elasticities of demand and supply are less than unity. It can also be seen from Table 4.9 that the differences between the models become smaller at higher price elasticities. It can also be seen that while price and earnings become more stable, quantity remains as stable as before. Thus equal proportionate increase in the price elasticities of supply and demand will leave the instability of quantity unchanged. In a market in which supply shift predominates, an increase in the price elasticity of demand relative to that of supply will destabilise quantity and vice versa.

In view of the low price elasticities of supply and demand prevailing in most commodity markets, the above numerical illustrations suggest that at the world level, the prices of most commodities would fluctuate more than their quantities. This confirms the findings reported in the earlier section that at all levels of aggregation, price instability appears to be greater than volume instability, when the price, volume and earnings instability of individual commodities are compared. In fact at the world level, price instability

Table 4.9: Standard Deviations of Price, Quantity and Earnings (Percentage)
b = price elasticity of demand; d = price elasticity of supply

| Model | b = 0.3; d = 0.2 | | | b = 1.5; d = 1.0 | | |
	Price	Qty.	Earnings	Price	Qty.	Earnings
Conventional	40	10	38	8	10	12
Cob-web	89	23	88	18	23	26
Adj-Lag	73	12	73	21	12	22

Note: The algebraic description of these three models together with the derivations of the variances of price quantity and revenues are given in Appendix B. Var u = 0.022; Var v = 0.018. Var u and Var v are the variances of supply and demand shifts respectively.

exceeds volume instability in 34 out of 37 major commodities. However, at the level of individual countries, it is in only 9 out of 34 commodities that price instability exceeds volume instability in more than half of the countries involved [13]. This suggests that at individual country level, volume tends to be more unstable than price. This is not surprising in terms of the three models under study, since it is likely that the price elasticity of demand facing individual countries would be very high and certainly in excess of unity. In all three models, the variance of volume would tend towards the variance of domestic supply as price elasticity of demand tends to infinity. The large volume instability of small individual countries reflects to a large extent the instability of their supply.

Low Price Elasticities: Reasons

Low price elasticities of supply and demand at world level clearly do provide one of the most important explanations for price and earnings instability. There are a variety of reasons for the price elasticities of the demand for and supply of individual commodities to be low. The demands for beverages and other food products are price-inelastic because these commodities have few substitutes, they form a small part of consumers' budgets and they have low income elasticities according to Engel's law. The demands for agricultural raw materials and metal ores may be inelastic, particularly in the short run, because expansion in their consumption may require investment in plants which take time to install. Furthermore, the demands for these commodities are 'derived' demands so their price elasticities ultimately depend on the demand elasticities for the final products for which they are raw materials. The demands for their processed forms (e.g. cotton goods and jute goods) may be inelastic. The demand for natural rubber may depend more on the stock of cars, and metal ores, on existing metal processing capacities, than on their prices in the short to medium term. Both the stocks of cars and processing capacities would be unlikely to vary much in response to changes in rubber or ore prices.

Price elasticities of supply for most primary products tend to be low for several reasons. It is usually difficult to vary the production of commodities in the short to medium term. For annual crops, the area may be determined in the previous year and hence short-term variation in output is only possible through changing inputs of fertilisers and pesticides which affect yields and through varying picking and harvesting techniques. Of course, prices must fall considerably before they fail to cover harvesting and transport costs. For tree crops, current production may largely depend on the plantings made five to eleven years earlier. Production can be changed by varying the harvesting techniques but with some detrimental effect on the long term yield of the trees themselves. For example, both undertapping and over-tapping can adversely affect rubber trees.

Even in the longer run when the area under cash crops can be varied, farmers in many LDCs have few options. In Bangladesh and India jute farmers may grow rice if the price of jute falls relative to rice. But what happens if the prices of both jute and rice fall? Their land, knowledge and local markets may all severely limit their ability to switch to other crops. Even in areas with several suitable crops if farmers are to respond sensitively to changes in the relative prices, they must be able and willing to grow different kinds of crops on the same land areas. But, the majority of farmers in LDCs are small, vulnerable and risk-averse and often they are poorly informed on production techniques for crops other than the few they traditionally grow. These factors will limit the response of crops to changes in relative prices even when these are substantial.

Of course, if there is storage, output needs not equal sales - and supply elasticity would be higher if farmers store some output in years of general abundance to sell in years of general shortage. Supply elasticity would also be higher if family labour is sent to other areas in bad years (when returns to labour in the farms are low) to return in good years (when such returns are high). However, in practice, farmers in most LDCs seldom store for such a purpose and farm workers tend to move to other areas only on a long-term basis. Once moving to other rural areas or cities, farm labourers rarely return to work on family farms again.

As for the production of metal ores, output in the short to medium term does not respond well to price movements because, with few exceptions, most of the costs are overheads which remain fixed when output varies. If demand is high and mines are working to capacity, it is impossible to raise output without new shafts, new machinery and other equipment - all of which may require several years to obtain. On the other hand, if the demand is low, there is little incentive to reduce output as the savings would be mainly labour and energy costs which tend to be quite small relative to the total mining costs including overheads. A fall in demand may lead to a fall in output only if the price falls to such a low level that it fails to cover the low marginal (variable) costs of production.

In practice, producers, consumers and traders would, as arbitrageurs, increase the stocks of the storable primary commodities they hold when their prices fall below the expected future levels by a margin exceeding storing costs. Where a large futures market exists, arbitrageurs can always hedge the spot purchases to hold as stocks by selling them forward as futures. Thus, in normal times, arbitraging stock activities would help to reduce the amplitudes of price fluctuations. In essence, stock demand/supply raises the overall demand/supply price elasticity.

However, as elaborated later, price can easily be destabilised when there are large speculative funds flowing into the futures markets because when large funds are involved and large profits and losses may be made at margins, the commodity speculators can be very nervous and easily over-react to false rumours about factors such as wars, strikes, droughts etc. which affect future supplies.

Price Elasticities: Estimation Problems

We have discussed above the various reasons for expecting price elasticities of demand and supply to be low for commodities. But how low are price elasticities of demand and supply in practice? To estimate the price elasticity of demand for a given product from real world data one has to find a way of holding all other things constant while price varies. In practice stocks and price are jointly determined by a host of variables, none of which can strictly be held constant. The statistical technique of multiple regression has been widely used to try to isolate the effects of price changes on the quantity demanded from effects of changes in other variables, such as income, prices of substitutes and complementary goods and taxes, but problems remain.

The Identification Problem

The estimated equation may or may not be the demand equation, depending on whether the identifiability condition for the demand equation is fulfilled. If it is not, then the coefficient of price in the estimated equation need not be a measure of the slope of the linear demand function but a mixture of the slopes or price elasticities of the demand and supply functions and their shifts. If the identifiability is met, then the demand equation can be estimated using one or the other of the econometric estimation methods.

It can be shown that for the demand equation to be identified, the total number of endogenous and exogenous variables present in the model but excluded from it must not be less than the number of equations in the model less one. It also helps to identify the demand function if we can tell with experience or prior knowledge either that the demand and supply shifts are independent, or that the demand (or supply) shifts are the predominant source of market fluctuations. It is not enough that certain variables are present in the model but not in the demand equation for it to be identified. Those variables omitted from the demand equation must also have moved sufficiently in the sample period for their influences on endogenous variables other than demand to be felt in order for the demand equation to be strongly identified. For example, if weather remains very stable over the period under study, so that supply does not shift very much, the identification of the demand equation can be said to be weak.

Simultaneous Equation Bias Problem

To estimate the demand equation, the popular method used is the so-called classical least-squares or ordinary least-squares (OLS) method. This method produces estimates which are unbiased and have minimum variances (and are hence considered 'best') if certain assumptions are fulfilled. These include the assumption that the residuals are uncorrelated with the explanatory variables. In the demand (and supply) equation one of the explanatory variables is price, since price is not independent of the dependent variable (quantity), it cannot possibly be independent of the residual term in the equation determining quantity. This means, therefore, that the assumption of independence between the residual and each of the explanatory variables is violated and OLS yields, as a result, biased and inefficient estimates, and the bias does not decrease with the sample size. Many other estimation methods are proposed (e.g. two-stage least squares, three-stage least squares) which produced estimates with better properties than those of OLS for large samples. However, the superiority of these other methods over OLS for small samples has not been clearly supported by results from Monte Carlo experiments to warrant the replacement of OLS by any of the alternative estimators as far as small samples, which are generally the case, are concerned.

Low Price Elasticities: Evidence

There are a large number of studies providing econometric estimates of price elasticities of demand and supply. For example, Askari and Cummings (1975) and Labys and Hunkeler (1974) each report estimates from about 200 studies. For each product, there may be as many as 100 different estimates, using different methods and covering different regions and countries. Labys and Pollak (1984) have recently given a long bibliography, consisting of hundreds of more recent studies in which elasticities are presented. However, with a few exceptions the estimates generally tend to bunch. Behrman (1977) gives the median of the estimates for each elasticity together with his own estimate. His own estimates tend to be lower than these medians because some of the price elasticities are cross-elasticities and because they usually are with respect to local prices and not the world market price. To give an idea of the magnitudes of price elasticities of supply and demand with respect to world prices in practice, the estimates by Behrman are reproduced in Table 4.10 below.

The short-run price elasticities of supply of developing countries are about zero for the four commodities coffee, cocoa, sugar and rubber, only 0.1 for tea, sisal and cotton and 0.2 for jute. Long-run price elasticities of supply of developing countries are, as expected, considerably higher, ranging from 0.1 for cotton, 0.3 for coffee and cocoa to 0.8 for sugar with 0.4 for rubber. The long-run price elasticities of demand by developed countries are below 0.5 for 5 of the 6 commodities listed, ranging from 0.0 for sugar, 0.1, 0.2, 0.3 and 0.4 for tea, coffee, cocoa and cotton respectively. Thus, according to a reliable source of estimates, price elasticities of supply for developing countries and price elasticities of demand for developed countries are sufficiently low to support the view that low price elasticities are largely responsible for the high price instability for commodities.

Supply Shifts

While large changes in the supply of a commodity in response to its price movements, i.e. high price elasticity of supply, are stabilising, large changes in supply caused by other variables including the prices of rival commodities and inputs can be shown to be destabilising. The supply of a commodity export represents the difference between production, on the one hand, and domestic demand plus the change in stocks (which could be positive or negative), on the other, in each exporting country. While export supply may fluctuate because of changes in domestic demand and/or changes in stocks, in most cases the main cause of fluctuations in export supply are changes in production. For agricultural products, production changes from year to year for any one or more of the following reasons: (i) natural factors such as rainfall, frosts, diseases or pests, plant exhaustion and production cycles; (ii) variable availability (or instability in the prices) of inputs such as fertilisers, seeds, fuels used in irrigation, etc; (iii) government policies, e.g. those which affect output prices received by growers or input prices paid by them (taxation, subsidies land tenure laws); (iv) other man-made interruptions to production, transport or storage facilities or strikes; and (v) delayed response of output to price changes (e.g. trees yield crops only many years after planting).

Production can usefully be conceived as the product of area and yield. While (i) - (ii) can affect production via their effects on the yield in the current year, (iii) - (v) can affect production, via their effects on the areas planted one or more years earlier. Thus, production in this year may be low because of a reduction in areas made several years ago as a result of low prices, strikes or wars at the time.

Table 4.10: Short-run and Long-run Price Elasticities of
Supply and Long-run Price and Income
Elasticities of Demand for Selected Commodities

	Price elasticity of Supply		Demand elasticity with respect to:	
	Short-run	Long-run	Price	Income
Coffee				
Developed			-0.2	0.2
Developing	0.0	0.3	-0.3	0.4
Socialist			-1.3	1.5
Cocoa				
Developed			-1.3	0.0
Developing	0.0	0.3	-0.1	1.4
Socialist			-0.6	1.2
Tea				
Developed	0.0	0.1	-0.1	0.0
Developing	0.1	0.2	-0.1	0.4
Socialist	0.0	0.7	-0.5	0.0
Sugar				
Developed	0.0	0.2	0.0	0.3
Developing	0.5	0.8	-1.1	1.1
Socialist	0.0	0.7	-0.5	0.4
Cotton				
Developed	1.4	1.4	-0.4	1.2
Developing	0.1	0.1	-0.2	0.5
Socialist	0.0	1.0	-0.1	0.0
Rubber				
World	0.0	0.4	-0.5	1.0
Developing	0.0	0.4		

Source: Behrman (1977), Table 4, p. 59.

An interesting example is the recent history of the
supply shifts of one commodity, coffee. World coffee production has fluctuated widely in the last three decades,
largely as a result of output variations in Brazil, where the
average absolute year-to-year change in production was 39
per cent for the period 1961-80. Brazil is the largest
producer of coffee whose share in world coffee production was
about a third in 1982. Brazil's production declined sharply as
a result of the tree eradication programme in the 1960s,

127

recovered somewhat after the coffee replanting programme in 1969 and increased (after the 1975 frost which caused real world coffee prices to triple) dramatically, from less than 17-22 million bags in the late 1970s to more than 32 million bags in 1981/82. Two other major producing countries, Colombia and Indonesia, increased their production by 40-50 per cent during the same period. With this increase in world production coffee prices fell until 1981 when another severe frost hit Brazil. Coffee's experience illustrates how government policies, natural hazards and lagged responses of output to prices cause upheavals in production and price.

Demand Shifts
The demand for primary imports represents the difference between domestic consumption on the one hand and domestic production plus changes in stocks on the other in the importing countries. Domestic consumption is influenced by factors such as income, population, industrial production, technology, taste and prices and availability of substitutes. Changes in stocks can be affected not only by changes in interest rates, insurance and warehouse charges but also speculation about future prices. Both domestic production and consumption can be affected by changes in tariffs, quotas, taxes and subsidies. Activities of large transnational corporations can also affect both supply and demand quite considerably.

The Predominant Source of Market Instability:
Supply Versus Demand
The identification of the main source of market instability arouses interest because it has important implications for the effects of price stabilisation. For example, in the context of a linear market model with additive disturbances, producers (consumers) gain from price stabilisation when the predominant source of market instability is shifts in supply (demand) [14]. In the context of a log-linear model with multiplicative disturbances, complete price stabilisation increases earnings instability only if the main source of instability is supply shifts and the price elasticity of demand is greater than half of one minus the price elasticity of supply [15]. Partial price stabilisation (within a ceiling and a floor or according to an alternative rule) will destabilise earnings in the supply-induced instability case only if demand is price-elastic.

Recently, several authors attempt to make inferences about the main source of market variation from the sign of covariance of the deviations of price and quantity from trends. According to them a positive (negative) covariance suggests that demand (supply) shifts are the dominant cause of instability [16]. An early user of this method for locating the main source of instability was the United Nations (1952, p. 58). From it they deduced that changes in demand tend to be the main source of instability for industrial raw materials while changes in supply tend to be the main cause of instability for foodstuffs. Two symposia in a well-known economic journal testify to the unquestioned acceptance of the method [17]. A renowned development economist, Ragnar Nurkse (1958), implicitly assumed its legitimacy in contending that the parallel movement of export prices and export quantities reflects unmistakably the dominant role of demand conditions and provides conclusive proof that the export fluctuations of primary producing countries originate in the world's industrial centres.

Unfortunately the method used by the UN and these authors is valid only in the very special case in which the price elasticities of supply and demand are equal. Recently Nguyen (1979a) has shown that for the demand (supply) to be the predominant source of market instability the covariance of the deviations of supply and demand must be greater (smaller) than the product of the variance of price (around trend) and a half of the difference between the price elasticities of supply and demand (with the price elasticity of supply minus that of demand) [18]. This means that the influence of demand shifts are the main cause of instability if the covariance of price and quantity is positive is valid only if the price elasticity of supply is less than or equal to that of demand. If the price elasticity of supply exceeds that of demand then we can infer from a negative covariance of price and quantity that supply shifts are the main source of fluctuation without knowing the exact magnitudes involved [19].

Residual Nature of the Commodity Markets

Since the supply of and the demand for exports are the residual difference between domestic production and consumption plus stock changes, changes in production and/or consumption in the export (import) countries would lead to proportionately much larger changes in the volume supplied or demanded. Consider the case of sugar. In 1980, the gross exports of LDCs were only just over one-fifth of sugar production and the gross imports of MDCs were about two-fifths of sugar consumption. For the world as a whole, internationally traded sugar is about one-quarter of production or consumption. This residual nature of sugar trade can be seen even more clearly if we look at a group of countries such as the EEC and in terms of net rather than gross imports or exports. Thus in 1961, EEC had net imports of sugar of 1.7 million tons. In 1980, it had net exports of sugar of 2.7 million tons. This change from being a net importer to a net exporter was caused by a much faster growth of production than consumption. Total production and consumption of EEC was 13.0 million tons and 10.3 million tons respectively in 1980 [20]. Quite a small change in either produces a large swing in net exports.

Furthermore, the prices of large quantities of some goods like sugar and aluminium are governed by long-term contracts (e.g. under 20 per cent of world's sugar ever reaches the free market). This too tends to exaggerate any instability in the residual free market.

Futures Markets and Speculation

For most commodities, as pointed out above, there is a long lag between the decision to invest and the achievement of the output. This lag may be a year for annual crops and several years for tree crops. The longer is this lag, the greater is the uncertainty about whether the investment will turn out to be more (or less) profitable than expected. Since most commodities must pass through one or more intermediary and processing stages, the buyers must often also plan well in advance. In such cases, buyers and sellers cannot know the prices likely to prevail on the date of delivery. Conventional insurance finds it difficult to cover for these risks so some alternative mechanisms have evolved to help buyers and sellers to reduce them.

Forward contracts provide one such device in that they allow producers to know in advance of planting a crop, i.e. while it is growing, the quantities they can sell at a negotiated price by contracts between themselves and dealers or final buyers. This price may be termed the forward price. The forward contracts in the physical market clearly help to reduce uncertainty. But they do not eliminate it altogether and are also inflexible in that difficulties occur if either party fails to meet his obligation. It is to deal with such difficulties that futures contracts have developed and the futures markets emerged.

A producer can use the futures market instead of a forward contract. In selling a futures contract, a producer simply sells his promise to deliver on a certain date at a specified place - a given quantity of the standard quality specified in the contract. The person who buys this contract will probably not hold it for long but will resell it to take advantage of any change in price meantime. The contract may change hands many times before delivery is due. The volume of 'paper' may relate to very much greater quantities of the commodities than are actually traded and most futures contracts are indeed cancelled (i.e. by contracts to buy off-setting contracts to sell) before the delivery date. The parties to a futures contract either deal directly on the futures exchange or via a broker. On most markets, they usually are liable to margin payments of about 10 per cent of the contract value. This allows clients to make large profits and losses from a small movement in prices. For example a 4 per cent rise in the underlying value of the futures contract represents in effect a 40 per cent return on the initial outlay. This attracts gamblers who wish to make money fast but have limited means.

Apart from producers and manufacturers who may wish to hedge their position to reduce risks by selling futures contracts, merchants holding stocks may also wish to hedge against an unexpected fall in the spot price by selling futures. There is an incentive for merchants to buy stocks now to resell later as long as the futures' price exceeds the present spot price by a margin exceeding the storage and interest costs.

Speculators

Speculators will buy futures as long as the spot price expected to prevail in say three months exceeds the three months' futures' price. Different speculators may hold different views about the expected spot price. Let us assume that at any given time there is a frequency distribution of expected prices held by speculators and this distribution has a mean and a variance. Let us call this mean the expected (spot) price. It is clear that the greater is the excess of the expected price over the futures' price, the greater is the quantity of futures the speculators would offer to buy.

Is Speculation Stabilising or Destabilising?

The spot price in each period is related both to demand for actuals for direct use as consumption and to demand for actuals to hold as stocks for later resale. But as the spot price itself also influences the amounts of futures sales offered by merchants to hedge their stocks purchases, it can be seen that the physical or actuals market and the futures market are interdependent. The spot price, futures price and the various quantities involved therefore have to be solved simultaneously. To help to examine the role of speculation on the instability of the spot price, a simple integrated spot-future market model is developed in Appendix G. But less formally we can consider the effect of an increase in the expected future spot price. It would lead to an increase in the demand for futures by speculators, pushing up the futures' price, causing arbitrageurs to buy more stocks which in turn raises the spot price, reducing consumption and encouraging production. A fall in the expected price will systematically have the opposite effects of lowering the price of futures and actuals and reducing production, while encouraging consumption. An increase in the rate of interest (or storage cost) will raise the price of futures via a reduction in

131

the supply of futures, but will reduce the demand for stocks and lower the current spot price. Thus, with the presence of arbitrageurs, speculators and the futures market, movements in the current spot price are seen to be affected not only by supply and demand shifts but also by movements in the rate of interest and expectations concerning the future spot price.

If the expected future spot price is stable and reflects the underlying long-term equilibrium spot price well then the presence of speculators in the futures market has a stabilising influence on the spot price. Suppose there is a windfall increase in output due to a good harvest and the spot price falls below its long-term equilibrium level, arbitrageurs will step in to buy spot for resale later (since the spot price is lower than the futures' price) and simultaneously they will sell futures to hedge their spot purchases. The fall in the futures' price will induce speculators to buy, as long as the expected future price for actuals remains higher than the futures' price. The increase in the speculators' purchase of futures prevents the futures price from falling further and so stimulates arbitrageurs' demand for actuals. In the absence of the speculators, merchants might not be willing to increase their stocks by so much, despite the low current stock price, because of their risk-aversion. Here, the activities of speculators can clearly be seen to have a stabilising effect on price.

On the other hand, it is possible for the speculators to anticipate a further rise in the spot price when it rises and expect a further fall in the spot price after it starts to fall, i.e. the expected future spot price is unstable and bears no relation to the long-run equilibrium spot price. In such a case, the spot price will become more unstable as a result of the buying and selling of the speculators in the futures market. On balance, there appears to be a consensus that in normal times, speculation stabilises the market, whereas in times of large shortages or surpluses, it tends to accentuate the instability of the market [21].

CAUSES OF EARNINGS INSTABILITY:
THEORETICAL CONSIDERATIONS

The causes of instability of export earnings which have been considered by several investigators are: (i) high commodity and geographical concentration of exports; (ii) specialisation in primary commodities (which are more unstable than manufactures); (iii) small economic size; (iv) a high degree of openness of their economies; and (v) a high rate of growth of exports. Many of these factors were thoroughly investigated by Massell (1970). Such studies try to explain the variation in the degree of instability across countries in terms of the characteristics of their economic structures. Theoretical explanations of differences between countries' instability easily become unnecessarily vague and misleading if exact mathematical relationships are not spelt out. To avoid this risk we first develop the following mathematical relationships before assessing the causes. (See Appendix F for a derivation of these relationships.)

Let S_t^2 and C_t^2 denote the variance of total earnings and the square of the Gini-Hirschman index of concentration respectively and $\tilde{S}_t^2$, a weighted average of the variances of the earnings from individual commodities, S_t^2 can be shown to be the product of C_t^2 and $\tilde{S}_t^2$, i.e.

$$S_t^2 = C_t^2 \cdot \tilde{S}_t^2 \tag{1}$$

where

$$C_t^2 = \sum_i^m w_{it}^2 \tag{2}$$

($w_{it} = \bar{X}_{it}/\bar{X}_t$; $\bar{X}_{it}$ and $\bar{X}_t$ being trends of the earnings of commodity i and total earnings respectively and m, the number of commodities), and

$$\tilde{S}_t^2 = \sum_i^m v_{it} S_i^2 \tag{3}$$

($v_{it} = w_{it}^2/\sum_i^m w_{it}^2$; S_i^2 being the variances of the earnings from commodity i, assumed <u>constant</u> over time t, for simplicity).

Commodity Concentration

Let us consider first the relationship between commodity concentration which may be represented by C_t^2 defined by equation (2), and instability, S_t^2. It can be seen from equation (1) that the smaller is the possible range of values for $\tilde{S}_t^2$, the stronger is the relationship between commodity concentration C_t and instability S_t. Equation (3) shows that the range of values for $\tilde{S}_t^2$ depends on the range of values of S_i^2 and varies inversely with C_t^2. In other words, the relationship between concentration and instability is the weaker, the wider the dispersion of the instability of individual commodities and the higher is the concentration. It should be noted that although w_{it} appears in both definitions of C_t^2 and $\tilde{S}_t^2$, C_t^2 and $\tilde{S}_t^2$ need not be correlated.

It is possible for C_t^2 to remain the same while S_t^2 varies substantially and vice versa. For example, consider a country exporting only two commodities, i.e. m = 2, and in a given period 1, these are in the proportions $w_{11} = 0.3$ and $w_{12} = 0.7$, while in a later period 2, $w_{12} = 0.7$ and $w_{22} = 0.3$ and the variance of each good remains constant over both periods so that $S_1^2 = 0.16$ and $S_2^2 = 0.01$, then $C_1^2 = C_2^2$ but the variance of total export proceeds differs substantially with $S_1^2 = 0.033$ while $S_2^2 = 0.137$. It can also be seen that in the limit S_t^2 is perfectly related to C_t^2 if S_i^2 is the same for all i, since in such an event, $\tilde{S}^2$ would remain constant even when C_t^2 varies substantially. Note that the commodity structure $w_{it}^* = \frac{1}{S_i} / \sum_j \left(\frac{1}{S_j}\right)$ which produces the lowest value for S_t^2 in general does not give a minimum value for C_t^2. Diversification can destabilise total exports if it involves moving w_{it} further away from w_{it}^* [22].

To focus attention on the effect of the dispersion of the instability of individual commodities on the relationship between commodity concentration and the instability of total export earnings, we make the neutral assumption that all the covariances [involving the proceeds of individual commodities] are zero. However, the pattern of intercorrelation of the movements of the proceeds from individual commodities do also play a critical role. Diversification into commodities which correlate negatively (positively) with the major ones can contribute to the stabilisation (destabilisation) of total exports. (See pp. 139-42 for an illustration of this.)

Geographical Concentration and Other Causes
The variance of U_{it}, i.e. S_i^2 can be taken to be a measure of instability of the earnings derived from commodity i. S_i^2 may in general be different for different countries. The more concentrated the markets for commodity i exported by a given country and the greater is the share of this country in the world export of commodity i, the smaller S_i^2 is expected to be. The relationship between S_i^2 and the geographical concentration is mathematically the same as that between S^2 and commodity concentration. The relationship between the instability of commodity i and its geographical concentration is the closer, the smaller is the variation of instability degrees across different markets for it. For example, in a period in which demand conditions are stable in most of the MDCs, the differences between the instability of markets would be small and hence one would expect the instability of every commodity and that of total export proceeds to be highly correlated (negatively) with geographical concentration.

The expected negative relationship between the instability of a given commodity i, S_i^2, of a country and its market share for this commodity is necessarily based on the assumption that market instability is largely supply-induced. In such a market, for a country with a large market share a negative correlation between the volume it sells and the price it receives is likely, so that its earnings will tend to be more stable than either its price or volume. But for countries with small market shares and supplies which may not correlate well with world supply prices may as often move in the same, or the opposite, direction to quantities. Insofar as a small market share is associated with specialisation in unstable markets, a negative correlation observed between market share and instability might simply reflect the fact that market share acts as a proxy for specialisation in unstable markets.

Since countries with small export size tend to have small market shares and higher geographical and commodity concentration, they are expected to be more unstable than countries with large export size. Thus, export size may be observed to correlate negatively with instability because it associates positively with variables which are inversely related to instability. Another reason for an inverse relationship between export size and instability is that countries with large exports tend to experience less supply instability because with larger exports, the number of independent producers/exporters within each sector increases and this increases the chance for offsetting movements of supplies (e.g. adverse weather conditions need not affect all producers equally if they are spread over a large area).

It is clear from equation (1) that given the commodity concentration (C_t^2) and the instability of each commodity $i(S_i^2)$, the instability of total export proceeds (S_t^2) can be high or low depending on whether the large weights $(v_i s)$ in the determination of $\bar{S}_t^2$ are given to commodities which are relatively unstable or stable. In so far as primary commodities are more unstable than other exports, large shares allocated to them (i.e. specialisation in primary exports) would cause total exports proceeds to be relatively unstable. Similarly, one would expect instability to vary inversely with the shares of manufactures in total exports, since manufactures are expected to be more stable than all other exports.

It is not clear how openness to trade, defined as the share of exports in GNP, should affect the instability of total export proceeds. Some authors have maintained that the countries which are more dependent on trade are likely to suffer more export instability than those which are less dependent on trade. Other authors have claimed the exact opposite. In terms of equation (1) above, openness to trade can only affect instability of total exports via their effect on the instability of individual exports (i.e. the S_{is}^i). Brundell and Svedberg (1981) demonstrated with the help of a simple model that greater openness tends to stabilise export earnings if instability is largely demand-induced and stabilise or destabilise export earnings depending on price elasticities if instability is largely supply-induced. When the elasticities assume values within the plausible ranges suggested by empirical literature, greater openness produces more unstable export earnings in the supply-shift case. In general, without knowing the predominant source of instability, one cannot say

135

whether an increase in the dependence on trade would stabilise or destabilise export earnings.

CAUSES OF EARNINGS INSTABILITY: EMPIRICAL EVIDENCE

This section will give a brief critical survey of the results produced from major empirical studies on the links between export instability and its main causes. Results may often be sensitive to the time periods in question, the formulae for measuring instability and concentration and the samples of countries selected.

Commodity Concentration

Coppock (1962) and Massell (1964) found no support for the association between instability and commodity concentration. Using samples of 66-69 countries, Coppock obtained correlation coefficients in the range of 0.02 and 0.11 for his index of instability and each of four measures of concentration. His index is chosen to approximate the average year-to-year percentage variation in earnings from exports of goods and services adjusted for a constant percentage trend. Massell used indexes of instability corrected for trend and Gini coefficients to represent concentration and found the regression coefficients between the instability and concentration indexes statistically non-significant. Michaely (1962) found a significant rank correlation coefficient of 0.4 between an average annual percentage change uncorrected for trend as an instability index and a Gini coefficient index of concentration but expressed surprise at the relative weakness of the association and attributed this to the deficiencies in the measure of concentration (peculiarities in classifying products) and the high intercorrelation in the price movements of many goods. Since Michaely's instability index is questionable (because it is not corrected for trend), the results of his tests lose much of their significance. MacBean (1966) found the rank correlation coefficients between each of two indexes of instability, i.e. deviations from moving average and Coppock's index, and the concentration index (Gini-coefficients) to be negative, small and statistically insignificant ranging from -0.0011 and -0.0754.

Subsequently, Naya (1973) produced a number of multiple regression equations involving instability (defined as average yearly fluctuation around a trend) as a dependent variable and commodity concentration (Gini-coefficient) among the explanatory variables for a group of 17 Asian countries (periods 1950-60 and 1960-69) which showed statistically non-significant partial regression coefficient for commodity concentration. In contrast with the above findings, Massell (1970), Knudsen and Parnes (1975) and Sheehey (1977) found

significant relationship between instability and export concentration. Sheehey used a sample of 95 countries, instability
index (defined as the annual percentage deviation from the
exponential trend) and concentration index (Gini-Hirschman
coefficient) and produced multiple regression equations
(giving instability as a dependent variable) which show that
the partial regression coefficients of commodity concentration
are statistically significant for all periods 1955-75, 1955-65
and 1965-75. However, Soutar (1977)'s multiple regression
equations relating instability (defined as the normalised
standard error - involving the mean of squared residuals from
a log-linear least square line) to its causes show that the
coefficients of commodity concentration (Gini-Hirschman coefficients) are not statistically significant even at 10 per cent
(despite his apparent conclusion to the contrary). More
recently, Brundell and Svedberg (1981) (using a large sample
of 139 countries, data for the 1965-77 period and a model
involving instability on the one hand and 12 explanatory
variables on the other, which include a measure of concentration) showed that concentration is a significant cause of
instability for the complete sample but is not significant when
20 oil-exporting countries are excluded. The results with the
exclusion of the oil-exporting countries make more sense
because over this period the quadrupling of the price of oil
over a few years have caused oil exporters to appear both
highly unstable as well as highly concentrated in one
commodity - oil. Thus, Brundell and Svedberg's study
appears to provide evidence against rather than for the
association between concentration and instability. Finally,
Lawson and Thanassoulas (1981) use various concentration
indices proposed by Tuong and Yeats (1976) - to avoid the
problem caused by the sensitivity of the Gini-coefficient to
the level of aggregation in trade data - and found that concentration as measured by different indexes, is not a significant cause of instability.

Thus, the empirical evidence reviewed clearly demonstrates a very weak, if any, association between commodity
concentration and instability. The explanations for the weakness or absence of the positive relationship between the
degree of commodity concentration and export instability have
been that (1) export proceeds from individual commodities
exported by countries with a high degree of commodity concentration tend to move in offsetting fashion and (2)
countries with a high degree of commodity concentration tend
to specialise in relatively stable commodities. To these two
explanations we have come up with two additional ones in a
recent article [23], (3) there is a wide dispersion of instability of individual products and (4) countries, particularly
LDCs, tend to have a high degree of concentration.

One of the main objectives of the empirical studies on
the causes of earnings instability is to find out whether

diversification policy would be effective in reducing it. Weak evidence on the association between concentration and insta- bility across countries is taken to throw doubt on the efficacy of diversification. If countries with a high degree of con- centration are on the whole only slightly (if at all) more unstable than countries with a low degree of concentration then it appears that unstable countries cannot hope to reduce their instability very much by diversifying their exports. This does not in fact follow. The above explanations for the weak international association between instability and concen- tration only suggest that diversification per se need not necessarily reduce instability. They do not imply that un- stable countries cannot substantially reduce their instability by diversification. It depends on what they diversify into. Diversifying into relatively stable commodities and/or into commodities whose proceeds tend to move in offsetting directions to the main exports are almost certain to be stabilising. Since unstable countries are largely unstable because they specialise in unstable commodities, diversification by these countries would probably stabilise their total export proceeds.

A Detailed Country-by-Country Examination

The above points are logically plausible. But, are they also empirically significant? To check this requires detailed trade data on individual countries. The data used were for 23 commodities (consisting of the IPC 18 commodities plus 5 others, namely rice, maize, tobacco, zinc and lead) for 105 developing countries for the 1962-78 period. Using the model described earlier we have produced not only a value insta- bility index for each commodity exported by each country and the correlation coefficient between the deviations from trends of every pair of commodities exported by each country, but also the instability indexes for the aggregate of these commodities for each country, using the actual (trend) shares as well as hypothetical shares to represent various diversifi- cation policies.

For illustration, the detailed results for two countries, Kenya and Costa Rica are presented in Table 4.11. Kenya is a typically unstable country, exporting seven of the commodi- ties covered, whereas Costa Rica is a relatively stable country, also exporting seven. Each figure under the heading 'share 1' represents the historical percentage share of each commodity in the country's total export for the seven commodities. The figures under 'share 2' represent the hypothetical shares resulting from a partial diversifying programme in which the share of the main export is reduced by 30 per cent of its magnitude (e.g. the share of Kenya's coffee is reduced from 56.25 per cent to 39.38 per cent) and the shares of the rest increased by equal absolute increments (e.g. the share of each of the other six commodities exported by Kenya increases by 2.81 percentage points) provided that this does not cause the shares of the next one or two commodities to become larger than that of the first. Whenever this occurs, then the shares will further be reallocated along the same principle, but excluding the first one and so on (e.g. see Costa Rica's shares in Table 4.11). In the limit, the shares of all commodities exported by each country can be made equal and the resulting instability of the total earnings can be compared with the historical instability to see whether and how much instability of total earnings may be reduced by a complete diversification programme.

The results are very different between Kenya and Costa Rica. For Kenya, the instability index of total export earnings falls from the historical level of 63 to the hypothetical levels of 49 and 25 associated with partial and complete diversification programmes respectively. Thus diversification policy has great scope for stabilising Kenya's total export proceeds. Diversifying helps in the case of Kenya because first and foremost Kenya happens to specialise in an unstable commodity - coffee, with an index of 88. Only two other commodities exported by Kenya have comparable degrees of instability - maize (92) and hard fibres (78). The rest have indexes in the range of 22-53. Hence on balance, diversification means for Kenya diversifying into relatively more stable commodities.

How far is the efficacy of diversification affected by the pattern of intercorrelation between the movements of the proceeds from individual commodities. To investigate this, all indexes are recomputed on the assumption that the correlation coefficients of each pair of commodities are zero. The indexes associated with the historical shares and those of the partial diversification fall by about the same amount (10 percentage points), whereas the index associated with those of complete diversification is reduced by less than one percentage point. These results suggest that on balance, the high positive correlation (0.98) between Kenya's two most important exports, coffee and tea, is sufficient to swamp the effects of the weak negative correlation between hard fibres and both coffee and tea and the strong negative correlation between cotton and coffee and tea, which had only a tiny share in total export. Thus, Kenya's total export proceeds are un- stable partly because it specialises in an unstable commodity (coffee) and partly because the proceeds from its second most important export (tea) have moved up and down very closely with those of coffee. Because of this high correlation between tea and coffee, transferring export share from coffee to tea would not help much to stabilise total exports. To stabilise exports, the shares of the other commodities, particularly cotton, should increase more than that of tea. This is reflected in complete diversification in which the shares of tea

139

Table 4.11: Instability Indices, Historical Shares and Hypothetical Diversifying Shares of Costa Rica and Kenya (1962-78)

	Index	Share 1 (GC1)	Share 2 (GC2)
Costa Rica			
Coffee	51.83	44.79	31.35
Bananas	20.42	35.00	31.35
Bovine Meat	16.38	9.69	13.11
Sugar	52.08	7.04	10.46
Cocoa	68.03	2.45	5.86
Rice	172.47	0.59	4.01
Cotton	99.25	0.44	3.86

Index 1 = 29.76; Index 2 = 20.58; Index 3 = 45.08; Index 4 = 24.69; Index 5 = 20.38; Index 6 = 31.83; CG1 = 58.15; CG2 = 48.08; GC3 = 37.80.

Correlation matrix:

	Bananas	Cocoa	Coffee	Cotton	Bovine Meat	Sugar	Rice
Bananas	1.00	0.45	0.45	0.04	0.52	0.44	0.23
Cocoa	0.45	1.00	0.91	0.43	0.48	-0.29	0.81
Coffee	0.45	0.91	1.00	0.45	0.51	-0.41	0.80
Cotton	0.04	0.43	0.45	1.00	-0.22	-0.40	0.18
Bovine Meat	0.52	0.48	0.51	-0.22	1.00	-0.12	0.34
Sugar	0.44	-0.29	-0.41	-0.40	-0.12	1.00	-0.20
Rice	0.23	0.81	0.80	0.18	0.34	-0.20	1.00

Kenya

Coffee	88.04	56.25	39.38
Tea	52.72	27.08	30.79
Hard Fibres	78.03	8.05	10.87
Maize	52.09	3.45	6.26
Bovine Meat	22.45	1.72	4.53
Cotton	33.92	1.40	4.21
Oil Seeds, Oils	46.63	1.15	3.96

Index 1 = 62.59; Index 2 = 49.02; Index 3 = 25.23; Index 4 = 52.16; Index 5 = 39.71; Index 6 = 24.30;
GC1 = 63.48; GC2 = 52.06; GC3 = 37.80

Correlation matrix:

Coffee	1.00	-0.78	-0.12	0.59	0.48	0.98	-0.36
Cotton	-0.78	1.00	0.10	-0.26	-0.46	-0.77	0.00
Hard Fibres	-0.12	0.10	1.00	0.22	0.36	-0.13	0.08
Bovine Meat	0.59	-0.26	0.22	1.00	0.29	0.62	-0.21
Oil Seeds, Oils	0.48	-0.46	0.26	0.29	1.00	0.33	0.08
Tea	0.98	-0.77	-0.13	0.62	0.33	1.00	-0.40
Maize	-0.36	0.00	0.08	-0.21	0.08	-0.40	1.00

Note: 1 – Index 1, Index 2 and Index 3 are total export instability and GC1, GC2 and GC3 are Concentration Indexes associated with historical shares, partial and complete diversification shares respectively.

2 – Index 4, Index 5 and Index 6 are total export instability associated with the above three sets of shares when all the correlation coefficients are assumed zero.

Source: Data used are supplied from the UNCTAD Secretariat.

141

and coffee will be reduced and hence the high positive inter-correlation between tea and coffee no longer plays a signifi-cant role in raising the instability of total exports. This explains why the change in the instability index of total exports associated with complete diversification is so small when the zero correlation assumption is imposed.

In marked contrast to the above results for Kenya, the results for Costa Rica illustrate how diversification could destabilise total export proceeds. The instability of total proceeds increases from the historical level of 30 to the hypothetical levels of 31 and 45 associated with partial and complete diversification respectively. This is due to the fact that two of the three major exports of Costa Rica, bananas (20) and bovine meat (16), are the most stable and coffee (52), the most important export, is more stable than the remaining five commodities, sugar (52), cocoa (63), rice (172) and cotton (99). It is also due to the fact that earnings from different commodities tend to move in phase as reflected in the predominance of positive correlation coefficients. In other words, diversification for Costa Rica largely means diversify-ing into unstable commodities and commodities with little offsetting movements. This suggests that Costa Rica could not reduce its export instability much by simply diversifying.

These results suggest that unstable countries are likely to be unstable to a large extent because they specialise in exporting unstable commodities. Any attempts at diversifi-cation by them would probably increase the shares of relatively stable commodities and so stabilise total exports. On the other hand, stable countries are stable largely because their major exports are relatively stable, so diversification may destabilise their total exports just because the chance of diversifying into unstable commodities is higher. To investi-gate these two related hypotheses, results for nine highly unstable countries (three from each continent) and nine very stable countries - all exporting five or more commodities - are given. It can be seen from Table 4.12 that partial diversifi-cation will reduce the instability of total exports for all nine unstable countries (the reductions are considerable for five) and complete diversification produces greater stability for all nine. On the other hand, as expected, partial diversification slightly reduces total export instability for five of the stable countries and raises it for the other four, whereas complete diversification destabilises total exports for all except one country, Peru. The results are in a sense comforting, because countries which cannot benefit from diversification are usually already fairly stable and so have little need for greater stability, whereas countries which are most unstable have great scope for reducing instability by diversification. Of course, in practice, stability of export earnings is but one objective, another equally important objective is growth in export earnings and countries are unlikely to diversify into stable but stagnant commodities even if this increases stability. Stabilising by diversification may increase or decrease export growth, depending on the demand pattern facing each country's individual commodity exports and given the resource constraints and the country's pattern of comparative advantage, the country may have to face at some stage the trade-off between growth and stability of its total exports in searching for an optimal diversification programme.

The summary results for all 105 countries are given in Table I.1 in Appendix H. By comparing the means for all countries, it can be seen that partial diversification on average is more effective than complete diversification though the reduction in instability is very small.

Geographical Concentration and Other Causes

The empirical results, once again, did not provide clear support for the relationship between geographical concentration (i.e. lack of diversified markets) and total export instability. While earlier on, Coppock (1962), MacBean (1966), Massell (1964) and Naya (1973) obtained a small but negative association between the indexes of geographical concentration and total export earnings instability and Massell (1970) and Kingston (1976) found a positive but statistically insignificant one, Knudsen and Parnes (1975) and Soutar (1977) found evidence which suggests a significant relationship between these two indexes. On a priori grounds, one can expect a stronger relationship between geographical concentration and instability than between commodity concentration and instability, because variation in the instability across different markets for the same commodity is likely to be less than variation in the instability across commodity exports. However, for commodity exports in which demand fluctuations are the main cause of instability, demands in different markets tend to go up and down together following the trade cycle so fluctuations in demand in one region may do little to offset changes in demand in another region. In these cases, market diversification may not stabilise total export proceeds very much and hence one may fail to observe a weak relationship which may nevertheless exist between geographical concentration and instability.

As large exporters of a commodity are more likely to trade it in more markets, the instability index of this commodity is expected to be smaller for them than for small exporters insofar as a strong link exists between geographical concentration and instability for each commodity. However, evidence does not reveal any clear relationship between market shares and instability, i.e. large exporters of each commodity appear to be no more stable than small exporters.

Again there is no clear evidence on the connection between primary product specialisation and instability.

Table 4.12: Instability and Commodity Concentration Indices* of 9 Most Stable and Unstable Countries** Exporting Five or More Commodities

	Index 1	Index 2	Index 3	GC1	GC2	GC3	Share***	M
Unstable Countries								
Guinea	98.7	72.2	36.0	76.6	58.2	44.7	54.8	5
Morocco	65.1	50.0	24.8	81.3	59.1	35.4	44.6	8
Kenya	62.6	49.0	25.2	63.5	52.1	37.8	41.1	7
New Hebrides	47.1	39.4	31.3	80.2	60.5	44.7	61.3	5
Papua New Guinea	43.8	37.9	35.2	53.1	46.0	44.7	68.0	5
Indonesia	43.3	43.2	38.7	48.1	41.1	35.4	31.2	8
Paraguay	59.9	49.6	48.0	46.1	40.0	37.8	54.2	7
Guatemala	44.8	40.4	33.8	60.6	49.0	37.8	65.2	7
Dominican Republic	35.5	30.8	29.7	64.4	50.3	37.8	77.8	7
Average of unstable	55.6	45.8	33.6	63.8	50.7	39.6	55.4	6.6
Stable Countries								
Congo	21.6	20.5	26.7	69.7	53.0	37.5	37.5	8
Zaire	22.6	20.2	20.4	74.3	54.5	30.2	82.1	11
Angola	23.8	27.1	31.6	66.6	49.5	30.2	45.8	11
India	16.8	20.4	23.6	43.2	37.2	31.6	35.4	10
Philippines	23.6	21.4	27.8	48.2	41.4	35.4	69.7	8
Malaysia	28.6	30.0	37.7	53.7	47.4	37.8	70.9	7
Peru	13.5	12.8	10.9	45.6	39.9	35.4	59.7	8
Mexico	16.1	15.1	16.4	44.2	38.0	27.7	33.9	13
Jamaica	19.4	21.8	24.0	65.9	56.1	44.7	44.2	5

Average of Stable | 20.7 | 21.0 | 24.3 | 56.8 | 46.3 | 34.5 | 53.2 | 9

* Instability Index: RMSD, Concentration Index: GC1, GC2 and GC3 are Gini coefficients associated with historical, partial diversification and complete diversification shares respectively
** Three from each continent
*** Share of the commodities included here in total export of all commodities

Coppock (1962) found the total of world trade value in manufactures to be more unstable than that in primary commodities for the period 1948-58. In a more refined classification of goods, Coppock showed that some classes of primary goods were more, some less, unstable than manufactures. Capital goods, for example, were relatively unstable whereas food and agricultural raw materials were relatively stable over the period. Using a sample of thirty seven countries, MacBean (1966) found low and non-statistically significant relationship between instability and the ratio of primary to total exports. When the influences of commodity and geographical concentrations are allowed for in multiple regression analysis, only a weak partial relationship between specialisation in primary products and instability was observed. Massell (1964)'s multiple regressions also revealed weak though significant relationships between instability and primary product specialisation. These findings were also reaffirmed by a more recent study by Massell (1970) and one by Naya (1973) of Asian countries. In fact, over the period 1950-66, Massell (1970) found a negative and highly significant relationship between instability and the ratio of food to total exports. These findings simply reflect the wide diversity of experiences concerning instability within each broad group of primary products and manufactures. For example, of primary products, food, agricultural raw materials and petroleum were relatively stable, whereas minerals were not and of manufactures, capital goods and chemicals were unstable, while others were not.

How do we reconcile the findings that countries more dependent on primary products were no more unstable than those less dependent on primary products with the results given in Table 4.7 which shows that the prices of individual primary products were considerably more unstable than those of manufactured products, except for chemical products? Two possible explanations are: (1) greater price stability in manufactures is obtained at the expense of greater volume instability; this reflects high price elasticities of demand and supply for manufactured products; (2) instability is largely induced by demand variation in the case of manufactures - because few uncontrollable forces operate on supply - causing price movements to reinforce those of quantity to produce unstable earnings movements. Moreover, the price instability indexes of manufactures given in Table 4.7 are for the 1971-80 period, whereas the findings of the various studies reported above are for an earlier period. It is possible that the prices and earnings of manufactures were more unstable in the earlier period than in the 1971-80 period. In fact, using a sample of 121 non-oil exporting countries, Brundell and Svedberg (1981) found a statistically significant negative partial relationship exists between the ratio of manufactures to total exports and instability thus confirming the greater stability of both price and earnings of manufactures in the more recent (1965-77) period.

There is quite strong evidence supporting a significant negative relationship between a country's size (as measured by its GDP or total export value) and instability. Erb and Schiavo-Campo (1971) and Lawson (1974) found a significant link between instability and country size. Naya found that this applied to the Asian countries he investigated. Although Mathieson and McKinnon (1969) and Khalaf (1976) found no relationship between country size and instability, on the basis of a small sample of countries their findings were contradicted by the more recent study by Brundell and Svedberg (1981), using a much larger sample, which shows that export size had a significant coefficient with the right expected sign. On balance, it does appear that countries with large exports tend to have more stable earnings. Brundell and Svedberg explained this in terms of greater stability of supply in countries with large export sectors. It is possible that countries with large exports tend to have more offsetting movements between price and quantity. However, results from Tables 4.5 and 4.6 give only weak support for these two explanations in that for each commodity, countries with large market shares do not seem to have much more stable earnings than countries with small shares.

For the period 1950-68, Mathieson and McKinnon (1974) obtained a non-significant coefficient for export size in a multiple regression equation explaining export instability. However, their sample of only 12 countries is really too small. Using a much larger sample of 121 non-oil exporting countries for a more recent period 1965-77, Brundell and Svedberg (1981) found that the degree of openness is one of three variables (the other two - already mentioned - are export size and ratio of manufactures) which are significant and have the right expected signs.

POLICY IMPLICATIONS

Developing countries are found to have significantly more unstable export earnings than developed countries in all three decades since 1950. The LDCs are no doubt more dependent on the exports of primary products and tend to have higher degrees of commodity and geographical concentration than MDCs. Researchers have hoped to find remedies for instability in their attempt to determine its causes. However, little useful policy implications can be drawn from cross-country regression analyses. For example, we have shown from our detailed study of each of 105 countries that diversification policy can help to stabilise the export earnings of many of these countries which experience the most severe degrees of export instability, despite the absence of a significant cross-

147

country relationship between instability and the degree of concentration. The findings that countries with large exports have more stable export earnings provides no help to the majority of unstable small countries. Countries which are more open to trade are also more vulnerable to the damaging effects of export instability and hence the observed relationship between instability and openness to trade simply reflects the greater need and effort of these countries to adopt measures to stabilise their export earnings. Finally, most LDCs in the process of development would become more and more industrialised so that their ratio of manufactures to total exports are bound to increase over time, irrespective of whether this would lead to more or less stable export earnings. Export earnings would be stabilised if countries diversify into stable products, irrespective of whether these are manufactures or primary products.

In short, given the high degree of price instability at the international level over which each country individually has no control, individual countries cannot reduce the instability of their earnings much by stabilising their supplies alone. The only domestic measure for reducing export instability open to them, appears to be diversifying into stable products, if these can be identified. At the same time, they may, if they have not already done so, adopt measures to reduce the harmful effects (if any) of export instability on their economies and individual export sectors. At the international level, apart from price stabilisation via international commodity agreements and complementary financing schemes, export instability can be greatly reduced by better exchange of information on future production in exporting and importing countries. Fluctuations in the production in the importing countries can be an important source of demand shifts and better information flows will make better forecasts and production planning possible. Therefore, better information flows about future supplies world-wide would help to remove most of the regular but large swings in the supply and demand for each commodity. Even the apparently less predictable, uncontrollable and occasional, large shifts in demand and supply can become more foreseeable if information flows are freer and the more regular types of fluctuations moderated.

COMMODITY INSTABILITY: CONSEQUENCES

The evidence over the three decades 1950-80 clearly supports the proposition that LDCs suffer more violent fluctuations in export earnings than MDCs. Large fluctuations in export prices and earnings are still generally believed to have adverse short-term effects on income, investment, employment and the price level and detrimental effects on their economic growth. The general acceptance of the harmful effects of export instability by governments is evidenced de facto in the existence of the Compensatory Financing Facility of the International Monetary Fund (IMF-CFF), the EEC STABEX scheme of the Lome Convention and the various international commodity agreements.

According to a priori reasoning, export instability affects development adversely through such variables as imports, savings, investment, employment, government revenues and national income. It also generates uncertainty which impedes effective planning and investment, forces countries to hold greater reserves which have opportunity costs and/or results in interrupted flows of imports of intermediate and capital goods and aggravates inflationary pressures in both LDCs and MDCs. To deal with the administrative and balance of payments problems arising from it diverts skilled manpower from production activities and reduces the growth rate of export earnings of LDCs insofar as higher risks induce producers and consumers to switch from unstable commodities to more stable substitutes.

It has, on the other hand, been maintained by several authors that export instability may have favourable effects on savings. They argue that savings and investment in a boom period are not matched by disinvestment in the subsequent slump or that as savings take place from transitory income more instability permits more investment.

THEORETICAL CONSIDERATIONS

There is no question that large export fluctuations are at the very least a nuisance and their reduction would benefit all countries. However, schemes for stabilising export proceeds impose resource costs and hence it is important to know not only whether the benefits of stabilised exports are positive but also whether they are large enough to justify the costs of adoption of such schemes. The benefits of export earnings and price stabilisation rest on preventing the harm caused by export instability. In practice, the consequences of export instability are not easy to measure because they depend on policy reactions of government and on the diverse economic circumstances of each country. Export instability presents a problem to the export sector itself and this problem may spread to the rest of the economy, in the form of instability in GNP, investment and consumption generally. But stabilising measures pursued by a government may succeed in more or less insulating the rest of the economy from export fluctuations. Insofar as this occurs, statistics may not reveal much domestic instability resulting from export instability. The damage to the rest of the economy is largely prevented in such a case, but the cost of export instability then becomes the resources and skilled manpower involved in operating the stabilising measures.

Before plunging into statistics on consequences of export instability, it helps to explore the expected repercussions of, for example, an export shortfall (below trend deviation) in one year followed by an overage (above trend deviation) of the same size in the following year. Export overage is beneficial, whereas export shortfall is damaging. To show that each country is better off with stable exports than with unstable exports requires that the harm from the shortfall exceeds the benefit from the overage (of equal magnitude). For convenience of exposition, let us assume that export earnings have no trend, i.e. they are on average neither rising nor falling over the relevant period, so that an export shortfall would in fact appear as a fall. With a rising trend, a shortfall can occur even if exports in fact rise (but at a slower rate than trend).

Effects of an Export Shortfall
Let us consider first the effects on an economy of an export shortfall under various policy reactions by the government. The existence of a shortfall does not mean that all export sectors have shortfalls. The shortfall in total exports is the net result of shortfalls in some sectors and overages in others.

Effects on the Foreign Exchange Receipts
The occurrence of an export shortfall will reduce the foreign exchange receipts of the country but not by the full extent because in the export sectors there may be large foreign firms which repatriate a large proportion of export proceeds as profits and payments for imported inputs. Thus insofar as foreign firms are inclined to maintain their payments to domestic factors and to government while letting overseas payments fluctuate with their export earnings, the net foreign exchange receipts of the country will fall by a smaller percentage than total exports.

Effects on Export Sectors
In sectors exporting commodities such as tea, sugar and rubber, where large proportions of output come from large plantations owned by the state or foreigners, output and employment may not fall very much because variable costs may be small relative to total costs. Output in plantations will be reduced in response to a fall in prices/earnings (in the same year) only if prices fall below harvesting costs (a very rare occurrence). Similarly in mining, e.g. tin, copper, lead, bauxite, iron ore, where overhead costs are large relative to

the total costs of mineral extraction, varying short-run
output by continually laying off and recruiting labour or
closing down and reopening mines (or processing plants)
would seldom be economic so that employment and wages are
unlikely to fall much in response to a fall in mineral prices
and earnings. But the extent that employment and real wages
are reduced, in response to the export shortfall, the labour
force would suffer. If local investors have diversified port-
folios they may not be much affected. For them, low returns
in some investments could be offset by high returns in
others.

For sectors exporting commodities such as cocoa, coffee,
groundnuts and jute, a large part of output is produced by
small farmers whose money income would normally fall as a
consequence of export shortfall. These are the people most
likely to suffer the most from an export shortfall unless there
are marketing boards, stabilisation funds or other measures to
help them to smooth consumption through savings or changes
in the prices of the goods they consume moderate fluctuations
in their real incomes.

Effects on the Economy at Large
Faced with a shortfall in the net foreign exchange receipts
associated with exports, there are several possible policy
reactions. An export shortfall will have two main effects: (a)
pressure on the balance of payments and (b) a downward
multiplier effect on income and expenditure. Insofar as the
export shortfall is temporary, the external imbalance which it
causes is also temporary and does not really call for adjustments in the exchange rate or in the aggregate level of
expenditure. The appropriate approach appears to be either
to run down reserves or to borrow to finance the balance of
payments deficit, while at the same time using fiscal and
monetary measures to insulate the economy from the effects of
export instability.

Use of Reserves or Borrowing to Deal
with a Temporary External Imbalance
If the country adopts such an approach, then the cost of
export shortfall on instability would be little more than the
cost of maintaining adequate reserves of foreign exchange or
of international borrowing. The more unstable the exports,
the larger is the cost of holding adequate reserves or the
cost of international borrowing. For a country which behaves
in this way, income, investment and employment may remain
relatively stable even if exports are unstable.

Similarly for export sectors in which a large proportion
of output is produced by small farmers who suffer real hardships when their incomes vary with export prices and

earnings, marketing boards, variable export taxes and subsidies or stabilisation funds may help to moderate the fluctuations in their incomes. The operation of these domestic income stabilising schemes by a country, however, involve expenditure in foreign exchange which may be considerable in a year of widespread shortfalls and would require either the holding of larger reserves or larger foreign borrowing.

Use of Other Measures to Correct an External Imbalance

If a country chooses to respond to a balance of payments deficit by one or more of the following: (i) import restriction; (ii) exchange rate depreciation; and (iii) deflationary policy, either because it cannot afford access to adequate international liquidity or because its government is unconvinced that economic instability is harmful, then the following repercussions may occur. Suppose imports of raw materials and capital goods are allowed to fall. If the country cannot produce many of the capital goods itself, investment would fall. A reduction in imported raw materials would probably reduce output and capacity utilisation. The fall in investment and expenditure by the export sectors reduce income via the multiplier. But, if both investment and exports have sizeable direct import contents and the marginal propensity to import is large, these together with the marginal propensity to save and tax may produce a multiplier not much greater than unity so that income is likely to be considerably more stable than exports, i.e. the effect of export instability on income may be less than expected. Because the effect on income is 'dampened', the effect of the price level could also be limited even if prices and wages are flexible downward. The effect on employment would be small. Employment will of course fall less if wages are flexible.

Given that a large proportion of tax revenue is derived from export taxes, the shortfall in exports would produce a shortfall in tax revenue directly as well as indirectly via the fall in income in the rest of the economy. The government can choose to maintain its expenditure by deficit financing or borrowing from abroad. However, a government which chooses not to borrow to finance a temporary balance of payments deficit is unlikely to borrow to finance a budget deficit. Its expenditure would probably fall in response to a fall in its tax revenues. This may mean a cut in the public investment (e.g. roads, transport, provision of energy or irrigation, etc.). The cut in public investment programmes would affect adversely the expected yields of past and future investments and reduce the productivity of investment as well as its level.

Exchange rate depreciation may produce little improvements in the balance of payments because of low short-term price elasticities of demand for exports and imports. Furthermore, uncertainty generated by frequent changes in the exchange rate may reduce inward investment and fear of depreciation may diminish foreign firms' willingness to reinvest profits in the country.

By not taking measures to offset the effect of an export shortfall on the economy, the government has implicitly pursued a deflationary policy. However, since the multiplier reduction in income cannot reduce imports sufficiently in response to the export shortfall to remove the external imbalance, the government might then take measures which would reduce income further. In such a case, export instability would produce a more pronounced effect on income, investment and employment and the adverse consequences of export instability would be magnified by the policy measures adopted to correct a temporary external imbalance.

The consequences of an export shortfall thus depend mainly on policy reactions. With sufficient reserves or access to international credit, a country can largely neutralise the adverse domestic consequences of export instability. The cost is no more than the interest paid on borrowings or opportunity costs of reserves and skilled personnel to monitor stabilising devices. Only if a country cannot afford to, or chooses not to, hold reserves or borrow, will the adverse consequences of export instability occur and be observable.

Effects of an Export Overage

Suppose in the following year, the country's exports rise above average. If reserves were run down in the previous year because of shortfall, they are now restored. If the excess of imports over exports was financed by borrowing, then it can be repaid this year. Thus imports may be allowed to stay more or less on trend. Taking the export upward and downward changes together, the cost of borrowing or holding reserves is the greater, the greater is the overall amplitude of the export changes.

If imports were allowed to fall in the previous year, then symmetrically they are allowed to rise in this year in response to the export overage. Imported capital goods increase, investment increases, so do producers' income and expenditure in the export sectors and income and employment in the rest of the economy. Government expenditure also increases in response to higher tax revenues and this stimulates investment further.

Effects of Export Fluctuation on Investment and Growth

The changes in the level and efficiency of investment in response to an export overage may proportionately be smaller than those in response to an export shortfall, i.e. the

153

responses of investment to an upswing and a downswing in export could be asymmetrical. In such a case, the detrimental effect of export instability on economic growth can readily be measured in time series analysis; however, it is quite possible for the effects of export instability on investment to appear symmetrical. In such a case, the adverse effects of instability may still exist but assume a form which is more difficult to assess. For example, taking the two years together, investment may be larger and more efficient without fluctuations than with them for the following reasons: (i) with unstable incomes, it is more difficult to estimate the expected returns on yields; export fluctuations encourage business speculation and miscalculation and generate risks and uncertainty for entrepreneurs; (ii) fluctuations in government expenditure on the infrastructure and the stop-go policies resulting from export instability raise the risks associated with investment and cause inefficiences in delayed construction work etc; (iii) fluctuations in import of capital goods and raw materials result in fluctuations in investment which would reduce the efficiency of investment; (iv) insofar as wages and prices are inflexible downwards (but not upwards), export instability increases inflationary pressures, with inflation encouraging spending, discouraging saving and possibly distorting the allocation of resources further away from optimum; (v) the country may under-produce the unstable commodities in which it has comparative advantages and thereby forgo some of its potential trade gains. Of course, high risks associated with investment for reasons (i) - (iii) above would reduce foreign investment in the country and at the same time make foreign borrowing more expensive.

However, it has also been contended that export booms generate optimism leading to increased investment which is not matched by disinvestment in years of export slumps. According to Reynolds (1963, p. 108) investors in the export industry (copper mines) regard upswings as beginnings of trends rather than as temporary phenomena, and behave accordingly; downswings, on the other hand, are apparently considered short-run phenomena, since no major disinvestment occurred for any of the companies even during the severe depression of the 1930s. If for comparative advantage or profitability reason, an industry is to expand, then we would expect it to increase its investment during booms unmatched by disinvestment during slumps when faced with unstable income rather than to maintain investment continuously at a high level, irrespective of the movements of its income. Thus, increased investment in upswings unmatched by disinvestment in downswings may simply reflect two facts - the industry is growing and its income unstable. Instability produces this stop-go pattern of investment but the reason for growing capital formation may be long-term profitability rather than instability. Hence, investment in the boom unmatched by disinvestment in the recession cannot be regarded as convincing evidence of a higher average level of investment being associated with more unstable earnings [24].

The view that export instability favours investment was also held by Sir Sidney Caine (1958, p. 188) who maintained: 'There is in fact plenty of evidence on the other side in, for example, the high level of investment which has prevailed in such countries as Malaya and Indonesia during periods of very sharp fluctuations in the prices of their principal products'. Investment is expected to be related positively to the expected mean of returns and negatively to risks (as indicated by the variance of returns). High level of investment on Malaya and Indonesia during periods of high risks (owing to unstable prices) may reflect high expected returns rather than high risks – thus investment in these periods may be high despite rather than because of high price instability.

Effects on Savings

Higher risks and uncertainty would induce firms and individuals to hold larger precautionary balances and to raise these, savings have to be higher. This view is stressed by Knudsen and Parnes who contended, on the basis of Friedman's permanent income hypothesis, that a large variance in transitory income (caused by export instability) would stimulate savings and so investment since savings are the primary source of capital formation in LDCs. However, while it is true that savings are necessary for investment, it does not automatically follow that a decline in consumption will induce capital formation, for the fall in consumption could contract the market and so discourage private investment. Even if this did not occur, most of these savings would, as we suggested above, be held in the form of liquid assets and could fail to be turned into long term investment. Generally saving from a transitory increase in income in one period could be matched by dissaving to support consumption in the next. Furthermore, income instability leading to a high level of demand for precautionary balance would increase savings only temporarily while this balance is being built up but would not raise long-term saving.

Difficulties in Measuring the Adverse
Effect of Instability on Growth

The above analysis suggests that whether export instability generates observable adverse consequences on the domestic economy or not depends a great deal on the policy reactions of governments. The adverse consequences can largely be avoided if the country holds adequate reserves (or is willing and able to borrow in the international money market) and pursues domestic stabilising policies to insulate producers in the export sectors and the rest of the economy from the effects of export instability. The cost of export instability - which in this case is simply the cost of borrowing or holding reserves - appears to be lower than that incurred in the form of unmitigated adverse consequences of export instability spreading throughout the economy. In the latter case, adverse effects of export instability can probably be observed in the forms of fluctuations in income, investment and employment and possibly higher inflation. The marginal costs of holding reserves are the opportunity costs involved in forgoing investments which would have been undertaken less the returns on the overseas assets in which reserves are held - say the interest on dollar countries.

Where investment and its efficiency are allowed to be affected adversely by export instability, it is still by no means easy to measure the detrimental effect of instability on economic growth in practice either by cross-country comparison or time series analysis.

Cross-country Analysis

Even if we exclude from the sample all countries which choose to isolate the effects of export instability on their economies by holding large reserves etc., the multiplier effects of export fluctuations can be very different for different economic structures and a cross-country regression (or rank correlation) analysis may not reveal any relationship. A given export instability may produce different income and investment instability in different countries. The effect of a given investment instability on its efficiency may also be very different for different commodity sectors. The efficiency of investment and the investment income ratio and hence the rate of economic growth may be determined by many factors which are more powerful than export instability. Fast technological changes and mobile international capital flows have recently transformed the pattern of tastes, factor endowments and comparative advantages of individual countries and these are likely to be more powerful determinants of the economic growth of each country than export instability. Other powerful influences on economic growth may be the savings habits of the people, tax and trade policies pursued by the government and the level and pattern of investment carried out by the government. Suppose a country suddenly finds itself possessing substantial comparative advantage in the production of a number of commodities with stable export markets, then its economic growth would be high and its exports would be stable. By comparing only growth and instability across countries, we will then wrongly attribute its high economic growth to its export stability. Conversely, had these commodities had unstable markets, then the country will have both a high growth rate and high export instability and we would conclude, equally wrongly, that export instability if anything favours growth. Thus, cross-country comparison can easily fail to reveal the relationship between economic growth and export instability.

Time-series Analysis

Could time series analysis of each country do better? Suppose we examine the case of a small country, e.g. Zambia, which derives most of its export earnings from a single commodity, e.g. copper, but by virtue of its small size, it contributes only a small fraction of world exports of this commodity, so that for all practical purposes, it is a price-taker in the world market for this commodity. The most satisfactory approach to studying the effects of export instability on it appears to involve the construction of an econometric model for it, consisting of the sector exporting this commodity with links to a macro-model of the whole economy. Since short-run output can be treated as very inelastic with respect to price, i.e. output moves more or less along a trend, fluctuations in export earnings would largely reflect fluctuations in export prices (which are exogenously given). By comparing the results for GDP levels and growth rates in two simultaneous runs - one with stable export prices and one with unstable export prices around the same smooth trend - one could, in principle, measure the effects of export instability on the economic growth of this country [25].

The question is how do we model the effects of export instability on investment and its efficiency? A priori, we would expect random fluctuations in export prices/earnings to produce results different from those of a smooth trend because of risk aversions on the part of producers and consumers, disruption to investment programmes, the presence of non-linearities (arising from summing up of the constraints), lags in the functional forms and rigidities in the money wage or asymmetric response of certain variables to export fluctuations. It is possible for investment to respond symmetrically to an export shortfall and overage and yet at the same time to be lower say because of frequent disruptions to capital goods imports - reasons mentioned above. Hence, the effect of export instability on investment may not be reflected in asymmetric responses of investment (or other variables) to export swings. In the absence of such asymmetric responses, simulation runs would probably fail to detect any effects of export instability on investment or economic growth.

To measure the effect of instability or the efficiency of investment in time series analysis requires say annual measurements of instability and investment efficiency. But instability is usually measured over a period of several years, so how do we have annual series of this available? Furthermore, there is also the problem of finding a suitable time series for investment efficiency. The obvious choice of a measurement for the efficiency of investment is the ratio of year-to-year change in income to investment but this includes a large random component and is therefore a rather poor proxy for it.

In any case, export instability may have a significant long-term impact on investment and its efficiency but a negligible short-term (year-to-year) impact. The presence of lagged responses of investment level and efficiency and income growth to export instability make it very difficult to observe or measure the impact of export instability on growth when other variables affecting growth and investment are also changing and have lagged effects on them.

Effects on MDCS as Importers of Commodities

Export price and earnings instability is expected to destabilise the import flows of developed countries, add further pressure to inflation in these countries and generate uncertainty over the long-term development of their sources of supply.

According to Behrman (1977), the effect of export price instability on developed countries via inflationary pressure may be sufficiently harmful so that the 'gains from the reduction of inflation pressures for consuming nations (mostly developed countries), may be substantially greater than the revenue gains to producing nations (mostly developing countries) and the deficit of buffer stock operations' (p. 38). Since this argument, if true, would provide a very strong rationale for MDCs to support international measures for reducing export price instability, a brief summary of Behrman's arguments leading up to this conclusion is warranted.

Behrman noted that according to the Project Link model [26], a 33 per cent increase in prices of non-fuel commodity exports from the LDCs is required to raise the inflation rate in USA by 1 per cent. This underestimates the effect on inflation in USA by considering only the proportion of commodities exported by LDCs and by failing to take into account the substantial number of oligopolistic industries which use commodity price rises to implement 'cost justified' increases in their own prices. Revising by the Project Link estimate upwards for the above reasons, but also downward to take account of the fact that this estimate relates to more commodities than the ten core ones which Behrman was interested in, Behrman suggested that increases of about 30-60 per cent in the prices of the ten core commodities might cause 1 per cent rise in the US consumer price index. Assuming this range of impact and the historical trends in commodity price increases, he estimated that holding the prices within the proposed ± 15 per cent bands might reduce the US inflationary rate by 0.2 to 0.4 per cent per two or three years in the course of a decade of operation. Such numbers become substantial when they are converted into real output equivalents, using inflation - unemployment trade-offs along a Phillips curve. Thus 'in order to avoid such a degree of inflation, available Phillips curve estimates suggest that unemployment would have to be increased to about 0.03 to 0.3 per cent (Perry (1970) and Wachter (1976)). Okun's (1962) law suggests that this translates into about 0.1 to 0.9 per cent of real GNP. To be somewhat conservative, consider the middle of this range. It implies a gain of about $9 billion in each such year for the US economy.' On the conservative assumption that such a gain is experienced only twice in a decade, Behrman estimated that the discounted value of the US gain alone would amount to about $15 billion, depending of course on the discount rate. The gains to other industrial countries, which could similarly be calculated, would also be substantial.

Since the Phillips curve was never a precise relationship and since the 1970s shifts about so widely that it virtually ceases to exist, it is no longer meaningful to use Okun's law and the Phillips curve to translate a given reduction in inflation pressure into an equivalent increase in real output. Moreover, to equate a reduction of only 0.2-0.4 per cent in the rate of inflation with an increase in real GNP of 0.1-0.9 per cent appears excessive. The average annual inflation rate in the industrial countries over the period 1960-80 was over 12 per cent. Similar calculations for industrial countries would suggest that a reduction of inflation rate from 12 per cent to 6 per cent (the present level) would cause real GNP to fall by 20 per cent. Surely this is unbelievably large. In fact Behrman did not claim that his above calculation is transferable to 12 per cent inflation level and was much more qualified about it than the above brief account appears to suggest.

It appears that stabilising the prices of commodities, which are suitable for buffer stock operations, i.e. the ten core commodities, will have a very small effect on the inflation pressure in MDCs. MDCs would only find it worthwhile to support the international schemes for stabilising the prices of these commodities if the resource costs involved were small [27]. The general lack of MDCs' close participation in existing ICAs may simply reflect that they are unconvinced that the benefits of ICAs in terms of reducing inflation would cover costs.

REVIEW OF EVIDENCE ON THE EFFECTS OF
EXPORT INSTABILITY

Although it appears that the case for instituting national and international measures to reduce export instability and to insulate domestic economies from its adverse effects has been widely accepted in principle, these measures would be even more attractive to governments and policy makers at all levels if export instability could be shown in practice to have adverse short and long term effects on LDCs' economies.

The work of MacBean (1966) was an early attempt to assess the economic effects of instability. It covered a wide range of the issues and its unexpected results undermined the consensus. It served as a trigger for much subsequent research. A brief summary of its major findings provides a starting point for a review of empirical literature [28]. A rank correlation between export and income instability indices of a sample of 35 developing countries over the period 1946-58 revealed no evidence of association between the two. A time series analysis - counting the number of years when the deviations from trends of exports and GNP had the same sign for a sample of eleven countries, chosen on the basis of high trade ratios and therefore probable sensitivity to export fluctuation - appeared inconclusive, since deviations of exports and GNP had the same signs in only 61 cases out of 99 with no time lag and 45 out of 89 with a one year lag. This test is, however statistically inefficient because it implicitly treats all deviations with the same or opposite signs as of equal importance, irrespective of the magnitudes of the deviations. Thus, it is possible for income in a given year to fall considerably in response to a fall in exports and yet remain marginally above trend and exports marginally below trend so that their deviations have opposite signs. Regression would provide a more powerful test. Using regressions and MacBean's trend corrected series, Maizels (1968) found a close association between export and GNP fluctuations in 5 out of 11 countries in MacBean's sample. The relationship is less close for the other countries but on inspection this appears to be due, in most cases, to special circumstances on one or two years, which obscure the underlying relationship. Thus, Maizels was probably correct to conclude that the time series analysis would seem to support the view that short-term fluctuations in national income, at least in these trade oriented countries, is associated with variations in their export proceeds. However, these cross-country and time series results taken together with an ECLA study (1962) which MacBean quotes appear to support MacBean's conclusion that in response to export fluctuations, fluctuations in GNP tend to be heavily dampened.

The relationship between investment instability and export instability gains weak support from a cross-country regression analysis carried out by MacBean, involving a sample of 20 LDCs, over the 1950-9 period. The correlation coefficient is only 0.34 which is not significant even at the 10 per cent level.

This relationship was tested by MacBean against the time series data for 10 Latin American countries for which data were available over the period 1948-58. Unfortunately while the investment data were in current prices in domestic currencies, exports were valued at current dollar prices. This discrepancy could blur somewhat a relationship between the two variables which may exist. Perhaps, as Maizels (1968) suggested, this is responsible for MacBean's arriving at results which appear somewhat contradictory. On the one hand, MacBean found 'a fairly consistent relationship' between fluctuations of exports and imports of capital goods and 'a statistically significant relationship' between those of capital goods imports and investment - suggesting an association between export and investment instability; on the other hand he found, on the basis of rank correlations for each country, that very little consistent relationship exists between fluctuations in export and investment. However, MacBean's results are not necessarily inconsistent in a statistical sense. There can be a statistically significant but weak relationship between two variables (i.e. with a large sample size, the correlation coefficient may be numerically small but statistically significant). If there is a weak association between two variables A and B and between B and a third variable C, then there may be little association between A and C.

If export fluctuations are powerful generators of instability in income and investment, then we should find, in time-series or cross-country analyses, some significant associations between the fluctuations of export and those of income and investment. Evidence produced by MacBean suggests that export instability has only a weak destabilising effect on income and investment. This may be due to the fact that the majority of LDCs hold higher levels of reserves of foreign exchange and hence can adopt policy measures which reduce the effects of export fluctuations on their economies. In fact, MacBean found changes in foreign exchange reserves to have generally been compensatory and that LDCs tended to hold on average about 20 per cent more reserves (relative to imports) in 1956-7 than MDCs. However, countries with more unstable exports do not appear to hold more reserves relative to imports than those with less unstable exports. Hence, countries with more unstable exports may have to experience somewhat greater income, import and investment instability, though the effects of export changes may be heavily dampened because of the high average holdings of reserves.

By far the most important question is whether export instability hinders economic growth. The cross-country regressions, produced by MacBean using a sample of 25 countries, indicated a non-significant positive relationship (rather than the expected significant negative relationship) between an index of export instability and the growth rates of domestic capital formation. Simple regressions show that neither the ratio of investment to income nor the rate of growth of investment is negatively related to export instability. In fact, multiple regression with the growth rate of import capacity as an additional explanatory variable shows a positive relationship between the growth rate of investment (the dependent variable) and export instability.

MacBean's analysis of the effects of export instability on growth have been criticised on several grounds: the sample is said to be too small; some special cases should have been excluded; the index of instability (i.e. percentage deviations from a five year moving average trend) used is defective; the period 1950-8 may be too short and hence reflect unduly the workings of special factors; the instability index of export and growth rate of investment are not measured for an identical period (i.e. series are not articulated). Maizels by excluding five countries from MacBean's sample of twenty-one LDCs and relating the growth rate of GDP to export instability and the growth rate of fixed investment (rather than that of import capacity), produced an equation which would appear to provide 'a reasonably good explanation of inter country differences in rates of economic growth' and which 'also strongly suggests that highly unstable exports are likely to be a significant constraint on the rate of economic growth of many developing countries'. Unfortunately Maizels did not provide any rationale for replacing the growth rate of import capacity by that of investment [29] and insofar as export instability affects income growth via its impact on investment, the inclusion of both export instability and the growth rate of investment as two explanatory variables in determining income growth appears to be somewhat confusing. Furthermore, the grounds for excluding the five countries from MacBean's sample were not given. In general, the exclusion of observations which weaken one's chosen hypothesis without strong justification is not an acceptable scientific procedure. For these reasons, perhaps the results from Maizels' regression should best be disregarded.

Using a slightly larger sample of countries a different index of instability and two decades of data (1950-66), Kenen and Voivodas (1972) found that their results in general do not contradict those of MacBean. They found no consistent association between export instability and economic growth. What they found was that instability hindered investment in the 1960s even though it appeared, contrary to expectation, to stimulate investment in the 1950s. One possible weakness of their study is that the chosen index of instability is objectionable. Their instability index of export earnings is a measure of 'forecast errors' rather than of fluctuations around a trend, since deviation is measured around a 'forecast' which contains, in addition to a time trend, a component associated with the previous year's export earnings. The use of this forecast in the place of a smooth time trend in the definition of the instability index suggests that only <u>unpredictable</u> changes are included in the definition of instability. As pointed out before, although predictable changes may be easier to deal with than unpredictable changes, both types of change have repercussions on the economy depending on policy reactions and hence should be included in the definition of instability. Thus, an instability index should measure <u>unstable</u> earnings rather than <u>unpredictable</u> earnings.

Another weakness of their study is the inclusion of a coefficient of autocorrelation in all their regression equations. Such an inclusion seems difficult to justify. The forecast used in the instability index is obtained by regressing current export earnings against previous year's export earnings and time. The resulting regression coefficients of the previous year export earnings, R, is called the 'autoregressive coefficient'. To avoid the estimation bias which arises because of the dependence between lagged export earnings and the residual term, Kenen and Voivodas in fact obtained the estimates for the growth rate and the autoregressive coefficient by regressing the first difference of exports (i.e. current exports minus the previous year's exports) against the first difference of exports lagged by one year. They refer to the coefficient of this lagged first difference as R' and use R' in all of their multiple regressions which also include the instability index for exports and a measure of inflation. R' is used as a measure of the <u>duration of export disturbances</u>. But the economic rationale for including R' is not obvious and is not given.

By contrast. Glezakos (1973) found that export instability appears to have a significant negative effect on the real income <u>per capita</u> growth rate of the LDCs included in the sample over the 1953-66 period. However, some doubts can be raised about the validity of his results. First, seven of the forty countries placed in the LDC sample were Cyprus, Greece, Iceland, Portugal, Spain, Turkey and Yugoslavia. These countries are not normally considered to be LDCs. Second, while per capita growth rates were in real terms, there is no indication that the instability indices relate to exports in real terms. Mixing of monetary and real variables could cause serious bias in Glezakos's results. Instability indexes calculated in current prices may differ from those calculated in constant prices. Third, although for most purposes per capita income is a better indicator of welfare than national income, there are reasons for doubting its suitability as the dependent variable in this case. The plausible relationship is that growth of income should be influenced by the growth of the working force which in turn is related to the growth of population, and other variables such as export growth and instability. To regress per capita income's growth rate on export instability implicitly assumes that the partial elasticity of income with respect to population is unity which is unlikely. It should be pointed out that ten countries whose imports were found not to depend on their exports were excluded and this has helped to strengthen the negative relationship between instability and growth. The reason given for exclusion was that most of the effects of export instability on economic development stem from its impact on imports. Hence, countries whose imports were not sensitive to their exports were excluded because, apparently, their economic growth is not likely to be affected by export instability. The relative insensitivity of imports to exports in a country suggests that it has been insulating its economy from export instability by policy measures. This would mean that in such a country the effects of export instability on risks, uncertainty and growth may have been largely prevented. Hence, if valid a priori grounds clearly suggest that some countries' economic growth would not be affected by export instability, then these countries should be excluded and Glezakos has set a good example by restricting his sample in this way. But one should remember that one can no longer generalise the results to LDCs in general.

Note that Glezakos used the term 'import capacity' rather than 'imports' when he explained his criterion for excluding the 10 countries. However, his footnote 9 on p. 673 begins with the sentence: 'The primary criterion for the exclusion of countries from subsequent testing was the significance of the regression coefficient of imports on exports of the same year or on exports of the previous year'. This really suggests that Glezakos in the text of his paper, wrongly referred to imports as 'import capacity', which normally means the ratio of total foreign exchange inflows to the unit value of imports [30].

Using a sample of 28 developing countries, Knudsen and Parnes (1975) found a non-significant rank correlation between export instability and domestic instability (defined as the instability of GNP net of exports) in the 1960s. In a multiple regression equation with income growth as a dependent variable and both of these indices as independent variables, they found that the coefficients of these indices are positive and statistically non-significant. They also found that the coefficient of a weighted average of these two indices (with export instability weighted by export share in GNP and domestic instability, one minus export share) is positive and statistically significant. They maintained that a positive effect of instability on growth is not surprising because transitory income is largely saved, not consumed, and therefore adds to investment. This point is not convincing. If savings are higher out of positive transitory income than out of permanent income, then dissavings should also be higher out of negative transitory income and over a long period of time with negative and positive transitory incomes the effects on saving should even out. There is no reason to expect greater transitory incomes to generate larger savings [31]. Instability may also increase the need for a larger precautionary cash balance and hence savings but, as argued earlier, this is a stock change and need not lead to a higher flow of savings or investment over time.

Recently, Lancieri (1978, p. 147) used a large sample of 101 countries over the period 1961-72 to test the relationship between export instability and GDP growth rates (both in real terms) and obtained a negative rank correlation of -0.33, which is significant at the 1 per cent level. Lancieri (1979, p. 304) also tested the relationship between real GDP growth rate and instability of real total agricultural exports using a sample of 70 countries for the period 1961-72 and obtained an even higher rank correlation of -0.59 per cent, which is significant at 1 per cent. Lancieri's results, for a more recent period, reinforce Glezakos's earlier finding of a negative impact of instability on growth. However, since his results are based on a simple correlation between growth and instability, they can be objected to on the ground that instability (the independent variable) may spuriously capture the effects of other influences on growth which are omitted from the equation. Moreover, although the relationship between GDP growth rate and export instability is statistically significant, variation in instability explains only 11 per cent of variation in growth (implied by a correlation of -0.33), a rather small proportion. This suggests a rather weak relationship between growth and instability.

Lam (1980) produced statistical results which show significant, positive rank correlation between export instability and export growth for a sample of 15 Western Pacific countries and 9 developed countries for two time periods, 1961-72 and 1961-74. This positive correlation between export instability and export growth was later shown by Glezakos (1983) and Tan (1983) to be the result of a systematic bias caused by the manner in which the instability index was calculated.

The instability index used by Lam is the 'normalised standard error of estimate' of the 'linear regression of exports against time'. Examination of the data for merchandise export values of the countries in the sample reveals that they are in fact non-linear with respect to time. The standard error of estimate derived from fitting a linear trend to data with a non-linear trend will result in countries with a higher export growth rate tending to have larger standard errors of estimate. Hence, the instability index as calculated by Lam contains a positive bias in that countries with higher rates of growth of exports will have spuriously higher instability indexes. In order to test whether suitable correction for bias in the instability index affects the results reported by Lam, Tan fitted non-linear trends to the export values of all the countries in his sample, using the same data sources and covering the same time periods and found that there is no statistically significant correlation between export instability and export growth or income growth. Glezakos (1983) also re-estimated the instability indexes for the 14 Western Pacific countries over the 1961-72 and 1961-74 periods, using both linear and exponential trends and found that, over the 1961-72 period, export instability is negatively correlated to income growth (but not significant) when either an index with exponential trend or an index with the trend being linear or non-linear depending on the 'best-fit' criterion used. Over 1961-74, the correlation of export instability with these same indices become positive but statistically non-significant. Thus, Lam's study and the comments by Tan and Glezakos illustrate how the choice of a linear or non-linear trend in the calculation of an instability index can seriously affect the results.

More recently, Moran (1983), on the basis of a cross-section analysis for a sample of 30 countries found that export instability (as measured by several formulae to give emphasis to different aspects of instability) does not have a significant effect on domestic savings or income growth over the 1954-75 period as a whole. However, the effect of export instability on domestic savings and income growth was found to be negative and statistically significant over the 1954-65 period, but not significant over the later 1966-75 period, suggesting that the results are highly sensitive to the period of analysis.

Savvides (1984) used the same method as Glezakos to estimate the three variables income growth (Yr), export growth (Xr) and export instability index (I_x) for the same sample of countries but for the later period 1967-77 and found that in a regression equation relating to Yr to Xr and I_x, the coefficient of I_x is positive and non-significant and that of Xr is positive and significant in marked contrast to the earlier results of Glezakos. However, in a reply, Glezakos (1984) drew attention to the inordinately high real per capita GDP growth rates reported in the statistical Appendix of Savvides' paper. On closer examination of Savvides' data, a number of countries (Chile, El Salvador, Ethiopia, Ghana, etc.) - known to have had stagnating economies during the time period under consideration - are shown to have real per capita growth rates ranging from 4.5 per cent to 11.5 per cent per annum. Such growth rates are high by any standards and are hence incompatible with stagnation. Also, according to Savvides' data over 60 per cent of the LDCs attained annual real per capita growth rates of over 10 per cent. This bias could be due to Savvides' attempt to convert each country's

COMMODITY MARKET INSTABILITY

GDP from domestic currency into dollars, using foreign exchange rates which could be inappropriate, rather than using the UN Basic Series of National Accounts in constant (1975) US dollars. Using the latter data series and a different instability index (which is based on the trend, linear or non-linear, which best fits each country's time series of exports), Glezakos obtained an equation determining the growth rate of per capita income which shows a significant negative coefficient for export instability and a significant positive coefficient for export growth rate for the 1967-77 period, i.e. results which basically confirm those of his previous study for the earlier period, 1953-66.

Limitations of the Cross-country Approach
Most of the studies reviewed above investigate the effect of export instability (as well as inflation and export growth) on economic growth using a cross-country approach. Adams and Behrman (1982, p. 44) considered these studies as 'reduced-form representation of the impact of changes of commodity exports (or total exports) on various summary statistics relating to the macro-economic goals of the developing countries'. Unfortunately, Adams and Behrman did not explain what they meant by 'reduced-form representation'.

Suppose export instability does not affect income growth directly, but we can derive an equation relating income growth to export instability by substituting the equations relating investment efficiency and investment share in income into the equation relating income growth to the efficiency and income share of investment. We shall henceforth call such an equation a derived equation rather than a reduced-form equation as it should still be considered to be of structural form since it contains more than one endogenous variable. It is misleading to call it a reduced-form equation since in doing so, one destroys the usefulness of the reduced-form concept in making it mean two quite different things. The concept of reduced-form equation should better be reserved for the equation which involves only one endogenous variable, i.e. according to its strict econometric meaning.

Comments on Adams' and Behrman's Criticisms of the Cross-country Approach
The parameter of the derived equation relating income growth to export instability and other variables are combinations of the parameters of the original equations. Adams and Behrman (p. 50) suggested, as a criticism of the cross-country approach, that the parameters of the derived equation may be unstable even if the original parameters are stable. The converse is also possible (though not as probable) that, owing to offsetting movements in original parameters, the

167

derived parameters may turn out to be more stable than the original ones. Instability in parameters is a problem for both original and derived equations.

In most of the cross-country studies, very few variables apart from export instability are included in the equation determining economic growth. The omission of important variables determining economic growth would reduce the explanatory power of the overall equation (R^2) but need not necessarily cause a bias in the estimate of the effect of export instability, unless the omitted variables are correlated with export instability. A simple example may help to make this point clear. Let X_1, X_2 and X_3 represent income growth, export instability and export growth respectively. The effect of X_2 on X_1 may be measured by the partial regression coefficient $(b_{12 \cdot 3})$ of X_2 on X_1, given X_3, which can be shown to be related to the simple correlation coefficients between X_1 and X_2 (r_{12}), X_1 and X_3 (r_{13}) and X_2 and X_3 (r_{23}) as follows [33]:

$$b_{12 \cdot 3} = \frac{r_{12} - r_{13} \, r_{23}}{1 - r_{23}^2} \quad \frac{S_1}{S_2} \tag{5}$$

where S_1 and S_2 are the standard deviations of X_1 and X_2 respectively. Suppose X_2 and X_3 are largely uncorrelated so that $r_{23} \approx 0$, then equation (5) reduces to:

$$b_{12 \cdot 3} \approx b_{12} = r_{12} \left(\frac{S_1}{S_2} \right) \tag{6}$$

Hence, provided X_2 and X_3 are uncorrelated, the omission of X_3 will produce no bias in the estimation of the effect of X_2 on X_1, since in such a case $b_{12} = b_{12 \cdot 3}$, according to equation (6).

Equation (5) is also useful in throwing light on another issue. Suppose a spurious correlation between X_2 and X_3 arises because the index of instability used is incorrectly based on a linear trend when an exponential is called for (e.g. the above-mentioned case of Lam (1969)), what is the effect of this spurious correlation on the effect of X_1 on X_2, with X_3 also included? Suppose $r_{12} < 0$, $r_{13} > 0$, an increase in r_{23} will increase the absolute magnitude of the negative value of the numerator and at the same time reduces the (positive) value of the denominator and hence will apparently increase the estimate of the negative impact of export instability, X_2, on income growth, X_1. Hence a spurious correlation between the export instability index and income growth could result in a significant negative impact for export instability on growth when the 'true' impact may be non-significant.

Insofar as the omitted variables are in fact correlated with export instability, their omission from the equation will produce a bias in the estimation of the effect of export instability, but in the absence of a clear knowledge of the signs and magnitudes of these correlations, one cannot say anything about the direction of the bias. In other words, omitting other important influences on economic growth may result in a spurious positive effect for export instability on growth, when its true effect is significant and negative, or in a spurious significant negative effect for export instability, when its true effect may be small and non-significant. Although this criticism may be valid against particular cross-country studies it is not valid against the cross-country approach as such. The bias caused by the incorrect omission of variables is as much a problem for time-series analysis or country modelling as for cross-country analysis. Hence, Adams and Behrman (p. 50) were not correct to regard this as a problem peculiar to the cross-country approach.

It may be argued that as the cross-country derived equation tends to be specified with fewer variables than those specified in the time series country modelling, the bias due to omitted variables would be greater for the former than the latter. However, in fact, this bias depends on the correlation between the set of omitted variables and export instability rather than on the number of omitted variables and it is not at all obvious that this correlation should increase significantly with the number of omitted variables. There may be little independent variation in the set of exogenous variables included in the time series country model, many of which may contain significant time trends.

The main purpose of most of the studies is to determine whether export instability hinders economic growth. For this purpose, the simpler derived form of the estimated equation would do. Although for other purposes mentioned by Adams and Behrman, knowledge of the original parameters may be required, it is not correct for them to criticise the derived form of the equation on the ground that it is not helpful for purposes which were not intended in these studies using the derived form.

Their criticism that the derived form 'suppresses the overall constraints on the economy due to factor availabilities, national identities, government and central bank budgets, and so forth' is similar to their above criticism. Of course, the derived form only answers the very limited question it is designed to do, it can hardly be criticised for not providing other answers, however useful they might be. The coefficient of the export instability in a cross-country equation determining economic growth may well reflect all the above constraints and identities mentioned above.

Insofar as export instability is endogenous rather than exogenous, application of ordinary least squares to the

169

multiple regression equation would produce biased and inconsistent [34] estimates. However, this is again a problem facing both time-series and cross-section analysis. What one is concerned with is the likelihood of getting small estimate errors relative to large ones, i.e. the variance of the estimate around the true value (or mean-square-error). On the basis of mean-square-error, ordinary least squares may perform almost as well as other so-called consistent estimators (such as two-stage least squares, limited information maximum likelihood, three-stage least squares or full information maximum likelihood methods) in several Monte Carlo studies [35]. Ordinary least squares may perform reasonably well on the basis of the mean-square-error criteria because its inferiority on the basis of bias criterion is compensated by its superiority on account of having a minimum variance.

Of course, as pointed out earlier, both high export instability and low income growth may largely be caused jointly by a set of exogenous variables and hence an observed negative relationship between them need not indicate any direct causal relationship between them. This is true but is quite another matter. In practice, we always have an identification problem, i.e. the problem of distinguishing a structural relationship we are interested in estimating and that of a mongrel equation representing a combination of other equations in the model. The identification problem again applies equally to both time-series and cross-section approaches.

The final criticism made by Adams and Behrman, is quite valid. They correctly pointed out that 'even if the underlying structural relations have the same form across countries, the reduced forms may differ because of different structural parameters or different predetermined variables'. Moreover, owing to different policy reactions by the governments in different countries, the underlying structural relations may well have very different forms. Hence, the coefficient of export instability in the derived form equation relating it to income growth would be likely to vary a good deal across countries and hence, even if it is significant and negative for every country, the estimate of it on the basis of an across-country regression would probably have a large variance. Consequently the probability is that this estimate is not significant and even if it turns out to be negative and significant, it is probable that this is due to some spurious reasons, e.g. export instability and income growth jointly determined by some other powerful factors. This is an important weakness of the cross-country approach which has already been discussed. Despite this weakness, the approach may still be useful to assess the kinds of impact export instability has on growth which time series country modelling approach would normally fail to estimate, e.g. the effect of export instability on investment and growth via its effect on risk and uncertainty facing investors and entrepreneurs, and its effects on import flows, inflation, government expenditure, etc. Insofar as different foreign trade regimes in a country producing different degrees of instability and growth rates in, say, different decades, it is difficult to infer much about the casual connection between instability and growth because it may be impossible to distinguish the effects of instability from those of other trade measures under different regimes. In other words, even if there has been sufficient within-country variation in foreign trade regimes, it remains difficult (of not impossible) to detect the above-mentioned kinds of impact of instability on growth. Moreover, unless the experiences of many countries are pooled, the changes in the trade regimes occurring in each country are too few to permit a reasonable estimate of the relationship between instability and growth. There are just not enough degrees of freedom for estimation purpose.

Country Modelling Approach

This approach relies on the estimation and simulation of econometric models of the national economies, the commodity sectors and, sometimes, the commodity markets to assess the impacts of export instability on the various goals of the countries. This approach appears successful in estimating the short-run effects of changes in commodity prices, quantities or earnings on the main macro variables of interest but largely fails to measure the long-term impact of instability on the trends of these variables.

When the econometric model is used to estimate what would happen when export prices are first stable over a number of years, and then unstable, domestic income, investment, the price level and other macro variables may show considerable differences in fluctuations between the two cases, but the trends in these variables may show little or no difference. This could simply be reflecting non-linearities, constraints, lags and the weakness of any ratchet effects.

Rangarajan and Sundarajan (1976) estimated very aggregate macro-econometric models for 11 LDCs. They obtained long-run export multipliers above 2 for 9 out of 11 countries and found growth rates improved with greater export stability in about half of the cases. Their results suggest that while export growth assists economic growth, export instability is just as likely to help as to hinder economic growth.

Rangarajan and Sundarajan's approach is superior to the cross-country approach in the sense that they at least allow for some structural differences among countries. However, their model can be criticised for being grossly oversimplified since it is an extreme Keynesian demand - determined one, without supply constraints normally considered relevant for

171

LDCs. Furthermore, usual policy reactions are ignored and overall fiscal and monetary constraints are left out of their models. Given these weaknesses, it is not exactly clear what their results really show [36]. Their approach may reveal even less about the relationship between economic growth and instability than does the cross-country approach, which is based on much larger samples of countries and where the estimate of the cross-country coefficient of export instability and its distribution reflects in part the different policy reactions among countries.

The recent country studies by Adams et al. (1979) (coffee and Brazil), Priovolos (1981) (coffee and the Ivory Coast) and Nziramasanga and Obidegwu (1981) (copper and Zambia) have overcome some of these weaknesses by investigating the impacts of export instability within the wider context of econometric models in which the relevant primary sectors and their linkages with the rest of the economies are explicitly specified. Adams et al. (p. 168) demonstrated, on the basis of simulations, that 'fluctuations in the coffee market have magnified impacts on the macro variables of the Brazilian economy'. The predominant effects are through the demand linkages, with some supply impacts via capital formation, because 'the Brazilian macro model does not contain capacity constraints on industrial and tertiary sector output, reflecting the significant industrial under-utilisation which exists in Brazil'. However, Adams et al. made no attempt to measure the impact of instability on economic growth. Priovolos and Nziramasanga and Obidegwu found that fluctuations in commodity prices (coffee for the Ivory Coast and copper for Zambia) had little impact on the growth of their respective economies. According to Nziramasanga and Obidegwu (p. 108), while fluctuations affected the value of output of mining from the export sector negatively, 'the rest of the economy is insulated by the net international reserves, the foreign share of net export revenues, and balance on current account. They seem to absorb most of the up-and-down movements, leaving the real variables on their long-term trend rate.'

Adams and Behrman (1982) summarised, in a book, the major results of the country and commodity studies by Priovolos and Nziramasanga and Obidegwu, already mentioned, as well as those by Adams and Priovolos (1981) (coffee and Brazil), Siri (1980) (coffee and Central America), Lasaga (1981) (copper and Chile) and the commodity models by Pobukades (1980, copper) and Ford (1978, coffee). On the basis of simulation exercises designed for comparing the combined effects of an upward and downward movement of 10 per cent in the prices of coffee and copper, they arrived at a number of very useful conclusions which warrant summarising here. The direct impact on the commodity sector varies a good deal depending on whether 'the passive commodity -

COMMODITY MARKET INSTABILITY

sector policies exacerbate (e.g. Brazil) or mitigate (e.g. Ivory Coast) the international fluctuations'. 'The total effects of an international price shock are fairly large in most cases, although smaller for the Ivory Coast than for the other countries because of the automatic policy attenuation through the price-stabilisation fund in this country.' These total effects are the combination of three relatively small direct sectoral effects and the often larger indirect impact on the rest of the economy. Since in the estimated models of which we are aware, there is generally little evidence in support of the existence of significant asymmetries in the private sector or in government policy responses to upward versus downward shocks, the combined impact of an upward followed by a downward change in price of the same size is small.

Explorations with larger price shocks (than 10 per cent) revealed 'decreasing returns' to the amplitude of price shocks because of the constraints in the system. However, if there are a series of shocks of the same sign in a row before there are opposing shocks within the cycle, the effects may become substantial. However, further simulations also showed that a series of n shocks in the same direction have less than n times the impact of one shock. Again this reflects a kind of 'diminishing returns' to such price shocks.

Turning to the simulated effects of a sustained price change on goal attainment of LDCs, they showed that the direct impact on the commodity sector itself can be very large, building up dramatically as the sustained price changes affect production and, in some cases, influence the world market price. However, results vary across countries, reflecting in part differences in policy goals, in the behaviour responses of the private sector and the government and the technological structures. For sustained changes, as for fluctuations, passive fiscal and monetary policies play a major role in transmitting fluctuations in the commodity sector to the rest of the economy in the form of indirect impacts. These indirect impacts are often larger than the direct ones because of under-utilised capacities, foreign exchange constraints and the way expectations are formed. Generally, while a sustained increase in commodity prices may produce favourable effects on capacity utilisation, growth and balance of payments goals, it may produce adverse effects on inflation (but not for Chile) and relative distribution goals on the other. Hence, recognising the effects on the multiplicity of goals, a sustained increase (decrease) in the international prices is not an unmixed blessing (curse).

In short, they report many very important detailed results. Depending on policy reactions, the direct and indirect impacts of an upward (or downward) change in the international price of a commodity, or a sustained change in direction, can be very large for most countries, but the impacts of a combined upward and downward change of a

173

given size on the macro variables are small, suggesting that ratchet effects are negligible as transmitters of the effects of export instability on investment and growth. A sustained increase in a commodity price, however, powerfully assists investment, growth and capacity utilisation but has adverse effects on inflation and income distribution.

It appears that these studies fail to detect the adverse effects of instability on investment in the form of asymmetrical responses of investment (or other macro variables) to instability and insofar as this is because asymmetrical responses are weak or absent in practice, any time-series analysis will fail to measure the adverse effects of investment, because if long-term investment is lower with high export instability than with low instability for various other reasons mentioned earlier such as higher risk discount and lower incentive to invest because of frequent disruptions to imports of capital goods over a long period of time, the adverse effect of instability can only be picked up in a cross-country analysis and not in a time series analysis, involving relationships between annual observations on different variables. Thus, the fact that Adams and Behrman's analyses were not able to show the effects of instability on growth does not necessarily mean that the effects are weak or absent. The effects might well exist and were significant and yet were not detected either because of insufficient variation in instability in the period considered or because adverse effects were not primarily reflected in the form of asymmetrical responses of investment.

Finally, Dick et al. (1984) used a computable general equilibrium model (ie. a comparative static framework of the Johansen type) to investigate the short-run effects of fluctuations in commodity prices on the economies of Colombia, Ivory Coast and Kenya. Their results showed that these economies are destabilised by fluctuations in commodity prices, but the effects of the price shocks can be confined to the relevant commodity producing sectors by a policy of fixed domestic absorption in the face of the price instability. This however requires a large reserve of foreign exchange. They recognised that the adjustment costs of frequent exchange rate changes to attempt to maintain the balance of payments by shifting resources between domestic sectors and export sectors, would be substantial. They conclude that the use of foreign exchange adjustment to maintain the trade balance appears to be rational only when the price shock could be considered as representing a shift in the price trend. They did not attempt to assess the long-term effect of price instability on growth because their analytical framework does not explicitly recognise the effects of uncertainty associated with the export instability on the behaviour of key economic agents - producers, consumers and governments - effects which they rightly claimed that econometric time-series studies failed to capture satisfactorily in their estimated models.

The main strength of their comparative static approach lies in the wealth of details concerning the disaggregated linkages between the relevant commodity sectors and the rest of the economy. Its main weakness is that, as a comparative static approach, it allows no lags in the relationships. When the variables of a model contain substantial trends, it is no longer meaningful to talk in terms of <u>static</u> equilibrium values, since with trends, the expected values of all endogenous variables are continually 'disturbed' by the trends in the endogenous variables and so can never attain their equilibrium values. One can however still talk in terms of long-term equilibrium trends in these variables. These long-term equilibrium trends are in fact steady-state paths (provided by the particular solution of the difference equation with all residuals taking the expected value of zeros), around which the actual values of the variables tend to fluctuate. Because these steady state paths usually include the lag-coefficients as determinants, solutions in the comparative static models by ignoring all lag coefficients may produce very poor approximations to these paths. However, despite the shortcomings of this approach, the study by Dick et al. still provides valuable insights on the immediate impacts of price instability at the disaggregated sectoral levels and on the transmission of the effects from these sectors to the rest of the economies. The authors expressly refer to the impact of price instability that their study attempts to investigate as <u>short-term</u>. However, it is by no means obvious that the effects they considered are necessarily short-term. A comparative static approach compares two sets of equilibrium values in determining the effects of 'price shocks' without being concerned with the length of time that would have to elapse before the economy and markets can reach another equilibrium. The effects are presented either in full or zero, whereas in the real world they are somewhere in between and have each a particular time pattern. Therefore, it is difficult to interpret comparative static results or draw practical policy conclusions from them.

CONCLUDING REMARKS ON CONSEQUENCES OF INSTABILITY

Empirical evidence in the form of time series analysis and country modelling together with a priori reasoning clearly suggest that any upward or downward change in the commodity export prices or earnings would have important effects not only on the export sectors but also, if the export sector is large, on the rest of the economy unless offset by policy actions. Such offsetting policies backed by adequate reserves of foreign exchange and/or easy access to international borrowing could substantially mitigate the impact on

175

the rest of the economy of changes in export prices or earnings.

A priori reasoning suggests that where the adverse effects of export instability on growth take the forms of ratchet effects (e.g. asymmetrical responses of investment to an upward vis-a-vis downward change in exports), time series analysis could capture them but where these effects take the forms of reducing the trends of variables affecting growth (e.g. the investment/income ratio and investment efficiency) the time series analysis and country modelling would normally fail to detect them. In such cases, only cross-country analysis can hope to capture any such adverse effects of instability on growth using suitably chosen samples of countries which are homogenous in terms of economic structures and policy reactions.

Since in general there are other more powerful influences on economic growth than export instability, responses of relevant variables such as investment and imports may be very different for different countries and policy reactions in different countries may also be very different - it is unlikely that the effects of instability on economic growth would consistently be revealed in different cross-country studies, using different samples of countries, over different periods of time.

Indeed, this review of empirical literature on the relationship between export instability and economic growth, using a cross-country approach, suggests some support for instability being an obstacle to growth but the results are shown to be sensitive to the samples of countries, the periods under investigation and the manner in which export instability and the trends in exports are measured. The differences in the results produced by different studies do not appear surprising - they simply confirm the difficulty of capturing, in practice, adverse effects (which could be slight) of export instability on economic growth, even though a priori grounds suggest some adverse effects are likely.

The difficulty of proving the detrimental effect of export instability on economic growth does not mean that we should abandon the view that risk and uncertainty, stop-go-policies, disruption of imported capital goods or public investment programmes, and investment fluctuations have adverse effects on the level and efficiency of investment and hence growth rates. The evidence exists in other fields of economics that higher returns are required for investments with higher risks and that repeated disruptions to investment programmes reduce their attractiveness to investors. Even in the absence of direct evidence confirming the detrimental effect of export instability on economic growth, a priori reasoning and indirect evidence still strongly suggest that those countries whose economies seem likely to be sensitive to export fluctuations should be encouraged and assisted to insulate their economies from the effects of export instability. The costs of instability to them and to the international community at large may considerably outweigh the cost of such devices as a generous international compensatory financing scheme. Failures of countries to insulate their economies may reflect any one or more of the following: (a) shortages of resources; (b) deficiency in information concerning the costs and benefits of insulation; and (c) higher priority given to non-economic goals. The case for introducing further resources - using international schemes to help these countries to insulate must rest on the argument that such countries have underestimated the true benefits of such insulation because of (b) and (c); otherwise with (a) alone, it is a matter of transferring the resources to them and let them use the resources how best they wish.

NOTES

1. Index involving the average of absolute values of percentage deviations:

$$I_1 = (1/n) \sum_i^n (|X_i - \hat{X}_i| / \hat{X}_i)$$

Index involving the root of the average of squared percentage deviations:

$$I_2 = \sqrt{(1/n) \sum_i^n ((X_i - \hat{X}_i) / \hat{X}_i)}$$

where X_i and $\hat{X}_i$ are actual and trend values in period i = 1, 2, ..., n.

2. For convenience of exposition, the discrete time interval discussed is a year, i.e. annual observations are considered, although in practice, a week, a month or quarter may be relevant because data are weekly, monthly or quarterly.

3. In the former case, it is said to be heteroscedastic, i.e. has non-constant variance, and in the latter case it is said to be serially correlated or just autocorrelated.

4. In the sense of having large variances, i.e. there is a greater chance of producing large errors.

5. The least-square formula for the variance of the estimate underestimates its correct size.

6. This also means that stabilising a time series would reduce its arithmetic mean over any finite sample period.

7. Alternatively the index should be:

$$I_2 = \sqrt{(1/(n-2))\ \sum_{i}^{n}\ (w_i - \bar{w}_i)^2}$$

For a mathematical derivation of the mean and variance of a log-normal variable, see Appendix D.

8. Let $w_t = (|X_t - \hat{X}_t|)/\hat{X}_t$, where X_t and $\hat{X}_t$ are the actual observation and its trend value in year t. The mean of w_t is:

$$\bar{w} = (1/n)\ \sum_{t}^{n}\ w_t \qquad\qquad (1)$$

Since, by definition MAD = $\bar{w}$ and RMSD^2 = (1/n) Σw_t^2, we must have : Var w = RMSD^2 – MAD^2.

9. See House of Lords Select Committee on Commodity Prices Report (1977) vol. I, p. xxiv and pp. ci-cii, Tables 3.4a and 3.4b. For example, out of a total number of 66, 45 and 15 correlation coefficients between EUVs of major exporters and quoted prices (1964-74) for coffee, cotton and cocoa respectively, 22, 19 and 9 respectively are less than 0.65.

10. Assuming that the demand and supply for a commodity can be expressed as follows: q = ep+u and q = np+v, where u and v are two random variables with zero means and constant variances, p is the logarithm of the deviation of price from its trend and e and n are price elasticities of demand and supply respectively. It can be shown that:

var p = (n^2 Var u + e^2 Var v)/(e + n)^2 and

var q = (Var u + Var v)/(e + n)^2

assuming for simplicity that cov(u,v) = 0.

Solving these two equations for Var u and Var v in terms of Var p and Var q and subtract Var u from Var v gives: Var v – Var u = 2((e + n)/(e – n)) (Var q – (e^2 + n^2)/2 Var p).

Since e and n are both likely to be less than unity, (e^2 + n^2)/2 < 1 and with Var p > Var q, we must have Var v > Var u if e < n.

11. Note that the usual 't' test for the difference between two means cannot be used here because instability index has a X^2 distribution rather than the required normal distribution and the F test is not a useful test because the stringent assumptions on which it is based may not strictly hold. The Mann-Whitney U test is one of the most powerful of the non-parametric tests. For a description of the Mann-Whitney test see, e.g. Sidney Siegel, <u>Non-parametric statistics for the behaviour sciences</u>, pp. 116-27. It is

demonstrated there that this test is an excellent alternative to the t test and without the restrictive assumptions and requirements associated with the t test. Whitney (1948, pp. 51-6) gives examples of distributions for which the U test is superior to its parametric alternative, i.e. for which the U test has greater power to reject H_0.

12. The Mann-Whitney U test produces the following values for the standard normal: 7.6, 8.2, 7.3 and 7.2 for the periods 1950-60, 1960-70, 1970-80 and 1950-80 respectively.

13. UNCTAD, TD/B/1029, Table 3, p. 7.

14. See Massell (1969).

15. Let b and d be price elasticities demand and supply respectively, then complete price stabilisation would destabilise proceeds if b > (1/2)(1-d). See Nguyen (1979).

16. See Brook and Grilli (1977) and Murray (1978).

17. See F. Rudolf et al., eds. (1958, 1959).

18. See Nguyen (1979c). Let Var u, Var v, Var p and Cov(p,q) be the variances of demand shifts, supply shifts and price and the covariance of price and quantity respectively, then Var v ⪌ Var u only if Cov(p.q) ⪋ (n-e)/2-Var p, where n and e are price elasticities of supply and demand respectively.

19. The invalidity of the inference about the source of instability from the covariance of price and quantity had in fact been demonstrated earlier by Porter (1970), whose analysis is however more complicated than necessary.

20. The implication of these figures for the EEC can best be illustrated with the help of a simple arithmetic example. Let Q, C and X represent a region's production, consumption and export then, we have X = Q-C. Let a be the average ratio of C to X and hence 1 + a be the average ratio of Q to X. It can be shown that the variance of X would be equal to a^2 times the variance of C plus $(1 + a)^2$ times the variance of Q, assuming Q and C are independent. Now suppose a = 4, i.e. consumption is four times as large as net export, and let the standard deviation of Q and C be the same at 10 per cent. Then, the standard deviation of X would be 64 per cent, i.e. almost six and half times as large, i.e. export is considerably more unstable than production or consumption. Proof: X = Q - C, hence $\Delta X = \Delta Q - \Delta C$ and since Q = X + C, we can write Q/X = 1 + C/X = 1 + a, where a = C/X. Let x = $\Delta X/X$, q = $\Delta Q/Q$ and c = $\Delta C/C$; Var x = $(1 + a)^2$ Var q + a^2 Var c, assuming the independence of q and c.

21. See House of Lords Select Committee on Commodity Prices Report (1977), p. lxxii.

22. See MacBean and Nguyen (1980) for a detailed demonstration with numerical illustration of this.

23. See MacBean and Nguyen (1980). We have also briefly mentioned these points in the earlier section under the heading of commodity concentration.

24. Asymmetrical expectation on the parts of investors

concerning the upswings (as permanent) and downswings (as temporary) is really not rational. However, as long as the expansion of the industry is profitable, this expectation will appear to be justified ex-post.

25. See Nziramasanga and Obidegwu. From the results of simulations of an econometric model of copper and Zambia, the authors concluded that stabilising copper price has no impact on the Zambian economy, since the rest of the economy is insulated by the net international reserves and the foreign share of net exports. Unstable copper price has no adverse effect on economic growth (p. 109).

26. Project Link refers to the world econometric model LINK (under the direction of L.R. Klein). Overall the LINK system consists of 18 models for QECD countries, 8 models for centrally planned economies and 4 regional models for developing countries and a residual model for 'the rest of the world'.

27. However, by assisting developing countries to stabilise their import capacity, say via contributions to international compensatory financing schemes, developed countries can gain substantially, as commodity importers, from the continuity and growth of their supplies and, as exporters, from more stable imports from developing countries. The review of empirical literature is not begun with an earlier study, Coppock (1962), because for a number of reasons listed below, little weight can be placed on Coppock's results. Apart from using a peculiar index of instability (with trend estimated on the basis of only two observations), Coppock mixed together LDCs and MDCs and focused on bivariate not multivariate relations. For what it may be worth, he reported a positive correlation between instability and income growth.

28. The fact that Maizels replaces growth of import capacity by that of investment has often been overlooked when his results are quoted.

29. For example, MacBean (1966, p. 110) defined import capacity as the total value of exports plus net invisibles and net capital transfers divided by an index of import prices.

30. See Adams and Behrman (1982, p. 49).

31. See Lim (1976, p. 318).

32. For proof, see Johnson (1969, p. 59).

33. An estimate is said to be inconsistent if its bias and its variance do not fall towards zero as the sample size increases indefinitely.

34. See Bassmam (1958). See also Johnson (1960, p. 294) for a summary comment on Bassmam's study.

35. See Adams and Behrman (1982, pp. 41-2).

Chapter Five

POLICIES FOR DEALING WITH PRIMARY COMMODITY
INSTABILITY

The major problems involved are (1) the instability of prices
characteristic of commodities and the effect these are believed
to have on the welfare of producers and consumers; (2) the
poor prospects which face many primary products in terms of
slow growth in demand and declining trends in real prices;
(3) the obstacles which restrain exports of commodities and
more especially processed forms of commodities to the markets
of the industrialised nations. The main proposals which are
currently on the World's agenda for alleviating these problems
are those contained in various resolutions of the UNCTAD,
from the Nairobi meeting in 1976 to the Sixth UNCTAD in
Belgrade in 1983. Many have a much longer history and have
recently been reviewed in considerable detail by Fiona
Gordon-Ashworth (1984).

THE INTEGRATED PROGRAMME FOR COMMODITIES (IPC)

The focus of international discussion has been the Integrated
Programme for Commodities launched at UNCTAD IV in 1976 as
part of the plans for the establishment of a New International
Economic Order. At UNCTAD IV it was agreed that the members should enter into negotiations for the setting up of a
Common Fund to finance international buffer stocks or internationally co-ordinated national buffer stocks, within the
framework of international commodity agreements. The objectives were stabilisation, 'just and remunerative pricing,
taking into account world inflation', and a number of others,
including expansion of processing in LDCs, diversification of
exports, stabilisation of export earnings by means of compensatory financing and improved access to markets of MDCs.
The Programme covered 10 core commodities: cocoa, coffee,
tea, sugar, copper, tin, rubber, cotton, jute and jute products, hard fibres plus a further eight to be included at a
later stage: bananas, vegetable oils, meat, tropical timber,

181

iron ore, bauxite, manganese and phosphates, with possible further additions [1].

The intention of the Group of 77, representing the LDCs, was that a large number of ICAs using buffer stocks, but with possible back-up of controls on exports or production should be negotiated as soon as possible. The Common Fund, financed mainly by contributions and loans from the MDCs and the oil surplus exporting LDCs, was to provide the finance for the buffer stocks. There was also to be a smaller element for assisting other objectives such as diversification. It would act as a catalyst for the ICAs by removing the difficulties of obtaining finance and providing the integrating aspect of the IPC.

THE COMMON FUND

The Common Fund was the novel feature of the IPC. The UNCTAD Secretariat proposed that it have, initially, $3 billion, of which $1 billion would be contributed by governments and $2 billion borrowed. A second $3 billion would be raised when necessary in the same proportions.

The arguments put forward in support of it were that its existence would speed up the negotiation of new ICAs, and the re-negotiation of existing ones, as it would remove the obstacle of finance which had proved a serious hurdle in the past. In terms of equity, it would be an improvement because importing nations would now be contributing to the costs of price stabilisation which was in their, as well as the producers' interests. Previously the responsibility of financing buffer stocks had fallen entirely on exporting nations. It would provide a pool of finance on which the ICAs would be able to draw as necessary. It would economise on the total finance required because : (1) movements in commodity prices were to some extent offsetting so that some ICAs would be repaying while others were borrowing from the Common Fund; (2) a central fund would be able to obtain better borrowing terms partly because of pooling risks and partly because of economies of scale and greater bargaining power in dealing with banks than would individual ICAs.

The Group of 77 proposed an element of independence for the Common Fund in that it could initiate actions itself e.g. finance national stocks outside the framework of the ICAs and some other measures in or outside that framework. They also insisted on a controlling voice for LDCs in the decision making structure of the Fund.

The MDCs, particularly USA, Germany, Japan and the UK were not particularly sympathetic to these proposals. They appear to have been suspicious that the Common Fund would be used to support measures which would raise commodity prices rather than simply smooth out their fluctuations

about long run trends. The USA and Germany were philo-
sophically opposed to anything which interfered with free
market forces, despite their own extremely interventionist
policies in domestic agriculture, regional policies and protection of industries such as steel and textiles.

This inconsistency has aroused much criticism from
liberal commentators. But of course it can be argued that it
is their bitter experience of the effects of such policies in
terms of mountains of wheat and butter and lakes of milk and
wine which makes MDCs so suspicious of schemes which may
claim to be about stabilisation but turn out to involve price
supports. Toleration of the inefficiencies and budgetary costs
is the price they pay to placate powerful domestic lobbies.
There is no similarly powerful force in the international
sphere to induce acceptance.

The developed countries argued against a strong Common
Fund with independent finance and an ability to act on its
own. They proposed instead a pooling arrangement, whereby
the surplus cash balances of individual ICAs would be deposited with the Fund. The compromise eventually reached,
after prolonged negotiations, lay much closer to the MDC
model than to the Group of 77's ideal. The June 1980 Agreement on the objectives, capital structure and mode of operation of the Common Fund envisages an emasculated version of
the original proposal. Instead of a $6 billion fund under its
control, a mere $500 million is to be available for assisting in
the original buffer stocking objective. A second window,
however, has been added to finance measures other than
stocking such as diversification, productivity improvements
and marketing. The finance for this has to be raised by
voluntary contributions by governments. The Fund is not
empowered to intervene in commodity markets itself. Although
LDCs have a majority in the voting structure, the MDCs have
a 'blocking vote' in discussions with 'significant financial
implications' and in 'other important decision.' The hopes of
the more optimistic supporters of the original scheme are
placed on the possibility that once operational it will evolve
through time and gain more resources, as have the World
Bank and the IMF over the years since their creation [3].
But the Common Fund has yet to come into operation. Several
deadlines for ratification have come and gone. To date (July
1986) insufficient numbers have ratified the Agreement and
paid the necessary contributions. The USA in particular
seems unlikely to ratify.

INTERNATIONAL COMMODITY AGREEMENTS

Despite the hopes and expectations of the Group of 77 for
many new ICAs the results have been disappointing. In the
nine years since UNCTAD IV only one new price stabilising

agreement, that for natural rubber in 1982, has emerged. Two other new agreements have been negotiated, for jute and tropical timber, but they have no price provisions and are concerned mainly with research and circulation of information. Other agreements, which were in existence before the Nairobi meeting have been re-negotiated, but have faced many difficulties and may actually be weaker now than before. The longest lasting agreement - that for tin - ran into problems when the Sixth International Agreement, which was to have come into force in July 1982, failed to achieve sufficient acceptances from producers and consumers (80 per cent of production and consumption). Although the signatories did go ahead it was without the participation of the US, the world's largest consumer, and Bolivia the third largest producer. Subsequently (October 1986), the Agreement ran out of funds in a vain endeavour to support prices and the tin market collapsed. A brief account of this episode is given below, p 196.

In sugar, which has a long history of agreements, the 1977 International Sugar Agreement signally failed to stabilise world sugar prices. For most of its period of operation the price ruling on the free world market was below the floor price of the Agreement. The exception was in 1980 when it was above the upper price range. The Agreement was re-newed in 1984 but only as an administrative arrangement without means for intervention in the market (Smith, 1983, p. 316 and The Times, 1985).

The first Cocoa Agreement came into being in 1972 after ten years of negotiation. Its provisions included a buffer stock and export quotas. Its history is of repeated failure to contain cocoa prices within the target range. Most of the time it was virtually non-operational because it had no stocks. The attempt to renegotiate it in 1979 ended in failure. The 1980 Agreement had no production or export quotas and neither the USA, the major importer, nor Ivory Coast, a major exporter joined. It accumulated over 100,000 tons in its buffer stock but was unable to maintain the floor price. Attempts to renegotiate in 1984 failed to reach an agreement and were adjourned to February-March 1985. Despite signs to the contrary, a new agreement was negotiated in the Summer of 1986, with flexible pricing provisions included. (Ashworth, 1984, The Times 1985)

In the Coffee Market attempts to control prices have swung between international commodity agreements involving both producers and consumers and cartel arrangements among groups of producers. The first truly international commodity agreement for coffee was set up in 1962. It provided for export quotas and certificates of origin for coffee from members to aid control of the MDC markets. During its lifetime, up to renegotiation in 1967, it met its price objective of holding prices above the 1962 level but only at the cost of accumulating large national stocks and stimulating increased coffee production. The fast growing producers in Africa pressed for larger quotas and Brazil bore the brunt of restraining exports. In an attempt to reduce oversupply the 1968 Coffee Agreement included a Diversification Fund. Over the 1962-72 period of these Coffee Agreements prices were probably more unstable than previously. One commentator, A.D. Law (1975) suggests that price instability was as much as 50 per cent greater than it would have been in the absence of the 1962 and 1968 Agreements.

The withdrawal of the US, because of high coffee prices and what was seen as unfair pricing of processed coffee from Brazil, severely weakened the ICA and the Agreement, although renewed until 1975, contained no economic provisions. Instead, quotas imposed by Latin American and African producers became the main instrument of control. The 1976 Agreement's economic provisions were inoperative until 1980. Producers again formed cartels, first the Bogota Group of eight Latin American producers and then a multinational company, Pancafe, with an initial capital of $500 million to finance trade withdrawals. But despite its activities Pancafe failed to combat a continuing fall in coffee prices due to declines in consumer demand for coffee. This led to yet another attempt at co-operation with consuming nations which bore fruit in the activation of the 1976 Agreement's economic provisions. It had wide membership, 99 per cent of world production and over 90 per cent of consumption. It has been successful in supporting coffee prices but again only by withholding some 12 million tons of coffee at a cost of about $1 billion. A replacement agreement on similar lines was negotiated in 1983 and continues in force.

The international Coffee Agreements may have held prices higher than they would have been in the absence of such controls and exporters have gained extra revenues as a result, but the underlying structural problems of excess supply have not yet been tackled. Neither the diversification scheme nor export promotion measures have had any significant impact and it is debatable whether or not the ICA acted to reduce fluctuations in coffee prices. (Ashworth, 1984, chapter 10)

There have been various attempts to control the international market for wheat. From 1949 to 1967 successive agreements sought to control the market via multi-lateral long term contracts guaranteeing agreed quantities of exports and imports at specified prices. While introducing some stability into part of the market one effect has been to destabilise the residual free market as it became the market into which excess demand and supply were decanted. On the basis of a weighted average of prices within and outside the International Wheat Agreement the effect was probably stabilising, but it is difficult to know how much of any improvement should be attributed to the Agreement and how much to the activities of the large national stores of wheat held by USA and Canada (MacBean 1966, pp. 265-7, Ashworth 1984, Chapter 7).

Since 1971 the Wheat Agreement has had no price provisions. It has become a food aid convention for emergency relief of famine.

The International Rubber Agreement of 1979 aims to stabilise prices and to achieve a balanced growth between demand and supply. It has no quota provisions. Intervention is by a buffer stock which purchases or sells according to whether the market price falls within the lower or upper intervention zones. The trigger action prices are 20 per cent above and below the reference price, but there is another band defined by upper and lower intervention prices which are 15 per cent above and below the reference price. There is provision for automatic revision of the reference price, and the accompanying price range, in relation to movements in the daily market price and the size of the stock. This operated to reduce the reference price by one per cent in May 1982 much to the indignation of producers who felt the reference price was in any case too low to cover the costs of most producers. It is too early to assess the effectiveness of the Agreement, but it is clear that producers are unhappy. There were large scale buying operations in the summer of 1981 which were widely believed to have been a unilateral attempt by Malaysia 'to raise prices in the run up to a general election in April 1982.' Malaysia has threatened withdrawal and newspaper reports in October 1982 suggested that Malaysia, Indonesia and Thailand had agreed to a producer controlled scheme for cutting supplies (Ashworth 1984 p. 200). They are also reported to be seeking the addition of export quotas to the Agreement. This is referred to as one likely source for a renegotiated ICA for rubber in a recent UNCTAD bulletin (UNCTAD, 1984, p. 6).

In Sum
The recent history of ICAs is clearly not one of unqualified success. Only tin, cocoa and rubber have provisions for international stocks. Both tin and cocoa have back-up quota provisions and the producers are seeking similar provisions in a renegotiated Rubber Agreement. Long delays in negotiations have normally been followed by the rapid development of several difficulties leading to renegotiation or abandonment of the economic provisions. Actual market prices during the period of operation of ICAs have often as not been outside the agreements' specified ranges.

The problems which face ICAs in the real world are a mixture of the political and the economic. Conflict between producers and consumers over the choice of the reference

POLICIES: PRIMARY COMMODITY INSTABILITY

price and the intervention prices is the most common cause of
difficulty and delay in negotiations, and of the breakdown of
the agreements. Conflicts between producers with different
costs, different prospects for expansion or diversification,
different levels of dependency, different technologies and
different levels of foreign participation form further difficulties. Most agreements have a multiplicity of objectives:
price stabilisation, increasing export earnings, raising consumption of the commodity, ensuring fair labour standards, to
prevent unemployment, to encourage wider participation in
processing, to improve market access, to promote economic
growth, to increase competitiveness, to increase purchasing
power of exports. Most of these figure in several Agreements
(Tin, Coffee, Cocoa, Sugar, Rubber for example). But they
seldom contain provisions for their attainment. Most are
simply pious hopes. Even if price stabilisation is singled out
as the key objective, the methods set out for achieving this
leave a great deal to be desired. The reference prices are not
fixed by systematic forecasting methods using all available
information. They are set by political bargaining which may
be only slightly influenced by rather informal forecasting.
The intervention prices are mainly the outcome of bargaining
strengths. While they are reviewed periodically this is not
done systematically save in the Rubber Agreement where
there are provisions for lowering or raising the reference
price by 5 per cent if the average Daily Market Indicator
Price, which takes into account three grades of rubber and
the four main markets, is either below the lower intervention
price or above the upper one over the six months prior to
review. But this can be, and has been, over-ridden by a
special vote. It also has a stock trigger. If buffer stock
purchases or sales of 300,000 tons take place then the reference price is automatically adjusted down or up by 3 per
cent, unless a special vote decrees otherwise. A special vote
requires a two-thirds majority of producers and consumers
voting separately. In the other agreements managers operate
with even more crude rules of thumb. Normally the funds
provided are inadequate to carry enough stocks for sufficiently long periods to even out large swings in supply and
demand.

A serious problem which faces any price stabilising
agreement in a world characterised by flexible exchange rates
is that stabilising a price in dollars or sterling can involve
destabilising its price in all other currencies if the dollar or
pound fluctuate against a basket of other currencies. Buffer
stock actions which help to stabilise export prices for one
group of LDCs where currencies are pegged to the dollar may
be destabilising for others whose currencies are pegged to
the franc, the pound or the yen. These risks are clearly
demonstrated in a study by Alexander Yeats (1985). In these
circumstances it is a serious problem for an ICA to decide in

187

which currency to denominate the price of the commodity it wishes to stabilise.

The examination of history is a useful, indeed essential part of evaluation of ICAs, particularly in revealing the complexities which surround their negotiation and demise. But assessing their technical feasibility from their past history is complicated by the political factors and by the difficulty of establishing the necessary counterfactual situation of absence of the ICA over the same period, yet this is the only true comparison. To take a real commodity and its associated agreement and attempt to model the 'with and without' situations is very difficult. This is partly because the existence of a buffer stock or quotas may have altered the structural relationships in unpredictable ways, but also because other random or systematic factors, not captured by the model, may have influenced the behaviour of supply and demand during the period of the ICA's operation.

It is, in fact, a very complicated business to identify the appropriate trend. Yet this is the key to success for any ICA whose objective is to smooth price fluctuations. First there is the problem of the choice of the appropriate trend: short, medium or long-term (3-5, 5-10 and 10 plus years say). A trend value for the price has to be projected, say, each year for one year ahead to provide the basis for fixing the reference price and the upper and lower intervention prices. The data required go beyond the series of past prices for they are in part the result of previous official interventions. Even if the particular commodity price series were free of such contamination it could be inefficient to project purely on that basis because information on determining variables such as population, income, acreages, new mines etc. may be available and should be incorporated in the projection. The more 'good' information used, the more efficient should be the trend estimate. An econometric model should be used to generate hypothetical historical price series on the basis of (a) absence of the ICA and (b) data on exogenous variables which are used to estimate prices and privately held stocks. The hypothetical price series is then used to estimate the trend by least-squares regression.

The longer is the chosen trend projected the more stable would be the stabilised price resulting from, say, buffer stock operations, but the larger would be the required stock and its cost. If a short-term trend is chosen the reference price would adjust more quickly to any changes in economic forces. This would mean less stability would be achieved, but the costs of the stock would be smaller and the risks of running out of funds or stock would be much less. If the authority runs out of stock, or funds so that it has to suspend operations, the resulting price instability may be greater than if it had not operated at all, or had operated with more modest aims.

Suppose in a free market a price fall occurs. It could be the result of any one of the three possibilities:

(i)   a sudden, unexpected but temporary increase in supply, such as a bumper crop, or sudden temporary fall in demand e.g. a dock strike in USA. This would be modelled by an unusually large value for the random residual in the supply or demand function

(ii)   a sudden but permanent increase in supply (with no change in the growth rate afterwards) e.g. a once-over shift to a more productive variety of the crop; or a sudden permanent drop in demand e.g. a technological development which leads to a once over drop in the raw material component of finished products. This would mean a shift in the intercept of the supply or demand function

(iii)   an increase or decrease in the growth rate of supply or demand e.g. a technology change phased in over time. This would involve a change in the co-efficient relating supply or demand to time in the relevant function.

The immediate price fall/rise would be large with (i) or (ii) and moderate with (iii). The change in price could be cumulative with (ii) and (iii) but would quickly reverse itself with (i).

The implications for the buffer stock agency depend crucially on whether the cause of the price change is known. Strictly speaking, the trend of price is unaffected by (i) and so the buffer stock should sell or buy sufficient to keep within the pre-arranged margins for the reference price without changing the reference price.

If (iii) is the cause the reference price can be adjusted fairly quickly to take account of the new situation as the change occurs quite gradually. So the buffer stocks should not run out, or reach excessive heights.

The most serious problem is (ii). Without intervention the price would fall/rise permanently to the new trend level. But if the authority does not reduce its reference price (in the fall case) because it does not diagnose the cause it could quickly run out of funds. Price would collapse dramatically as private stockholders would dispose of stocks until prices fell low enough to induce them to start holding stocks again.

Real world data cannot be used to illustrate these issues because the real causes of price movements are never certain, nor can we ever be sure of the correct specification and estimation of the underlying model that generates historic prices. A plausible model would require a system of simultaneous, non-linear, dynamic, stochastic equations. Such a model is in general very difficult, if not impossible to solve by analytical methods.

To avoid these difficulties one possible approach is to perform an experiment with an imaginary product. To examine the technical and financial implications of a buffer stock we construct a model in which the parameters are known. We feed in controlled exogenous changes of the three types considered above and investigate the effects with, and without, the operation of the buffer stock. In this way it is possible to measure precisely the reactions of price and stocks. It would be easy to extend this to repercussions on export revenues, producers' incomes, inflation etc. by marrying the commodity market model to a macroeconomic model of an exporting economy, but the exigencies of time and space confine us to the simpler version in this chapter.

The Model

This is at the world market level for the commodity. It reproduces the underlying characteristics of the World Bank model for tin. Both current demand and supply are assumed to be related to the previous year's level and price, and to the relevant sets of external influences in the current year. Plausible price elasticities of supply and demand are used. The price equation is in fact an inverse form of the demand for stocks. The equations are in log-linear form i.e. the logarithms of the variables are linearly related. The supply of stocks function is just a definition expressing the equality between current stocks, on the one hand and the last year's stocks plus the difference between last year's supply and demand. Stocks are assumed not to deteriorate. Current stocks exceed last year's stocks by the amount by which supply exceeds demand during last year. But this last function is in actual values not logarithms. Because of the mixture of linear and log-linear equations this model is not easy to solve analytically. But it is easy to obtain numerical solutions with the aid of a computer. The model is set out in Appendix H. Graphical representation of the numerical data are show in Figures 1 to 4 below.

PRICE FLUCTUATIONS AND BUFFER STOCK RESULTS

Figure 1 depicts the sources of the fluctuations. For convenience, the combinations of all the external influences on demand and supply are represented by the variables X (demand shift) and Z (supply shift). They are defined to include random terms U (demand error) and V (supply error). X, Z, U and V are shown for a period of 50 years in Figure 1. The magnitudes of U and V are deliberately exaggerated in the graph to make it easy to identify when their abnormal values occur. Note that these are multiplicative, not additive disturbances, i.e. the shift in the demand function, for

Figure 1:   Experiment 1: Sources of Fluctuations

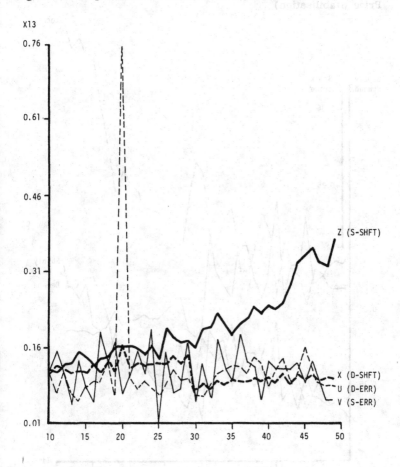

Figure 2:   Experiment 1: Price, Demand, Supply, Stocks (No Price Stabilisation)

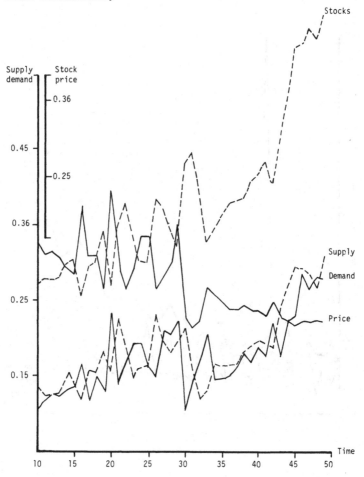

Figure 3: Experiment 1: Complete Price Stabilisation

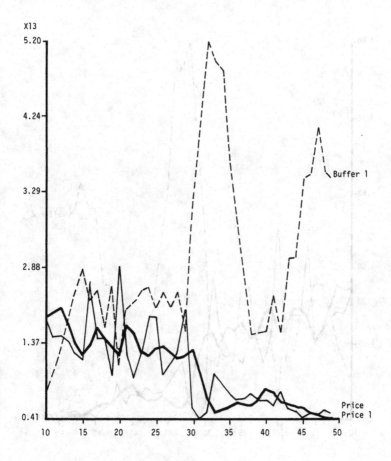

Figure 4:   Experiment 1: Partial Price Stabilisation

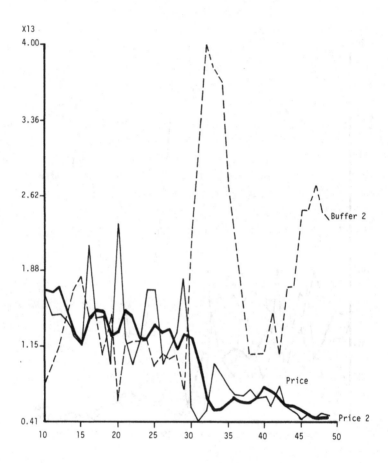

example, is proportional not parallel. They occur for U in year 20 and for V in year 25. The shift variables X and Z include not only the random terms U and V but systematic trend and cyclical elements. The length of the cycle for supply (Z) is 8 years and for demand (X) it is 5 years. The growth rate of the trend in supply suddenly jumps to a higher value in year 35, whereas that of demand remains the same throughout. In year 30 there is a sudden downward shift in the intercept for demand (X).

In Figure 2 the results of these are depicted in the absence of any intervention. The graphs show the paths followed by supply, demand, price and private stocks. Price and stocks vary inversely as expected, with stocks rising over time as price follows a downward trend. Note the stock peak in year 30 when price reaches a trough, with the downward shift in demand which occurs in that year. Price recovers a little subsequently and then falls gently in response to the higher growth in supply after year 35.

In figure 3, the buffer stock aims at completely stabilising price at its reference level given by Price 1. It is successful in doing so: Price 1 follows a steadier path than Price, the free price. Note that the changes in stocks are relatively small until year 30. Then in attempting to hold the price stable in the face of what turns out to be a permanent downward shift the stocks level, Buffer 1, shoots up over the next two years, to about 3 times its previous average level. It subsequently falls gently over years 32, 33 and then sharply in 34 and 35.

Figure 4 shows the buffer stock operating to hold price within a band 15 per cent either side of the reference price. It shows the time paths followed by the stabilised price, Price 2, the free market price, Price and the effects on the buffer stock, Buffer 2. Price 2 is more stable than Price and the buffer stock, Buffer 2, is at a lower average level and fluctuates less than Buffer 1 in Figure 3. Their path is however fairly similar.

This first experiment demonstrates the large swing in the buffer stock level when a permanent downward shift in demand occurs. In the next experiment we have an upward shift in demand in year 30 and a decrease in the growth rate of the supply trend after year 35 and one consequence is that the buffer stock agency runs out of stocks in trying to hold price. Despite its best endeavours it fails. The price, Price 2 is no more stable than the free market price, Price, would have been. When the buffer stock is permitted to become negative and aims at completely stabilising the price, Price 1, at its reference level, it does make Price 1 more stable than the free market price but this is only achieved by vast sales and purchases.

THE TIN CRISIS OF OCTOBER 1985

Our model analysis of an ICA was carried out some time before the failure of the International Tin Agreement in 1985/86. We chose tin as our representative commodity simply because it has characteristics which lend itself to an international buffer stock, because the World Bank had an econometric model of the tin market for its projection work and because, with tin agreements going back to 1931, it is the longest lasting ICA and has often been claimed to be a success. Picking this most stockable commodity and assuming that its market parameters were known enabled us to highlight the risks which attach to ICAs of the buffer stock variety, especially when set up for less ideal commodities. However, any model is an extreme simplification of the real world. It is constructed to focus attention on the issues considered crucial and to ignore other factors on the (often heroic) assumption that their joint effects are random and tend to be small.

The full explanation of the collapse of the Sixth ITA has yet to be revealed. It must necessarily be much more complex than our model, but the main events and elements of an explanation seem clear. Its negotiation was fraught with conflicts. The US wanted a purely buffer stock agreement with no use of export quotas. Producers, particularly Malaysia argued that a large buffer stock tended to depress market prices. The outcome was a compromise. The buffer stock was increased from the 20,000 tonnes of previous agreements to 30,000 with an additional stock of 20,000 tonnes to be financed by borrowing, 'using as security stock warrants, and, if necessary, government undertakings.' (Sixth ITA, Article 21). The stock was to be financed equally by producing and consuming nations, a radical departure from previous ITAs where producers had sole responsibility for finance. Contributions to financing were on the basis of shares of production or consumption of tin and the amounts on the basis of the floor price at the time when contributions were called for. In the upshot, the largest consuming nation, the US, and the third largest producer, Bolivia, decided not to join. In the case of the US the reason was that it regarded the stock provisions as inadequate; while for Bolivia, the objection was to a too low price range. (Gordon-Ashworth, 1984, p. 125). Events swiftly revealed the flaws in the new ITA.

From the second quarter 1981 until November 1985 the buffer stock was a net purchaser of tin, from 1982 onwards on a large scale. At the end of the Fifth ITA on 30th June 1982, the buffer stock held over 48,000 tonnes. At the end of 1984, now under the Sixth Agreement, it had reached nearly 56,000 tonnes. Export controls were instituted in April 1982 and remained in place from then on.

A major cause of the collapse was the choice of an unsustainable floor price in 1982. It was too high for a world in which the trend growth rates of consumption had dropped sharply from past rates, and prospects of restoration of world growth were poor. The problem can be partly attributed to a campaign of support purchases of tin conducted by an unidentified group, widely believed to represent tin producers. This pushed prices to record levels of over $9,000 (Malaysian) per metric tonne in March 1982. But, when the campaign ended, the price dropped to $7,035, throwing the burden of support back on to the ITA buffer stock.

These high prices encouraged non-members to expand production and the export quotas of member countries were breached by smuggling. Tin of 'unspecified origin' reached over 16,500 tonnes in 1983, most of it from South East Asia. Production of tin in Brazil rose from 8,000 tonnes in 1982 to over 17,500 tonnes in 1984. Production also rose in UK, Canada, Peru and Burma. World supplies of tin surged at a time when consumption was dropping sharply, to a level nearly 25 per cent lower than the 200,000 tonnes annually consumed in the late 1970s. A major contributory factor was the substantial increase of the substitution of aluminium and plastic cans for tin-coated steel cans and in other uses. These were largely due to technological changes which are unlikely to be reversed. In terms of our model this type of situation is shown in Figure 3 for the 30th year. But in the real world, the situation was still worse because of the growth in production from new mines and re-opened old ones. Some of these may not go out of production even with a very low price for tin.

With this combination of cyclical and trend movements against tin the buffer stock manager was forced to buy considerable amounts of tin for stock. To increase the impact of his limited funds on the price of tin he entered into substantial commitments in tin futures and borrowed heavily from a range of sources. Promises from the Association of Tin Producing Countries to provide the manager with an additional £60 million were not met. As a result he ceased operations in October 1985 with debts estimated at the time at £600 million owed to metal traders on the LME, and another £300 million to other ITC creditors (The Times, November 8th 1985, p. 23). The security for these debts was the stock of tin held by the ITA plus the obligations of the member governments defined in the Agreement. When the ITA suspended operations the Tin Market was immediately closed to avoid the total collapse in tin prices and allow time for a negotiated solution to be worked out between the ITA and its creditors. In fact, to date no solution has been forthcoming.

The fundamental reason for the failure of the ITA was that its target price range was not adjusted downwards in response to adverse changes in the supply and demand for

197

tin which, for the most part, were not merely temporary and reversible changes. But the failure of the ITA need not have had such a catastrophic effect upon the market for tin. The severity of the crisis was exacerbated by the promise of funds to continue to back an unrealistic price and by the very large futures market commitments which the ITA undertook. One can make a rough assessment of how large these were from the fact that even at the peak price the physical stock of tin held by the ITA implies purchases of at most £500 million but the outstanding debts in November 1985 were £900 million.

This points up the risks which are involved in making extensive use of the futures market to support the spot price of a commodity. It should in more normal circumstances induce increased holdings of private stocks (see ch. 4 pp. 129-32) but if speculators sense that the price is being supported at an unrealistic level they may be prepared to supply futures sales contracts to an almost infinite amount.

The dramatic collapse of the tin market has had a quite profound effect on public attitudes to international commodity agreements. The governments of the USA, West Germany and the UK were supplied with further ammunition to attack such interventionist policies. Whether it is just that the credibility of internationally controlled buffer stocks should be totally undermined by this one event depends on how far one believes it to be the result of fundamental flaws in the basic mechanism or merely the result of human error and unusual circumstances.

Implications of the 1985 Tin Crisis for ICAs

Shifts in demand and supply do occasionally occur and it is generally difficult to predict them even under ideal conditions. Simulation runs of our model show that if the buffer stock manager fails to lower the floor price promptly in response to a downward shift in demand, then he will soon run out of funds in attempting to defend an excessively high floor price - not to mention the encouragement to substitution and the consequent direct reduction in demand. When he runs out of finance, the price would drop sharply and price instability could on the whole be considerably greater with than without the buffer stock actions. The recent tin crisis underlined two further problems which arose because the ITA could and did borrow to finance more stock and to intervene in the futures market in an attempt to support an excessive floor price. With the presence of a large supply of speculative funds, an attempt to maintain the spot price by raising the futures price significantly above the future spot price expected by speculators generally could cause a financial loss with magnitude not only potentially larger than that involved in spot activities alone but also difficult to predict in advance. Because the ITA could borrow partly on the security of tin stocks and partly on the strength of member governments' implied guarantees, there was a lack of financial constraint on the size of its future commitment. Its eventual loss in future dealings was consequently larger. Of course, several other factors contributed to the crisis:- support buying campaign and record high tin price which tended to encourage production while consumption remained low, decision by the US to sell tin from the strategic stockpile and failures of export and production controls to contain the expansion of tin production.

The collapse of the Sixth Tin Agreement has serious implications for other ICAs particularly because the history of tin agreements has often been looked upon as a success story in commodity price stabilisation schemes. The lessons for other ICAs are: (i) if shifts in demand and/or supply cannot be detected promptly, inappropriate stock activities could destabilise price, (ii) ability to borrow could simply lead to cash crises and result in insolvency, (iii) intervention in the futures market could be a very costly affair and (iv) it is often difficult to make export and production controls effective, especially where there are important newcomers.

CONCLUSIONS

The rationale for ICAs is that the existing markets produce excessive price fluctuations which have harmful micro and macro effects on the economies of exporting and importing nations. Hence, the first and the direct objective of ICAs is to stabilise price via buffer stocks and other back-up measures. Other desirable outcomes are expected to flow from stabilising prices: reduction of risks to producers and users of the commodities, reduced instability in earnings of foreign exchange and in producers' incomes, government revenues, increased investment and growth. Empirical evidence has failed to show that damage to LDC exporters or MDC importers is in general significant. We have set out reasons including the problem of fluctuating exchange rates, why the ultimate objectives may not be achieved by stabilising prices even if this were successful. Our survey of post-war ICAs, backed up by an attempt to model a buffer stock operating in the rather favourable situation of an ideal commodity market, ideal in the sense that its structural parameters are precisely known, have illustrated the enormous difficulties which face attempts to stabilise price around its long-term equilibrium path. It appears that if commodity exporting LDCs are to be helped to achieve greater stability in their ability to import, other means must be sought. Of these, extension and improvement of compensatory financing is likely to be the most important, but improved technology to reduce fluctuations in production and improved information flows to make speculation more stabilising and encouragement to producers to use the futures markets seem other promising lines for development.

THE COMPENSATORY FINANCING FACILITY (CFF) OF THE IMF

I. Rationale for Compensatory Financing

The premise on which a compensatory financing scheme, such as the IMF-CFF, is based is that the stabilisation of import capacity around trend benefits each country by assisting its growth, contributing to the stability of its income and employment and reducing its rate of inflation. Import capacity may be defined as total foreign exchange inflows divided by an index of import prices. The foreign exchange inflows consist not only of export earnings but also workers' remittances and tourism, aid and foreign borrowing including the scheme's compensatory payments. It is implicitly assumed that with stable import capacity, a country can maintain a steady flow of the imports of capital goods and intermediate goods regarded as essential for the success of its development programmes and can insulate its domestic economy from fluctuations in its export earnings, e.g. by offsetting government expenditure.

If a country stabilises income when faced with an uncompensated export shortfall, it will incur a balance of payments deficit. As the deficit arising from an export shortfall is temporary in the sense that the export shortfall is expected to be reversed, it calls for no corrective measures which may disrupt steady economic growth. Instead the appropriate policy should be to borrow externally to finance this deficit. In practice, many developing countries, particularly the poorest, do not find it easy to borrow on reasonable terms and hence are obliged to deflate or use import controls which involve sacrifices in their economic objectives. Access to compensatory finance could permit such countries to pursue policies appropriate for long-term development, uninterrupted by the frequent need to take damaging short-term measures to deal with a temporary external imbalance.

This in principle suggests: (i) that the objective of the scheme should be the stabilisation of foreign exchange receipts in real terms around a fairly long-term trend (i.e. the period over which the trend is calculated should be long enough for the sum of expected shortfalls to equal the sum of expected surpluses over trend, or 'overages') and (ii) that only countries with both export shortfalls and a balance of payments need (i.e. a balance of payments deficit and/or a critically low level of international reserves relative to annual imports) should have access to compensatory drawings under the scheme. The logic of the scheme should also require that repayments be made when exports are above trend and the country concerned has no balance of payments problem. (This ability to repay test is symmetrical to the balance of payments need test applied as a condition for borrowings from the CFF). In practice, many countries may have persistent balance of payments problems because their currencies are overvalued or their investment programmes are over-ambitious. Such countries may not have to repay at all if 'no balance of payments problem' is a necessary condition for repayment. Furthermore, the 'balance of payments need' condition also becomes a redundant constraint on compensation. Hence, these conditions would be inappropriate unless all countries with access to the scheme can be required to adopt appropriate corrective measures to achieve long-term equilibrium on their balance of payments.

As the description below of the main features of the CFF shows, its apparent objective is the stabilisation of foreign exchange receipts in nominal, not real terms around a medium-term, not a long term trend. Furthermore, while compensatory drawings are tied to export shortfall and subject to a balance of payments need test, repayments are not directly tied to export averages and are not subject to any ability to repay test. The CFF is also open to a number of criticisms which are discussed below.

II. Main Features of Current CFF

According to an IMF - Staff Report (1984, p. 1), the purpose of the compensatory financing facility is to provide financial assistance to members experiencing balance of payments difficulties resulting from export shortfalls or cereal import excesses that are temporary in nature and due largely to factors beyond the member's control.

The CFF was established by the IMF in 1963, but it was not until its conditions were liberalised by the Executive Board Decision No. 4912(75/207) of December 1975 that substantial assistance to IMF members could be given. That decision increased the amounts available, while leaving the rules unchanged.

(i) Eligible countries. All members of the IMF are nominally eligible to draw under the CFF, but most developed countries' members have refrained from using it.

(ii) Compensation base of shortfall calculation. The shortfall on which compensatory drawings were based was related to a source of foreign exchange receipts which may be called the base of shortfall. This base was originally total merchandise exports. It was later expanded in 1979 to include earnings from services (workers' remittances and tourism) and in 1981 to include cereal imports. Once a member chooses to base its request on earnings that include or exclude receipts from workers' remittances and tourism, it is bound by that choice in any subsequent request for a period of 5 years. Similarly, once a member elects to base its request on data that include cereal imports, then it is bound by that option for a period of 3 years. In the case of the inclusion of cereal imports in the basis for compensation, compensation is related to the sum of export shortfalls and cereal import overages (either of which can be positive or negative). For convenience of exposition, the base of shortfalls is henceforth referred to as total merchandise exports, except where it is necessary to spell out explicitly whether it includes workers' remittances, tourism and cereal imports.

Compensation conditions. To qualify for a drawing, a country must satisfy all of the following conditions, in addition to the existence of the export shortfall:

(a) there must be a balance of payments need;
(b) the export shortfall must be (i) temporary and (ii) largely beyond the control of the member;
(c) the Fund must be satisfied that the member will co-operate with the Fund in efforts to find, where required, appropriate solutions for its balance of payments difficulties;
(d) each drawing must not exceed a maximum of 85 per cent of quota for export shortfall (or 83 per cent for cereal imports excesses) and total outstanding drawings must not exceed 105 per cent of quota.
[(d) is usually referred to as 'quota restrictions'.]

The guidelines on co-operation with the Fund have remained largely unchanged throughout the years of the facility's operations. The co-operation requirements associated with drawings in the lower tranche (when outstanding drawings are below 50 per cent of quota) are less strict than those associated with drawings in the upper tranche (when outstanding drawings are above 50 per cent of quota).

The shortfall formula. The shortfall in export earnings on which compensation is based is the amount by which total export earnings in the shortfall year are below a trend value calculated as a geometric average of earnings in the five-year period centred on the shortfall year. To calculate the trend value, judgemental forecasts of the export earnings in the two post shortfall years are used. The 1975 decision discarded previously applied forecasting limits, so that the calculated shortfalls could increase. Until December 1975, the export earnings for the two years after the shortfall year were subject to a forecast limit in the sense that projected earnings could not exceed the average earnings of the two years before the shortfall year by more than 10 per cent. Judgemental forecasts can in principle be (and probably have been) used to limit the size of the calculated earnings shortfall. Inevitably such forecasts are difficult to produce and are subject to an important margin of error; it can be shown that a small percentage forecast error can produce a substantial difference in the size of the shortfall. The rules allow 'judgemental forecasts' for the two post shortfall years to be taken to be equal to 'earnings in the two pre-shortfall years multiplied by the ratio of the sum of earnings in the most recent three years to that in the preceding three years', if the result of such a trend appears reasonable.

Nominal terms trend. All calculations relating to the use of the CFF are made in special drawing rights (SDR) at current prices. The Executive Board of the IMF has, on several occasions, considered the possibility of calculating shortfalls from a <u>real term</u> trend (i.e. the five year moving geometric average of export earnings deflated by an appropriate price index of imports, centred on the shortfall year) but has each time rejected it largely on the ground that accurate import price indexes are not available for all countries and their release is likely to be subject to a longer delay than those of export earnings in <u>nominal terms</u>.

(iii) <u>Repayment conditions</u>. Repayments of CFF drawings must be made in equal quarterly instalments during the period beginning 3 years and ending 5 years after the date of drawings, unless the Fund approves a different schedule. Earlier repayment may be expected on the basis of an improvement in the member's balance of payments and reserve position (or when the member is subsequently found to be over-compensated because of under-estimation of export earnings in the shortfall year). In other words, each CFF loan is expected to be fully repaid within 3-5 years. For each CFF loan, a service charge of 0.5 per cent is imposed by the IMF. The interest on outstanding balances now stands at 6.6 per cent per annum.

III. Evolution of the CFF
Since its establishment in 1963, the CFF has been reviewed in 1966, 1975, 1979 and 1981. The major aspects affected are: (i) access; (ii) method of estimating trend and (III) bases of shortfall calculations.

Access. The limit on outstanding drawings was 25 per cent of a member's quota in 1963. This limit was raised to 50 per cent in 1966, with drawings in any 12-month period limited to 25 per cent of quota. At the same time, a two-tranche system was established concerning the requirement, whereby a stricter test was associated with requests that would raise outstanding drawings above 25 per cent of quota. In 1969, with the establishment of the buffer stock financing facility, a joint limit of 75 per cent of quota was introduced on outstanding drawings under the CFF and the buffer stock financing facility (BSFF). In December 1975, this joint limit on CFF and BSFF was removed and the limit on outstanding drawings under the CFF was raised to 75 per cent of quota, with no more than 50 per cent in any 12-month period; the threshold for the upper-tranche co-operation requirement was raised to 50 per cent of quota, where it has remained ever since. In 1979, the limit on outstanding drawings was raised to 100 per cent of quota and the limitation on drawings in any 12-month period was removed. When financing of cereal import excesses became possible in 1981, the 100 per cent of quota limit on outstanding drawings was also applied to cereal drawings, with a joint limit of 125 per cent of quota on outstanding export and cereal drawings. Finally, in 1984 when there were major quota increases for members, the separate limits on outstanding export and cereal drawings were reduced to 85 and 83 per cent respectively of the new quota with a joint limit of 105 per cent of quota.

Total potential supply of CFF in nominal terms has therefore expanded considerably since 1963. The potential supply of CFF resources for 120 countries (obtained as the product of aggregate quotas and quota limits on outstanding CFF drawings) increased from under 2 billion SDRs in the early 1960s to over 20 billion SDRs at present.

Trend. The Fund's method for calculating the medium-term trend value for export earnings has changed several times since 1963. Under the 1963 decision, the trend value was estimated by combining the results of a formula with those of a judgemental approach. Under the formula, the trend value was estimated by applying weights of 0.25 to exports in each of the two pre-shortfall years and 0.5 to exports in the shortfall year. The judgemental part involved combining actual export earnings for the three years and forecasts for the two post-shortfall years based on market appraisal and available information. In the 1966 review, it was decided to rely mainly on the method involving judgemental forecasts. In the 1975 review, an extrapolation formula for estimating the trend value (as described above) was introduced but, unsurprisingly, the formula produced 'unsatisfactory' results in practice and was abandoned in favour of the judgemental method.

Upper and lower limits on export forecasts were introduced in the 1966 review, but were removed in the 1975 review. The arithmetic average of exports for the five years centred on the shortfall year was used as the estimate of the trend value up to the 1979 review, when it was decided that it should be replaced by a geometric average. (The estimated export shortfall is invariably smaller when the geometric average is used than when the arithmetic average is used.)

IV Evaluation of the CFF

(i) Quota limits. While the benefits to members can be raised quite considerably by rational changes in the key features of the CFF, the most important determinant of total benefits from the CFF is the partial supply of its resources in real terms. The progressive relaxation of quota limits on CFF drawings and the increase in the overall quota in 1981 have produced about a ten-fold increase in the potential supply of the CFF's resources in nominal terms since 1963. However, in real terms, because of a high rate of inflation, particularly in the 1970s, the CFF's supply of resources increased much less. Even in nominal terms, the CFF's resources grew rather less than world trade and far slower than the world payments imbalances. In 1966-68 total IMF quotas represented about 16 per cent of deficit developing countries' export earnings and 64 per cent of their current account deficits but only 6 per cent and 12 per cent respectively in 1978-81.

(ii) Calculation for shortfalls method for estimating trend. While a five-year moving average centred in the mid year can be used to estimate the trend value for any year up to two years before the current year it is hardly appropriate for estimating the trend value for the shortfall year as it then requires forecasts for the exports in the two post-shortfall years (i.e. in the future). This makes the calculated shortfall highly sensitive to forecasting errors. But the trend value for the shortfall year need not be based on forecasts. An exponential, or linear, trend value can be estimated, using the least-squares method with data for the last five years for medium-term trend or seven to ten years for estimating a long term trend. There is advantage in using a known formula rather than a qualitative judgemental approach to calculate the trend value in that each member can judge in advance with less uncertainty the amount it is entitled to draw from the CFF. Undue uncertainty concerning drawings from the CFF reduces the incentives of each member to incur the foreign exchange cost involved in its domestic stabilisation. Lack of automaticity in the members' drawing right also increases uncertainty and may deter countries from using the CFF.

The fact that the geometric average is smaller than the arithmetic average is no ground for criticism. Since trend of nominal exports is likely to be exponential rather than linear, the use of the geometric average to produce the estimate for the trend value appears justified.

Real versus nominal. The inappropriateness of the use of a trend in nominal terms in shortfall calculation has been recognised by everyone, including officials of the IMF and members of the Executive Board. A member with a shortfall in nominal exports but no shortfall in real exports needs no compensation; on the other hand, a member with no shortfall in nominal exports but with a shortfall in real exports does require compensation - if one accepts that the objective of the CFF is to stabilise the import capacity of member countries. Hence, giving compensation on the basis of shortfall from a nominal trend would often result in giving assistance to members when it is not needed and denying assistance when it really is. The essential aim of any stabilisation programme is to provide short-term assistance at the time it is needed. The CFF can be seen to miss its objective by not compensating shortfall from the real export trend. Furthermore, in so far as the sum of shortfalls over a few years tend to be same in real terms or in nominal terms there are no extra resources required by the CFF by using real terms calculation.

(iii) Conditionality. The high level of use of CFF by developing countries may suggest that drawings on the CFF are not subject to a high degree of conditionality. However, it can be seen from Table 6.1, where the outstanding CFF drawings are shown as a proportion of countries' IMF quotas, (July 1982) for 111 developing member countries are presented, 58 countries have no outstanding drawings. The most plausible explanation for the fact that over half of LDC members have made no drawings from CFF is that the existence of conditionality (i.e. the lack of automaticity) has made them reluctant to pursue domestic stabilisation programmes involving a certain increase in the foreign exchange expenditure which they are not certain will be covered by subsequent CFF loans.

In principle, the side condition of a balance of payments need does make sense. The only problem is that in practice balance of payments need may be open to different interpretations when it refers to so many things, e.g. current account deficits, reserve position and its trend. Whether there is a balance of payments need should not be a matter for the IMF alone to judge case by case. There must be a clear rule about how balance of payments need is to be interpreted so as to reduce uncertainty about what it implies to members.

The most disliked condition is the requirement of co-operation, particularly for requests in the upper tranche when evidence of the adequacy of past co-operation has to be produced. Why should co-operation with the Bank be required for CFF drawings? In principle, by the definition of an export shortfall, the balance of payments problem arising from it is temporary and requires no corrective measure.

It has been reported that in some cases CFF drawings have been used by the IMF to induce members to 'toe-the-line' in other matters. This tendency is a serious cause for concern, as it would in effect introduce indirectly upper credit tranche conditionality into the approval of compensatory drawings.

(iv) Repayments. If compensatory drawings require simultaneously an export shortfall and a balance of payments need, then it must follow, as a matter of symmetry, that repayment should be made only when there is simultaneously an export overage and a favourable balance of payments situation. It has been stated that the reason for not relating repayment to export overage is that this would have required forecasts of export earnings at regular intervals (e.g. quarterly) for every country with debts to the CFF. However, if the IMF method of trend estimate is replaced by the least-square method, then no forecasts would be required to calculate overages at regular intervals and hence repayments can then be tied to overages, as required by a priori considerations.

(v) Effect of CFF operations on 'export instability.' Finger and Derosa (1980) attempted to measure the impact of the CFF on the stability of participating countries' foreign exchange receipts and found that the CFF has not stabilised foreign exchange receipts. Up to January 1979, 71 countries have drawn from the CFF. Using the data on exports and CFF drawings and repayments, Finger and Derosa estimated the instability indexes both for export receipts and export receipts plus CFF compensations (or minus repayments) - which they referred to as export instability 'with CFF' and export instability 'without CFF.' They found that no matter how CFF transactions were treated, their effect on 'export instability' was very slight. When CFF drawings were added to and repayments were subtracted from export receipts in the year they were actually made, they found CFF transactions have in fact raised export instability for half of the LDC countries (62) and 5 out of 9 MDCs, which have used the facility. The impact was however always minimal. For only 8 LDC users did CFF change export instability by as much as 5 per cent and 5 out of these 8 changes were in the wrong direction - i.e. towards more instability. Across all users, there was a net increase of instability by 0.1 per cent. Their measure of instability, the standard errors of the regression of the natural logarithm of export receipts against time, is a perfectly acceptable one.

These results seem to be due to the fact that repayments are not related to overages and that drawings frequently do not take place in the shortfall year because of time lags. Eliminating the effect of the time lapse between the shortfall and receipt of the drawings and excluding the effects of repayments they found that CFF transactions reduced export instability in just over two-thirds of the LDC users of the CFF. But the overall average reduction of export instability over the 62 LDC users was still only 1.5 per cent and for the DC users, the net effect was an increase of export instability. Thus even when the effects of the time lag between shortfall and drawings and repayments were ignored. CFF transactions were still found to have a negligible effect on export instability. This suggests that the method used by the IMF to calculate the medium term trend has produced trend values which are almost as unstable as the actual export values themselves. The use of a moving-average should help to smooth out the series, but this is offset by the use of forecasts in the moving-average which contain large errors absent in the actual series.

The results reported by Finger and Derosa should be considered as strong evidence against both the trend estimation method adopted by the IMF, and its repayment schedule because it is unrelated to the occurrences of export overages.

V.   Proposals for reform of the CFF
In view of these shortcomings of the CFF several proposals can be made to enhance its usefulness to members. These include proposals for: (i) increasing the CFF compensatory drawings as a proportion of total shortfalls, i.e. the implied rate of compensation; (ii) calculating shortfall around a real term trend rather than a nominal term trend; (iii) lengthening the trend itself, i.e. using more years in the calculation of the trend value, (iv) making repayment conditional on overages and the passing of 'an ability to repay test' - in terms of reserves and/or balance of payments position (but given the fulfilment of repayment conditions, repayment is immediately required, i.e. without the two years space period) and/or lengthening the repayment period; (v) making the system of compensation and repayment completely automatic so that no other conditions are required and countries need no longer feel inhibited about drawing on CFF for fear of Fund imposed conditions on their economic policies.

It is worth repeating here that the switch from nominal to real term calculations would have a marginal effect on the total outstanding drawings from the CFF over say a decade and would not require an increase in the CFF resources. The reluctance to change to real term calculations cannot be justified on that account, nor on the belief that reliable import price indexes are not available for most countries. Comprehensive statistical information on import prices - in the form of the unit value index of total imports - is available in the United Nations system. Furthermore, an improvement of import price statistics for individual countries could be achieved with relative ease, particularly, if, where necessary, countries receive technical assistance from an institution such as the IMF. In any case, the deficiency in the information on import prices is an argument for improving import statistics rather than one for continuing to provide compensatory financing services which do little or nothing to help the countries to stabilise their real imports and income. The adoption of any of the other proposals (i.e. (i), (iii) - (v)), could substantially raise the need of CFF for more resources. Given the present international political and economic climate these are unlikely to be forthcoming. But their adoption would require a smaller increase in the resources of CFF if the rate of interest were nearer the real opportunity cost of capital.

THE EEC STABEX SCHEME

The Lome I Convention, signed in February 1975, by EEC members and 46 African (37), Caribbean (6) and Pacific (3) (ACP) states, established the EEC scheme for the stabilisation of export earnings (or EEC - STABEX scheme) initially for the period 1975-79. The list of non-EEC members has been expanded to include 19 additional countries. The scheme was subsequently revised and applies for the period 1980-84 covered by the Lome II Convention signed in October 1979. Negotiations for the Lome III Convention are presently underway and some features of the system are likely to be modified.

I. The aim of STABEX
Stabex is a commodity-specific compensatory financing system of a regional nature, in principle limited to trade flows of basic agricultural commodities from ACP countries to the EEC. Its stated aim is set out in Article 23 of Lome II as follows: 'With the aim of remedying the harmful effects of the instability of export earnings and to help the ACP States overcome one of the main obstacles to the stability, profitability and sustained growth of their economies, to support their development efforts and to enable them in this way to ensure economic and social progress for their peoples by helping to

209

safeguard their purchasing power, a system shall be operated to guarantee the stabilisation of earnings derived from the ACP States' exports to the Community of products on which their economies are dependent and which are affected by fluctuations in the price or quantity or both these factors.' Under Lome I, the ACP governments had only to inform the European Commission ex-port as to the use to which Stabex transfers had been put; under Lome II they have to agree in advance of the transfer the projects to which the Stabex funds are to be allocated and on which they are ultimately spent.

Stabex was allocated an amount of 375 million ECUs for the 1975-79 period and 550 million ECUs for the 1980-84 period. These funds are part of the European Development Fund (EDF) for the ACP countries which amount to 5 billion ECUs under Lome II Convention. [Under Lome I Convention, the funds allocated to Stabex represented one-eighth of the resources of EDF.]

II. Main Features of STABEX

(i) Eligible countries. The beneficiaries are the 64 developing countries in Africa, the Caribbean and the Pacific (ACP countries) overseas countries and territories, under Lome II. [Previously under Lome I Convention, the eligible countries were 46 ACP countries.]

(ii) Compensation Base of shortfall calculation. The shortfall on which compensation (usually referred to as a transfer) is based is the gross sum of the shortfalls in the individual exports of 46 agricultural products to (a) EEC for 51 states and (b) the world for 13 states - the term gross sum is used in the sense that in summing across shortfalls, overages are not deducted. [Previously, under Lome I prior to 1980, the list of commodities covered by the scheme consisted of only 19 primary products of which 18 were agricultural commodities and 1 mineral, iron ore.] Thus, the number of products covered has been increased to include most tropical agricultural raw materials of current interest to the ACP countries (except for sugar and tobacco) and some processed agricultural products.

Compensation conditions. To qualify for compensation from Stabex, each ACP state must certify:

(a)   that their products are included in the list of products covered by the scheme and that they were exported to the EEC. These conditions may impose some administrat-

ive burden on the ACP countries and the scheme;
(b) each product involved is at least 6.5 per cent [7.5 per cent under Lome I prior to 1980] of total export earnings to all destinations (5 per cent for sisal and 2 per cent for least developed states);
(c) the shortfall in the export of the product to the EEC (or to all destinations for 13 states) was at least 6.5 per cent [7.5 per cent, prior to 1980, under Lome I] below reference level (2 per cent for least developed countries) and
(d) the shortfall was not the result of a trade policy measure adopted by the country which reduced its exports to the EEC.
[Conditions (b) and (c) are usually referred to as dependency and trigger thresholds respectively.]

The shortfall formula. The shortfall is calculated as the amount by which actual export earnings (of a commodity to EEC) fall below a 'reference level', defined to be the average nominal export earnings over four years previous to the shortfall year. In certain cases (e.g. new line of production), the average is calculated on the basis of three years instead of four years. The basis of the transfer is the shortfall plus 1 per cent for statistical errors and ommissions.

(iii) Repayment Conditions. The ACP countries are required to repay any transfers made to them if for a given year and a given product the unit value of the exports is above the reference unit value, the quantity of exports to the EEC is not less than the reference quantity and the value of exporters is no less than 106.5 per cent of the reference level of the export value. If these three conditions are met, the amount repaid is equal to the difference between actual earnings of exports to the EEC and its reference level in the previous year [2]. [Previously, provision of Lome I required the amount repaid to be equal to the reference quantity multiplied by the difference between the actual and reference unit value.]

If these conditions are not fulfilled, the amount is paid at the rate of one fifth per year after a deferment of two years. If, on the expiry of the seven-year period, these payments have not been made in full, the Council of Ministers will decide whether to require that they be made in one or more instalments or to waive the rights to repayment.

POLICIES: PRIMARY COMMODITY INSTABILITY

Interest rate on outstanding balances: none

Resources limitation. The resources allocated to Stabex for
the period 1980-84 are 550 million ECU. This is divided into
five annual instalments. For each of these years, resources
available consist of the annual instalment of 110 million ECUs
(minus any amount already spent in the previous year) plus
any amount left over from the previous year, plus any repayment of loans, plus up to 20 per cent of the following year
instalment. Should the amount prove insufficient, it is for the
Council of Ministers to decide whether (i) to authorise the
use in advance of a maximum of 20 per cent of the following
year's instalment or (ii) to reduce the amount of the transfer
to be made.

Special concession for the least developed countries. The least
developed countries received a more favourable treatment than
other ACP countries in three respects: (i) they do not have
to repay transfers; (ii) their dependency threshold is lowered
to 2 per cent and (iii) their trigger threshold is lowered to 2
per cent.

Evaluation of the Stabex

Performance of Stabex. In the period 1975-82, Stabex has
made 205 transfers to 44 ACP countries, amounting to 761
million ECUs and has turned down 90 transfer requests. In
fact, Stabex transfers were larger than aid flows from the
European Development Fund (EDF) in several cases - and
represented a significant proportion (10-66 per cent) of the
aid flow from EDF for just under half of ACP countries.
There has been little repayment of Stabex funds by borrowing
countries largely reflecting the high proportion of transfers
in the form of grants to the ACP least developed countries
and the generous repayment terms.
    An examination of Stabex operations under Lome I for
years 1975-79 shows that 123 transfers were made to 37 (out
of 57) ACP states and two overseas countries and territories
for shortfalls in earnings from 24 different commodities [3].
The 3 main beneficiaries - Senegal (for groundnuts),
Mauritania (for iron ore) and Sudan (for groundnuts) -
received about 30 per cent of total transfers. Benin, Niger,
Uganda and Tanzania received another 20 per cent of Stabex
transfers, largely for shortfalls in cotton, groundnuts, sisal,
tea, palm and palm kernel oils. The ACP least developed
countries received two-thirds of total transfers, all in the
form of grants; the remaining third was distributed as loans
in 21 transfers, nine of which have been paid back so far in
part or in full. Over three-quarters of the transfers were for

shortfalls in the earnings of only 4 commodities - groundnuts (40 per cent), iron ore (16 per cent), cotton (11 per cent) and wood (10 per cent).

Annual total transfers from Stabex vary considerably, ranging from 34 million ECUs in 1977 to 164 million ECUs in 1978. These have to be compared with the annual instalment/ tranche of Stabex resources of 75 million ECUs over the 1975-79 period. The large differences in the calls on Stabex resources in different years might reflect the relative import- ance of a few commodities in the total ACP/EEC trade of all commodities covered. Thus, five commodities (coffee, cocoa beans, rough wood, iron ore and tea) represent 75 per cent of the imports of the commodities covered into the EEC, with coffee and cocoa beans accounting for over one-half. The high concentration of value on a few products has important implications for future Stabex payments. The simultaneous occurrence of shortfalls in the exports of two or more of these commodities in a given future year could cause a large increase in Stabex transfers in that year. Although provisions for reducing payments existed during the period covered by Lome I, no recourse to them was found necessary. In fact some 6 million ECUs in unused funds and repayments have been transferred to the new Stabex.

Of the total value of Stabex transfers, it was estimated by the Commission that compensation for losses due to local circumstances (e.g. drought, cyclones, plant diseases, mine closures) and weakening economic situation in EEC countries accounted for 69 per cent and 31 per cent respectively.

While the funds appeared to be sufficient to meet eligible claims in the 1975-79 period under Lome I, Stabex was not able to meet all the claims on it during the period 1980-84 under Lome II, especially in 1980 and 1981. The proportions of eligible claims actually paid were only 53 per cent and 43 per cent respectively for 1980 and 1981 respectively. For 1982, all eligible claims were met.

Depending on the uses to which each beneficiary actually allocated Stabex transfers, useful gains have been observed. When transfers were used in the export sectors for domestic price and income schemes for farmers, they proved adequate and efficient in stabilising the sectoral income. Most transfers were, however, used for development purposes such as sustaining agricultural earnings, completing projects of infra- structure, communications, food production and storage. Other uses of transfers included debt servicing and payment for administrative costs. In fact Stabex transfers have been a significant supplement to aid for many ACP countries because they are interest-free to all and outright grants to some countries.

More information is required on their impact on the ACP recipient countries. In particular, there is an obvious need for a more detailed investigation for each major recipient of the effects on the country's import needs, the production, organisation, and export earnings fluctuations, of those commodities covered by the scheme, because the benefits depend to a large extent on the use made of Stabex transfers.

Limitations of Stabex. While there is clear evidence that Stabex has yielded important benefits to the ACP recipients, it has several important limitations. First, being a regional system, it is limited to ACP countries and with respect to trade only with EEC (except for 13 states). Second, with the phasing out of iron ore, it covers merely agricultural products which include only 10 of the 18 IPC commodities. [However, it should be mentioned that a new minerals facility (MINEX) has been launched by Lome II, covering copper, cobalt, phosphates, manganese, bauxite/aluminium, tin and iron ore. The dependency threshold is 10 per cent of total export receipts for least developed countries and 15 per cent for other ACP countries; whereas the trigger threshold is 10 per cent (i.e. shortfall must be at least 10 per cent of total export earnings). The granting of transfers, which requires not only earnings shortfall but also evidence that production is endangered, is highly discretionary. The resources allocated to Minex were 280 million ECUs for 1980-84 period, to be divided into four equal tranches.] Third, its method for calculating shortfalls tends to underestimate shortfalls when nominal export earnings follow a rising trend, fails to take account of changes in import prices (since the reference level relates to nominal export earnings) and represents a very short-term trend (since only four years are used for calculating the reference level). Fourth, the manner in which the dependency threshold applies separately to each commodity could result in excluding some countries (with more diversified exports) from the benefit of the facility even though their dependence in the listed commodity exports, taken together is quite significant. Fifth, the imposition of the dependency and threshold conditions may marginally reduce claims on Stabex but, at the same time, may cause significant administrative costs and delay to both the scheme and the requesting countries. Sixth, the most important limitation of all is that the resources at its disposal are very limited and have probably not improved in real terms, if account is taken of world inflation in the last five years.

To facilitate comparison between the two existing compensatory financing schemes, their key features are summarised in Table 5.1 and the annual flows of compensatory loans repayments and the number of countries involved are presented in Table 5.2. From Table 5.1, it can be seen that CFF differs from Stabex in almost all aspects. CFF aims to compensate for shortfalls in total export earnings, whereas

Stabex aims to stabilise the shortfalls of the export earnings of individual products covered on a gross basis. Almost all LDCs have access to CFF but only 64 ACP countries have access to Stabex. Only drawings from Stabex are subject to threshold conditions. The trend formulae of CFF and Stabex also differ - CFF's five-year moving average rightly centres on the shortfall year but requires forecasts of the two post-shortfall years, whereas Stabex's four-year moving-average wrongly centres on the middle of the second and third of the four pre-shortfall years but requires no forecasts; both are in nominal terms. Both impose different side conditions on compensatory drawings:- CFF requires the existence of balance of payments need, co-operation and non-violation of quota limits; Stabex requires that the fall in earnings is not caused by national policy. Neither imposes restriction on use. The period of repayment is the same - i.e. repayment after 7 years, after two period grace but there are differences in interest charges on loans - CFF charges 6.6 per cent whereas Stabex is interest free.

It can be seen in Table 5.2 that while the number of transfers differed little on average, the total value of CFF transfers each year was many times as large as that of Stabex transfers. In other words, although Stabex appears to be more generous in its terms of compensation, the magnitude of its average transfer was small largely because the ACP countries are generally quite small.

PROPOSALS FOR AN ADDITIONAL COMPENSATORY FINANCING SCHEME

The governments of United States, Sweden and Germany as well as the UNCTAD secretariat have made proposals for an additional compensatory financing scheme. After the circulation of a study on the scheme proposed by the UNCTAD secretariat, there was extensive intergovernmental discussion on the UNCTAD proposal, leading up to the report of a group of top-level experts on this issue.

I The need for an additional facility.
The rationale for establishing an additional complementary facility for compensating commodity related export earnings shortfalls is based on two arguments: (i) the instability problem exists at two levels - at the level of total export earnings of a country and at the level of export earnings of individual commodity sectors - and reduction of instability at both levels is deemed beneficial to both developing and developed countries and to require different kinds of foreign exchange assistance and (ii) the international schemes for stabilising export earnings (i.e. IMF-CFF and EEC -

Table 5.1: Summary of Major Features of the IMF-CFF and Stabex

Key features	IMF/CFF	STABEX
I OBJECTIVE	Compensation for temporary shortfalls in export earnings when these cause balance of payments difficulties and are largely beyond the control of the country.	Stabilisation of earnings from exports by ACP States to the Community of certain products (...) which are affected by fluctuations in prices/and or quantities.
II ACCESS - Eligible countries	All members of IMF, particularly primary exporters.	63 ACF States and overseas countries and territories.
- Exports covered	Merchandise exports + optional inclusion of: a. Receipts from travel and workers' remittances b. Cereal imports	Individual exports of 46 agricultural products to: a. EEC for 51 states b. The world for 13 states
- Thresholds	None	Dependency: commodity must be at least 6.5 per cent of total earnings from exports to all destinations (5 per cent for sisal and 2 per cent for 35 least developed States) Fluctuation: commodity shortfall for trade with EEC (all destinations for 13) at least 6.5 per cent below reference level (2 per cent for least developed).
- Formula for shortfall	Geometric average of nominal export earnings for a 5-year period centre on shortfall year; may also include excesses on cereal imports.	Reference level: average nominal export earnings over four years previous to shortfall year.

III MODALITIES

- Conditionality	1. On eligibility of transfer:
	  a. Existence of balance-of-payments need.
	  b. Drawings <u>up to</u> 50 per cent of quota - must co-operate to find solutions to balance of payments difficulties, where required:
	  - Drawings <u>over</u> 50 per cent of quota - must have been co-operating with Fund to find solutions to balance of payments difficulties, where required.
	2. On use: none
		1. On eligibility of transfer:
		  a. Before 31 March of year after shortfall year.
		  b. Fall in earnings from exports to EEC must not be due to national trade policy.
		2. On use: none, but some indication of probable use given before transfer agreement signed and report on actual use due within 12 months of signing.

- Repayments	1. 2-year grace period, repayment within 5 years, usually in quarterly instalments. 2. Interest charges: 6.6 per cent. 3. Service charge: 0.5 per cent per transaction.	1. 2-year grace period, repayment within 7 years, 5 equal instalments. 2. Both unit value and quantity higher than respective average of 4 preceding years and earnings at least 106.5 per cent of its average. 3. No interest charge.
- Special concessions for some countries	None	35 Least developed countries receive transfers as grants.
- Conversion of loans into grants	None	Converted if loan not repaid in 7 years and after consideration of balance-of-payments, exchange reserves and external indebtedness.

IV RESOURCES

- Origin	IMF resources through quotas.	EEC member State contributions.
- Structure	Revolving fund.	Fixed revolving fund, 5 equal annual instalments, but can advance 20 per cent in any year except last.

217

Table 5.1: (continued)

Key features	IMF/CFF	STABEX
- Amount	A maximum of 105 per cent of country quota but not more than 85 per cent for export shortfall or 83 per cent for excess cereal imports.	ECU 550 million (1980-4).
V POLICY AND INSTITUTIONAL ISSUES		
- Importance of developing countries in decision-making process	Depends on quota distribution.	Established by joint ACF-EEC negotiations. Arrangements for consultations for problem areas but administered by EEC Commission.
- Periodicity of review	Periodical and ad hoc (1963, 1966, 1975, 1979, 1981 and 1983)	Five years, but product and country additions can be made in between.

Source: UNCTAD (1984) (TD/B/AC.37/3)

218

STABEX) and the international commodity agreements (ICAs) are insufficient (because of limitations) to deal effectively with this dual level instability problem. It is convenient to consider these two arguments in the reverse order.

(a)   Limitations of ICAs, IMF-CFF and EEC-STABEX

ICAs. We have established earlier in this chapter that ICAs may not succeed in achieving their immediate objective of stabilising prices. However, even if they do, and do so at reasonable costs, the need for an adequate facility for compensating commodity export earnings shortfalls would still remain because (i) there would remain a substantial residual of uncorrected earnings instability due to quantity variations arising from supply sources; (ii) many commodities important to the LDCs exports cannot be covered by ICAs based on buffer stocks owing to their perishable nature and other characteristics; and (iii) even when they are physically suitable for buffer stocks operations, it may be impossible to conclude ICAs for a variety of other reasons. Only 5 commodities - coffee, cocoa, sugar, natural rubber and tin - are so far covered by ICAs with price provisions. Two other ICAs for jute and tropical timber, concluded since the adoption of the Integrated Programme for Commodities in 1976, contain no price provisions. The progress of the negotiation and/or renegotiation of all such agreements have been slow and their economic provisions have been rather weak.

IMF-CFF. The CFF is designed to help LDCs to deal with general balance of payments problems but not for specific sectoral instability. Indeed, the CFF has features which limit the extent to which it could be used to assist in commodity sector stabilisation. If the features of the CFF could be so improved that CFF drawings could be confidently anticipated by LDCs' governments and used for assisting sectors with shortfalls, then it could play an important role by enabling LDCs to stabilise or assist their commodity sectors.

Even then, the need for an additional facility would remain because of the quota limitation on CFF resources. At present, the rate of interest charged on CFF drawings of only 6.6 per cent is well below the international market rate, the difference represents a concessional or aid element. But this aid-element makes it unlikely that the resources of the IMF can be increased sufficiently to meet the growing need of LDCs for compensatory funds, as their export trade expands. Of course, even with the present funds, the CFF can be made more beneficial to LDCs if its shortfall formula is replaced by another. This formula would involve the calculation of shortfalls and averages around a longer-term trend of

219

Table 5.2: Use of IMF-CFF and Stabex

	1963–1965	1966–1975[e]	1976	1977	1978	1979	1980	1981	1982	Jan–Oct 1983
1 Amount outstanding	87	722	2713	2756	2921	2859	2791	3272	5398	7473
2 New purchases	87	1134	2308	241	578	572	980	1243	2268	2639
3 Repurchases	–	499	317	198	413	643	1039	762	502	563
4 Net purchases	87	635	1991	43	165	–71	–59	481	2126	2076
5 Average rate of compensation %										
(a) based on new purchases			40.0	42.2	51.2	52.1	75.8	50.2	61.5	82.5
(b) based on net new purchase[a]				41.3	50.3	41.4	60.4	41.6		
6 Number of countries purchasing	3	34	45	13	15	19	15	29	25	22
7 Number of purchases	3	54	48	14	15	23	15	29	28	22

STABEX (ACP)[d] (million ECU)[b]

	1966–1975	1976	1977	1978	1979	1980	1981	1982
1 Transfers:								
(a) Grants	43.05	30.18	34.99	91.54	63.16	69.95	28.29	42.75
(b) Loans	40.90	10.25	0.20	72.70	2.85	73.12	154.56	25.97

2 Repayments	-	0.61	4.18	0.49	1.14	-	c	-
3 Net transfers	83.93	39.82	31.01	163.75	64.87	143.07	182.85	68.63
4 Major products	Wood (47); Coffee (17); Cotton (13)	Ground-nuts (30); Sisal (19); Cotton (11)	Ground-nuts (35); Sisal (24); Iron Ore (21)	Ground-nuts (45); Iron Ore (28); Cotton (17)	Ground-nuts (40); Cotton (17); Coffee (39)	Ground-nuts (46); Coffee (39); Cocoa (28)	Coffee (44); Cocoa (27); Ground-nuts (16)	Coffee (29); Copra (16)
5 No. of countries receiving transfers:								
(a) Grants	16	13	13	18	13	23	18	18
(b) Loans	10	6	-	3	1	6	8	3
6 No. of transfers	35	26	19	26	17	33	36	33

a Calculated on basis of net new purchases by countries purchasing in given year, after deducting their repayments.

b Based on information available as of 21 November 1983, two claims outstanding and repayments yet to be decided.

c Five countries had outstanding Lomé I transfers offset against current claims.

d Including EEC overseas and territories.

e 1975 only for STABEX.

Source: UNCTAD (1984) (TD/B/AC.37/3)

export earnings in real terms, with the trend estimate based solely on actual data without forecasts.

EEC-STABEX. From the point of view of LDCs generally, the Stabex scheme has a very limited impact because it is limited to ACP countries' trade with EEC, omits many commodities of major interest to LDCs and has very limited resources. Furthermore, its formula for calculating shortfall not only produces the wrong amount of transfer but also causes it to be given at the wrong time, because (i) the moving-average is centred not on the shortfall year but on the middle of the second and third of the four years prior to the shortfall year and (ii) the reference value is calculated on the basis of export earnings in nominal terms, ignoring the movements of the import price index facing each individual LDC. It has been contended that, apart from these limitations, Stabex has an important advantage over the CFF, from the point of view of commodity sector stabilisation:- while the CFF is designed for providing assistance for balance of payments problems arising from shortfalls in the total export earnings of a country, Stabex is designed for stabilising the export earnings of individual commodity sectors in each of the eligible countries. As noted earlier, the majority of Stabex transfers have been used for general development-related purposes (e.g. completing or continuing projects which would otherwise have been delayed or remained uncompleted), some of which contribute to a reduction in the domestic supply-related cause of instability. When such transfers were used promptly in the sectors with shortfalls, they were effective in maintaining these sectors' income.

(b) The 'two-levels' of instability problem. The literature on export instability examines this problem largely at the level of aggregate total export earnings of a country. It is concerned with the causes and consequences of fluctuations in total export earnings and not with those of individual commodity sectors within each country. Thus, the shortfall in the total export earnings of a country is supposed, on the one hand, to have multiplier effects on income, employment, investment, etc., and, on the other hand, to produce a shortfall in foreign exchange earnings, leading to a fall in imports, investment and disruption to the process of development (because of the dependence of the country on imported goods). The literature recognised that shortfall in total export earnings implies shortfalls in individual sectors and that producers in the shortfall sectors have to endure hardships which vary considerably across commodities, depending on whether they are largely produced by small family firms, or large foreign-owned or state-owned enterprises. But in looking at total export earnings, it ignores the fact that each sector's income can be very unstable, while all sectors' income in aggregate (i.e. total export earnings) may remain relatively stable.

Gross versus net shortfall. Given a small shortfall in total export earnings (net shortfall), the sum of the shortfall of sectors with shortfalls (gross shortfall) can be large or small, depending on the magnitude of the total of overages of the sectors with overages (gross overage). Since by definition, net shortfall is equal to gross shortfall minus gross overage, a given small value for net shortfall can conceal a very large gross shortfall associated with a large overage.

Let us consider the case of a country in which total export earnings are relatively stable, but sectoral incomes are highly unstable. Since total export earnings are stable and so is the total income of the export sector as a whole, there is apparently no foreign exchange problem at aggregate level and no instability problems for macro variables such as income and investment associated with export instability. However, individual commodity sectors suffer considerable fluctuations in their incomes and these fluctuations could seriously reduce the levels, trends and productivity of their investments. Insofar as commodity sectors are important in the economies of LDCs because of their sheer size, their linkages with the rest of the economy and their role as a major source of savings, the negative impacts of the instability of individual sectors' earnings could be significant. By investigating the problems of instability only at the level of total exports, the literature on this subject may have in fact neglected a rather important problem facing some LDCs.

(c) Foreign exchange implication of commodity sector stabilisation. Even if one recognises the need for stabilising income at the individual sector level, it is still not clear how assistance in terms of foreign exchange from an international scheme can be calculated. Let us consider first the case of providing assistance for stabilising income and imports of a country suffering from highly unstable total export earnings. Suppose the country has only a minimum of foreign exchange reserves and no access to foreign borrowing so that it has to adjust its imports to its exports every year and let us assume that it does so by adopting fiscal measures to vary the income level. For convenience, let us assume that exports (and hence imports) have no trend so that a shortfall is also a fall. Let us now consider the effects of a fall in total export.

With no compensation. Without compensatory drawing, the change in its income ΔY would be equal to $\Delta X/m$, where ΔX is a fall in export (or overall shortfall) and m is the marginal propensity to import. (Note that the change in import M is equal to $m\Delta Y$; hence equating ΔM to ΔX as required by trade balance equilibrium yields $\Delta Y = \Delta X/m$, as noted.) In other words, the change in export has a large multiplier effect on income.

With a compensation based on net shortfall. Suppose now the country can count on compensation equal to ΔX, it can ignore the need to maintain the trade balance and in principle can maintain its imports, i.e. $\Delta M = 0$. To maintain its imports, the change in income must also be zero. i.e. $\Delta Y = 0$. This is possible given $\Delta X < 0$ only if the fall in export is exactly matched by an increase in autonomous expenditure ΔG of equal size to the fall in export, i.e. $\Delta G = -\Delta X$. Otherwise, income and imports would fall and the country would appear to be over compensated. Hence, if the aim of the compensatory financing scheme is the stabilisation of income (and imports), then there must exist in the country a system for stabilising aggregate expenditure so as to neutralise the effect of export fluctuations on income.

This means that on receiving foreign exchange equal to ΔX, the government should spend all of this on something. If the benefits from sectoral stabilisation are deemed more important than, say, those from completing existing projects or starting new ones, then they can use all of this compensation, plus what they can obtain from the sectors with overages, in the form of repayments of past compensatory loans, interest charges or taxes, to make compensatory loans to the sectors with shortfalls. The sectors with shortfalls may not receive full compensation for their shortfalls, insofar as gross overage exceeds repayments plus tax payments (out of overages), but in most years the proportion of uncompensated shortfall is likely to be small. A domestic compensatory scheme for sectors which was financed by foreign assistance equal to net shortfall could therefore reduce income fluctuations for individual sectors.

Governments could fully compensate sectors with shortfalls by reducing expenditure elsewhere by an amount equal to gross overage minus repayment. In doing this, both income and imports could be maintained with a foreign exchange requirement no greater than the net shortfall. Compensation on the basis of the shortfall in the total export earnings of the country would be adequate.

But if compensatory drawings are used to stabilise sectoral earnings, they may do little to reduce the root causes of supply-related sectoral instability - if anything stabilised incomes tend to reduce rather than increase the incentive for sectors to stabilise output and yields. This means that sectoral instability has to be reduced not via income stabilisation schemes but indirectly via investment in irrigation schemes and agricultural programmes designed to encourage producers to adopt techniques which would reduce vulnerability to such forces of nature as frost, drought and pests.

With two types of compensation - one of which based on net shortfall. Suppose the country pursues a scheme which fully compensates each shortfall sector while leaving expenditure elsewhere unchanged. Since the additional net expenditure arising from sector compensation - which is equal to gross shortfall (GS) minus total repayment (R) from sectors with overages (assuming no taxes) - exceeds net shortfall (NS) [or shortfall in total export earnings], both income and imports will increase as a result. The increase in income would be equal to $\Delta Y = k (GS - R - NS) = k (GO - R)$, where $GO = GS - NS$ represents gross overage and k is the multiplier. The increase in imports will be equal to $\Delta M = m\Delta Y = mk (GO - R)$ and the need for foreign exchange, implied by the trade imbalance, will be equal to $-\Delta B = -(\Delta X - \Delta M) = NS + mk (GO - R)$. Thus if an international scheme such as the CFF compensates NS in full, the country still requires an additional amount of foreign exchange equal to $mk (GO - R)$, where 'mk' can be referred to as the direct and indirect foreign exchange content of sector expenditure. This suggests that, in addition to the CFF, a new supplementary facility would be required to compensate the country for the extra foreign exchange cost associated with sector stabilisation. Note that R is in general less than GO because one pre-condition for repayment is the existence of previous debts and not all sectors with overages have previous debts. Since repayment is also limited to the outstanding debt balance, even overage sectors with debts may repay less than the full amount of their overages. In fact the steeper the trends of sectoral earnings, the greater would be the difference between GO and R and the greater would be the demand by the country for assistance from the new facility.

However, there are now two problems:- first, the operation of the additional facility together with full compensation of shortfall sectors will destabilise income, employment and imports (as compared to the case in which the country receives compensation only equal to NS, fully stabilises income and only partially compensates shortfall) and second, compensation from the additional facility would be related not to the gross shortfall (as in the case of Stabex or the proposed UNCTAD scheme) but to overage net of repayment, which seems rather paradoxical and appears to make little sense. Furthermore, m and k will vary from country to country and their product is likely to be considerably less than unity. For example, on the base of a simple model, let marginal propensity to import m be 0.2 and the marginal propensity to spend e (i.e. marginal propensity to consume plus marginal propensity to invest) be 0.8, then $k = 1/(1 - e + m)$ would be 2.5

and mk = 0.5, i.e. this suggests an appropriate compensation rate of 50 per cent.

Thus, it can be seen that compensatory transfers on the basis of <u>net shortfall</u> (such as provided via the CFF) can be used not only to stabilise income and imports at the aggregate level but also to stabilise the income of the sector quite considerably. On the other hand, full compensation of sectoral shortfalls would <u>destabilise income and imports</u> (and a host of other macro variables related to income) and would in any case require extra foreign exchange assistance - not on the basis of <u>gross shortfall</u> - but on the basis of <u>gross overage</u> net of total repayment (as the analysis above clearly suggests). Would governments seriously consider compensations which relate to overages rather than shortfalls? Furthermore the proportion of gross-overage net of repayment to be compensated should be estimated for each requesting country on the basis of its multiplier and marginal propensity to import neither of which is easily estimated. To use a simple compensation rate for all countries would tend to over-compensate some and under-compensate others.

II <u>Intergovernmental discussion and proposals by the governments.</u>

From 1963, when the Fund first established the CFF, governments have shown interest in an additional compensatory financing facility to supplement the CFF by dealing with problems of export instability of a nature and duration which could not be adequately dealt with by short-term balance of payments support. At the invitation of UNCTAD I, the World Bank staff prepared a study on such a scheme, which was subsequently examined by an Intergovernmental Group on Supplementary Financing. In its report in 1969, the Group affirmed the feasibility of the proposed scheme. It recommended that the supplementary facility should be administered within the World Bank in consultation with the IMF but stressed that 'it would be of little value merely to direct available resources from basic development finance for the purpose of supplementary financing.'

The UN Trade and Development Board endorsed the recommendations of the Intergovernmental Group and invited the Bank to work out arrangements for supplementary financing. But the World Bank informed the Board that it had decided to postpone consideration of the additional scheme, owing to the very limited support for it among potential donors. UNCTAD III in 1972 renewed its invitation to the World Bank to work out detailed arrangements for the additional facility [Resolution 55 (III)] and again in July 1973 but with no result.

Proposals by Some Governments

The US proposal. In 1975, at the Seventh Special Session of the General Assembly, the United States proposed a new development security facility to stabilise overall export earnings, not in addition to but as a replacement for the IMF-CFF. It was proposed that this facility would 'give loans to sustain development programmes in the face of export fluctuations of up to $2.5 billion and possibly more in a single year, with a potential total in outstanding loans of $10 billion.' Later, the United States further proposed that additional IMF compensatory financing loans be made to LDCs for shortfalls in export earnings for a specified number of commodities (the 10 'core' commodities plus 5 perishable ones). Loans were to be made through a special Trust Fund after utilisation of full quota limits under the CFF, when there was a serious balance of payments problem arising from a shortfall in total export earnings from the commodities covered, subject to policy conditions, including those related to commodity supplies. Special concessions to low-income countries in the form of lower interest rates (2-3 per cent) and longer repayment periods (10-12 years) were to be made and financed by the proceeds of IMF gold sales. For other LDCs, compensatory drawings were to be financed from medium term borrowing, with repayment periods of 5 - 8 years.

The Swedish proposal. In 1977, the Swedish Government put forward a scheme for compensating shortfalls in total export earnings from commodities falling within SITC groups 0-2, 4 and 68 (i.e. almost all primary commodities except fuels, gold and precious stones) for non-oil exporting countries. The loans were to be given without any conditionality save prior use of the IMF-CFF and were to be based on shortfalls from a real medium-term trend. Repayments were to be related to the variance of overages and subject to no time limit, with interest rate concessions for the poorest countries. The source of finance would consist of borrowing from international financial markets (75 per cent) and direct capital contributions (25 per cent) from the aid budgets of the aid-giving countries.

The German proposal. In 1978, the Federal Republic of Germany proposed a scheme for compensating shortfalls in total export earnings from 25 commodities involving loans for 8-10 years, at low interest rates and with concessional treatment for the least developed countries. The resources of $5 billion were to be raised from international borrowing against government guarantees and direct government contributions.

The UNCTAD secretariat's proposal. At UNCTAD V (1979), the Secretary-General of UNCTAD was requested to prepare a detailed study for the operation of a complementary facility to compensate for shortfalls in earnings of each commodity. In the period 1980-83 the UNCTAD secretariat produced a series of documents which contain (i) estimates of shortfalls in the export earnings of commodities in a list (which includes the 18 IPC commodities plus 5 others) at individual LDCs level as well as at the aggregate level of LDCs as a group, (ii) a feasibility study of the complementary facility (TD/BB/C.1/222) and (iii) proposals for setting it up. At UNCTAD VI held in Belgrade in July 1983, the Secretary-General of UNCTAD was asked to convene, after consultation with interested governments, an Expert Group on the compensatory financing of export earnings shortfalls. In its report in December 1984 (TD/B/1029), the Expert Group presented 'a prototype of a facility which links the uses of commodity - specific compensatory finance to the needs of supply adjustment based on the features previously identified.' They hoped that the descriptions of the nature, main characteristics and mode of operation of such a facility in concrete terms would help the governments to visualise and discuss how it could be designed.

Thus, unlike the governments, the UNCTAD secretariat has not made a proposal for a scheme. All it has done has been (i) to focus attention on the need for an additional facility and on the types of features which may be considered desirable largely from the point of view of LDCs as commodity exporters, (ii) to gather as much information as possible on the financial requirements of such a facility (with various optional features) and on its projected impacts on individual LDCs and on the World at large and (iii) to keep up the process of negotiations for its establishment by encouraging intergovernmental discussion and government participation in the selection of modes of operation and features. Since in the last resort, almost all the features of the new facility are a matter for negotiations among the governments, their views are of paramount importance. Since the views of the Group of Academic Experts largely reflect economic considerations and consequently may not take into account internal and international political implications of the scheme, they may be influential but are not necessarily crucial. The views of the governments of 6 developed countries and 10 developing countries and the EEC are reproduced in Annex IX to the Expert Group Report and a summary of their views together with the proposals by United States, Sweden and Germany and UNCTAD (81), is given in Table 5.3 below. Although the UNCTAD secretariat has not specifically proposed a scheme with a particular set of features, one can infer a scheme with a range of features and options from the arguments presented in UNCTAD documents. It is convenient to refer to this scheme with the set of features recommended by the Expert Group as the UNCTAD proposed facility or just UNCTAD facility for short.

Main features of the UNCTAD facility

The Expert Group emphasised the following four key features of the facility:

(i) Compensating loans are to be based on the shortfalls in the proceeds from specific commodities (i.e. this can be taken to refer to compensating being based on gross shortfall).

(ii) The loans are required to be used to reduce supply-caused instability (i.e. loans may not be used merely to maintain shortfall sectors' income).

(iii) The uses of the loans should be consistent with international commodity objectives and arrangements – (very vague, since there is no consensus on what these are!).

(iv) The facility would be operated basically on self-financing, commercial principles, except for providing concessionality in certain cases – (this means that a commercial interest rate would be charged to all eligible countries, except perhaps the least developed countries which might be required to pay a lower concessional rate of interest – which might have to be financed from aid).

The Group maintained that 'these last features were also common to compensatory financing schemes put forward in the past and to many of the proposals and suggestions submitted by Governments for the present purposes.' (In fact, apart from referring to commodities, none of these features can be said to be common to the facility proposed by the governments of United States, Sweden or the Federal Republic of Germany – since in all these other proposals, compensation is on the basis of net shortfall, loans are not tied to specific uses and interest charged on loans would be considerably lower than commercial rates.)

The features concerning eligible countries, commodity coverage, shortfall formula, repayment conditions, interest charged and concessions to the least developed countries as well as issues such as capital structure and institutional options are summarised in Table 5.4. It is useful to review the key features recommended by the Group to see how far they reflect the four basic principles which, as the UNCTAD secretariat proposed at UNCTAD V, should form the basis of a new complementary facility (TD/229/Supp.1, p. 21), namely:

(a) shortfalls should be measured in real terms and calculated with reference to the long-term trend;

(b) countries should be compensated for the full extent of their shortfalls;

(c) no conditions should be attached to drawings;

Table 5.3: Main Characteristics of Proposals and Suggestions
in Connection with Additional Commodity-related
Compensatory Financing Facilities

Proposed by and date	Country coverage for access to drawings	Commodity coverage	Compensation criterion
United States 1975 (current status not known)	Developing countries	15 commodities (including IPC 10 core)	
Sweden 1977 (revised 1983)	Developing countries	All primary commodities (except fuels) i.e. SITC 0-2 4 and 68	Medium-term trend value of commodity export earnings in real terms
Federal Republic of Germany 1978 (revised 1984)	Developing countries	25 selected commodities	Based on IMF-CFF formula. Full compensation for shortfalls above threshold level
UNCTAD secretariat 1981	Developing countries	All primary commodities (except fuels, gold, diamonds and precious stones) or some selective list like the IPC 18 commodities	Based on medium-term trend value in real terms

230

Table 5.3: (continued)

Capital structure	Terms and concessionality	Relations to IMF-CFF	Conditions
IMF Trust Fund Financed in part out of proceeds of IMF gold sales and from medium-term borrowing	For poorer countries 2-3 per cent interest rates and 10-12 years repayment periods. Other developing countries: interest rate to cover cost of financing and repayment period of 5-8 years	Must have fully utilised the initial 25 per cent of quota available under IMF-CFF	Existence of a balance-of-payments problem. Policy conditions, including commodity supply conditions
A scheme based on 25 per cent capital contributions from Governments and borrowing on international capital markets	In principle, repayment based on overage. For poorest countries compensation loans outstanding after 5 years to be written off. Subsidisation of 5 per cent interest	Must first make use of all means to obtain compensation from IMF-CFF	
$5 billion over 10 years. Government contributions and funds raised in capital market with government guarantees as backing	Loans running 8 to 10 years at interest significantly below market rates. Special treatment for the poorest developing countries	Account to be taken of payments under IMF-CFF	Some international monitoring (or conditionality)
Based on 10 per cent government paid-in capital and borrowing on private capital markets, backed by callable	Based on overage and fixed maximum repayment period of 10 years. Highly concessional terms for least devel-	Account to be taken of drawings under IMF-CFF to avoid double compensation	Mutual agreement between facility and client countries on use of credits relating to commodity problems and root causes of

231

Table 5.3: (continued)

Proposed by and date	Country coverage for access to drawings	Commodity coverage	Compensation criterion
Finland 1983	Least developed countries and countries most dependent on commodity export earnings	Commodity sector	Based on overall losses in earnings in commodity sector. In nominal terms, with fluctuation and dependance thresholds
Sweden 1983	Poor and very commodity-dependent countries		
Norway 1983	Low-income countries with heavy dependence on commodity exports	All IPC at a minimum	
Senegal 1983	Developing countries	IPC + food products	Compensation for recorded production losses and coverage of costs of durable solutions to eliminating causes of these losses
Federal Republic of Germany 1984	Developing countries obtaining at least half of	All non-energy commodities	Aggregate decline in commodity exports to all countries, due to events outside

Table 5.3: (continued)

Capital structure	Terms and concessionality	Relations to IMF-CFF	Conditions
capital subscribed by Governments	oped countries For other countries rates approaching average interest cost of borrowing		commodity supply instability
	No transfer of real resources	Compensation must be additional, with due account taken of existing facilities	Due consideration paid to need for structural adjustment policies and appropriate production planning in developing countries
	No transfer of real resources more favourable terms for least developed countries		Market orientation, including necessary structural adjustments
Identify all sources (government contributions, borrowing on capital market, auto-financing etc.)	Some concessionality	Full use of existing schemes first	
By developed countries plus levy on verified overages from commodities covered in countries benefiting from system	Repayments linked to level of surplus, within 10 years maximum period		Financing arrangements should be such as to permit durable solutions to be found to eliminating the root causes of production shortfalls
Revolving fund open to all countries; 1/3 government con-	Loans of 8-10 years maturity, repayments also if exports above	Avoid double compensation	Repayment obligations should offer exporting countries an additional incentive

Table 5.3: (continued)

Proposed by and date	Country coverage for access to drawings	Commodity coverage	Compensation criterion
	their total earnings from commodities		control of country: use of IMF-CFF formula, or average of past data; possibility longer reference period: 10% trigger threshold (2.5% for LDCs). Compensation, 100% of shortfall for LDCs, 60-80% for others, depending on ceiling for funds
France 1984	Priority to least developed countries		Favours the establishment
Switzerland 1984	In order of priority: least developed countries, low-income developing countries and other developing countries strongly dependent on export of commodities	All primary commodities except fuels, gold and precious stones (SITC 0,1,2,4 & 68)	A formula which has proven itself, e.g. the calculation method used in the framework of the IMF-CFF, adapted to the commodity sector; partial compensation for shortfalls in commodity-related export earnings; consider using real values

Table 5.3: (continued)

Capital structure	Terms and concessionality	Relations to IMF-CFF	Conditions
tributions. 2/3 from capital market, with fixed ceiling; contribution scale based on formula similar to the UN scale; contributions split into several instalments	trend (10% above mean value). Interest rate below market rate (lower for LDCs). Some remission of debts for poorest countries		to eliminate the cause of their loss of export earnings themselves, as far as it is in their power to do so

of a 'distinct' facility along the lines of STABEX

Loans, based on government contributions and guarantees and borrowing on capital markets	More favourable terms to LDCs; repayments when overage in earnings occur, with fixed ultimate time limit	Additional: avoid double compensation	Loans should encourage a producing country to adjust its production structure, mainly by its own means, in order to avoid that the situation deteriorates to the point that a large-scale International action becomes necessary; loans should also support structural adjustment programmes which are in process, but the realisation of which is hampered by shortfalls; possible use of national stabilisation funds to carry out and co-ordinate policies

Table 5.3: (continued)

Proposed by and date	Country coverage for access to drawings	Commodity coverage	Compensation criterion
Austria 1984	Least developed and other low-income countries heavily dependent on export earnings from commodities	Commodities exported by these countries representing a crucial source of income (except oil and precious stones)	

Source: UNCTAD (1985) (TD/B/1029/Rev. 1, Annex viii)

Table 5.3: (continued)

Capital structure	Terms and concessionality	Relations to IMF-CFF	Conditions
Contribution from as many countries as possible (industrialised plus oil exporters) representing finance additional to current development assistance	Overall ceiling per country for drawings from all facilities.	Complementary to existing facilities; avoid double compensation	Necessary adjustment processes undertaken

Table 5.4: Summary of the Basic Features of an Additional Facility

Features	Recommendations of the Expert Group for the main features of the facility	Quantitative features used in the illustrative simulations
A Basis for compensatory loans		
1 Country eligibility	All developing countries	134 developing countries
2 Commodity eligibility	All primary commodities (SITC 0+1+2+4+68)	29 commodities
3 Eligibility for loans	A shortfall according to the formula in a commodity sector	
(a) Shortfall formula	Based on an exponential, or linear, trend value over a ten-year period in nominal terms	Exponential trend value
(b) Thresholds	Application of dependency and fluctuation thresholds, both set at 5 per cent	idem
4 Size of loans		
(a) Compensation rate	Not predetermined. It would depend, inter alia, on the diagnosis of the causes of the commodity sector shortfalls, and on the multi-year commodity stabilisation programme as agreed between the facility and the recipient country	Average rate of compensation of 50 per cent
(b) Basis for the calculation of total loans	Sum of the loans as calculated above in each affected commodity sector (i.e. gross basis)	idem

B Main operational characteristics

5 Lending

(a) Lending policy	Loans will be based on a multi-year commodity stabilisation programme as agreed between the facility and the recipient country	
(b) Lending terms	Lending interest rate would be based, inter alia, on the cost of funds to the facility and on its own borrowing rate	Lending rate at 2 per cent below market rate
	Repayments with a fixed maturity and accelerated repayments whenever overages reach a predetermined level	2-year grace period and repayments of principal in 10 equal annual instalments
6 Concessionality for the least developed countries and other low-income countries	Possibility of lower thresholds, higher compensation rate, grants, longer grace period, lower interest rates, greater access to technical assistance. Subsidisation of interest rate will only be made to the extent agreed by Governments and will be financed through a special interest rate subsidy account	Thresholds = 2 per cent Compensation rate = 75 per cent Grace period = 4 years Interest rate = 0 per cent (applied to least developed countries)

7 Borrowings

(a) Borrowing policy	Borrowings will be the main source of funds of the facility, which should therefore be managed in a commercial way to secure market support. Most borrowings will be long and medium-term at competitive market rates	
(b) Borrowing terms		Borrowings with an average 2-year grace period and repayment in 10 years

Table 5.4: (continued)

Features	Recommendations of the Expert Group for the main features of the facility	Quantitative features used in the illustrative simulations
(c) Limit on borrowings	Debt < Callable capital + cumulated net income	idem
8 Relations with other facilities		
(a) Co-operation	Based on formal co-operation agreements	
(b) Avoidance of double compensation	The facility will consider the other facilities' drawings in relation to a commodity, as well as additional export earnings of that commodity, in its own calculations	A global average rate of compensation of 50 per cent was considered as a sufficient protection in assessing the additional resources needed for an additional facility, avoiding double compensation
9 Sources of funds	The facility is to function as a self-financed, commercially managed entity. Its main sources of funds are the paid-in-capital, cash generated by its operations, repayment of loans (which will reconstitute its resources), and borrowings in financial markets	idem

C Capital structure

10 Special accounts

(a) Special interest rate subsidy account	To finance the reduced interest rate to countries eligible for concessionality. Funded by voluntary contributions
(b) Special technical assistance account	To finance technical assistance to countries eligible for concessionality. Funded by voluntary contributions

11. Total capital

(a) Ratio of paid-in to total capital	A minimum of 1:5
(b) Distribution of government contributions to the paid-in capital	Along the lines of that of the Common Fund for Commodities

Source: UNCTAD (1985) (TD/B/1029/Rev. 1. Annex xi)

(d) terms of repayment and interest charges should be related to the ability of the recipient to repay.

Glancing through the features given in Table 5.4, one can see that apart from the retention of the idea of a long-term trend, none of the above principles has escaped the surgical knife of the Expert Group. Shortfalls are to be measured around a nominal terms trend; compensation rate would depend, inter alia, on the diagnosis of the problems of the commodity sector and on the commodity stabilisation programme as agreed between the facility and the recipient country; drawings would be subject to threshold conditions; lending interest rate would be based not on the ability of the recipient to repay but on the borrowing rate or the cost of the fund to the facility, and repayments would have a fixed maturity and increase when there were sizeable overages and would apparently take no account of the ability to repay.

In the light of the earlier discussion, the replacement of real trend by nominal trend in the calculation of shortfalls is particularly unfortunate. The reason the Group gives for doing so is simply a repeat of the reason given by the IMF for not changing over to the real trend - namely, the practical difficulty of obtaining import prices of individual countries. But, given the consensus on the appropriateness of the real trend in the calculation of shortfall, recognition that there are statistical problems with data import price should lead to a recommendation to improve the statistics rather than to completely ignore the influence of import price movements on the stability of import capacity.

The compensation rate linked to the foreign exchange cost of measures for stabilising sector income or for reducing causes of unanticipated and unplanned quantity variation would vary across countries with different commodity compositions and economic structures. Furthermore, as the commodity export structure and economic structure of each country change over time, there is also a need to adjust its compensation rate. To carry the argument further one would require a different compensation rate for each commodity sector in each country. The research and administrative costs involved could be significant. Hence, this idea is essentially unworkable in practice. In theory, in the light of an earlier discussion, it may reduce the benefits of the facility to the recipient, since it assumes quite arbitrarily and probably incorrectly that no other uses of the drawings can yield equal or higher benefits to the country than those arising from the stabilisation of sector income.

Countries need assurance that if they use resources for stabilisation they will be reimbursed. But compensation is paid only after the statistics are available which usually means a year or more's delay, so countries have to anticipate its receipt. This is what lies behind UNCTAD's demand for compensation to be free of side conditions. Such conditions can be the source of dispute and create doubt as to whether and how much compensation the country will receive. It is true that the threshold conditions can also reduce the burden to the facility of administering large numbers of very small claims. But making many very small claims is a nuisance to countries too, especially if they add up to little. Even without threshold conditions, countries may not make many very small claims. In any case, in a computer age, provided the process of dealing with claims is sufficiently automatic, the system can be computerised and the burden of dealing with more claims may be unimportant.

The recommendation that loans should be charged at an interest rate reflecting the borrowing cost to the facility and that repayment should be made within a fixed period, taking into account overages but not the ability to repay does make good sense. If there is no balance of payments need test applying to compensation, then there should be no ability to repay test (involving balance of payments and reserves position in reverse) applying to repayment. Fixed terms of repayment and lending interest rate reflecting borrowing cost are necessary conditions for the facility to become a viable commercial banking enterprise. The scope of its operation and hence its financial resources can expand faster to keep up with the growing need of LDCs, only if the facility remains viable without requiring a large inflow of grants or soft-loans from aid-giving countries. If its objective is to provide compensation on a large scale to LDCs, then it should not be another aid institution so all concessional elements should be kept to the minimum.

Finally, the Group maintained, without elaboration or supporting arguments, that 'calculation of shortfalls on a gross (i.e. commodity-by-commodity) basis is more appropriate than that on a net (i.e. aggregated) basis in relation to the objective of reducing instability in individual commodity sectors.' We have demonstrated above, with the help of a simple example, the invalidity of the idea of basing compensation on shortfalls on a gross basis, even when a system for giving full compensation to each shortfall-sector is actually pursued by the recipient country. Basing compensation on the shortfall, on a net basis makes more sense in relation to the objectives of income (and import) stabilisation as well as of sectoral stabilisation. Furthermore, there is a case for making the compensation rate (when the basis is net shortfall) uniform at 100 per cent. This is an important advantage because it removes the need for estimating different compensation rates for different countries associated with compensation on gross shortfall. A further advantage of net shortfall as the basis is that it eliminates the need for threshold conditions to reduce very small claims. Without such side conditions, compensations become more automatic and more certain. One

243

Table 5.5: Shortfalls and Compensations of Existing Facilities and of an Additional Facility: 1977-82 (billions of dollars)

Facility		1977-82	1977	1978	1979	1980	1981	1982
IMF-CFF[a]	Shortfalls	11.89	0.56	1.03	1.18	1.68	2.97	4.47
	Compensations	7.34	0.31	0.55	0.81	0.90	1.65	3.12
	Average compensation rate[b] (percentage)	61.7	51.8	52.1	68.0	57.9	58.4	71.4
	Number of countries		14	26	23	30	43	37
Stabex[c]	Shortfalls	1.34	0.04	0.23	0.09	0.37	0.51	0.10
	Compensations	0.79	0.04	0.22	0.09	0.16	0.18[d]	0.10
	Average compensation rate[b] (percentage)	58.9	100.0	91.0	100.0	53.7	40.4	100.0
	Number of countries		14	21	14	29	27	24
Additional facility[f]	Shortfalls	47.42	4.12	5.06	5.21	7.21	13.43	12.39[e]
	Compensations							
	- 75% comp. rate	35.56	3.09	3.79	3.91	5.41	10.07	9.29
	- 50% comp. rate	23.69	2.06	2.53	2.60	3.60	6.71	6.19
	Number of countries		64	70	73	80	90	94

a The data are restricted to the developing countries included in Table 5.1. The shortfalls and the drawings under the IMF-CFF are often calculated for 12-month periods not necessarily coinciding with calendar years. In order to obtain comparable figures with the other facilities, the shortfalls (and the drawings) were allocated to calendar years on a pro rata basis.
b The annual rates of compensation were calculated in the currency of the original data.

244

c Stabex data cover ACP States and EEC member States' overseas territories.
d Including transfers that were financed by EEC from extra-budgetary resources.
e Provisional.
f Country coverage: 134 developing countries and territories. Commodity coverage: 29 commodities (see notes to Table 5.1). Trend formula in nominal terms: exponential over a ten-year period. Dependency and fluctuation thresholds set at 5 per cent (2 per cent for the least developed countries). Calculations on a gross basis.

Sources: IMF (for CFF data), Commission of the European Communities (for Stabex data), UNCTAD data bank and UNCTAD secretariat calculations

Table 5.6: Simulation of the Operations of the Additional Facility: 1977–81 (millions of dollars)

	1976	1977	1978	1979	1980	1981
A Operations with recipient countries						
1 Cash flows with countries						
Shortfalls		4 112	5 066	5 211	7 215	13 430
Compensatory loans		2 105	2 677	2 752	3 839	7 021
Payments by countries:		–	157	532	926	1 390
Repayments of principal		–	–	196	420	666
Interest payments		–	157	336	505	723
Net cash outflows		2 105	2 521	2 220	2 913	5 631
2 Net situation with countries:						
Outstanding debt		2 105	4 783	7 339	10 758	17 113
Subsidy (cumulative):		–	54	201	450	847
Developing countries (in general)[a]		–	42	142	303	548
Least developed countries[b]		–	12	59	147	299
B Sources and Uses of the facility funds						
1 Uses of funds (cumulative)						
Disbursements on compensatory loans	3 456	2 105	4 782	7 534	11 373	18 395
Repayments of borrowed funds	0 186	–	–	3	240	701
Investment		1 728	1 728	1 728	1 728	1 728
Special investment account		204	213	188	125	–
		4 038	6 724	9 454	13 467	20 824

2 Sources of funds (cumulative)

Special interest subsidy account [a] [b]	186	204	213	188	125	–
Resources provided by the paid-in capital	3 456	3 456	3 456	3 456	3 456	3 456
Net income		346	684	1 002	1 301	1 562
Repayment of compensatory loans		–	–	196	616	1 282
Borrowings		32	2 371	4 612	7 969	14 524
		4 038	6 724	9 454	13 467	20 824

C Operations with the financial markets

1 Cash flows with the financial markets leaders

Annual borrowings		2	2 339	2 241	3 357	6 556
Payments to the financial markets leaders:		–	3	240	698	1 235
Repayment of principal		–	–	3	237	461
Interest payments		–	3	237	461	773
Net cash inflows		32	2 336	2 001	2 659	5 321

2 Net situation with the financial markets

Outstanding debt		32	2 371	4 609	7 728	13 823
Investment		1 932	1 941	1 916	1 853	1 728

a Subsidy due to the small interest rate differential (2 per cent) between the market rate and the lending rate to developing countries in general.

b Subsidy due to the 0 per cent interest rate granted to the least developed countries (as compared to the interest rate charged to developing countries in general).

Source: As for Table 5.7

Table 5.7: Basic Elements of the Balance Sheet of an Additional Facility: Illustrative Simulation for the Period 1977-81[a] (millions of dollars)

	1976	1977	1978	1979	1980	1981
A Assets						
Investment[b]	3 456	1 728	1 728	1 728	1 728	1 728
Special investment account[c]	186	204	213	188	125	–
Loans (outstanding)		2 105	4 783	7 339	10 758	17 113
		4 038	6 724	9 255	12 611	18 841
B Liabilities						
Debt[d]		32	2 371	4 609	7 728	13 823
Paid-in capital	3 456	3 456	3 456	3 456	3 456	3 456
Net income[e]		346	684	1 002	1 301	1 562
Special subsidy account	186	204	213	188	125	–
		4 038	6 724	9 255	12 611	18 841

Basic capital structure

Total capital	17 280
Paid-in capital	3 456
Callable capital[c]	13 824
Subsidy[c] (paid as a lump sum)	186

a The hypotheses used in the simulation are those of Table 5.6. Specific hypotheses for the period 1977-81 are:
- Average borrowing rate of the facility: 10 per cent

b – The facility borrows and lends to the market at the same rate (i.e. no 'liquidity costs')
It is supposed for simplicity that the facility will maintain for the end of each year a minimum level of highly liquid investments equal to one half of its paid-in capital.

c The special investment account, and its revenue, are intended to finance the special interest rate concessionality to the least developed countries (i.e. 0 per cent). Everything therefore happens as if those countries were subject to the lending rate applied to the other countries (i.e. 8 per cent). Unused funds of the subsidy account are invested in the market at the prevailing interest rate.

d It should be noted that the debt of the facility at the end of the period is equal to the callable capital. At the end of the period, therefore, the facility would not have exhausted its borrowing capacity (limited by the callable capital plus net income).

e These figures do not take into account the administrative expenses of the facility and should be adjusted downward. Net income = interest on (investment + loans - borrowed funds) + subsidy account transfers.

Source: UNCTAD data bank and UNCTAD secretariat calculations

cannot over-emphasise the importance of this. By making compensatory drawings more automatic and dependable LDCs are encouraged to stabilise their national and sectoral incomes by their own devices.

The hypothetical financial acquirements of UNCTAD facility for the period 1976-81

The actual shortfalls and compensations of existing facilities, IMF-CFF and EEC-STABEX, and the hypothetical shortfalls and compensations of the UNCTAD facility for the period 1977-82 are given in Table 5.5. It shows that over the period the total CFF drawings amounted to $7.3 billion, or about 62 per cent of the shortfalls calculated by the IMF, the total Stabex transfers amounted to $790 million, representing 59 per cent of Stabex calculated shortfalls and the hypothetical compensatory loans from the UNCTAD facility amounted to $23.7 billion, representing 50 per cent of UNCTAD calculated shortfalls. Thus loans from the UNCTAD facility would have been about three times the CFF drawings and 30 times total Stabex transfers.

To make compensatory loans of this amount requires that the UNCTAD facility be run on a commercial basis, where financial viability is of critical importance. Any aid-element would have to be financed not by borrowing but very large direct contributions from rich countries. But grants or soft loans of such large amounts would not be attractive to donor nations, especially via an institution over which they had little control. If they were made, it would probably be at the expense of development aid. The developed countries would be unwilling to raise their total aid bill each time they agree to a new international scheme. Hence, the dilemma that if the UNCTAD facility involves a large transfer to resources, then it seems likely to receive little support from the donor nations whose contributions are vital for its survival, but even if somehow it gains their support, it may disenchant the developing countries if they fear that its establishment would be at the expense of existing aid.

The financial requirements of the UNCTAD facility depend not only on the annual flows of compensatory loans but also on other features such as repayment conditions, interest rates, and concessions to the least developed countries. Given the features recommended by the Expert Group, the UNCTAD secretariat produced detailed simulated results for the operations of the UNCTAD facility for the period 1977-1981. These results are summarised in Table 6.6. It can be seen that, after five years of operations, the outstanding debt of the recipient countries in 1981 would be $17.1 billion (i.e. just over 70 per cent of the cumulated compensatory loans) and the countries would repay about $4.3 billion, of which $1.3 billion represents interest payments. The total subsidy (arising from the fact that lending interest rate is lower than the borrowing interest by 2 per cent per annum and is zero for least developed countries) would amount to $847 million, of which about $300 million would go to the least developed countries.

Sections B and C of Table 5.6 also illustrate the sources and uses of the facility funds and the operation with the financial markets. It can be seen that the resources of $3.5 billion provided for, initially in 1976, by the paid in capital are assumed to be invested and only a small part used in the operations of the facility. By 1981, the facility shows an outstanding debt of $13.8 billion with the financial markets but with total assets - consisting of $17.1 billion worth of debt of LDCs and $1.7 billion worth of investment - worth about $18.8 billion, i.e. a net worth of $4.9 billion which exceeds the initial capital of $3.5 billion it started with in 1976. Hence the facility is shown to be financially viable. Its net worth increases because of this special annual interest subsidy in the years 1976-80 which accumulates to $806 million. This amount plus interest earned on its investment exceeds the total subsidy given to the users. Clearly the facility would remain financially viable as long as its subsidies to the recipient countries are covered by the interest it earns on its investment plus the interest subsidy contributed annually from the governments.

What the governments might be asked to contribute was not only the $3.5 billion of paid-in capital but also to provide callable capital or guarantees to enable the facility to borrow an amount of 13.8 billion in the financial markets in 1981. There would be less need for government's guarantees if the financial markets can reasonably be sure that all the facility's loans to the countries would be repaid within a fixed term. Table 5.7 presents the basic elements of the balance sheet of the facility. It can be seen that to enable the facility to borrow $13.8 billion a callable capital of the same size had to be subscribed from the governments.

NOTES

1. Developing countries as a group accounted for two-thirds of world exports of the 10 core commodities on average (1973-74). They were chosen as prima facie candidates for stock control policies.

2. Empirical analysis does show some evidence of negative correlation between movements of primary commodity prices, but not a lot. See House of Lords, (1976).

3. See UNCTAD, 'Commodity Issues : a review and proposals for further action' (Belgrade - June 1983, TD/273) paras. 42-47 for a Secretariat defence of the new Agreement and hopes for the evolution of the Common Fund to a position of influence.

Chapter Six

PROSPECTS AND POLICIES FOR THE 1990s

As set out in Chapter 3 the most likely prospect for the mid-1990s is that there was no overall scarcity of food and raw materials. In terms of real prices the non-oil commodity prices in general are expected to be lower than their averages for 1979-81. However, there is a wide variety of expected future relationships between demand and supply among different commodities. There are also changes in the pattern of consumption and production, exports and imports, among the main groups of nations, expected to take place by the mid 1990s. The appropriate caveats to be borne in mind when using these projections were set out in Chapter 3.

Table 3.6 in Chapter 3 summarised the projected real prices for various commodity groups. In this section we discuss in a little more detail some of the more important metals, food and agricultural raw materials in terms of their consumption, production, export and import.

PROSPECTS FOR METALS AND MINERALS

In recent years it has become clear that the growth in demand for most of the traditional metals is likely to be much slower than was formerly believed. This is not merely because expectations of world growth have been lowered, but because the increasing shift in the composition of the national product in the MDCs towards services lowers the requirements for traditional industrial materials. Also the increased costs of energy have reduced the average size and weight of cars in the interests of fuel economy, and technological changes have increased the availability of substitutes for metals. Finally, environmental policies designed to reduce pollution, such as the lowering of lead additives in petrol and controls on smelting and refining activities have reduced demand directly or through raising costs. These factors together have lowered the demand prospects for copper, lead, steel and tin. Currently there is a great deal of surplus capacity in both

mining and processing of most minerals. This is partly due to
the earlier pessimism about the long term availability of
non-renewable resources which encouraged conservation, a
search for substitutes and exploration and investment in
mining and refining. But probably the more important cause
is the sharp reduction in growth since the mid-1970s. Successful efforts to reduce costs and the effects of weak
demand have produced the recent low prices in the markets
for the major metals apart from aluminium.

The recent experience and projections to 1995 for several
metals, important in world trade, and of particular importance
to a number of developing countries whose fates are closely
tied to exports of these metals are set out in Table 6.1.

For the reasons set out above, the rates of growth of
exports for all of these metals, save lead, are expected to
decline substantially compared with the 1961-82 period. The
developing countries' projected shares in world exports are
shown as declining for bauxite and manganese, rising for
copper, iron ore and nickel and stationary for the others
when compared with their 1979-81 averages.

Table 6.1: Growth of World Exports of Metals and Export
Shares of LDCs

	Rate of Growth		LDCs Export Shares per cent			
	1961-82	1979/81-95	1964-66	1979-81	1985	1995
Bauxite	4.0	1.7	91.6	75.8	65.9	69.0
Copper	3.3	1.5	61.5	62.6	67.9	67.2
Iron Ore	4.5	0.7	46.6	46.9	45.5	50.8
Lead	1.6	1.9	49.0	33.0	33.2	33.6
Manganese Ore	2.1	0.9	83.6	74.8	73.0	70.9
Nickel	3.2	0.8	7.1	29.9	30.7	32.5
Tin	0.5	-1.1	83.9	87.1	84.8	86.3
Zinc	2.9	2.2	38.0	25.4	25.5	25.9

Source: World Bank, Economic Analysis and Projections
Department (1984)

253

Copper

Because copper both looms large in trade, over $10 billion in 1979/81, and is of particular importance to several LDCs such as Chile, Zambia, Zaire and Peru among others, it may repay some more detailed attention. Its intensity of use has dropped from 1,100 kg per million dollars of GNP (1980 constant prices) from the early 1960s to less than 840 kg around 1980, in the industrial nations, while it has risen from about 540 kg in 1960 to 720 kg in 1980 in the developing countries. Substitution against copper is an important and continuing influence e.g. aluminium in electrical power transmission, in telecommunications and in car radiators; plastics in plumbing pipes; fibre optics and satellites in telecommunications. The expectation is that this process of reducing intensity will continue in the MDCs, that there will be a slight increase in intensity in the LDCs and a slight decrease in the CPEs as the economy of Russia matures.

These factors lead to estimates of growth in consumption of refined copper between 1985 and 1995 of 0.9 per cent per annum in MDCs, 3.4 per cent in LDCs and 2.1 per cent in CPEs, adding up to 1.6 per cent average for the whole world and implying a consumption of 11.8 million tons around 1995 compared with 9.0 million tons in 1982. This is a good deal slower growth than for 1970-82.

On the supply side the critical factor in the long run is mining capacity. This is difficult to determine, because of varying estimates of which shut-down mines can return to production and which have effectively been lost, and is even more difficult to project. The best estimates show respectively a decline from about 3.04 to 2.87 million tons per year from 1982 to 1995 for the MDCs and an increase from about 4.2 to 5.3 million tons per year in the LDCs. The CPEs play a relatively minor role in trade in copper, meeting their own requirements, but with only minor surpluses for export.

Copper Trade

Some countries export in one form and import it in another at a different stage of refinement. As a result gross exports are considerably higher than net. The projected gross exports for the World have been increasing at 3.4 per cent per annum 1961-81, while those of LDCs have been rising faster at 3.6 per cent. For 1985-95, projected export growth for the world is 1.3 per cent per annum, made up of 1.4 per cent for MDCs, 1.2 per cent for LDCs and 2.1 per cent for CPEs. The share of refined copper in developing countries' total copper exports is expected to rise from 54 per cent (1979-81) to 63 per cent by 1995.

Price

By historical levels the copper prices 1983-85 have been extremely low. High stocks, hanging over the market have been a major factor in this. These stocks are now expected to decline and prices to recover somewhat. But chronic over-supply tendencies are likely to continue to depress prices below past levels over the next few years. Around 1990 some further adjustment of capacity to slow demand growth could have occurred and the London Metal Exchange (LME) prices could rise in 1983 constant dollars to about $1580 per ton in 1990 and about $1720 per ton by around 1995.

Policies

The Intergovernmental Council for Copper Exporting Nations (CIPEC) was formed in 1967 by Chile, Peru, Zaire, and Zambia. Since then it has been joined by Indonesia, as a full member, and by Australia, Papua New Guinea and Yugoslavia as associate members. CIPEC has made attempts to initiate joint cutbacks in exports, particularly during the surplus period 1974-77, but with little success. The UNCTAD IPC included proposals for stabilising copper prices, but no agreement has been reached on measures to do so. Scrap recovery in the MDCs, their own mining capacity and their ability to substitute other materials in many uses limits severely the possibility of gains to LDCs from cartel action. Some importing nations, e.g. USA and Japan have official stockpiles of copper, but apart from 20,000 tons in the US strategic stockpile (1985) these are negligible. The US copper industry has been forced to cut production sharply as a result of low prices and increased competition from imports. As a result it has sought protection, but so far the US government has resisted its demands.

Although, in the market economies, the largest 20 companies account for 75 per cent of mining, ownership seems to be sufficiently dispersed to ensure reasonably effective competition in the industry. Over 40 per cent in the developed market economies and 70 per cent in the LDCs of mining capacity is controlled by governments. Vertical integration is common in both state controlled and private companies.

Tin

Tin is a much smaller item in world trade than copper but its production is concentrated heavily in the developing countries of Malaysia, Thailand, Indonesia, Bolivia, Zaire, Nigeria and China. In 1982 they accounted for 74 per cent of world production. Output has been declining in Bolivia, Malaysia, Zaire and Nigeria, but expanding in Brazil, Indonesia and Thailand. Consumption has been increasing in the LDCs and CPEs, but declining in industrial countries. Prospects are poor because it is expected that the substitution of tinplate by aluminium, plastics, chrome steel and tin-free-steel will continue.

255

Excess supply of tin over the demand for it led to rising stocks up to 1983 when stricter export quotas under the International Tin Agreement (ITA) and production cutbacks in 1983 produced some fall in stocks. Recently, with the collapse of the ITA, tin prices have fallen from over $8,000 per ton in October 1985 to around $6,000 in early 1986. ITA stocks remain high and if sold off quickly could push prices below $4,000 per ton. Even if some salvage operation can be mounted export controls are unlikely to hold in the face of expanding production in newcomers such as Brazil. Prices could be much lower than presently projected by the World Bank.

Bauxite and Aluminium

Bauxite is the main metallic ore from which alumina (aluminium oxide) is refined. Alumina, in turn, is the basic raw material of the aluminium industry. It is converted into aluminium in electrolytic smelters operated by electric power. The availability and cost of electricity is a key determinant of the location of aluminium plants. Recovered scrap provides about 25 per cent of world aluminium.

Aluminium's lightness, strength, resistance to corrosion, electrical conductivity and relatively low melting point give it a wide variety of uses. Transport, construction and packaging absorb just over 20 per cent each, electrical engineering about 10 per cent and 25 per cent in other miscellaneous uses.

The known economic reserves have increased from 5,700 million tons (1963) to 22,600 million tons (1983). Bauxite mining capacity is widely dispersed among the industrial market economies, the developing countries and the CPEs. The LDCs have about 50 per cent of the world capacity of 114 million tons per year (1983). Most of this is in Jamaica, Guinea, Suriname, Guyana and Brazil. Guinea has the largest and most rapidly growing exports of bauxite, 9.8 million tons (1979-81) growing at about 3 per cent per annum. Jamaica's exports have been falling 1961-85 but are expected to reach over 5 per cent per annum growth 1985-95. Jamaica has been processing bauxite to the alumina stage increasingly since the 1960s and this is expected to continue, while Guinea's production of alumina is quite small and growing slowly. The production of primary aluminium has been growing fast in LDCs; 13.9 per cent per annum, 1961-82 and 6.7 per cent per annum, 1980-85, but from a small base. It is expected to continue to grow but at a slower rate of 4.6 per cent per annum, 1985-95.

As Table 6.2 shows the LDCs have, and are expected to continue, to process locally an increasing proportion of bauxite into alumina or primary aluminium.

Table 6.2: Production in Million Tons

	Bauxite			Alumina			Primary Aluminium		
	LDCs	World	%	LDCs	World	%	LDCs	World	%
1969–71	36.6	60.0	61%	4.9	21.2	23%	0.8	10.2	8%
1979–81	50	90.3	55%	7.9	33.7	23%	2.4	15.6	15%
1985	44.1	87.8	50%	9.2	34.1	27%	3.3	16.1	20%
1990	50.0	95.7	52%	10.8	38.4	28%	4.0	17.8	22%
1995	64.4	114.5	56%	13.6	44.4	31%	5.1	20.7	25%

Source: World Bank, Economic Analysis and Projections (1984)

This is a commodity in which the increase in value added from processing which could accrue to LDC producers is potentially large according to UNCTAD studies (1984e). But most of the planned expansion in aluminium capacity 1985-90 is in Canada, Australia and Brazil, and in alumina capacity Brazil is the only country in the world planning to expand. The major difficulty is that existing capacity is probably more than adequate to meet expected demand right through the 1980s. Additional problems facing LDCs who aspire to move up the processing stream are that the investment requirements are very high, the energy requirements are great, particularly at the aluminium refining stage, the industry is largely vertically integrated so that most trade is intra-firm with a small free market and there are trade barriers facing exports in processed forms. A major worry for all producers of primary aluminium is that recycled aluminium from scrap recovery is expected to take about 35 per cent of the market in the industrial economies by 1995.

The Other Metals

Iron Ore
In the industrial nations the demand for iron ore is likely to remain almost stationary up to 1995. All the expansion is likely to take place in LDCs where demand should grow at 3.1 per cent per annum. This will lead to a shift in the trade pattern so that trade will increasingly be between LDCs.

Nickel
As about 60 per cent of nickel is used in the steel industry its fortunes are tied closely to the demand for steel. As the outlook for steel is fairly stagnant for reasons given in the introductory section nickel consumption is expected to grow at only about 1.5 per cent per annum up to 1995.

Manganese
Like nickel, demand for manganese stems mainly from the iron and steel industries. Their slow growth combined with increases in the efficiency with which they use manganese has already substantially reduced their requirements for manganese ore. The main source of demand in future will be the iron and steel industries of Korea, other South East Asia, the Middle East and Latin America in the developing world. Overall growth of demand 1980-85 will be just under one per cent per annum. Reserves seem ample for the foreseeable future. Most exports will continue to be from South Africa and the developing countries.

Lead

The main use for lead is in batteries. This, plus the use of lead additives in petrol makes the demand for lead dependent on the car and truck industries. Reduction in the rate of expansion of the motor industry, reductions in the size of cars and the emphasis on weight reduction for economy plus the anti-pollution campaigns to reduce lead use in petrol and an increase in lead scrap recovery for refining have already lowered demand for lead concentrates significantly. Even with resumed growth the rate of increase in demand for lead 1985-95 is projected at only 1.2 per cent per annum. The share of developing countries in exports of lead concentrates is expected to decrease from 55 per cent in 1982 to 43 per cent in 1995, but more refining in LDCs should lead to some offsetting increase in exports of lead metal. Canada and Oceania are likely to increase their share of world exports of both lead concentrates and metal.

Zinc

World demand for zinc is expected to grow more rapidly than for most of the other metals. The demand for improved protection of steel surfaces from corrosion is expected to lead to increased use of zinc in the industrial nations. New applications for zinc are currently under development.

The trend in LDCs to process their own concentrates and an increase in MDCs dependence on metal imports will be the major influences on trade in zinc. Imports of zinc metal are expected to rise at 4.3 per cent per annum (1985-95) while concentrates grow at a lower rate of 2.1 per cent per annum.

Conclusion on Metals

Earlier worries about depletion have been overtaken by the facts of slower growth in industrial production, the increased use of substitutes and increased efficiency in use. Although non-renewable natural resources must by definition eventually run out if demand for them continues, the history of minerals up to now shows a clear tendency for proven reserves to grow faster than demand. The known reserves of most metals today are vastly greater than say, 20 years ago. Mining companies do not normally undertake expensive exploration until they are fairly sure that demand will grow fast enough to justify development. For this reason proven reserves are much smaller than the potential reserves. Moreover, as the price of any one metal rises substitutes are found both among other metals and synthetics. Modern production and consumption are so complex and varied that they present a near infinite combination of consumption possibilities and a considerable range of input combinations for producing most

259

goods and services. Probably no mineral is truly indispensable. The probability of growth being choked off by lack of mineral resources seems remote. Decreasing returns in mining seem likely to continue to be offset by advances in technology.

Disruption, however, seems much more of a risk. Major wars or civil wars in say, Southern Africa, could have serious effects on OECD imports of chromium, manganese, platinum and uranium.

Another worry is that LDCs may fail to capture a sufficient share of the world's production and export of minerals and metals. Reasons for this include TNCs fears of expropriation or unilateral changes in contracts which would damage the profitability of exploration and development of mines in LDCs. This would not matter too much if LDC governments were able themselves or through national companies to carry out these tasks themselves. A number of LDCs clearly can: Brazil, Mexico, Venezuela, The Philippines, Korea etc. But for many of the smaller and poorer LDCs the task of mounting their own exploration and development in mining and refining is too formidable. Nowadays the investment costs are so huge that even the large TNCs form consortia. The expertise is difficult and expensive to obtain outside of the TNCs.

Various solutions to these problems are possible. They range from treaties involving guarantees and insurance for TNC investments to consortial arrangements involving multilateral institutions such as the World Bank with the LDC governments and the TNCs in joint ventures. A number of successful forms of agreements have been devised and are reported in Mikesell (1979) and suggestions of solutions in Bosson and Varon (1977). The Third LOME CONVENTION on co-operation between the EC and Afro-Caribbean states includes a number of articles emphasising the importance of technical assistance, training and EC funding for exploration and development of mining in the LDC partners (Articles 78-83). It also includes a special financing facility for mining assistance (SYSMIN) to help ACP States which are dependent on mining (Articles 176-184) [The Courier, No. 89 Jan-Feb. 1985].

PROSPECTS FOR AGRICULTURAL RAW MATERIALS (NON-FOOD)

Like the minerals, the demand for most of these materials is tied closely to the growth of industrial production and the development of synthetic substitutes for them. This is the case for the fibres: wool, cotton, jute and hard fibres such as sisal, abaca and henequen and for timber. For tobacco, population, per capita income and health fears are the main factors influencing demand. If world economic growth continues to be slow prospects for all of them are poor. Past and prospective growth rates of several key agricultural material exports and the export shares of the developing countries are shown in Table 6.3.

For most of these products LDCs are substantial consumers and importers. As they continue to develop processing capacity for raw materials to create jobs and increase local value added the proportion available for export in raw form will decline for all such commodities.

PROSPECTS FOR FOOD AND BEVERAGES

There are two main issues involved in world production and trade in food. These are the question of food security in the developing countries, particularly in Africa and some parts of Asia, and the question of agricultural protection in the industrial nations. They are both of fundamental importance to the world's future and they are not unrelated.

FOOD SECURITY AND INTERNATIONAL TRADE IN FOOD

The Issues
As far as the global figures are concerned recent projections, at least from the World Bank, take a much less pessimistic view than the earlier studies such as FAO's Agriculture: Toward 2000. At least to the end of the century, according to Bank experts, world food production can easily outpace population growth and probably exceed demand (Bale and Duncan, 1983). Overall food prices are unlikely to rise in real terms. Real export prices for grains from the USA have in fact fallen over both the long and medium term as shown in the following graph (6a). World cereal production has consistently exceeded population growth. Between 1960-70 population grew at 2.0 per cent per annum while cereal production grew at 2.0 per cent while 1971-80 the rates were respectively 1.7 per cent and 2.6 per cent.

Developing Countries
As Table 6.4 makes clear the Developing Countries as a group have succeeded in increasing food production faster than population growth. In the last few years India and China have had quite dramatic successes in increasing food output - to some extent by increasing or restoring incentives to farmers. Taking 1974-76 as 100, food production per capita for China and India were 128 and 110 respectively by 1982-84 (World Bank, 1986, Table 6). China's fertiliser consumption has risen from 418 grams per hectare of arable land in 1970

261

Figure 5: Real Export Unit Values for Wheat and Corn, USA, Selected Years 1910-82 (1967 US dollars per metric ton)

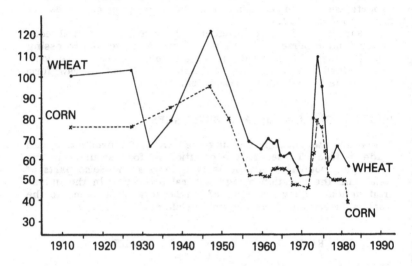

Source: World Bank Tables based on US Dept. of Commerce Statistical Abstract of the United States, various issues

Table 6.3: Growth of World Exports of Natural Rubber, Cotton, Tobacco and Sawn and Veneer Logs

| | Rate of growth | | LDCs Export Shares per cent | | | |
	1961-82	1979/81-95	1964-66	1979-81	1985	1995
Rubber	2.3	2.2	97.2	98.6	98.8	99.9
Cotton	1.0	0.6	62.9	67.7	44.6	44.4
Tobacco	2.4	1.9	49.1	50.2	55.4	56.0
Logs	5.1	-2.6	92.6	94.9	92.7	92.5

Source: World Bank, Economic Analysis and Projections Department (1984)

PROSPECTS AND POLICIES FOR THE 1990s

Table 6.4: Growth of Cereal* Production per capita (%) per
annum 1970-82

World	0.5
Industrial Market Economies	1.6
East European CPEs	-0.2
Developing economies of which	0.9
East Africa	-2.2
West Africa	-0.8
Middle East and North Africa	-1.2
East Asia and Pacific	+1.8
South Asia	+0.3
Latin America and Caribbean	+0.8

* Although other foods are of increasing importance the weight
of cereals in LDC diets in general is so high as to represent
a reasonable proxy for basic foods.

Source: World Bank calculations based on USDA data.

to 1,806 grams in 1983 (Ibid). Both now export cereals. For
low-income economies as a group the index of food production
per capita has risen from 100 in 1974-76 to 116 in 1982-84.
The major problem area is Africa - the scene of repeated
famines and of chronic hunger. Food production there has
failed to keep up with the growth in numbers. But even
within the nations where food production has grown significantly faster than population hunger persists. The reason
usually is poverty. There are groups who neither have the
resources to grow enough food for themselves and families nor
adequate incomes to buy food. Most such groups are in the
bottom decile of income distribution and most live in rural
areas. But there are also quite large groups who are undernourished in the towns. Usually they are the newcomers from
rural areas. They have problems finding work and their
incomes are low and erratic. In many cases, the cause of
hunger is not physical shortages of food, it is the lack of
income which is the result of low productivity and high
unemployment. As A.K. Sen's studies of famines in Bengal,
Ethiopia, the Sahel and Bangladesh have shown, even during
some of the most grave famines there has been enough food if
it had been more evenly distributed. The trouble was that the

263

small farmers and the landless labourers had no employment or other source of income to pay for food (Sen, 1981). What then are the most promising approaches to the alleviation of chronic hunger and catastrophic famines?

Food security can be defined as a situation where all individuals and households can have access to adequate sources of nutrition for an active and healthy life. Ideally that means that people should either be able to feed themselves from their own produce or have enough income to buy food. But it would also require mechanisms for emergency relief when disaster strikes. This applies equally to nations. They either have to be self-sufficient in basic foods or self-reliant, i.e. be able to earn enough through exports to pay for food imports. For them too there have to be arrangements to deal with emergencies. Two kinds of food insecurity need to be distinguished: chronic and transitory. Chronic food insecurity is a continuously inadequate diet. Transitory food insecurity occurs when there is a temporary, often acute, decline in households' access to food. It stems from instability in food prices, food production or households' incomes. It can mean famine. Debate centres around the question of what are the optimum solutions to chronic and transitory food insecurity both at the level of the family and the nation. The major questions debated are:

1. Should nations aim at self-sufficiency or self-reliance?
2. Should fluctuations in domestic production be met by the accumulation and decumulation of domestically held stocks or by exporting surpluses and importing to meet deficits?
3. Does the world community need to invest in public international stocks of basic foodstuffs or is an increasingly integrated, well-informed world market and its privately held stocks (plus the public stocks of USA, Canada, Australia and the EEC) adequate to meet all foreseeable emergencies?
4. Given the widely dispersed rural communities and poor transport links typical of much of Africa, do regions within countries have to be self-sufficient in production and hold their own emergency stocks or would it be more efficient for them to maximise incomes, improve transport and rely on trade to meet both normal and emergency food needs?
5. Can countries which take the self-reliant route depend upon the international financial system including the IMF's Compensatory Financing Facility and its Food Financing Facility, to provide adequate credit for food emergencies?
6. Within each country can farmers and their workers who specialise in export crops rely upon credit to buy food

when either their revenues drop or food prices shoot up unexpectedly?

These issues have been considered in many reports by officials of the World Bank, the UN Food and Agriculture Organisation, in conference papers and in academic writings. As the way in which the questions have been posed hints, there is a broad division between those who believe that the main solutions require direct government participation in the production, stockpiling and distribution of food and those who believe that government policies have been, and often still are, the main cause of the problem. The latter group tend to favour the restoration of government farms and parastatal marketing organisations to the private sector and such policies as the restoration of incentives to farmers to produce those crops which are most profitable. That they and their countries should specialise along the lines of their (dynamic) comparative advantage, i.e. farmers and nations should do the things that will earn them the highest (social) rate of return on the resources at their disposal. This does not mean simply looking at current costs, but involves looking to the future, allowing for risk and uncertainty, making intelligent guesses about future trends in demands and costs and keeping an eye on the competition. For some countries, it would mean putting more resources into food production whether to replace imports or to develop exports. For others the most efficient use of resources may be to grow export crops, develop or expand mineral exports, shift resources into processing, or increase manufactured exports and by these means obtain more food indirectly through trade than they could by producing it directly for themselves.

The Market Approach
The role of government, as seen by this school, would be to make sure that its citizens and managers were faced with the right market signals or shadow prices so that their decisions would be made on the basis of full information about the costs and benefits of the strategies they adopt. Generally this would mean that prices as set in international markets should be the guide to domestic prices. If a good or service can be obtained more cheaply from abroad then very special reasons would be required to justify producing it at home, e.g. overriding defence, distribution or positive externalities such as a pronounced complementarity with some other socially profitable domestic production. Governments would also have a role in seeing that the poor are protected from hunger by distributional or employment policies.

Until recently practically all developing countries neglected agriculture. The resources invested there were much less than in other sectors. Research, particularly in subsistence crops was neglected. Marketing boards and other state organisations paid prices to farmers which were well below international prices. They did this on food crops in order to keep down food prices for urban workers and on major cash crops to raise government revenues. At the same time manufactured goods prices were kept high by severe restrictions on imports because of the desire to protect domestic industries and to ration the use of scarce foreign exchange. Overvalued exchange rates further lowered the incentives to export and distorted the prices of imported inputs (Bates, 1981, Part I; World Bank, 1983, Sections 4-7). The effects of such domestic distortions were to lower national output and slow growth with no apparent improvement in income distribution (World Bank, 1983, Section 6, 1986, chapters 4, 5 and 8).

Just how damaging government policies can be to a major export is illustrated by the case of the Ghana Cocoa Marketing Board. The Ghanaian Government's share of cocoa sales revenues rose from 3 per cent in 1947-48 to 60 per cent in 1978-79. In addition the Marketing Board took as much as 20 per cent to cover operating costs. As a result the cocoa farmers' prices by 1979 averaged about half their 1963 level, even after allowing for subsidies on seeds and other inputs. Farm prices also remained highly unstable. Cocoa production fell from 540,000 tons in 1965 to 250,000 tons in 1979. The volume of exports fell by 80 per cent and an estimated 45,000 tons of cocoa a year were smuggled to neighbouring territories where prices were higher. From being the dominant exporter in the world Ghana dropped below both Brazil and Ivory Coast. The foreign exchange loss to Ghana was about 15 per cent of average export earnings (World Bank, 1983, p. 77).

In terms of direct production of food Ghana's failures are equally dramatic. Taking 1974-76 as 100, food production per capita in Ghana in 1981-83 was 65 while Ivory Coast and Sri Lanka, two countries which have moved towards policies of efficient pricing and management, have achieved 108 and 127 respectively (World, Bank, 1985, Table 6).

Such observation, combined with a priori reasoning of neo-classical economics leads many economists to the view that long-term food security and long-term economic development can be achieved by the same policies. Countries which get their macroeconomic policies right, e.g. equilibrium exchange rates, no excessive government borrowing, non-inflationary monetary policies, on the one hand, and adopt pricing systems which reflect marginal social opportunity costs, should on average become self-reliant. They would argue that on the whole such policies would not have adverse distributional effects because most of the poor live in rural areas and have been discriminated against by past economic policies. Efficient pricing would give them better prices for their crops and would stimulate more labour intensive production. Better prices and more jobs would raise rural incomes. Higher prices would of course hurt the urban poor, but they would have more job opportunities and if necessary they could be assisted by job creation, income transfers or their food consumption could be subsidised through food stamp programmes, ration shops or subsidising the prices of their staple foods.

The major role of government is seen as being to provide the economic, social and stable political environment in which private actors will be stimulated by the profit motive to work, save and invest in ways that promote the country's social aims. This involves doing those things which the private sector will not do adequately, e.g. defence, health, education, policing, and quite a lot of research. As research in agriculture, particularly in Africa, has been seriously neglected this is an area for intensive public sector effort and international aid. The Consultative Group on International Agricultural Research is already producing a flow of new technology but is short of funds. Economists, of even quite laissez-faire outlook, would support international and governmental assistance for research in Africa where there is a serious gap in knowledge of how to raise yields and quality in both food and export crops.

Criticisms of the Market Strategy Approach to Food Security

Critics of the approach outlined above would stress its risks to both nations and individuals. For nations food insecurity can stem from fluctuations in domestic production of food, in world prices for food and from prices for exports. A policy of self-reliance may expose the nation to greater risks than one of self-sufficiency. Self-reliance requires that the country should always be able to obtain adequate supplies of food through trade. But if its need to import more food coincides with a year when world supplies to the international market have declined or demands from other nations have surged, the food deficit nation can be exposed to very high import prices or it may have to accept political, economic or commercial strings to get food. In the worst possible case its own export earnings could have declined in the same year. If it cannot pay for adequate food imports from current earnings and use of reserves it would have to borrow commercially, use IMF or other official concessionary borrowing facilities or seek food aid. Such resorts could prove costly in terms of treasure or political independence. These considerations may lead many developing countries to consider self-sufficiency the preferable policy.

It is also a worry to some governments and observers that a policy of devaluing exchange rates, reducing levels of protection and reducing taxes on exports may cause serious problems, for countries which rely mainly on a few primary commodity exports. If many LDCs simultaneously adopt such policies the volume of their raw material exports could rise fairly quickly. But these products generally face demands which are both slow growing and price inelastic. Their world prices would then drop sharply and their export earnings would fall. Given the high overhead costs of tree crops and mining this situation would not be remedied quickly by automatic responses of supply to the falling prices. These same conditions, plus the random shocks to supply and demand characteristic of such products, also make their prices and earnings relatively unstable. The result of unco-ordinated actions of producers responding to increased farmgate and minehead prices could increase both long and short term uncertainty and place their national food security in jeopardy.

Such considerations lead many governments of LDCs to aim to be nationally self-sufficient in food through increase domestic production and stocks held nationally, or by regional or UN organisations in which they have a substantial, if not controlling voice.

Rather similar arguments can apply to small farmers. Even if, on the average, the incomes earned from more specialised production of cash crops promised to be higher than from growing their own food many farmers, and particularly the poorer ones, might find the risks too great. They are the ones who find it hardest to obtain credit when their crop is poor or food prices exceed their current income. They cannot afford to place themselves in this double jeopardy.

Practical Policies
In food security as in all other areas of development economics it is essential to recognise the diversity of developing countries and of the families that live there. Each is faced by different opportunities and constraints. Such considerations argue the need for a very pragmatic approach to their problems.

Raising the rate of economic growth and reducing income inequality can reduce and probably eliminate food insecurity. But in the present world climate, for many LDCs growth cannot go fast enough to alleviate chronic food insecurity for some groups in the near future. Other policies to speed the attainment of food security are necessary. What are the most cost-effective ways of doing this?

Experts from the World Bank suggest that possible types of intervention are: (1) increase food supplies, (2) subsidise consumer prices, (3) create jobs for the poor or transfer income to them,

Changing food supplies can be achieved by increasing non-traded foods, by increasing imports or by reducing exports. But food security will only be improved by increasing supply if it increases the real incomes of the groups who go hungry. This requires either that it lowers the price of food for which they are net consumers or raises their income from producing food either as farmers or rural labourers. Increasing production of traded food may do nothing to lower food prices. It may simply replace imports or increase exports. Thus it will only necessarily improve food security if it provides income and employment for the poor. Policies which lower food prices will help the urban poor, but may harm the rural poor if they are net sellers of these foods. They may reduce effort or switch to alternative crops.

Policies of national self-sufficiency need not reduce food insecurity. It depends on their effects on the real incomes of the poor. National self-sufficiency policies may not even increase food availability. The increased food produced may simply replace imports or go into exports.

Subsidising food prices without lowering producer prices can help alleviate chronic food insecurity. But such policies have to be very carefully designed if they are to help the target groups without spilling over to the mass of the population and causing budgetary problems. Problems with such schemes include the difficulty of controlling access to the targeted group, the costs of administration, the incentives to fraud and corruption, the risk that food sold at low prices and intended for human consumption may be used to feed livestock or make alcohol. Food subsidy schemes work best if foods can be identified on which the poor are dependent; if the scheme can be confined to a geographically restricted area and if the food is of a processed type such as flour, bread or tortillas and where a few centrally located firms do the processing.

Transferring income to the poor by giving them cash, food or ration cards can be cost-effective means of improving food security. Usually such schemes aid only the urban poor through such methods as rationing food to a target group. The food can be sold at low prices through special shops or given free at health centres. It is more difficult with scattered rural populations, but subsidising farm inputs which are bought infrequently can effect income transfers to poor farmers. As with subsidised food prices, it is difficult to avoid leakages to non-targeted groups. There is a trade-off between reducing leakage and administrative costs.

Public employment programmes such as the rural public works schemes used in Pakistan and India can raise rural incomes by providing jobs when the seasonal demand for agricultural labour is low. They can construct feeder roads, irrigation ditches, flood protection, schools and village dispensaries. Potentially such schemes can be excellent. The main difficulty is the choice of projects and administration. Often funds are misappropriated, projects of interest to the local landlords, rather than the poor are constructed and the quality of the work is often very poor so that roads are washed away in the next flood. Sometimes schemes to provide employment prove extremely costly in relation to the benefits. One in Malaysian small scale dairy farming was costing over $3 for every $1 actually reaching the participating farmers.

Clearly the choice of approach depends on the characteristics of the groups who suffer food insecurity and on the administrative capacity of the country. Most countries will have a variety of target groups and therefore need a combination of measures. In sub-Saharan Africa most of the afflicted are food sellers, but there are also some urban poor and some landless workers. An appropriate approach is likely to be to raise producer prices, especially as they are usually below international prices, and complement this with food subsidy or ration programmes for the rural poor and job creation for the landless. But if, as in most Latin America, the food insecure live mainly in the cities and shanty towns, policy should aim mainly at lowering food prices, preferably through schemes targeted on the urban poor. If the numbers are large and the administrative costs of operating tightly controlled schemes are excessive a feasible approach could be to lower import prices of foods consumed mainly by the poor.

The main message of recent research on the alleviation of hunger is that a common sense approach which sees the existence of hunger as necessarily implying that a decline in food availability in the country is the cause can be misleading and dangerous. True it is often associated with a decline in food output per head as has been the case in the Sahel. But this is because in Africa food production is not just the main source of food supply but is also the livelihood for large sections of the population. In other developing countries food output has fallen even more without any sign of famine, e.g. between 1970-81, 24 per cent in Algeria, 29 per cent in Hong Kong, 30 per cent in Jordan and 38 per cent in Trinidad and Tobago, (Sen. 1985: World Bank, WDR, 1984, Table 6). As the work of Amartya Sen and others has shown famines can occur even when there is no decline in a country's overall food availability. Possible causes are loss of income through unemployment, a fall in the price of products which the hungry usually sell, or a rise in the price of the food that they depend upon. This has clear implications for policies for transitory as well as chronic hunger.

Dealing with Food Emergencies

Crises arise which lead to famine situations as a result of sudden changes which reduce food supplies, raise food prices beyond the capacity of the poor to pay, or reduce the incomes of the poor. In most of the recent famines war and civil war have also played a role in damaging production and disrupting transport and communications.

National buffer stocks are a frequently recommended policy for stabilising supplies and prices. But in developing countries they are a high cost method [1]. Storage facilities have to be built to a capacity which can hold the maximum required stock. But as buffer stocks rise and fall most of that capacity is unused most of the time. In tropical countries storage losses are high as also are the opportunity costs of capital tied up in stocks. Most countries would find it much cheaper to use exports and imports to balance food surpluses and deficits, relying on commercial or IMF CFF credit to pay for excess requirements of food imports. Even if they have to pay higher than normal prices for cereals when they need imports, over the long run this will normally prove cheaper than domestic stocks. Commercial, government and international stocks of grains and other foods are more plentiful and more widely dispersed than in the past. It is extremely unlikely that a developing country which has accessible ports and its own or borrowed foreign exchange could not now obtain supplies of food without paying an exorbitant cash or political price to obtain it. Recent events (1980/81) have proved the reliability of the trading system (Bale and Southworth, 1982).

Even for land-locked countries domestic buffer stocks should be a last resort. Measures to stabilise domestic production through irrigation and plant protection, together with improvements in information and distribution systems are more cost-effective. Regional co-operation in trade in food can help (Koester, 1985). Improvements in early warning systems which can enable swift identification of the early development of a crisis and the nature of its causes and likely effects are crucial. They would enable early placing of orders for shipments and arrangements for emergency transport systems when these are necessary. If such warning systems cannot be relied upon regional stocks at convenient locations may have to be held.

But even if supplies of food on average are adequate and prices stabilised, groups such as landless labourers, whose employment or wages are depressed by drought conditions, or farmers whose crops have failed or prices fallen, or the urban poor whose jobs have disappeared, need special help. They need income support with payments in cash or kind and if effective work programmes can be mounted - temporary public employment.

AGRICULTURAL PROTECTION

Trade in agricultural products is much more effected by protection than trade in manufactures. Governments justify this in the name of strategic, social and environmental objectives, but as was argued briefly in Chapter 1 most of

271

these objectives could be achieved at much lower cost by alternative policies such as direct income supports and sub-sidies to specific types of agricultural, forestry or other land uses which are deemed environmentally desirable. The attain-ment of self-sufficiency in basic foodstuffs is itself a questionable objective and certainly cannot justify the over-production and dumping of foodstuffs in world markets which is promoted by the European Community's CAP. The effects of agricultural protection are to: (i) raise food prices and tax levels in the industrial countries, (ii) lower international prices for food products, damaging the interests of developed and developing country exporters, (iii) destabilise their world prices. But contrary to the belief of most writers in this field the overall effects on the economic welfare of the developing countries are ambiguous. As the majority of LDCs have, in recent years, become substantial net importers of these foods the effects of such policies as the CAP are to lower the prices of their food imports. On balance, for LDCs as a group the net effects of liberalising food trade may well be adverse to the extent of $1 billion per year at current prices at least in the short term. For the world as a whole the reduction of agricultural protection would bring significant benefits.

The Nature and Measurement of Agricultural Protection

Successive rounds of tariff negotiations within the GATT have lowered tariffs on trade in manufactures to the point where they have ceased to be an important barrier to their trade. Apart from certain areas such as textiles, leather goods, steel, shipbuilding and automobiles barriers to trade in manu-factures are much lower than in the 1950s. The same cannot be said of agriculture (UNCTAD, 1986, Tables 4-6). There, barriers abound. Mostly they take a non-tariff form, save for Japan where tariffs also remain high on food imports (UNCTAD, 1983, p. 45). Tariffs on raw materials tend to be insignificant in all countries (Ibid, p. 46).

The main obstacles to agricultural exports are variable import levies, characteristic in the EC, quotas, quality and hygiene standards, and subsidies to domestic production. Because of their variety and lack of transparency it is exceedingly difficult to measure their effects on trade. Their protective effect in terms of discriminating against imports and switching domestic resources from other activities into agriculture would be best measured by the effective pro-tection rate (EPR). This is the difference in value added at domestic prices and value added at international prices as a proportion of value added at international prices. Value added is the difference between the price of the finished product and the cost of the variable inputs; raw materials, inter-mediate goods and energy. Value added is then the rewards, wages, profits and rent which go to the factors of production. The EPR measures the proportionate increase in the returns to local factors of production as a result of protection including subsidies or tax rebates and also tariffs or subsidies on inputs.

Most attempts to measure protection settle for a much less complete indicator. They simply take the difference between the domestic price and the international price for the same product as a measure of the implicit tariff. This as a proportion of the international price can be called the Nominal Protection Coefficient (NPC). To be meaningful any measure of protection has to allow for location, marketing costs and quality so as to make sure that the price comparison is fair.

Table 6.5 illustrates the very high levels of protection given in European Agriculture and also shows how for livestock fed on grain or other protected inputs, protection can actually become negative, as it does in the Table for UK poultry and eggs. Generally, the EPR is much higher than the NPC and shows just how large are the incentives to European producers to increase output.

While there is no doubt about the high levels of protection to agriculture in the developed market economies of Western Europe and Japan the actual numbers given in any tables must be taken with a substantial pinch of salt. There are several factors which explain the wide variety of estimates which appear in various studies. Firstly they vary greatly from one year to another. This is simply the result of fluctuations in both world prices and domestic outputs. Secondly, in the world of flexible exchange rates which reflect movements of capital more than trade, exchange rates are only by chance at the long run equilibrium level which is appropriate to measurement of protection. Both of these points suggest averaging several years is a sensible adjustment unless the objective is to draw attention to the exacerbation of instability in world prices due to constantly varying levels of protection. Another, practical problem is the sheer difficulty of locating a 'world price' for many commodities. There may be no world market or only one that involves so few buyers and sellers that the prices reached there are no guide to the competitive equilibrium price that is right.

The most serious problem, however, is that the prices in international markets are themselves partly the result of protection. If one is looking merely at a change in the level of protection for a small country this may not matter much. It could have a negligible effect on world prices. But if the question were what would happen if there were a substantial or complete movement towards free trade in agriculture then it would not be legitimate to assume that existing world prices would stay the same. They would certainly rise as production in the protected areas fell in response to reduced incentives.

273

Table 6.5: Protection Rates for Selected Commodities in West Germany and the UK, 1975-77

Protection measure	Commodity (%)							
	Wheat	Barley	Oats	Potatoes	Beef	Pork	Poultry	Eggs
West Germany								
NPC	86	65	49	32	–	75	28	30
EPR	*	*	593	473	–	*	144	150
United Kingdom								
NPC	63	37	36	19	54	35	9	5
EPR	581	158	236	110	833	64	(62)	(62)

Note: Figures in brackets indicate negative protection rates

Source: K. Harling (1983), 'Agricultural Protectionism in Developed Countries: Analysis of Systems of Intervention', Eur. Rev. Agric. Econ. 10:223-47

Levels of Protection

Despite these qualifications some indication of the comparative levels of agricultural protection can be drawn from empirical research. One useful study from Japan calculates nominal rates of protection for most of the OECD nations (Matthews, 1985, p.93). The estimates are shown in Table 6.6. In it the US is clearly the least protectionist while Swiss and Japanese agriculture compete for the label of most protected. The European Community's agriculture is highly protected compared with manufacturing, but apparently no more so than other industrial nations. However, as a large customs union, particularly after the most recent enlargement, the EC causes a great deal of trade diversion in agriculture from low cost producers in the rest of the world to relatively high cost producers within the EC.

Table 6.6: Nominal Rates of Agricultural Protection, Selected Countries, 1955-80

Country	1955	1960	1965	1970	1975	1980
United States	2.3	0.9	7.6	9.8	3.8	-0.1
France	23.8	18.5	21.9	30.6	21.9	22.8
Germany	21.9	28.9	31.9	30.7	26.4	29.6
Italy	29.5	29.9	34.7	37.1	23.3	32.9
Netherlands	10.7	18.1	23.5	25.7	22.4	20.2
U.K.	25.9	25.4	15.9	19.9	5.3	24.3
Denmark	4.3	3.1	4.3	13.9	15.5	19.6
EC	23.3	24.3	28.1	31.5	20.8	26.0
Sweden	23.8	28.7	31.7	36.8	26.8	33.6
Switzerland	34.7	35.5	39.4	45.7	46.5	53.1
Japan	15.0	29.3	40.3	42.1	42.7	45.5

Source: US Department of Agriculture World Agriculture: Outlook and Situation Report March 1984, quoting a Forum for Policy Innovation Research report (Japan) 1983

The Effects of Agricultural Protection

Agricultural protection in the industrial nations raises food prices to their citizens and lowers world prices. Through a variety of incentives in Western Europe and Japan which affect both their revenues and costs farmers are stimulated to raise output and productivity by all means at their disposal. Their net incomes are raised and the prices of their products made more stable. For the rest of the world prices are lowered and made more unstable, lowering farmers' incomes and increasing uncertainty. These effects are likely to lower world output of the affected crops. In terms of absolute magnitude the losses inflicted on world exporters are largest for the main temperate zone agricultural producers: USA, Canada, Australia and New Zealand. But the losses inflicted upon LDC's exporters are also large. Countries which are net importers of food, on the other hand, are better off because world prices are lower than they would be under free trade. As many LDCs are substantial importers of food the net effects of trade liberalisation upon developing countries' welfare are by no means clearcut. It has also to be borne in mind that many LDCs benefit from special arrangements with MDCs for exports. The most obvious beneficiaries are the African and Caribbean countries which have special access to EC markets under the Lome Convention. Liberalisation of trade in agriculture clearly would involve costs as well as benefits to LDCs.

There have been many attempts at quantifying the effects of agricultural protection, or of the effects of liberalising trade in agriculture completely or through some reduction in trade barriers. Fairly complete accounts of the main empirical studies can be found in UNCTAD (1983c) and (1986) and in Matthews (1985). Some of their more important findings are summarised below.

Effects on Consumers

Most studies have concentrated on production and trade effects but the World Bank, World Development Report (1981) p. 33 contains estimates of the costs of the Common Agricultural Policy to consumers in the EC during the 1970s. According to the Bank they had to pay between 1.4 and 5 times the world price for milk powder, 1.5 to 4 times for butter, 2.5 times for soft cheese, double for beef, and 1.5 to 2 times the world price for grains. In addition their taxes paid for subsidies to production and surplus disposal. Altogether the Bank estimated that EC agricultural policies cost consumers about $11 billion in 1976. Such a figure is of course sensitive to the year chosen as when world prices fall the EC protection and subsidies automatically increase. In a year when world prices rise the gap between their average level and EC domestic prices narrows. However, there is no doubt that over the 1970s and 80s EC consumers and tax-payers have paid heavily to support European farming.

Effects on Major Exporters

The effects upon the agricultural exports of USA, Canada, Australia and New Zealand are substantial and a major source of friction between these nations on the one side and the EC and Japan on the other. They have pressed for major changes in both the Kennedy and the Tokyo Rounds of GATT negotiations with little success. They will undoubtedly try again in the next GATT round of multilateral trade negotiations which seem likely to be started in 1987. They would be substantial beneficiaries from liberalisation of agricultural trade as they are the main suppliers of wheat, barley, maize, rice, meat and dairy products. These expectations are borne out by empirical estimates. A joint FAO, UNCTAD study of trade liberalisation on 10 major agricultural products showed net foreign exchange earnings gains of about $3.8 billion to developed country exporters (UNCTAD, 1983c, p.67).

Effects on Developing Countries

This is the aspect which has attracted most investigation and produced a wide variety of estimates. Differences in their approach and assumptions make it difficult to interpret and compare their results. There are three basic approaches; market shares, partial equilibrium and general equilibrium analyses. The first compares the market shares of exporters to the protected area e.g. the EC, before, and sometime after, its formation, comparing their subsequent share with an assumption of constant shares or shares predicted by trends or economic models. The effects of increased protection are assumed to be the difference between the predicted and the actual market shares. Problems are that this residual may be the result of far more than the protection. Income and independently caused price changes would have occurred and affected supply and demand for agricultural exports. In the case of the EC, all the nations which formed it had their own pre-existing systems of protection so that this approach cannot show the effects of liberalisation. The approach takes no account of exports from the EC or of the repercussions in food importing countries. Finally, various studies use different definitions of market shares. The conclusions vary from significantly damaging effects on LDCs from the CAP to negligible effects on LDCs (Matthews, 1985, p. 104; UNCTAD, 1983c, pp. 64-75).

The partial equilibrium approach models each commodity and uses supply and demand elasticities to estimates the changes which would result from the complete or partial reduction of protection. Some studies make no attempt to allow

277

for substitution among commodities resulting from the price changes while others allow for this. If the estimates are made for one commodity at a time assuming ceteris paribus the effects of liberalisation will be exaggerated because of the possibilities of substitution in both production and consumption. To capture all the possibilities, including income effects of the changes requires complex general equilibrium models. The results in terms of magnitude and distribution of the gains and losses to countries are sensitive to the sizes of the elasticities of supply and demand for each country, to the time allowed for adjustment and to whether countries pass on the price changes to producers and consumers.

One very influential study which has used this approach is by Valdes and Zietz (1980). It covered agricultural exports for 56 developing countries and estimated that a 50 per cent cut on OECD nations' tariff and non-tariff barriers would raise their value by $3 billion a year (in 1977 prices). The UNCTAD secretariat comment that this may be an under-estimate of the gains to LDCs because the study excluded a major sugar exporter, Cuba, excluded some products, such as fish, and concentrated on short run responses in LDC production (UNCTAD, 1983, pp. 66-7). But Alan Matthews considers that Valdes and Zietz probably overestimate the likely gains to LDCs from liberalised agricultural trade because they included some exports of processed foods while they excluded dairy products which are a significant import for many LDCs. They appear also to have neglected special preferences for LDCs e.g. under the Lome Treaty. Moreover the current situation differs from the period they studied in that LDCs are now much larger importers of temperate agricultural products and have greater benefits under the GSP (Matthews, 1985, pp. 107-8).

Valdes and Zietz themselves actually arrive at a net income gain for LDCs of only $400 million after allowing for costs of producing the exports and the increased costs of food imports. Some LDCs would be large gainers while others would lose. There would also be income distribution and employment effects which should be considered in arriving at some estimate of the welfare effects.

Four fifths of the export value gains would go to middle-income developing countries. Brazil, Argentina, India, Philippines, Thailand and Colombia share the largest increases. If the increased earnings were passed on to farmers, incomes of relatively poorer sections in LDCs would probably be raised and certainly increased output would create more jobs in rural areas which are socially needed and would reduce income differences between rural and urban dwellers.

Matthews has carried out a similar partial equilibrium study to that of Valdes and Zietz, using more up-to-date information and testing the sensitivity of the results to different assumptions on elasticities and other factors. As his interest is purely on the effects of the CAP on LDCs he confines his analysis to EEC trade with LDCs. He concludes that, depending on the assumptions used, there is a net loss to LDCs from total liberalisation of the CAP of between $0.3 and $1.0 billion (1985, Chapter 7, p. 229). The gainers would be mainly in Latin America and the losers mainly in Africa and Asia including oil exporters. The losses stem from the increased cost to LDCs of food imports and the loss of preferences for their exports in EC markets when trade becomes free. The study is carefully done and the author properly cautions his readers on the underlying assumptions and judgements which lead to this result (Chapter 7, pp. 228-31). As he notes, the results from CAP liberalisation would be more favourable for LDCs if their agricultural sectors were to become much more productive as a result of policy changes or in response to higher world prices. He considers this to be unlikely because domestic policies seem to him to be unlikely to change in the short run, international prices are not generally passed on to LDC farmers or consumers and that in LDCs farmers' aggregate response to prices is in any case rather low, especially in the short run. Moreover, even if energetic policies were undertaken to promote agriculture in LDCs this might still lead to increased food imports because it would raise the incomes of the rural citizens whose income elasticity of demand for food tends to be quite high.

Matthews' arguments are persuasive. But there are one or two counter-arguments to be made. One is that the opportunity cost of resources which would be drawn into both exports and domestic food production in LDCs as a result of liberalising agricultural trade is relatively low. This would be true if there were underutilised labour and even land in many LDCs. Reduced resource costs would raise the benefit to cost ratio from liberalisation. There could also be social gains if increased jobs in the rural areas slowed migration to the towns which has been an increasing and costly characteristic of most LDC economies.

A further possible gain arises from examination of the general equilibrium effects of liberalising the CAP and other protection. In the EC and Japan resources would be released from agriculture and the need to pay for more food imports would force the EC and Japan to sell more manufactured exports at lower prices. This should benefit the majority of LDCs who are net importers of manufactures. A recent general equilibrium study by Burniaux and Waelbroeck (1985) suggests that cheaper manufactures from Europe would improve LDCs' terms of trade and raise their income by 2.9 per cent. But their estimates are on the basis of projections to 1995 and assume that very high levels of protection for European agriculture prevail then. That probably biases their results upwards. A number of other general equilibrium models produce varying results. The only conclusion which

seems to emerge from a survey of them is that they are all
subject to various objections but that 'Regardless of sign, the
impact on LDCs is generally shown to be small' (Matthews,
1985, p. 110).

A very recent study by Tyers and Anderson (1986)
reported in the World Bank's World Development Report (1986)
presents a much more elaborate study of the effects of trade
liberalisation on seven commodity groups: wheat, coarse
grains, rice, beef and lamb, pork and poultry, dairy products and sugar. It is based on a set of supply and demand
equations for the 'world' agricultural economy (thirty
countries or groups of countries). Its results are necessarily
limited by omissions and fairly restrictive assumptions. The
gains and losses which would have occurred with liberalisation
in 1985 in a 1980-82 base are summarised in Table 6.7.

As the study omits tropical products, the net effects on
LDCs from industrial market economy trade liberalisation are
more negative than in other studies (Valdes and Zietz, 1980).
But they show considerable gains from simultaneous liberalisation in both LDCs and the industrial economies for both
groups $18.3 and $45.9 billion respectively.

For the world as a whole the gains from reduced agricultural protection would significantly outweigh the losses. In
the protected countries of Western Europe and Japan lower

Table 6.7: Efficiency Gains from Liberalisation of Selected
Commodities, by Country Group, 1985 (billion of
1980 dollars)

Liberalisation by gains to	MDCs	LDCs	MDCs & LDCs
MDCs	48.5	−10.2	45.9
LDCs	−11.8	28.2	18.3
CPEs	−11.1	−13.1	−23.1
World	25.6	4.9	41.1

Notes: 1. Data are based on the removal of the rates of
protection in effect in 1980-82
2. MDCs, LDCs and CPEs above represent industrial
market economies, developing countries and East
European non-market economies respectively

Source: Tyers and Anderson (Background paper), reproduced in
World Bank (1986), Table 6.8, p. 131

food prices would directly benefit consumers. These benefits would be proportionately greater for lower income groups as they spend a larger proportion of their income on food. The price of agricultural land would be lowered making it easier for the sons of farmers and others to enter the industry, and some land would be released from food production to other uses; housing, forestry, nature reserves. As protection was progressively reduced, falling food prices would ease the inflationary pressures which continue to plague industrial nations despite the highest unemployment levels since the 1930s. In turn, any reduction in Western government's fears of inflation should allow them to increase demand and operate their economies at higher activity rates, increasing growth and lowering unemployment. As resources were shifted from their inefficient marginal agricultural activities into the manufacturing and service sectors of their economies in which their comparative advantage lies the nations' outputs would increase. They would demand more of all kinds of imports. Some of these increased demands would be met by developing countries which are food importers but exporters of anything from oil to manufactures. Such effects, though small, would probably be enough to outweigh the net losses to LDCs which the calculations of Matthews and others show to be, in any case, very small. If reduction in trade barriers included the reduction of tariff escalation on processed raw material and food products this would increase the probability of net gains to LDCs. If that were so then reduction of trade barriers in the field of agricultural products would certainly mean significant net gains for all major groups in the world save the centrally planned economies of East Europe which show little signs of ending their food deficits.

OUTLOOK FOR INTERNATIONAL COMMODITY AGREEMENTS

The outlook for trade in most primary commodities is one of continuing instability and declining real values. That is what emerges from the most authoritative studies and reasonable projections on the state of the world economy for the rest of the 1980s (see Chapters 3 and 4). But even if world economic growth recovers to rates closer to the 1960s changes in the composition of output towards services and continued technical progress in both commodity production and in the user industries seem likely to mean that earnings from the export of most primary commodities will be stagnant or grow very slowly. The fact that the Earth's natural resources are finite does not imply any likelihood of shortages and higher prices in the 20th Century, perhaps not even in the 21st.

While developing countries as a group are now much less dependent on primary exports, the poorest ones, particularly in Africa, continue to depend heavily on them for most of their foreign earnings. For many other low income countries in Asia and Latin America agricultural and mineral exports remain important. The industrially developed nations continue to have an interest in secure and growing supplies of raw materials and in more stable prices for them. What role, if any, are ICAs likely to play in alleviating commodity related problems and achieving the economic goals of both exporting and importing nations?

Stabilising

The survey and analysis of ICAs, both in post-war history and in theory suggest low probabilities for the creation of new or the revival of old ICAs to stabilise commodity prices or exporters' incomes. The reasons are a combination of technical, economic and political. The international buffer stock approach most strongly advocated in the UN's Integrated Programme for Commodities is technically possible only for commodities which are storeable at reasonable cost. This strictly limits the potential number of agreements using this approach and consequently the potential benefits to exporters and importers. But even for those technically possible the economics present very serious problems. For any ICA whether using buffer stocks, quotas or a combination of these, the fundamental problem is to forecast correctly the long term trend in price and to adjust intervention prices so as to keep in touch with it. If they fail to do this, if they fail to detect significant shifts in the trend, or if they fail to adjust to changed rates of growth in demand and supply then in a quota agreement the quotas will be set too high or too low and pressures on producers or consumers to break the agreement will build up and resources will be misallocated. In a buffer stock arrangement the agency controlling stocks runs out of funds or stocks. In our simulation of a buffer stock scheme, where the fundamental economic characteristics of the market are known, a buffer stock authority would find it exceedingly difficult to stabilise price. The proportional increase in stock required to stabilise price in the face of a given downward shift in demand becomes very large and presumably very expensive. This may strain the agreement to breaking point. When there is an upward shift in demand the authority runs out of stocks and fails to stabilise price.

In the real world the market parameters would not be precisely known and in any case can change for various reasons. The target and upper and lower intervention prices would be the outcome of judgement and bargaining between producer and consumer interests. The size of the stock would be limited by financial considerations. If quotas were used their size and allocation would be the subject of disputes between producers and consumers and among producers with different cost situations and different degrees of dependence on the product for export earnings and local employment. Where producing countries have the greater interest in the ICA there will always be a temptation to try to maintain a higher price than can be justified by the equilibrium path for price produced by demand and supply conditions over the long run.

The difficulties and dangers which are likely to afflict even the longest standing ICA are illustrated in the dramatic events surrounding the Sixth International Tin Agreement's failure in October/November 1985 (discussed in Ch. 5).

The failure of the Tin Agreement seems certain to reinforce a more widespread disillusionment with the stabilisation role of ICAs which formed their main rationale. This disillusionment had already revealed itself in the dissatisfaction expressed by Malaysia in the Rubber and Tin Agreements. This led Malaysia and other producing nations in 1982 to move towards independent producer action to raise tin and rubber prices, but with no lasting success. Lack of enthusiasm is also apparent in the laggardly progress in negotiating new ICAs under the Integrated Programme for Commodities and the absence of economic provisions in several of the later ICAs. Lack of support from some major producers, lack of interest by major importing countries, the sheer complexity of the commodity market for products like iron and manganese have made the negotiation of further agreements very difficult.

If the principal objective was macro-economic stabilisation for LDCs then that objective is more efficiently met by the compensatory financing of export fluctuations. Improvement of the existing schemes seems the best route to dealing with such instability. Suggestions for such developments are dealt with in the following section. Better information flows and improved markets as considered above are other ways of assisting price stability.

ICAs to support prices

The motivation of price support has always been a major reason for producer interest in ICAs but of opposition from importing nations. The asymmetric effects of quotas in the Tin and Coffee Agreements probably have held their prices higher than they would have been in free markets but the longer run consequences for tin have been very damaging. For coffee, where price elasticities of demand appear to be very low, the possibility of affecting revenue transfers to producing countries are real. But even here there are risks of promoting increased production in the longer run which will erode the market power of the producers' association. Apart from the tropical beverages and oil there seem to be no major internationally traded commodities which meet the required characteristics for successful action to raise prices.

Numerous studies have confirmed that judgement (Varon and Takeuchi, 1974; Corbet, 1975). Recognition by most producing nations that this is the case is perhaps the major reason for the declining support for ICAs. Improving LDCs' gains from exporting agricultural and mineral products can probably be more effectively achieved through reducing barriers to trade and increasing local processing.

Other Objectives for ICAs

Several recent ICAs have no price intervention provisions. Their activities have been confined to information gathering and dissemination, research, diversification and sales promotion. These have been supplementary objectives of other ICAs. Doubtless ICAs will continue and new ones may be formed with these sort of objectives in mind. It is not obvious that ICAs are required for these activities as existing UN agencies such as FAO, UNCTAD and the IBRD already disseminate such information and are willing to provide countries with technical assistance and finance for projects to diversify out of low return activities in agriculture or mining into more socially profitable activities. They also provide help with export promotion through agencies such as the GATT/UNCTAD International Trade Centre in Geneva. However, if producers and consumers want to share the costs of special organisations devoted to such activities some benefits may be derived from their specialisation and the resources costs are fairly low.

DEVELOPMENTS IN COMPENSATORY FINANCING

The Need for Stabilisation at Both Macro and Sectoral Levels

For many reasons, further improvements in the two existing compensatory financing schemes and the prospect of the establishment of the additional facility are inter-related. Hence to assess the likely developments in compensatory financing, it is important to review critically both the need for improvements in the existing compensatory schemes (i.e. IMF-CFF and EEC-STABEX) and the proposals for an additional facility for assisting LDCs in their stabilisation efforts at both macro and sectoral levels. In such a review, the conclusions of the Expert Group and the views of various governments on the issues are clearly important.

In Chapter 5, it was pointed out that apart from the need for stabilising the overall foreign exchange receipts of a country, there may also be a need for stabilising income and/or price at sectoral level. Empirical evidence in Chapter 4 clearly confirms the view that fluctuations in quantity form the predominant source of earnings instability at sectoral level. This suggests that dealing with the root-causes of quantity variation can stabilise sectoral earnings quite considerably. Furthermore, if enough countries, especially large exporters of a commodity, adopt measures to ameliorate quantity variations, then the world supply will be stabilised and thereby also the world price. Instability of income within sectors can be further reduced by domestic price-stabilisation programmes such as marketing boards and revenue - stabilising schemes such as variable tax rates on export crops and funds for lending to producers.

Neutralising the Effects of Instability versus Reducing Instability

From the point of view of each individual developing country, provided that continued foreign assistance for domestic sectoral stabilisation is assured, there may be little difference between neutralising the effects of instability via sector income stabilisation and eliminating the causes of instability via remedial measures dealing directly with the root-causes of the instability programme: as the adverse effects of instability are neutralised, instability ceases in effect to be a problem. It makes little difference to each sector whether the instability problem is dealt with by removing instability or by rendering it harmless.

However, from the world point of view, it makes some difference whether countries choose to neutralise the effects of instability or reduce unplanned quantity variations. In both cases, stable sector income in the exporting countries would probably (1) stimulate investment leading to a greater supply [this benefits importers at the expense of exporters, through a larger than proportionate fall in price, if demand is price-inelastic] and (b) reduce planned variation in output. In the former case, the neutralisation of the effects of price instability on producers' income reduces the fluctuations of area due to price movements; in the latter case, unplanned output changes are reduced by remedial measures. [This tends to increase both supply and demand and hence raise earnings.] Nevertheless, world supply fluctuations may be reduced much more in the latter case than in the former.

Measures for Reducing Quantity Instability and Foreign Assistance Required

Quantity instability can be reduced by many measures. These can be classified under three groups: (i) measured for stabilising the domestic prices, or ensuring the steady availability, of such inputs as fertilisers, pesticides, fuel, warehouse and market facilities, or transport (ii) measures for stabilising producers' prices and incomes and (iii) measures for stabilising yield fluctuations arising from natural factors such as vagaries of weather and crop disease e.g. irrigation, flood control and plant protection. Only (ii) requires increased expenditure and therefore foreign assistance when export shortfalls occur, (iii) requires steady investment expenditure and (i) requires expenditure which may not move up and down closely with export earnings. In terms of timing, only sectoral income stabilisation appears to require additional foreign assistance at the time of export shortfall. Other remedial measures require foreign assistance unrelated to the timing of shortfalls in the sector concerned.

The Case for Compensation on a Net-basis

However, according to the arguments in Chapter 5, even if the reasons for full compensation of sectoral shortfalls are accepted, there is still no case for an additional facility to compensate shortfalls on a gross-basis as long as the IMF-CFF compensates shortfalls adequately on a net-basis. The proper basis for compensation (in addition to full compensation of shortfalls on a net-basis), has been shown to be total overages net of repayments from the sectors with overages. The compensation rate has to be varied across countries, depending on their marginal propensities to import and multipliers. Moreover, if compensation of sectoral shortfalls is full rather than partial it will destabilise income and imports at the macro level. As was shown in Chapter 5, limiting total sectoral compensation to the amount equal to the net-shortfall means income and imports would be more stable than if total compensation exceeds this amount. Taking into account the needs for stabilisation at both macro and sectoral levels, there is a case for simply compensating aggregate export shortfalls on a net-basis. That is what the IMF-CFF does.

Two Alternative Solutions

This does not mean that there is no need for an additional facility. The CFF, as it stands at present, contains many unnecessarily restrictive features which prevent it from meeting the needs of developing countries for foreign assistance associated with their stabilisation efforts at both macro and sectoral levels. The international community is now faced with the choice between (a) keeping the CFF as it is with only minor improvements but also establishing an additional facility to complement it and (b) making major changes in the features of the CFF so that its assistance is more appropriate to the needs of LDCs.

Further Reforms of the CFF

If the proposal for compensation for shortfalls on a gross-basis can be 'dismissed' on the grounds discussed above, one important argument against alternative (b) is removed. However, other obstacles remain. These obstacles are described by the Group of Experts in the following passage:

> ... the scope for change [in the IMF-CFF] to deal with commodity sector stabilisation would be limited by policy and constitutional limitations on the Fund's operations. These include such factors as quota subscriptions and their distribution and the related drawing rights and limits, repayment rules, non-discrimination among members in terms of access to funds and loan conditions and the undesirability of the extension of conditionality on the use of CFF funds for sector-specific stabilisation activities... (UNCTAD document TD/B/1029, p. 22, paragraph 74).

Two of these obstacles present no problem. At present, there is no restriction on the use of CFF drawings. The use of funds to reduce future sectoral instability is unlikely to be discouraged by the IMF and so there is no reason for that to be a cause of conflict with the requirement for co-operation with the IMF. Provided the potential resources at the disposal of the CFF expand adequately, there is no valid reason for excluding MDCs. In practice, most MDCs have, up to now, refrained from using the CFF allowing it to devote its resources to LDCs.

The removal of quota restrictions on CFF drawings could present a serious problem because it would require some other form of rationing the Facility's limited resources. Of course, simply increasing IMF quotas in line with the expansion in world trade would meet that objection. But this would involve an increase in the amount of aid-transfers associated with CFF loans because of their concessional interest rate (at present 6.6 per cent compared to current market rates of 10 to 14 per cent).

For the CFF to meet adequately the needs for countries for stabilisation at both macro and sectoral levels, it is most important that CFF drawings be made as automatic as possible. In the words of the Group of Experts (p. 17, paragraph 53): 'It [CFF] could play a role in assisting to stabilise commodity sectors if Governments could finance their stabilisation efforts in the firm anticipation of being able to recoup through drawings on the CFF. But since eligibility and the size of drawings are not entirely predictable, Governments would be restrained in undertaking sectoral commodity stabilisation activities based merely on the potential financial assistance from this source.' The predictability of drawings, can be improved if side conditions are dropped and the present shortfall formula requiring judgemental forecasts is replaced by one which uses forecasts which simply entrapolate from past data. To improve the timing of CFF drawings (i.e. giving assistance when it is needed) and to meet the countries' need for medium-term loans (rather than short term) the trend on which shortfall as based should be in real terms and calculated on the basis of a longer series of past data. There is no problem in lengthening the trend if the IMF adopts say the more meaningful UNCTAD shortfall formula as a replacement for its present unsatisfactory formula. For the CFF drawings to be medium-term loans, not only has the trend to be lengthened, but the repayment period has also to be increased from say seven to ten years.

In principle, all obstacles to the reform of the CFF - to turn it into 'an appropriate mechanism' for tackling the instability problems at both macro and sectoral levels - can be overcome if the international community is willing to finance the required improvements. Actually, the amounts required would be small relative to total aid. For example, the interest subsidy associated with the outstanding debt of countries to the CFF of 3.3 billion SDRs in 1981, see Table 5.2, is only about 200 million SDRs. If all these reforms had been carried out in 1964 and total outstanding debt had then increased four-fold, the resulting subsidy in 1981 would still have amounted to less than 1 billion SDRs.

The Establishment of a New Facility

If, for institutional, political or practical reasons, it is not feasible to make the above changes in the features of the CFF, then there is a prima facie case for an additional facility. To meet a balanced need for stabilisation at both macro and sectoral levels, this facility should provide compensation for shortfalls on a net-basis (not gross-basis) and should have a number of appropriate features, which should be obvious from earlier discussion (e.g. the shortfall should be measured around a real, long-term trend; compensatory loans should be fully predictable in terms of size and eligibility, etc.).

In assessing the burden on the international community associated with such a facility, it is important to distinguish between paid-in capital which should be sufficient to cover the total subsidy resulting from compensatory loans being charged at a concessional interest rate and callable capital (a form of government guarantees) which should cover the total outstanding debt of the facility to the financial markets. While paid-in capital represents government grants transferred to the facility, callable capital involves no transfer, except when the facility fails to recoup funds from debt-defaulting countries. In subscribing callable capital, each government bears a proportion of the risk (of default) associated with compensatory loans to the beneficiary countries. The financial burden associated with a given amount of callable capital is equivalent to an insurance premium required for insuring an equal amount of loan to the eligible countries against the risk of their default. Thus, for example, if the expected average annual loss due to default is 1 per cent, then the equivalent annual financial cost of a $14 billion of callable capital (i.e. the estimated callable capital for the UNCTAD facility for 1981, after 5 years of operations) is $140 million.

So far, we have examined in logical terms the rational choice facing the international community concerning the various approaches for assisting developing countries in their efforts to stabilise aggregate income, and imports and sectoral earnings. Examination of the link between the assistance required from the facility and the stabilisation effort of the countries suggest the features which an improved CFF should possess. However, what happens may depend more on politics in the MDCs and the resistance of pressure groups within them than on the rationale of each approach.

The Views and Attitudes of the Governments

For example, under a different government, the United States not only supported a new commodity-related facility but also proposed its substitution for the present IMF-CFF in 1975. The present US government has opposed a new more liberal facility on the following grounds: (a) that it 'is likely to promote delay in correcting domestic economic policies which contribute to poor performance in export sectors', (b) that it is deficient because it does not deal with 'commodity shortfalls in an over-all balance-of-payments context' and disregards the nature of the causes of such shortfalls; (c) that it contains 'concessional elements which are inappropriate for balance of payments financing' and bears 'close resemblance to aid programmes, but with greater automaticity'; (d) that it 'would involve a duplication of existing activities which would dilute the effectiveness of already established institutions' and (e) that it entails 'a significant financial obligation which is presumed to be undertaken mainly by the industrial countries', each of which is experiencing 'domestic budgetary constraints which severely limit the availability of resources for expansion of existing facilities or establishment of new ones'. The US government concluded that 'complementary financing along the lines that have been proposed would conflict seriously with the objectives and modalities for temporary balance of payments assistance already available', tend to 'undermine the international monetary system' and would unlikely attract financial resources in the amounts required in the present economic climate. It maintained, '... given the deficiencies, chanelling scarce Government resources to a new facility would be a particularly inappropriate policy'.

Because of the importance of the US influence in international decision making it is useful to comment briefly on

289

each of these grounds for opposing the new facility. Ground (a) may be valid for a small number of countries but is not valid generally. Ground (b) is in part not applicable to the facility as 'proposed' by the Expert Group. Ground (c) overlooks the fact that existing CFF drawings already contain a significant interest subsidy, higher in fact than the rate proposed for the new facility. In fact, some MDCs governments which expressed support for the idea of a new facility in 1983 (e.g. Finland, Sweden) now opposed any transfer of real resources via subsidised interest rates. Ground (d) is an argument for the adoption of a means for dealing with double compensation rather than for not establishing a new facility (e.g. the coexistence of CFF and Stabex has already focused attention on the problem of avoiding double compensation). Finally, ground (e) is unquestionably valid and important. It may be the critical one responsible for delay or failure to reach agreement on the establishment of a new facility.

In view of the great reluctance of most governments to ratify any agreement which involves their contribution of vast sums of paid-in and callable capital, there may be a greater chance for an improved IMF-CFF, financed from proceeds of IMF gold sales and medium-term borrowing, without government contributions, than the creation of a new facility financed by government grants and government guaranteed borrowing.

Although the present US administration may be reluctant to see a substantial increase in the CFF resources, a lowering of conditionality and an increase in the automaticity of CFF drawings, it has in principle no reason for opposing such a move because none of its stated grounds against the establishment of a new facility really applies to the reform of the CFF along the lines proposed. Perhaps with sufficient political pressure from other governments, the US government could be persuaded to accept such a reform of the CFF.

A quick glance at Table 5.3 (Chapter Five) shows that the majority of MDCs, which supported the idea of a new complementary facility [to 'top up' the CFF], favoured the restriction of its access to the least developed countries, very poor countries and countries heavily dependent on commodity exports rather than all developing countries. Given that a new facility, if it ever comes into force, will probably have very limited resources, the proposed restriction of access to poor countries heavily dependent on commodity exports certainly makes good sense. As far as the MDCs are concerned, the prospects for agreement on the proposed additional facility would vary inversely with the size of its financial requirement. Although a new facility for all developing countries appears unlikely there is some ground for optimism for a scheme for a group of small and poor LDCs. Such a scheme could have better features than Stabex and a wider country coverage but like Stabex still involve relatively small resources. It is doubtful that the majority of LDCs, excluded from access to such a scheme, would show much genuine interest in it. Hence, like Stabex, a scheme with such a restricted access would have to be financed almost wholly from the contributions of MDCs' governments.

Despite the existence of Stabex which relates transfers to shortfalls on a gross-basis, all proposals from MDCs' governments support compensation related to shortfalls on a net-basis, i.e. shortfalls in the total export earnings of the commodities covered. However, some governments object to compensation on a gross-basis for wrong reasons. For example, the government of Canada (TD/B/1-29/Add. 1, p. 8, para. 34/5) questioned 'how these countries, unable to save to stabilise their earnings, will be able to save to pay back loans' and maintained: 'From the point of view of the development of recipient countries, a commodity-specific approach of compensatory financing could have major drawbacks by reducing the incentive for diversification, further processing and necessary economic adjustment. It could also discourage commodity producers in developing countries from responding adequately to the market signals of individual commodity markets'.

Since the points made by the Canadian government may raise undue doubts regarding the capability of LDCs to repay loans and benefits of sectoral stabilisation, it is important that each point raised by the government of Canada should be dealt with. Consider the first point, suppose a country provides full compensation for the shortfalls in each sector's income and borrows from the CFF and the new facility an amount exactly equal to the excess of its imports over exports (which is equal to net shortfall plus gross overage minus total repayment from sectors, other things being equal), then it can be shown that provided the rules of the domestic schemes for compensation and repayment (and interest charges) are the same as those applied by the international schemes, the country can repay the amount expected from it by using the excess of exports over imports in years when total imports are above trend. If the country receives foreign assistance in excess of need (in shortfall years), then whether it can fulfil its repayment obligation or not depends on the uses to which the excess foreign exchange is allocated and their yields in terms of foreign exchange over time. To save to stabilise earnings (i.e. to build up foreign exchange reserves in anticipation of need) may impose a bigger burden on LDCs than to save to repay loans (incurred as the need arises in the process of earnings stabilisation).

As far as the second point of the Canadian government is concerned, it can be pointed out that sectoral stabilisation in principle does not alter the trend of price or long-term profitability which is based on long-term comparative advantage. Hence it would not discourage diversification or further processing, which are based on long-term return considerations. Insofar as it reduces diversification based on risk associated with export instability, it may increase the country's trade gains, because the reduction of such diversification may lead the country to produce more of the commodities in which it has a comparative advantage.

Improvements in Stabex

So far we have discussed only the prospects for improvements in the CFF and the establishment of a new additional facility. Let us turn now briefly to the Stabex. The developed countries in the EEC have clearly recognised the need for assisting the least developed countries (whether they are ACPs or not) in their stabilisation efforts. Hence, unless a new facility in fact comes into force in the near future, the resources of the Stabex would be likely to be increased substantially in nominal terms and moderately in real terms. It is possible that country coverage and commodity coverage would be further expanded and the basis for compensation, which is at present only exports of certain commodities to EEC, may be extended to cover all destinations. Although the shortfall formula is unsatisfactory, the repayment terms are sufficiently generous, so that it is unlikely that these particular Stabex features would be changed. If a new facility with important concessional terms to the least developed countries is established, then the EEC may redirect their resource-transfers from Stabex to other aid-programmes and allow Stabex's resources at least to decrease in real terms.

Prospects of Compensatory Financing: Concluding Remarks

In short, although the new additional facility for all LDCs as 'proposed' by the Group of Experts contains desirable features which few governments, including that of the United States, could object to, it is most unlikely that it will ever come into force, because of the reluctance of governments to accept the need for a new institution or to make large capital contributions to it. A new facility, with access restricted to the least developed countries and other low income countries, with large concessions (to be financed out of total aid resources of MDCs), has a fair chance of being established since the total resources involved are probably small. There will certainly be further improvements of the IMF-CFF along similar lines as in the past. It remains most doubtful that the CFF's resources in real terms will be raised substantially. However, with sufficient pressure from developing countries, CFF drawings can become larger in real terms and more predictable in size and eligibility, especially if LDCs insist on this as a condition for abandoning the demand for a new facility. To make CFF drawings predictable requires a replacement of the IMF shortfall formula, with all its draw-backs, by another which involves no arbitrary forecasts of future values. Without the new facility, Stabex's real resources and scope of operations will probably also expand steadily. A new facility, involving no transfer of resources and viable in the commercial sense, is (though theoretically sound and attractive to MDCs) unlikely to be considered seriously in practice through lack of LDCs' general support.

PROSPECTS FOR PROCESSING OF COMMODITIES IN DEVELOPING COUNTRIES

There appears to be widespread international acceptance of the need to expand processing of raw materials in developing countries. A resolution to establish a framework of inter-national co-operation, for expanding in LDCs the processing of primary commodities before export was adopted at UNCTAD V without dissent. Underlying the widespread interest in the processing of the raw forms of commodities in LDCs are the beliefs that developing countries have a potential comparative advantage on processing the raw forms of commodities they produce and that they can expand their foreign exchange earnings considerably by exporting processed forms rather than raw forms. Industrialisation based on each country's resource endowment has been regarded as the only main route for development for many LDCs. For example, according to a Norwegian Government Report (1975, p. 52), if LDCs are to have any hope of escaping their unfavourable economic situation, 'they must work their way out of their position as unilateral suppliers of raw materials, develop and diversify their economy and to a greater degree achieve control over and process their own natural resources'. The main economic objective of LDCs is a self-sustaining process of growth and to achieve this, aid alone is insufficient. It has to be supplemented by trade if LDCs are to achieve the goal of long-term self-sustained development.

LDCs have made slow progress in the processing of raw materials for export. Partly this is because of all kinds of barriers, i.e. trade barriers (tariff and non-tariff barriers raised by governments), entry barriers (resulting from the operations of transnational corporations' (TNCs) market structures, economies of scale) partly because of the more general obstacles which exist in many LDCs such as lack of general and specific skills required for processing primary commodities or faulty incentive structures. The future prospects of increased processing of commodities for export in LDCs depend largely on the extent to which these barriers and other problems can be removed, reduced or surmounted. Removal of barriers depends crucially on the co-operation of the governments of MDCs. Although MDCs are committed to assist LDCs under various agreements such as the Charter of Economic Rights and Duties of States, the Declaration of the Establishment of a New International Economic Order and The Resolution on Development and International Economic Co-operation, it is still most unlikely that as a disunited group LDCs could obtain the necessary co-operation from MDCs to remove or reduce barriers to primary processing, largely because those MDCs which can do the most to help (in terms of the reduction of tariff and non-tariff import barriers and the regulation of TNCs by anti-trust laws) may be the least willing to do so, as they face the greatest sacrifices and difficulties involved in adjustment to an expansion in LDCs' exports of processed commodities.

Citizens in a country may identify their self-interest with their country's national interest or can be compelled to. In their relationships with one another, they usually observe the moral code of fairplay. But governments frequently do not identify their national interest with that of the world. In their negotiations with one another, the principle of fairplay generally prevails only when their national interests are not adversely affected. Within their own countries governments often seek to assist poorer and weaker sections of their community by redistributive measures through progressive taxes, social services and guaranteed farm incomes or measures to control the abuses of power such as anti-trust laws. But these same governments have made few efforts to support similar measures at world level. For example although many countries control monopolies and restrictive trade practices in their domestic markets, exporting is often exempted, i.e. anti-trust laws aim to protect citizens but not foreigners. Those governments which care less for the poorest and weakest people in their community, in their drive for efficiency and growth, may care even less for the poor and the weak in other countries.

Unless LDCs can arouse the conscience of the MDCs, persuade them it is their own interest, or produce a credible threat strategy, the MDCs are unlikely to reduce their barriers and substantial progress is unlikely to be made in LDCs' processing of their own primary commodities.

Documents produced by UNCTAD pinpoint the obstacles facing LDCs in their efforts to process their raw materials and show how these obstacles can be overcome with minimum sacrifices and resistances on the part of MDCs and TNCs. Since UNCTAD is not a Third World institution with its own secretariat, its documents cannot propose suitable collective strategies for LDCs to follow. However, while knowledge of the means of overcoming barriers is by itself insufficient, it is necessary. The series of studies on commodity processing and marketing produced by the UNCTAD constitute a useful source of information and providing insights into the problems facing LDCs in their attempts to industrialise via commodity processing.

As is common to all attempts at empirical investigation, these UNCTAD studies are not free from weaknesses in data and methodology, so governments who are worried about the effects of faster expansion of commodity processing in LDCs on their industries can adopt delaying tactics to avoid the embarrassment of either appearing unco-operative or rousing domestic opposition. They can delay serious inter-governmental discussion on the issue by simply complaining about these defects in the studies. The UNCTAD secretariat, while genuinely anxious to see their past efforts to help LDCs bear fruit, could do little to counter such tactics as it finds it difficult to resist the demands for more and better information. It is worth noting that governments had far less information on the earnings stabilisation issue when either the IMF-CFF or EEC-STABEX was established than they now have on primary commodity processing in LDCs.

Recent Progress in LDCs' Processing of Commodities

Available evidence shows that the commodity imports of MDCs from LDCs were much more concentrated on raw forms than those from other sources and that there has been little progress in LDCs' processing of raw materials for export. Table 6.8 gives the percentage shares of different stages of processing in MDCs' imports from LDCs and from all origins, and the percentage shares of LDCs' in MDCs' imports of each commodity, at each processing stage for the years 1970-72 and 1978-80. It can be seen from Table 6.8 that the share of raw forms in total imports of MDCs for these commodities from LDCs averaged 65 per cent in 1970-72 and 58 per cent in 1978-80, while those from all origins were 42 per cent in 1970-72 and 38 per cent in 1978-80. Furthermore, the shares of LDCs' in MDCs' total imports for those commodities were, at raw form stage, 51 per cent and 49 per cent and at all processing stages 33 per cent and 32 per cent in these two periods respectively. These figures provide an alternative illustration of the slow overall progress in LDCs' processing of raw materials for exports.

However, the degrees of concentration of imports in raw form from LDCs for these commodities and the changes in these degrees vary considerably for different commodities. For example, coffee, rubber, manganese, phosphates and tobacco had over 90 per cent of MDCs' imports from LDCs in raw form; whereas tin, copper, leather and jute had under 30 per cent. Under one-quarter of these commodities had a share of raw form under 50 per cent. By 1978-80, the raw-form shares of coffee, rubber and tobacco remained over 50 per cent but those of manganese and phosphates fell to 86 per cent. Tin, leather, jute, copper and lead had mixed fortunes

Table 6.8: The Structure of Developed Countries' Imports of Selected Commodities in Raw and Processed Forms from Developing Countries and the World; averages 1970-72 and 1978-80

Product by stage of processing	Percentage distribution of imports by stage of processing				Market share of developing countries (%)	
	Average 1970-1972		Average 1978-1980		Average 1970-72	Average 1978-80
	From developing countries	Total imports	From developing countries	Total imports		
FOODS AND BEVERAGES						
Cocoa						
1. Cocoa beans (0721)	83.2	53.0	73.6	46.7	98.2	97.5
2. Powder (0722)	1.3	3.5	2.9	7.0	22.5	26.0
3. Butter and paste (0723)	14.9	18.5	17.7	20.6	51.0	53.1
4. Chocolate (073)	0.6	25.2	5.8	25.7	1.4	13.9
Total value	711	1 137	3 707	5 993		
Total market share					62.5	61.9
Coffee						
1. Green, roasted (0711)	97.9	94.4	96.2	92.7	97.9	95.3
2. Extracts, essences (0713)	2.1	5.6	3.8	7.3	35.1	48.2
Total value	2 904	3 077	11 624	12 660		
Total market share					94.4	91.8

Copra						
1. Copra (2112)	59.6	55.3	24.9	23.5	98.3	99.5
2. Coconut oil (4223)	40.4	44.7	75.1	76.5	82.5	91.8
Total value	292	320	862	921		
Total market share					91.3	93.6
Fish						
1. Fresh, simply preserved (031)	86.7	78.3	87.1	83.4	29.3	37.1
2. Prepared (032)	13.3	21.7	12.9	16.6	16.2	27.5
Total value	712	2 6924	017	11 324		
Total market share					26.5	35.5
Fruit						
1. Fresh (051)	86.3	76.2	77.0	72.8	41.1	39.3
2. Preserved (053)	13.7	23.8	23.0	27.2	20.8	31.5
Total value	1 463	4 034	4 437	11 934		
Total market share					36.3	37.2
Groundnuts						
1. Groundnuts (2211)	54.3	58.8	32.3	56.5	68.8	27.6
2. Groundnut oil (4214)	45.7	41.2	67.7	43.5	82.6	75.1
Total value	280	276	424	878		
Total market share					74.5	48.3
Meat						
1. Fresh, frozen (011)	77.2	81.6	71.8	85.6	20.7	9.8
2. Prepared (013)	22.8	18.4	28.2	14.4	27.2	22.9
Total value	1 057	4 820	1 712	14 632		
Total market share					21.9	11.7

Table 6.8: (continued)

Product by stage of processing	Percentage distribution of imports by stage of processing				Market share of developing countries (%)	
	Average 1970-1972		Average 1978-1980		Average 1970-72	Average 1978-80
	From developing countries	Total imports	From developing countries	Total imports		
Palm kernel						
1. Palm kernel (2213)	64.5	53.6	22.4	20.0	100.0	98.3
2. Palm kernel oil (4224)	35.5	46.4	77.6	80.0	63.5	85.3
Total value	93	112	255	290		
Total market share					83.0	87.9
Sugar						
1. Raw beet and cane (0611)	54.7	50.9	50.7	45.0	64.2	59.5
2. Refined (0612)	45.0	41.5	48.2	40.6	64.7	62.8
3. Sugar preparations (062)	0.3	7.6	1.1	14.4	2.5	4.0
Total value	1 264	2 116	2 455	4 647		
Total market share					59.7	52.8
Tobacco						
1. Unmanufactured (121)	96.1	79.7	94.4	68.3	33.7	44.5
2. Manufactured (122)	3.9	20.3	5.6	31.7	5.5	5.7
Total value	405	1 446	1 471	4 565		
Total market share					28.1	32.2

Vegetables						
1. Fresh (054)	88.4	72.7	86.6	72.6	27.9	29.3
2. Prepared, preserved (055)	11.6	27.3	13.4	27.4	9.8	12.0
Total value	569	2 482	2 035	8 283		
Total market share					22.9	24.6
AGRICULTURAL RAW MATERIALS						
Cotton						
1. Raw cotton (2631)	45.6	24.4	16.3	11.9	69.7	52.0
2. Cotton yarn (6513)	4.0	4.2	7.6	6.2	35.3	46.4
3. Cotton fabrics (652)	13.6	22.2	10.8	19.0	22.8	21.5
4. Clothing (8411/8412)	36.8	49.2	65.3	62.9	27.8	39.4
Total value	2 213	5 943	9 829	25 928		
Total market share					37.2	37.9
Jute						
1. Raw jute (264)	29.7	26.5	13.3	11.1	92.0	87.2
2. Fabrics (6534)	62.0	59.0	58.9	53.9	86.2	79.6
3. Bags and sacks (6561)	8.3	14.5	27.8	35.0	46.7	57.7
Total value	424	517	511	702		
Total market share					82.0	72.8
Leather						
1. Hides and skins (211)	27.6	20.5	9.8	14.6	24.3	15.6
2. Leather (611)	34.1	18.8	25.7	15.6	32.7	38.4
3. Leather goods (612/831/851)	38.3	60.7	64.5	69.8	11.4	21.4
Total value	699	3 875	3 951	17 014		
Total market share					18.0	23.2

Table 6.8: (continued)

Product by stage of processing	Percentage distribution of imports by stage of processing				Market share of developing countries (%)	
	Average 1970-1972		Average 1978-1980		Average 1970-72	Average 1978-80
	From developing countries	Total imports	From developing countries	Total imports		
Rubber						
1. Natural rubber (2311)	98.0	34.4	90.6	29.6	96.4	97.9
2. Rubber products (629)	2.0	65.6	9.4	70.4	1.0	4.3
Total value	743	2 195	2 901	9 070		
Total market share					33.8	32.0
Sisal/Henequen						
1. Fibres (2654)	68.4	37.9	30.9	14.7	97.1	97.5
2. Cordage and manufactures (6556)	31.6	62.1	69.1	85.3	27.4	37.4
Total value	98	182	249	539		
Total market share					53.9	46.2
Wood						
1. Wood in the rough (242-2421)	60.9	30.6	55.0	28.6	52.8	52.7
2. Wood, shaped and plywood (243/631)	36.1	62.3	40.9	62.0	15.4	18.1
3. Manufactures (632)	3.0	7.1	4.1	9.4	11.1	12.0
Total value	1 786	6 742	6 783	24 744		
Total market share					26.5	27.4

MINERALS AND METALS

Aluminium						
1. Bauxite (2833)	41.7	12.1	33.5	8.4	73.3	71.8
2. Alumina (5136)	38.9	25.4	36.8	26.8	32.5	24.6
3. Unwrought aluminium (6841)	17.4	38.3	25.8	35.5	9.7	13.0
4. Wrought aluminium (6482)	2.0	24.2	3.9	29.3	1.7	2.4
Total value	660	3 110	2 344	13 100		
Total market share					21.2	17.9
Copper						
1. Ores, concentrates (2831)	15.5	13.3	29.4	17.8	55.4	68.2
2. Unwrought alloys (6821)	83.6	69.1	68.7	52.6	57.3	53.7
3. Wrought alloys (6822)	0.9	17.6	1.9	29.6	2.5	2.6
Total value	2 359	4 978	4 684	11 395		
Total market share					47.4	41.1
Iron						
1. Ores, concentrates (281)	81.6	23.7	67.1	19.0	46.6	44.7
2. Pig iron (671)	10.3	7.4	17.5	9.1	18.7	24.4
3. Steel ingots (672)	1.1	9.5	3.4	11.3	1.6	3.8
4. Rolling mill products (673 to 676)	6.9	56.5	11.7	57.2	1.7	2.6
5. Special steel products (677)	0.1	2.9	0.3	3.4	0.3	1.2
Total value	1 771	13 110	4 841	38 220		
Total market share					13.5	12.7
Lead						
1. Ores, concentrates (2834)	53.7	33.8	64.9	35.3	40.4	44.4
2. Unwrought alloys (6851)	45.5	63.9	34.7	62.1	18.0	13.5
3. Wrought alloys (6852)	0.8	2.3	0.4	2.6	9.1	4.0
Total value	121	477	467	1 936		
Total market share					25.4	24.1

Table 6.8: (continued)

Product by stage of processing	Percentage distribution of imports by stage of processing				Market share of developing countries (%)	
	Average 1970–1972		Average 1978–1980		Average 1970–72	Average 1978–80
	From developing countries	Total imports	From developing countries	Total imports		
Manganese						
1. Ores, concentrates (2837)	93.0	60.2	86.0	48.1	56.6	46.7
2. Ferromanganese (6714)	7.0	39.8	14.0	51.9	6.4	7.1
Total value	129	352	257	984		
Total market share					36.7	26.1
Phosphates						
1. Rock (2713)	91.9	82.5	86.2	73.5	61.1	63.2
2. Phosphoric acid (51335)	2.2	6.7	8.1	14.1	18.2	31.1
3. Phosphate fertilisers (56129)	5.9	10.8	5.7	12.4	30.2	24.6
Total value	270	492	1 075	1 994		
Total market share					54.9	53.9
Tin						
1. Ores, concentrates (2836)	18.7	18.3	10.3	11.0	84.5	77.9
2. Unwrought alloys (6871)	81.3	80.3	89.1	86.3	83.9	85.7
3. Wrought alloys (6872)	–	1.4	0.6	2.7	–	18.8
Total value	524	633	1 944	2 343		
Total market share					82.8	83.0

Zinc						
1. Ores, concentrates (2835)	76.1	47.9	76.4	43.7	34.7	31.2
2. Unwrought alloys (6861)	21.3	48.2	23.0	50.1	9.7	8.2
3. Wrought alloys (6862)	2.6	3.9	0.6	6.2	14.3	1.8
Total value	155	710	324	1 830		
Total market share					21.8	17.8
TOTAL VALUE	21 702	65 928	73 163	225 926		
Percentage in raw form	65	42	58	38	51	49
Market share: raw form					33	32
Market share: Total						

Source: United Nations Commodity Trade Statistics, Series D

while the raw form share of tin, leather and jute decreased from 19 per cent, 28 per cent and 30 per cent, respectively in 1970-72 to 10 per cent, 10 per cent and 13 per cent respectively in 1978-80, that of copper doubled over the same period, from 15 per cent to 29 per cent and that of lead, from 54 per cent to 65 per cent. Apart from leather, the most dramatic decreases in the raw-form shares were for palm kernel and cotton: their shares were 64 per cent and 46 per cent respectively in 1970-72 and fell to 22 per cent and 16 per cent in 1978-80. The proportion of commodities with a share of raw form under 50 per cent increased from one-quarter to two-fifths.

There was also considerable variation across commodities in the changes in the market shares of LDCs at semi-processed and full-processed stages. The commodities with favourable expansion in LDCs' market shares in semi or full-processed forms are coffee extracts and essences (35 per cent, 48 per cent), prepared fish (26 per cent, 31 per cent), palm kernel oil (63 per cent, 85 per cent), cotton clothing (28 per cent, 39 per cent), leather goods (11 per cent, 21 per cent), sisal goods (27 per cent, 37 per cent), chocolate (cocoa) (1 per cent, 14 per cent) and phosphates acid (18 per cent, 31 per cent). [Percentages in brackets represent market shares for 1970-72 and 1978-80 respectively.] Those in which LDCs had substantial decreases in market shares were three minerals: lead unwrought alloys (18 per cent, 13 per cent), phosphate fertilisers (30 per cent, 25 per cent) and zinc wrought alloys (14 per cent, 2 per cent) and two non-minerals: prepared meat (27 per cent, 23 per cent) and groundnut oil (83 per cent, 75 per cent).

The shares of raw forms in total imports of MDCs from LDCs in value terms tend to overstate the extent of processing in LDCs. For example, according to UNCTAD secretariat estimates (TD/B/C.1/253, p. 4, Tables 1 and 2) the percentage shares of raw forms of bauxite, zinc, iron and tin and raw material equivalent of volume of imports of main MDCs (i.e. EEC, USA and Japan) from LDCs were 52 per cent, 84 per cent, 97 per cent and 23 per cent respectively. These percentage shares in volume terms were considerably greater than the corresponding percentage shares calculated in value terms, which were 33 per cent, 76 per cent, 67 per cent and 10 per cent respectively.

Scope for Increasing Export Earnings by Processing Raw Materials

The view that LDCs can increase their export earnings considerably by processing commodities before export gains support from the results for individual minerals exported by LDCs produced by Bosson and Varon (1977). They compared the gross value added that is generated through existing local processing and the gross value added which would have been obtained had the whole production been semi-processed before export. Their results show that in 1970, LDCs obtained less than one-third of the total gross value added which they could have generated locally had they processed their minerals and metals up to the metal import stage before export. This percentage remained almost the same between 1950 and 1970.

The scope for additional gains in foreign exchange earnings by LDCs in the expansion of commodity processing before export is illustrated by the calculations made by the UNCTAD secretariat which are summarised in Table 6.9. Using a method similar to that used by Bosson and Varon, the UNCTAD secretariat showed that local semi-processing before export of the ten listed commodities, up to the stages considered, could raise LDCs' gross export earnings by $27.2 billion a year on the basis of 1975 trade figures, (an increase of 152 per cent). The gains in foreign exchange could be over twice as large once all non-fuel commodities are included in the list, since the ten listed commodities accounted in 1975 for about one-third of LDCs' total non-fuel commodity exports.

Table 6.9 shows that there are large differences between commodities in the potential gains from processing. They are greatest for bauxite, phosphate and natural rubber, where the ratios of additional gross earnings due to processing over the value of exports in raw form are 7.9, 2.6 and 2.2. They are also quite substantial for cotton (1.9), hides and skin (1.7) and non-coniferous wood (1.7), but low for copper (0.42), cocoa (0.21) and jute (0.13) and negligible for coffee (0.04).

For jute and copper there is little scope for increasing foreign exchange earnings by increased processing largely because their shares of imports in raw forms by MDCs from LDCs were already very low (13 per cent and 29 per cent respectively). For coffee or cocoa it is largely due to the relatively small value added in the processing of coffee or cocoa. In fact, despite the very high shares of raw forms in total imports for coffee and cocoa (96 per cent and 74 per cent respectively), efforts for promoting their processing should probably receive a low priority in view of their low impact on total export earnings for the countries involved. Removing the four commodities - coffee, cocoa, jute and copper - from the list of ten commodities considered would reduce the gain in the gross export earnings (attributed to processing) by only $1.8 billion. As the processing of bauxite alone accounted for $10.2 billion of the gains, investigating how to reduce barriers to LDCs' processing of bauxite should be a priority.

The results presented in Table 6.9 should, however, be viewed with caution. They only show 'the potential scope over

Table 6.9: Additional Gross Foreign Exchange Earnings of Developing Countries Through Increased Local Processing of Selected Commodities, 1975 (millions of dollars)

Primary commodity	Value of exports by developing countries	1st processing stage		2nd processing stage		Total additional gross earnings	Ratio of additional gross earnings to value of exports of primary commodities
		Product obtained	Additional gross earnings	Product obtained	Additional gross earnings		
Copper (ore, blister and refined)	2 865	Refined copper	230	Rods, wire, tubes sheets	970	1 200	0.42
Bauxite, alumina aluminium	1 300	Aluminium ingot	4 400[a]	Semi-manufactures (rolling and drawing)	5 800	10 200	7.85
Phosphate	1 480[b]	Superphosphates, phosphoric acids	3 800	-	-	3 800	2.56
Natural rubber	1 525	Sheet, plates, tubes	1 300	Rubber tyres	2 000	3 300	2.16
Cotton	2 091	Grey cotton yarn in bulk	1 300	Woven finished cotton fabrics	2 600	3 900	1.86
Jute	600[b]	Jute fabrics	80	-	-	80	0.13

Hides and skins	480	Finished leather	800	800		1.67
Non-coniferous wood	2 045	Plywood, veneer sheets, etc.	3 400	3 400		1.66
Cocoa	1 605	Cocoa butter and powder	340	340		0.21
Coffee	3 936	Coffee extracts and soluble coffee	170	170		0.04
Total	17 927	-	15 820	11 370	27 190	1.52

a Energy consumption would account for about 40 per cent of these additional gross export earnings if valued at world export prices of oil equivalent energy.

b Includes value of semi-processed products.

Source: UNCTAD secretariat estimates

time for gross gains from processing if all the processing stages listed were undertaken exclusively in LDCs for commodities produced and exported by them' (TD/229/Supp.2, p. 12, para. 25). They do not show net gain figures, which require data on foreign exchange costs associated with processing. These could be substantial in the case of bauxite where energy costs are high. Since bauxite is a high-bulk, low-value commodity, transport costs ought to play an important part in determining its location. But if energy costs are relatively low, a country is likely to have comparative advantage in processing its own bauxite into alumina before export because the share of transport cost on the gross value is much lower for alumina than for bauxite.

These results from the UNCTAD study are supported by the Joint World Bank and Commonwealth Secretariat Study (1983) for individual countries for five agricultural commodities: rubber, tropical hardwood, cocoa, coconut oil and tea and one mineral – bauxite. Of the agricultural commodities, value added and foreign exchange earnings are highest for rubber, followed by tropical hardwood and tea (e.g. tea bags) and relatively low for cocoa and coconut oil.

The net gains in foreign exchange earnings vary considerably across products based on the same raw materials. Of the rubber products, latex products yield between 55 per cent and 369 per cent of the hypothetical f.o.b. value of the rubber used. The net gain in foreign exchange earnings in processing motor rubber tyres are substantial though generally lower and vary considerably for different types of tyre, location of plant and year of production. For hardwood, the gross export earnings of the four major exporting countries of logs – Malaysia, Indonesia, the Philippines and Papua New Guinea – in 1978 (based on these logs) would have increased from the actual $1.8 billion to $3.0 billion, i.e. by 73 per cent if they had processed all the logs before export. By processing cocoa beans into cocoa products, the three major bean exporting countries, Ghana, Nigeria and the Ivory Coast, would have increased their foreign exchange earnings by 22 per cent, 32 per cent and 15 per cent respectively. As for coconut oil, the Philippines – which has an 80 per cent share in coconut oil exports from primary producers – would earn only 7-9 per cent higher for a unit of refined oil than for crude oil. Finally, India and Sri Lanka could have raised the foreign exchange earnings in 1979 by $3.49 and $2.97 per kg of tea respectively by exporting tea in bags rather than in bulk or blended form and by $1.09 and $0.21 respectively by exporting tea instant form rather than in bulk. The f.o.b. value of tea in bulk or in blended form in 1979 was between $1.38 and $1.63.

PROSPECTS AND POLICIES FOR THE 1990s

Barriers to the Expansion of Processing Raw Materials in LDCs

The expansion of processing in LDCs depends not only on their own policies but also on co-operation among LDCs and between LDCs and MDCs. The improvement of trade among LDCs, co-ordination of their investment and marketing, possibly selective restrictions on exports of certain products in raw form and incentives for expanding processing are all important determinants of further expansion in LDCs' commodity processing. Progress requires co-operation among LDCs to produce a well-co-ordinated package of policy measures. Furthermore, by acting together and enhancing their bargaining power, it is easier for LDCs, as a group and individually, to surmount the barriers to primary commodity processing, partly by inducing MDCs and TNCs to lower the trade and entry barriers. Knowledge of barriers and means of overcoming them is insufficient to stimulate expansion of primary processing in LDCs (because such knowledge need not be accompanied by MDCs' co-operation) but it is necessary. Fortunately UNCTAD studies [2] provide a good deal of information on these barriers.

It is useful to distinguish two groups of barriers. One group of barriers is erected by governments of MDCs in the form of tariff and non-tariff measures designed to restrict imports of processed commodities, primarily to protect their domestic producers against efficient external competition. The other group of barriers arise from industrial and market structures and private trade practices. This latter group includes a wide range of constraints and restrictive business practices which limit the access of LDCs, as newcomers, to markets in MDCs, to finance, information and technology.

Trade Obstacles Raised by Governments

Tariff protection in most MDCs against imports from third countries, particularly LDCs, has been increasingly reinforced by non-tariff measures designed to increase the effective protection given to domestic producers against foreign competition. To illustrate the magnitude of the overall effect of these barriers on LDCs' export earnings it has been estimated that the gross export earnings of LDCs would be $24 billion a year higher, by 1985, if all OECD trade barriers against manufactured goods from LDCs were removed [3].

Tariff Barriers

Imports of many products of export interest to LDCs into MDCs are still restricted by relatively high tariffs. Trade negotiations, such as the Kennedy Round and the Multilateral Trade Negotiations, have resulted in a reduction of tariffs mainly on products traded among MDCs. The Generalised

309

System of Preferences (GSP) neither covers all products of export interest to LDCs nor provides unlimited duty-free entry for all the products covered. Consequently, tariffs on the exports of LDCs are now, on average, much higher (by one-half) than those on the exports of MDCs [4]. Furthermore, it appears that one common feature of all tariff schedules of MDCs is that the nominal rates of tariff tend to increase with the degree of processing. For example, the raw forms of some commodities not produced in MDCs are admitted duty free, while progressively higher rates of import duty are imposed on their semi-processed and fully-processed forms. The widespread presence of a positive relationship between the nominal rate of tariff and the degree of processing has generated interest in the concept of effective tariff protection. The effective rates of tariff, not the nominal rates of tariff, are the relevant indicators of the extent of tariff protection afforded to processing industries in MDCs. It can be seen from Table 6.10 that the effective rates of protection are often many times higher than the nominal rates. For example, while the nominal rates for cocoa powder and butter are 1.6 per cent, 18.2 per cent and 12.2 per cent in USA, EEC and Japan respectively, the effective rates in these countries are 11.6 per cent, 126.6 per cent and 98.3 per cent, while the nominal rates for palm kernel oil in USA, EEC and Japan are 3.2 per cent, 8.0 per cent and 6.6 per cent, the effective rates in these countries are 37.5 per cent, 97.2 per cent and 80.0 per cent respectively. Apart from a few exceptions (5 cases), the effective rate increases with processing.

Trade in processed materials has been obstructed by tariff-escalation not only in the developed countries but also in the developing countries. Using a new comprehensive source of statistics on developing countries' tariffs, Laird and Yeats (1986) shows that the extent of the escalation is generally far greater in developing countries than in developed countries. In considering tariff-barriers to processing, the importance of escalating tariffs in developing countries should not be overlooked.

Even non-escalating tariff-structure can produce a significant bias against trade in processed products raw materials. The same tariff rate applied to both finished products and raw materials would reduce the share of finished products in total imports of both finished and primary forms because the demand for finished products is more price elastic than that for primary products. In a survey of empirical studies, Balassa and Kreimin (1976, p. 127) show that the average elasticity of demand for crude (unprocessed) materials in the United States, Canada, the EEC, EFTA and Japan ranged from a low of 0.2 in Canada to 0.39 in the United States, while that for processed products varied from 2.0 in Canada to 4.1 in the United States, suggesting that on average, the elasticities of finished products were about 10 times greater than for their materials. Suppose the price elasticities of demand for processed and raw forms of a commodity are respectively 4 and 0.4, their nominal tariff rates are the same at 20 per cent and their post-tariff trade values exclusive of tariffs are $20 and $80 millions respectively. It can be shown that the pre-tariff trade values of processed and raw forms would be $30 and $72 millions respectively. Hence, a non-escalation tariffs rate of 20 per cent reduces the share of processed products from 29 per cent to 20 per cent because of its higher price elasticity of demand. (Note that the pre-tariff trade value x* can be estimated from the post-tariff trade value x according to the following formula: $x^* = x(1-(1-e).t/(1+t))$, where t is nominal tariff rate and e is price elasticity of demand, e.g. given x, e and t equal 20, 4 and 0.2 respectively, $x^* = 20(1+3(0.2/1.2)) = 30$).

Yeats (1984) presents for 26 processing chains estimates for (neutral) tariffs that would be required if duties were to have an 'unbiased' influence on the import structure for each processing chain - in the sense that the share of each stage in the total trade of the chain remains unaffected by such tariffs. These estimates show that the neutral tariffs for primary products exceed the nominal rates on finished goods for all processing chains. For example, the nominal US tariff rates on cotton raw, yarn and fabrics were 1.9 per cent, 6.8 per cent and 7.4 per cent, for tariffs to have a neutral influence on US import structure, Yeats (1984, Table 1, p. 83) shows that the rates on raw cotton and cotton yarn should be 21.5 per cent and 12.4 per cent.

Thus, a de-escalation in tariffs on the primary and semi-processed stages would in fact be required to avoid any tariff-induced trade bias. In other words, in the attempt by LDCs to increase the shares of semi-processed and processed forms in their total exports of each product chain, even non-escalating tariff structures can be a serious constraint, because a given rate of tariffs tends to have a greater impact on import demand for finished products than for raw forms.

Non-tariff barriers

The common purpose of all non-tariff barriers is to contribute to the level of protection given to domestic producers against imports. Non-tariff barriers can be and have been used to offset the effect of tariff concessions. GATT have identified more than 30 types of non-tariff barriers, which are classified into the following broad groups:

(i)   Specific limitations on trade: quantitative restrictions; export restraints; health and sanitary regulations; licensing; embargoes; minimum price regulations, etc.

Table 6.10: Structure of the Tariff Protection - Nominal and Effective - in Developed Market-economy Countries on Selected Primary and Processed Goods Imported from Developing Countries (Post-Kennedy Round ad valorem rates or equivalent)

SITC heading by stage of processing	USA Nom.	USA Effect.	EEC Nom.	EEC Effect.	JAPAN Nom.	JAPAN Effect
Meat						
011 Fresh and frozen	4.6	4.6	17.8	17.8	6.2	6.2
013 Meat preparations	4.7	5.6	19.5	44.3	16.4	47.3
Cocoa						
072.1 Cocoa beans	0	0	3.2	3.2	3.0	3.0
072.2 072.3 Cocoa powder, butter	1.6	11.6	18.2	126.2	12.2	98.3
073 Chocolate	4.8	1.3	18.0	19.3	35.0	68.6
Leather						
211 Hides and skins	1.1	1.1	0	0	0	0
611 Leather	4.7	12.0	4.8	12.3	11.6	34.7
612.831 (a) Leather goods other than shoes	7.7	11.4	7.3	10.4	11.8	15.0
851 (b) Shoes	16.6	25.3	11.9	19.3	22.9	36.5
Groundnuts						
221 1 Groundnuts	25.7	25.7	0	0	20.0	20.0
ex 421.4 Groundnut oil, crude	24.1	-13.8	7.5	92.5	20.3	27.5
ex 421.4 Groundnut oil, refined	30.0	30.0	15.0	179.7	27.0	27.0

Code	Product						
Copra							
221.1	Copra	0	0	0	0	0	
ex 422.3	Coconut oil, crude	65.4	10.0	66.4	10.0	47.2	5.5
11	Coconut oil, refined	10.0	10.0	186.3	15.0	30.0	30.0
Palm kernel							
221.3	Palm kernel	0	0	0	0	0	
ex 422.4	Palm kernel oil, crude	80.0	6.6	97.2	8.0	37.5	3.2
ex 422.4	Palm kernel oil, refined	8.0	8.0	186.3	15.0	2.4	2.4
Palm oil							
ex 422.2	Palm oil, crude	8.0	8.0	9.9	9.9	0	0
ex 422.2	Palm oil, refined	8.0	8.0	180.0	14.0	0	0
Rubber							
231.1	Natural rubber	0	0	0	0	0	0
629	Rubber products	10.3	6.4	16.3	7.9	6.6	4.6
Wood							
242.2	Wood in the rough	2.3	2.3	1.1	1.0	0	
243	(a) Wood simply worked	8.5	2.9	4.0	1.6	0	0.3
631.2	(b) Plywood	25.4	14.0	19.6	11.3	13.8	8.5
632	Wood manufactures	23.2	11.5	16.3	8.7	13.6	6.7
Wool							
262.1	Wool, raw	0	0	0	0	9.7	9.7
651.2	Wool yarn	14.7	5.0	17.5	5.7	49.5	20.7
653.2	Wool fabrics, woven	21.3	10.0	38.1	16.0	60.9	20.7
ex 841.1(2)	Wool clothing	26.7	15.4	19.2	15.4	2.4	16.6

Table 6.10: (continued)

SITC heading by stage of processing		USA		EEC		JAPAN	
		Nom.	Effect.	Nom.	Effect.	Nom.	Effect.
Cotton							
263.1	Cotton, raw	6.2	6.2	0	0	0	0
651.3	Cotton yarn and thread	10.5	25.0	10.0	32.9	2.8	6.8
652	Cotton fabric, woven	13.8	24.6	12.0	19.1	7.9	17.8
ex 841.1(2)	Cotton clothing	20.0	35.4	14.0	20.8	14.7	27.5
841.4	Cotton clothing accessories, knitted	17.9	35.2	12.1	27.6	19.5	47.1
Jute							
264	Jute, raw	0	0	0	0	0	0
653.4	Jute fabric, woven	0	-0.6	19.6	53.3	20.0	54.4
656.1	Jute sacks and bags	3.6	10.7	15.5	14.0	12.5	2.7
Sisal, Henequen							
265.4	Sisal, henequen	0	0	0	0	0	0
655.6	Cordage	3.6	10.3	10.3	30.6	9.6	28.1
Iron							
281.3	Iron ore	0	0	0	0	0	0
671	Pig iron, ferro-alloys	0.7	0	4.0	3.5	1.9	2.9
672	Steel ingots	6.3	62.2	4.0	1.1	6.4	16.6
673 } 676	Rolling mill products	3.5	-4.8	5.5	11.5	8.9	20.5
677	Other steel products	4.0	6.3	7.5	19.5	7.8	8.6

Copper						
283.1	Copper ore, concentrates	0.3	0	0	0	0	0
682.1	Copper, unwrought	2.3	11.2	5.6	-5.6	7.0	43.1
682.2	Copper, wrought	4.2	5.4	8.0	10.5	17.8	34.9
Aluminium						
283.3	Bauxite	0	0	0	0	0	0
513.6	Alumina	0	0	5.6	11.1	0	0
684.1	Aluminium, unwrought	4.0	6.0	5.8	5.6	10.4	11.4
684.2	Aluminium, wrought	5.9	11.5	12.8	29.3	13.6	29.0
Lead						
283.4	Lead ore concentrates	6.0	0	0	0	0	0
685.1	Lead unwrought	8.3	42.7	7.2	33.8	6.5	29.4
685.2	Lead wrought	10.3	17.7	6.6	7.7	14.9	30.8
Zinc						
ex 283.5	Zinc ore, concentrates	12.0	0	0	0	0	0
686.1	Zinc, unwrought	6.6	2.5	5.8	13.4	6.5	14.8
686.2	Zinc, wrought	3.0	-0.3	8.3	13.0	14.9	30.8

Source: UNCTAD: 'The Kennedy Round. Estimated effects on tariff barriers', (TD/6/Rev.1) op.cit., appendix Table A.

(ii)   Charges on imports: variable levies; prior deposits; special duties on imports; internal taxes, etc.

(iii)   Standards: industrial standards; packaging; labelling and marking regulations, etc.

(iv)   Government interventions in trade: government procurement; stock trading; export subsidies; countervailing duties; trade diverting aid, etc.

(v)   Customs and administrative entry procedures: customs valuation; customs classification; anti-dumping duties; consular and customs formalities and requirements, and sample requirements.

Often one or more non-tariff barriers apply at the same time to the same import product.

Among the product groups subject to non-tariff barriers, the most often affected, in descending order, are meat, cocoa, wheat, barley, corn and rice. It can be seen from Table 6.11 that most of the non-tariff barriers are applied to food products or agricultural raw materials in raw and processed forms. Thus, almost all non-tariff barriers identified in Table 6.11 apply to commodities of export interest to LDCs.

As tariff barriers are reduced, non-tariff barriers appear to grow. Growing non-tariff protectionism also takes all kinds of 'negotiated' forms, e.g. 'voluntary export restraints', 'orderly marketing arrangements', 'organised free trade'. These are often market-sharing arrangements designed to protect ageing and inefficient domestic industries in MDCs against efficient foreign competitors, particularly in LDCs. The major example of these types of arrangements is the Multi-Fibre Arrangement of 1973, extended in 1981. The Arrangement is based on a system of bilateral quotas, which are even more restrictive than before and includes 'trigger levels' for further quotas which limit the scope for diversification of exports into new products. (Gerard Curzon et al., 1981)

Earlier, we discussed how increased in tariff escalations and import demand elasticities rising with the degree of processing may seriously hinder efforts of LDCs to increase the share of processed forms in the total values of their exports. This effort would also be hampered by escalation in the structure of non-tariff measures (NTMs). There is evidence (UNCTAD (1983)) that escalation in NTMs occurs in both developed and developing countries. The frequency indices for volume-restraining measures for 24 products (for different processing stages) of special export interest to developing countries are given in Table 6.12. Out of these 24 product groups, 14 and 5 face escalation and de-escalation respectively in the developed countries and 5 and 11, respectively in developing countries. For developed countries the numbers of NTMs increase for vegetables, fruit, coffee, oils, cocoa, tobacco, rubber, leather, wood, wool, cotton (up to and including yarn), jute, sisal and phosphates and decrease for meat, fish, sugar and aluminium. These figures support the view that developed countries, which are non-producers of the raw materials, are protecting their processing industries against low-cost processors in LDCs which may have a comparative advantage in processing their raw materials.

Protection given to domestic producers which limits imports from LDCs can also take the form of government subsidies to uncompetitive domestic industries. The importance of subsidies can be appreciated by a brief look at their total values in different MDCs. According to UNCTAD document TD/229/Supp. 2 (1979), total subsidies to domestic industries in 1976 amounted $5.1 billion in USA, $3.2 billion in Canada, $7.3 in Japan and $49.0 billion in EEC (of which France, The Federal Republic of Germany and UK accounted for $9.4 billion, $6.8 billion and $6.1 billion respectively).

Other Obstacles Raised by TNCs and Market Structures
Concentration of control through vertical and horizontal integration of operations has erected effective barriers to the entry of LDCs into the international markets for commodities at all processing stages. Restrictive business practices, e.g. cartel arrangements, often bind subsidiaries of cartel members in LDCs in matters relating to price fixing, market sharing and joint marketing and distribution. Although cartel arrangements may also be present in MDCs, they present more serious and widespread problems in LDCs than in MDCs. The adverse effects of such arrangements have been acknowledged by the OECD Committee of Experts on Restrictive Practices in Export Cartels (OECD, Paris, 1974) and Restrictive Business Practices of Multinational Enterprises (OECD, Paris, 1977). Other restrictive practices include not only price setting by a dominant firm in the market but also fixing different prices for the same product for different geographical areas or consumer groups. As mentioned above, these practices are often prohibited by national laws insofar as they affect domestic producers and consumers but not in regard to foreign producers and consumers.

The powerful control of TNCs over production, technology and marketing of many commodities of export interest to LDCs may seriously hinder the expansion of primary processing in LDCs. The extent of TNCs' control is clear and can be illustrated by considering some examples of the proportions of imports to or exports from various MDCs which were on an intra-firm basis (i.e. transfers within each TNC). Related party transactions accounted for about half of all imports into USA in 1977. Available data reveal that intra-firm transactions accounted for 29 per cent of Swedish exports in

Table 6.11: Summary of Non-tariff Barriers Applied by Developed Market-economy Countries on Imports of Selected Processed Commodities of Export Interest to Developing Countries

BTN Code		Non-tariff barriers imposed by		
		EEC[a]	Japan	USA
03.02	Fish, salted in brine, dried or smoked	-	DL	HS
7.04	Dried, dehydrated or evaporated vegetables	R/DL	-	-
8.11	Fruit, provisionally preserved	R/DL	DL	-
11.01	Cereal flours	VL	DL	GQ/BQ
11.02	Cereal groats and meal	VL	DL	GQ/BQ
11.06	Flour and meal of sago, and of manioc, etc.	VL	-	-
11.08	Starches and inulin	VL	DL	-
15.10	Fatty acids, acid oils from refining, fatty alcohols	R/DL	-	-
16.01	Sausages	VL/DL/HS	-	-
16.02	Other prepared or preserved meat	VL/DL/HS	DL	-
16.03	Meat extracts and meat juices	HS/BQ	-	-
16.04	Prepared or preserved fish	BQ	-	-
17.04	Sugar confectionery	VL/R	-	GQ/BQ
18.06	Chocolate and other food preparations containing cocoa	VL/HS	-	BQ
20.01	Vegetables and fruits, prepared or preserved by vinegar or acetic acids	L/BQ/GQ/HS	HS	-
20.02	Other preserved vegetables	DL/L/BQ/GQ/HS	-	-

Code	Description			
20.03	Fruit preserved by freezing, containing added sugar	VL/DL/L/GQ	–	–
20.05	Jams, fruit jellies, marmalades, fruit purée and fruit pastes	VL/DL/BQ/HS	DL	–
20.06	Fruit otherwise prepared or preserved	VL/DL/BQ/GQ/HS	DL	–
20.07	Fruit juices and vegetable juices	VL/L/DL/BQ/GQ/HS	DL	–
22.05	Wine	MP	–	–
22.07	Spirits, liqueurs and other spirituous beverages	R/DL/ST/GQ	–	–
24.02	Cigars and cigarillos	R/ST/DL/BQ/GQ	–	–
41.02	Calf leather	–	DL	–
41.03	Sheep and lamb skin leather	–	DL	–
41.04	Goat and kid skin leather	–	DL	–
53.07	Worsted yarn	DL/GQ	–	XR
53.11	Woven fabrics of sheep's or lambs' wool	DL/GQ	–	XR
55.05	Cotton Yarn	AITT[b]	AITT[b]	AITT[b]
55.09	Cotton fabrics	AITT[b]	AITT[b]	AITT[b]
57.06	Jute yarn	GQ/XR	–	–
57.10	Woven fabrics of jute	XR/BQ/GQ	–	–
58.02	Other carpets and carpeting (not of cotton)	DL/BQ/Q	–	XR
60.02	Gloves, mittens, etc. (not of cotton)	Q	–	XR
60.04	Undergarments, knitted or crocheted (not of cotton)	BQ/Q	–	XR
60.05	Outergarments, knitted or crocheted (not of cotton)	LL/DL	–	XR

Table 6.11: (continued)

BTN Code	Non-tariff barriers imposed by EEC[a]	Japan	USA
61.01 Men's and boys' outergarments (not of cotton)	DL/BQ/Q	-	XR
61.02 Women's, girls' and infants' outergarments (not of cotton)	LL/DL/BQ/Q	-	XR
61.03 Men's and boys' undergarments (not of cotton)	DL/BQ/Q	-	XR
64.02 Footwear with outer soles of leather	-	DL	-
69.11 Tableware of porcelain	DL/BQ/GQ/Q	-	-
73.01 Pig iron	DL/BQ	-	-
73.02 Ferro-alloys	DL/MP[c]	-	-

[a] Restrictions imposed in whole, or in part, by EEC member countries
[b] Trade limited in accordance with the GATT Arrangement Regarding International Trade in Textiles of 1973 (Multi-fibre Arrangement)
[c] On ferro-manganese since January 1978

Symbols: DL: Discretionary licensing; LL: Liberal or automatic licensing; L: Licensing of an unspecified character; BQ: Bilateral quotas; GQ: Global quotas; Q: Quota (method unspecified); XR: Export restraint; VL: Variable levies; MP: Minimum import price; HS: Health and sanitary regulations; R: Restriction unspecified; ST: State trading

Source: UNCTAD, 'Inventory of non-tariff barriers, including quantitative restrictions, applied in developed market economy countries to products of particular export interest to developing countries' (TD/B/C.2/115/Rev. 1 and Corr. 1)

1975, 30 per cent of UK exports in 1973 and 59 per cent of Canadian exports in 1971 [4]. According to Helleiner (1977), the shares of related party transactions in US commodity imports from LDCs in 1975 were 88 per cent for bauxite, 80 per cent for rubber (milk or latex), 68 per cent for bananas and cotton and 32 per cent for total of all commodities.

A useful illustration of limited access of developing countries to markets in developed countries is provided by the case of bauxite and alumina. In a recent study (TD/B/C.1/PSC/19/Rev.1, pp. 43-9) the UNCTAD secretariat concludes: 'Thus, most of the developing country-owned bauxite is being used not to supply the main TNC aluminium producers but either for domestic aluminium industries (Brazil, Yugoslavia, India), for sale to socialist countries (Guyana, Jamaica, Guinea) or for shorter-term sale through trading companies (Guyana - Philip Brothers)' and 'Market access for independent developing country suppliers of alumina seem to be limited at present to socialist countries (Jamaican and Yugoslav contracts) and domestic or regional aluminium smelters.' LDCs do not sell to TNCs or MDCs either because they find it unprofitable to do so or because they cannot do so owing to restrictions imposed by TNCs. This is, though not conclusive, highly suggestive evidence that TNCs restrict market access of LDC producers. The UNCTAD study also presents figures which clearly confirm the high degree of concentration of control in TNCs. Thus of total world capacity excluding socialist countries, six TNCs (Alcoa, Alcan, Reynolds, Kaiser, PUK and Alumisse) have control over 45 per cent for bauxite, 62.5 per cent for alumina and 52.5 per cent for aluminium; whereas the governments of LDCs have control over only 24 per cent, 4.1 per cent and 6.7 per cent respectively and private interests in LDCs, 1.2 per cent, 1.2 per cent and 2.5 per cent respectively for bauxite, alumina and aluminium.

Restrictions on the <u>Transfer of technology</u> are alleged to represent one of the most serious obstacles to the efforts of LDCs to industrialise. In the mineral and metal industries, and to a lesser extent in agricultural processing industries, the technologies involved, together with patents and licenses rights, are largely owned by TNCs. The more stringent the conditions for their transfer, the greater are the entry barriers. The cost of transferring technologies to firms in LDCs are beyond the reach of most of them and substantially reduce their competitiveness in the world market. It has been estimated by the UNCTAD secretariat (UN Publication, Sales No. E.75.II.D.2) that the attainment of an annual expansion in manufacturing output of 8 per cent could lead to a growth of the direct costs of transfer of technologies $1.5 billion in 1967 to $9 billion in 1980. Firms to which technologies were transferred have also been restricted in terms of total export volumes of the products covered to certain markets or

Table 6.12: Volume-restraining Measures Facing the Exports of Developing Countries in Selected Developed Market-economy and Developing Countries. Incidence on Primary and Processed Commodities (percentage)

Commodity	Stage of processing	CCCN[a]	Measures to restrain volume[b]	
			Developed market-economy countries	Developing countries and territories
Agricultural products	primary		25	31
	processed		26	25
Meat	fresh	0201-04,06	49	40
	prepared	1601-03	43	21
Fish	fresh	0301-03	35	47
	prepared	1604-05	31	27
Vegetables	fresh	0701-03,05,06,1204-06,08	39	26
	processed	0704,1103-06,1904,2001-02	48	16
Fruit	fresh	0801-09,0812	20	31
	processed	0810,11,13,2003-07	54	21
Coffee	green, roasted	0901	11	41
	extracts	2102	17	27
Oils	oil seeds	1201	33	45
	oils	1507	56	50
Sugar	raw	1701	78	50
	processed	1701,03,04,05	56	26

Cocoa	beans	1801	—	14
	processed, chocolate	1803-06	14	13
Tobacco	unmanufactured	2401	11	45
	manufactured	2402	22	37
Rubber	natural	4001	—	23
	processed	4005-09,15	6	22
	rubber articles	4010-14,16	14	27
Leather	hides, skins	4101	—	23
	leather	4102-08,10	13	17
	leather articles	4201-05,6401-06	26	24
Wood	rough	4403-04	6	25
	simply worked	4405-07,13	9	25
	manufactures	4408-12,14-28	12	26
Paper	pulpwood	4403	6	27
	papermaking material	4701-02	—	25
	paper products	4801-21	8	29
Wool	raw	5301	—	23
	carded, combed	5305	44	23
	yarn	5306,07,10	57	20
	woven fabrics	5311	72	37
Cotton	raw	5501	6	32
	carded, combed	5504	44	32
	yarn	5505,06	61	43
	woven fabrics	5507-09	57	38
Jute	raw	5703	—	18
	fabrics	5710	33	32
	sacks	6203	44	32

Table 6.12: (continued)

Commodity	Stage of processing	CCCN[a]	Measures to restrain volume[b]	
			Developed market-economy countries	Developing countries and territories
Sisal	fibres	5704	–	19
	cordage	5904–06	56	26
Mineral products				
	primary		8	32
	processed		12	25
Metallic ores		2601	17	41
Iron, steel	semi-processed	7301,02,04,05	10	25
	processed	7306–18	23	36
Copper	unwrought	7401–02	3	18
	wrought	7403–08	3	24
Aluminium	unwrought	7601	39	27
	wrought	7602–06	16	27
Lead	unwrought	7801	6	23
	wrought	7802–05	6	15
Zinc	unwrought	7901	22	23
	wrought	7902–04	9	17
Tin	unwrought	8001	–	18
	wrought	8002–05	–	14

		CCCN (a)	The number of 4-digit CCCN product groups affected by the given NTM	The ratio (b)
Phosphates				
	natural	2510	–	23
	phosphoric acids	2810	–	18
	superphosphates	3108	6	41

(This table is reproduced from Table 3 of UNCTAD (1983))

Notes: (a) CCCN stands for Customs Co-operation Council Nomenclature
(b) The ratio, in percentage forms, of the 4-digit CCCN product groups affected by the given NTM to the total number of 4-digit CCCN product groups in the given product category

Source: UNCTAD data base on non-tariff measures

generally. When the technology was transferred from a TNC to its subsidiary in a developing country, other firms in the country concerned have limited, or no, access to it. LDCs may also lack the skilled manpower required for implementing and maintaining a new technology and the high import costs of technical expertise would reduce further the competitiveness of firms in LDCs intending to enter world markets for processed commodities. (See UNCTAD documents TD/229/Supp. 2, p. 29, para. 57 and TD/B/C.6/1, Annex. III.)

Among the biggest obstacles to the industrialisation process in LDCs, except a few, is the control of TNCs over the supply of some important inputs to processing industries in LDCs and the market outlets for their outputs. Where they have such bargaining power, TNCs may charge processing firms in LDCs considerably higher prices for inputs and pay lower prices for their outputs than the prevailing world prices for inputs and outputs. In these circumstances, for each commodity group, new firms in LDCs would have to enter simultaneously all stages of processing in order to get round the entry barriers created by the TNCs. In view of the vast financial costs involved, the governments of the LDCs involved should closely collaborate, e.g. in collective dealings, to circumvent these entry barriers.

Insofar as LDCs have limited access to the international capital market because of their poor credit ratings or loans to them were considered to be more risky, the existence of important economies of scale is a major obstacle to their primary processing. To be competitive in the world markets, new firms in LDCs have to attempt to establish plants with sizes not much below the optimal levels. Average investment costs in mineral and metal processing are often too high for firms in LDCs to afford. These range from $80 million for a zinc smelting plant of 50,000 tons annual capacity to $1.2 billion for an aluminium plant of 500,000 tons annual capacity [6]. Average investment costs for agricultural products are generally lower. To process 17,000 bags of coffee a year (spray and drying), an investment of about $700,000 is required. The investment costs for a viable roasting and grinding plant for cocoa (the first stage of cocoa processing) are about $12-13 million - those for a plant producing cocoa butter and powder would be $1-2 million and $2-3 million respectively [7]. The costs of small and medium type plants would be about $10 million and $22 million respectively. Capital costs for processing cotton would be about $60-90 million. All these estimates, given in 1975, need to be revised upwards to take account of recent world-wide inflation.

Finally, for many commodities, the structure of transport costs appears to reinforce that of effective tariff protection in MDCs as a further barrier to the expansion of processing in LDCs. For these cases, freight rates increase with the degree of processing of a product and sometimes even exceed MFN tariffs. Furthermore, freight rates can be discriminatory against LDCs. According to Yeats (1977), freight rates appear to be higher to exports of certain LDCs than to similar exports from other LDCs and MDCs in the same geographical area. Insofar as higher transport cost of processed forms as compared to raw forms is due to the nature of the products involved rather than discriminating freight rates against LDCs, the case for locating processing plants near the source of raw materials is weakened. In any cost-benefit analysis to determine the location of processing plants, the calculation of transport cost should include the loss due to deterioration of the products during transport. For example, about 10 per cent of cocoa beans but almost none of cocoa paste or butter are spoiled during shipping. Therefore, a meaningful comparison of the transport costs of raw beans and processed beans should take account of this fact. Properly adjusted transport costs may favour processed beans even though unadjusted transport costs favour raw beans.

Obstacles Raised by LDCs' Governments

The governments in LDCs have also in many cases adopted policies which handicapped their domestic processors vis-a-vis their foreign rivals. Domestic processors are often obliged to buy raw materials and other inputs from local firms. This subjects them to several disadvantages. For example, they have to pay at higher prices than their foreign rivals for the same inputs or buy sub-grade raw materials at the f.o.b. price for quality grade. Their plants are underutilised in various months of each year because of supply shortages (in off-season).

Their competitiveness may further be reduced when processed products are taxed at higher rates than exports of raw materials (e.g. while there are no export duties on cocoa beans in major bean producing countries, exports of cocoa products such as cocoa paste and butter are subject to export tax). Moreover, shortages of spare parts for machinery due to foreign exchange bottlenecks and bureaucratic controls may cause low capacity utilisation of plants.

Thus, there are many things the governments of LDCs themselves can do to stimulate their processing industries. They can (i) ensure that the need of their domestic processors for low cost energy, spare parts, machinery and transport facilities and skilled personnel are more adequately met (ii) adopt measures to cause prices paid and received by domestic processors to reflect more closely social opportunity costs of raw forms and processed forms respectively, (iii) given processors, where appropriate, the freedom to buy raw materials from the cheapest sources and (iv) help them in matters relating to marketing (e.g. promotional activities, choosing intermediaries) and research (e.g. to find a more suitable intermediate technology, to improve quality - particularly of processed sub-grade products).

Framework of international co-operation on LDCs'
Commodity Processing

We have mentioned earlier that UNCTAD V adopted, in 1979, a resolution to establish a framework of international co-operation to assist LDCs to process raw materials before export. According to the UNCTAD secretariat (TD/B/C.1/253, p. 62, para. 130), this framework essentially involves 'drawing up a complementary set of principles, policies, measures, etc., which taken together would represent an effective response to the problems identified. These would be implemented through various international agencies, in bilateral or multilateral treaties and agreements and unilaterally by member governments.'

Assuming that broad agreement on the elements of the framework can be reached, governments then have to consider the nature and status of the proposed instruments of international co-operation. These may include: (i) international agreements (requiring national ratification) to be implemented through national laws and enforced at both national and international levels, e.g. ICAs, GATT codes, the Code of Conduct on marketing of commodities; (ii) General Assembly resolutions e.g. the Charter of Economic Rights and Duties of States, the International Development Strategy, the Declaration on the Establishment of a New International Economic Order and the Set of Multilaterally Agreed Equitable Principles and Rules for the Control of Restrictive Business Practices; (iii) Resolutions by intergovernmental bodies, e.g. the Lima Declaration and Plan of Action on Industrial Development and Co-operation adopted by the Second General Conference of UNIDO. Past experience has shown that little can be achieved through resolutions by UN agencies or intergovernmental bodies and it is in general difficult to enforce national laws controlling the international activities of TNCs. As yet, no ICAs include provisions concerning processing.

Concluding Remarks on Commodities Processing

The UNCTAD secretariat has elaborated, in at least two studies (TD/B/C.1/PSC/23 and TD/B/C.1/253), the elements of this framework together with specific proposals for dealing with each of the barriers investigated (see TD/B/C.1/253, pp. 57-62 for a summary). The set of UNCTAD documents on this issue have provided as much detailed information as can be expected on any subject or policy issue area. On the basis of this information, it can be seen that most of the barriers to expanding commodity processing in LDCs can be overcome by suitable measures if governments of both MDCs and LDCs so wish. However, it is implausible that MDCs most affected by the expansion of commodity processing in LDCs would favour action to promote or encourage the relocation to LDCs of processing industries. They would have to take a very enlightened, long-run view of their countries' interests to accede in this way. Hence, in the absence of a collective exercise of the bargaining power by LDCs as a group with the assistance of a Third World secretariat, it is unlikely that substantial progress will be made towards removing obstacles raised by the governments in MDCs, TNCs and market structures. However, by ensuring steady supply of raw materials to domestic processors at prices reflecting well opportunity costs and paying special attention to their need for adequate transport, warehouse and port facilities, the governments of LDCs can do much to stimulate their domestic industries to increase export earnings from further processing.

Removing trade barriers erected by MDCs' governments and obstacles created by transnational corporations would no doubt produce opportunities for an efficient shift in the location of processing. However, much of the potential benefit to LDCs would be lost if they fail to respond with positive policies to remove domestic price distortions and to ensure that their processing industries are not short of the required inputs.

Given the continued weak bargaining power of LDCs and their slowness to change policies adverse to their processing industries, the prospects for further expansion in their processing of primary commodities prior to export up to 1990 and beyond appear to be no better, or even worse, than they were in the 1970s.

With the removal of policy barriers, market power and unfavourable domestic distortions, returns to processing would likely be higher and would therefore encourage private entrepreneurs to expand processing in LDCs. This does not mean that there is less scope for expanding LDCs' export earnings in non-processing than in processing by removing obstacles to non-processing. There is no question that processing should expand at the expense of non-processing. The focus of attention on processing of raw materials in this study should not be taken to mean that expansion of production of manufactures in LDCs is considered to be less important. In any case, all industries use some raw materials or processed raw materials and in a sense all industries are processing industries. Therefore to help to expand LDCs' export earnings there is a case for removing obstacles and distortions to both processing non-processing to enable private returns in LDCs to represent better their true comparative advantages and leaving private entrepreneurs to decide on the location of processing and non-processing plants on the basis of these returns.

IMPROVEMENTS IN THE MARKETING SYSTEM FOR COMMODITY EXPORTS

As producers of primary commodities, LDCs are concerned about their low share of the price paid by the final consumers. Even for commodities involving little or no processing, the share of the producer in the final price can be rather small. For example, according to estimates by the UNCTAD Secretariat, on average only 12 per cent of the price paid by consumers for bananas in 1971 was actually received by the growers. Packing and transportation account for 38 per cent and ripening and distribution in the consuming countries account for 50 per cent [8]. The shares of exporting LDCs in the prices for tea, cocoa, coffee, jute and iron ore are shown on Table 6.13.

The low share of the final price received by commodity producers, mainly in LDCs, has usually been attributed to their weak bargaining power. Available evidence shows that most commodity markets consist of many freely competing sellers with little market staying power facing a few large buyers which are often collusively organised [8]. The large buyers are usually vertically integrated TNCs with control over finance, transport, promotional services, information and distribution channels, apart from some control over production itself. To illustrate the extent of TNCs' market concentration in commodities, Table 6.14 gives for each of eight commodities (bananas, bauxite, cocoa, coffee, copper, iron ore, rubber and tea) the number of leading TNCs and their joint market share in the World or major consuming countries (e.g. USA, UK).

It has been argued that even if TNCs have large market shares it does not necessarily mean that they exercise fully their power to minimise the price they pay to growers. TNCs are interested in long-term profits and are concerned with continued security of supply and hence would ensure that the price they pay to growers is sufficiently remunerative to generate adequate investment to maintain or expand production capacity. This argument is not totally convincing. If a firm has monopolistic power, it can, up to a point enhancing its profit beyond a competitive (normal) level by restricting its purchase and the extent to which it can do so depends on the price elasticity of supply. A simple model can help to illustrate this point.

Consider a profit-maximising trading firm which sells a commodity in a competitive market in the consuming countries but buys it from producers as a monopsonist. The firm has to accept the final market price as given but has control over the price it pays to producers (i.e. it faces a rising supply curve for the product it buys). Let P and C be the final market price and the producer's price respectively and let a and b be the price elasticity of the producer's supply

Table 6.13: The Percentage Share of LDCs' Producers in Retail Price in Major MDC Markets

Commodity	Average 1955-60	Average 1961-66	Average 1967-72	1973	Market
Tea	61	57	53	48	UK
	56	46	38	28	Netherlands
Cocoa	14	6	9	8	UK
	24	10	15	17	France
Coffee	46	43	43	50	US
	20	17	18	18	Germany FR
	38	35	34	33	France
Jute[a]	51	48	46	34	US
	32	35	32	25	France
Iron Ore	15	13	10	9	US
	12	10	8	7	France

[a] Wholesale price in the case of Jute

Source: UNCTAD document, Proportion between export prices and consumer prices of selected commodities exported by developing countries. (TD/184/Supp. 3 and Corr. 1)

Table 6.14: Market Concentration in Selected Primary Commodities

Commodity	Area	Year	Number of leading firms	Market share (%)	Level of processing
Bananas	World	1977	3	60	Banana imports
	USA	1977	3	90	"
Bauxite	MDCs	1974	6	69	Bauxite capacity
	MDCs	1974	6	76	Alumina "
	MDCs	1974	6	68	Aluminium "
Cocoa	USA	1967	4	77	} Chocolate
	UK	1967	4	78	} Manufacturing
Coffee	USA	1978	4	70	} Processing of
	Germany FR	1974	4	66	} green coffee
Copper	USA	1972	4	70	Refined copper
Iron Ore	MDCs	1976	15	50	Raw steel production
Rubber	USA	1968–69	5	78	} Tyre
	France	1968–69	3	85	} manufacturing
	UK	1968–69	4	82	}
Tea	MDCs	1978	5	75	Blending

Sources: UNCTAD document TD/229/Supp. 3, (1979), Table 1, p. 11

function and the share of distribution cost in final price respectively, then it can be shown that the producer's share in the final price, i.e. C/P, is equal to the fraction a(1-b)/ (a+1) [10]. Suppose the share of the distribution cost in the final price is 25 per cent and the price elasticity of supply is in the range 0.2 to 0.5, suggested by the empirical evidence, then the share of producers in the final price would be in the range 12.5 per cent to 25.0 per cent and the proportion of the final price which accrues to the firm as profit could be in the range of 50 per cent to 62.5 per cent. It can be seen that the producer's share in the final price varies negatively with the supply price elasticity. As this is higher in the long run than in the short-run, the producer's share is higher when trading firms attempt to maximise long-run profits than when they attempt to maximise short-run profits, but is still below the competitive norm as long as the long-run supply elasticity is less than infinity.

In practice, monopsonist buying may take various forms. Each of the few large enterprises dealing in each commodity may obtain its supply of the commodity from its own plantations [11] or subsidiaries in LDCs at a transfer price it can fix. It may buy direct from the producers of a number of LDCs (as one or two major buyers) often in the form of long-term contracts. Or it may buy from the commodity markets located in MDCs. For example in the case of bananas, marketing and distribution is predominantly controlled by three TNCs based in MDCs. These TNCs own plantations in LDCS, transport bananas in their own ships and sell them in MDCs through their own wholesale distribution channels. Fierce competition among the TNCs for larger shares in consuming markets tends to drive prices towards a competitive level. For cocoa, four major chocolate manufacturers with a joint market share of over three-quarters buy raw cocoa largely from dealers or brokers in the consuming countries on the basis of prices set in the terminal markets, all of which are located in the importing countries. (Manufacturing enterprises in socialist countries buy about one-third of their raw cocoa requirements directly from the producing countries and the rest from dealers.) In buying cocoa from the terminal markets, the four chocolate firms may each recognise the effect of its purchase on the cocoa price and so may refrain from driving it up by competitive buying. If a few large firms tacitly collude in buying, they act collectively as a monopsonist. As in practice the supply price elasticity is not known, the firms would attempt to find an optimal level of purchase on the basis of available information and past experience. What the firms purchase in total may exceed or fall short of the level at which joint profits would be maximised were accurate information available.

Thus, in a market in which there are only a few large buyers, there is an incentive for them to collude and act collectively as a monopsonist to extend their joint and individual profits. Insofar as they do exercise their monopsonistic power, the producers' share in the final price will necessarily be reduced, given the low supply price elasticities which empirical studies record. Their exercise of monopsonistic power is limited to a certain degree by the fear of new entrants. However TNCs can still reap excess profits by restricting purchases and minimise the risks of new entrants at the same time by imposing inter-firm and intra-firm arrangements which discourage entrants and/or effectively indicating they are prepared to start a price war to bankrupt new entrants before they can recoup their initial entrance costs.

Improvements in the Producer's Share in Final Price

In the light of the above analysis, it appears that there are two related ways of raising the producer's share in the final price: first to reduce the degree of concentration in trade and marketing and second, to increase the price elasticity of supply. The first way may require the producers to increase their participation in the marketing of their products, to induce an increase in the number of buyers of their products or to stimulate more competition among existing buyers. This may also include encouraging marketing firms (say, in Korea or Japan) to cooperate with the developing country producers to establish new market channels. The second way may involve the establishment of a marketing board for each commodity in each producing country (e.g. marketing boards for bananas in Jamaica, Somalia, Equador and Ivory Coast) and an association of producing countries (e.g. Union of the Banana Exporting Countries). The association of producing countries may follow the Trade Union example to set a minimum price level below which no country would sell, i.e. making supply price elasticity infinitely large at this minimum price.

By acting collectively, the producers can essentially exercise a monopolistic power to counter-balance the monopsonist power exercised by the TNCs. The share in final price would increase by their collective effort but the precise level to which their share could be raised would depend on their market power relative to that of TNCs acting together. While the market power of the producers depends on their control over their resources, their ability to manage total supply and the degree of concentration in production, that of the TNCs depends on the degree of concentration in trade and marketing, their control over transportation, market information, alternative sources of supply and supply of substitutes and the barriers to entry they erect via inter-firm and intra-firm arrangements. Even if producing countries succeed in organising themselves into a workable cartel, their ability to raise prices is still limited because of their relatively weak market position. Their bargaining power depends to a large extent on their ability to market directly to the final consumers themselves, if necessary. Their ability to do so is however hindered by their inferior access to market information and cheap transportation, apart from the obstacles caused by intra-firm arrangements set up by TNCS.

Commodity producers in MDCs can be expected to have better access to market information and cheap transportation and so have greater bargaining power (than those in LDCs) to raise their shares in the final prices of the products they export. Some recent evidence is at least suggestive that this is the case. Avramovic (1978) shows that the prices received by LDCs (as represented by their EUVs) for 19 commodities exported by them were on average only 88 per cent and 85 per cent of world market prices over the 1961-65 and 1971-75 periods respectively, whereas those received by MDCs for their primary commodity exports were close to or even exceeded world market prices over the 15 year period, 1961-75 [12]. Differences in quality and transport costs may to some extent explain these differences in the prices received by LDCs, but their weak bargaining power is another probable cause.

Recognising the need for positive actions to help LDCs' producers in marketing commodities UNCTAD V adopted without dissent resolution 124(V) in which it was agreed, inter alia, to establish within the context of the IPC a framework of international co-operation in the field of marketing and distribution of LDCs' commodity exports, with the objective of increasing their export earnings. In this context, governments also agreed to take into account, among other things, the following measures: (a) improvement in market transparency, including appropriate action to improve the functioning of the commodity exchanges; (b) increased technical and financial support for the development of national marketing and distribution systems of LDCs; (c) elimination of barriers to fair competition between marketing enterprises of MDCs and LDCs. Improvement in market transparency is the subject of the next section. Here only measures (b) and (c) are considered.

Despite this UNCTAD resolution, little progress has been made in each of the above aims. Negotiations in UNCTAD on a set of equitable principles and rules for the control of restrictive business practices have been dilatory. MDCS are slow to translate the agreed principles into laws and such laws are slow to eliminate entry barriers through intra-firm arrangements set up by TNCs. No existing International Commodity Agreements include measures on marketing and distribution. LDCs have not received much support from MDCs in setting up and operating multinational marketing enterprises. There have been only a few attempts by producers to strengthen their bargaining positions by forming and strengthening producers' associations and these attempts have had mixed and limited success. These associations may have improved the exchange of information among their members, furthered training programmes, helped to promote harmonisation of marketing policies and establishment of co-operative marketing and enterprises (e.g. the International Tea Promotion Association), but have not been too successful in raising producers' shares in the final prices. For example, five Latin American Banana producing countries which formed in 1974 the Union of Banana Exporting Countries (UPEB) agreed to adopt two measures: (a) to impose in each country an ad valorem tax on bananas and (b) to create in 1977 a joint marketing company for bananas (COMUNBANA). The strong and varying influences of TNCs have prevented the rate of this tax from being the same among these countries and owing to the entry barriers to markets in MDCs largely controlled by TNCs, the operations of COMUNBANA (effectively started in mid-1978) have appeared to be aimed at promoting exports to non-traditional markets such as in the CMEA countries and the Middle East [13].

It is worth pointing out that, in the context of the earlier simple model, the imposition of an export tax would leave the gross-of-tax share of producers in the final price unchanged, insofar as the price elasticity of supply is not affected by the tax. This means that the price received by the producers gross of tax increases proportionately with the final market price and the gross-of-tax export earning of each producing country would increase insofar as the final demand is price inelastic.

Many Western governments seem to recognise the small share of LDCs' producers in the final price and their difficulties for increasing this share. However, despite their apparent goodwill, progress in the establishment of the framework of international co-operation in the field of marketing and distribution of LDCs' commodity exports has been rather slow. The deliberations in the meetings of the UNCTAD Sub-Committee on Commodities discussing this framework were inconclusive [14]. At UNCTAD VI, July 1983, the UNCTAD Trade and Development Board was requested, under a resolution, to consider and decide on the basis of the further reports of the Committee on Commodities (on elaborating the elements of the framework) further action to be taken by the end of 1984. Thus, even after the elapse of five years since the agreement at UNCTAD V to establish the framework was made, governments have not yet reached the stage of discussing concrete proposals concerning its implementation. Moreover, while the existence of the framework helps, by itself, it can do little to improve the shares of LDCs' exporters in total retailed values. To make a real difference, producers of each commodity should co-operate closely through their national marketing boards or agencies to increase their collective bargaining power vis-a-vis TNCs and LDCs' governments should co-operate on issues covering several commodities rather than one at a time, since they have more to bargain with each other and so have more common grounds for collaboration when more commodities are involved in each negotiation.

IMPROVEMENTS IN MARKET TRANSPARENCY AND FUTURES MARKETS

As discussed earlier, one measure agreed at UNCTAD V was improvement in the market transparency and functioning of the commodity exchanges. Reliable information on past and current prices, quantities traded, and on the actual market agents as well as efficient forecasts of trends in consumption and production would help to improve decisions on resource allocation. Futures markets can add to market transparency by signalling changes in prices which affect not only current contracts but also future output plans.

Market Transparency

The quantity and quality of information varies among commodities largely because of differences in trading practices. For example, for commodities traded at auctions (e.g. tea) or on commodity exchanges (e.g. sugar and cocoa), information on current and past prices and quantities and active agents is available almost daily, whereas for commodities traded on long-term or annual contracts, direct or spot sales or on an intra-firm basis (e.g. iron ore, bauxite, manganese and jute products), information is neither easily nor quickly available to outsiders.

Information on various commodities is supplied by government departments (e.g. U.S. Bureau of Mines and Department of Agriculture). International commodity study groups such as the International Natural Rubber Organisation, the International Coffee Organisation, the International Sugar Organisation, the International Bauxite Association and major trading and/or consuming firms also publish regular reviews of market information and forecasts, Gill and Duffus (cocoa), Wigglesworth (hard fibres), H.D. Licht (sugar), Metallgesellschaft (minerals) are the best-known of these. Forecasts are produced by FAO and the World Bank. Information on minerals and metals are also reported in trade journals (e.g. Metal Bulletin, The Engineering and Mining Journal, Engineering and Mining Journal's annual survey of investments). However the information from all these sources is generally not sufficiently detailed to be

337

really useful to firms, particularly newcomers in LDCs, for making decisions on future investment projects.

Efficient decision making, particularly for new firms in LDCs, requires easy access to information on a wide range of subjects: traditional trading links, technological and structural trends, relative bargaining strengths of relevant transnational corporations in addition to prices. Reliance on second-hand information or the view of third parties may lead to poor decisions. Thus, it is not surprising that LDCs have so often repeated their demand for improved market transparency, for a better system by which reliable, up-to-date and relevant information would allow them to market their exports more effectively. But so far little has been done to make commodity markets more transparent. Since firms have incentives to keep much information private, market transparency can only be improved by government action in both MDCs (and CPEs) to make public relevant and timely information on trade flows, trade practices and production plans.

However, it is often the case that very little of such information is in government hands, and even if they want to assist LDCs, it is doubtful if they can readily and cheaply obtain it. In most democracies firms are entitled to keep private any information which is not clearly required in the public interest. Western governments tend to be reluctant to force disclosures which may be against the firms' interests. Without such disclosure the only way LDC firms can gain more information is by increasing their participation in commodity marketing.

Futures Markets

Lack of cooperation from governments does not rule out some improvement in market transparency. In making business decisions, the most important information is about future prices of outputs and inputs. If prices in futures markets provide good forecasts of commodity prices, the creation of new markets for futures contracts in more commodities and the improved functioning of existing futures markets would certainly help.

It may help to bear in mind our definition of a futures contract. It is an obligation to buy or sell at an agreed price a given amount of a specifically defined product at a specific future date. Parties entering such a contract have to pay a commission fee to the broker (if the broker is used) and a margin payment which usually amounts to 10 per cent of the value of the contract. One of the most useful services of the futures markets is the provision of hedging facilities to consumers, producers and merchants. As shown in Chapter Four (p. 130), they can transfer risk via dealings in the futures markets to less risk averse speculators. Often the hedging cost is relatively small (on average equal to the difference between the means of spot prices and futures prices). Though where small volumes are involved transactions costs can become prohibitive. If price uncertainty at harvest time is a problem to LDC producers, the question immediately arises as to why so few make use of the future markets to hedge their future sales. One reason given is that uncertainty about their production because the vagaries of weather, pests and so on make farmers unwilling to commit themselves to deliver a fixed amount (see, for example, Yamey, 1985, p. 32). But this uncertainty should affect physical contracts for future deliveries (i.e. forward sales) just as much as futures contracts. As it does not appear to deter farmers from dealing in these contracts, it should not deter them from hedging their future spot sales (as an alternative to forward sales). In any case, there is no need for them to do so. Indeed it may not be optimal for farmers to hedge the whole of their expected output. Furthermore underhedging or overhedging need not involve severe penalties. A more valid reason is that the usual size of the futures contract unit is more than the entire output of most individual LDC farmers. Any significant reduction in the size of that unit would probably make the costs of trading in futures too high.

This feature of the markets plus the fact that the average costs of trading in futures decline quite steeply with the volume of transactions (Yamey, 1985, p. 27), suggests that to enable their farmers to reduce risk via hedging, the governments of LDCs should set up schemes of cooperative hedging or empower commodity agencies such as marketing boards to hedge on their behalf. Once LDC governments recognise the benefits to farmers of using futures markets for hedging purposes, the next questions are (i) whether the supply of sufficiently long-dated contracts can be increased and (ii) whether more commodities of interest to LDCs can be covered by futures contracts.

It is rare for existing contracts to have delivery dates more than 18 to 24 months ahead. This is inadequate for producers of tree crops. Moreover, in most markets, the maximum contract is far less than this and the volume traded in it is often slight. This is because farmers, used to dealing with physical markets are often reluctant to consider transactions involving actual deliveries that commit them more than a year ahead and they have no experience with the futures market. There is no fundamental reason why contracts with longer maturity dates cannot be introduced if there is demand for them. Once producers can translate their need for long maturity contracts into effective demand via their governments, the markets will no doubt respond.

This is also true of the development of new markets. Their establishment and operation involves a sizeable overhead cost which has to be met from commissions and other charges.

This means that contracts for futures in a new commodity will be created only if a sufficiently large volume of business is likely to be attracted. According to Yamey (1985, p. 20), a futures contract is unlikely to attract much business unless there is a satisfactory level of demand for hedging. That depends on two factors: (i) risk as reflected in the degree of price instability in each commodity, (ii) the ability of users of the actuals market to participate efficiently in the futures markets. This suggests that there is no reason why new futures contracts should not emerge for sufficiently unstable commodities once the governments of LDCs make known their intention to hedge the sales of their farmers through futures contracts of appropriate maturities.

However, it has proved impossible in practice to predict whether a given contract will succeed or fail. Contracts may fail even when there seems to be strong potential trade interest. One possible explanation is the difficulty of attracting speculative interest. In the UK, for example, the commodity futures markets have traditionally been strongly rooted in the underlying trades - although a recent Bank of England survey (Ashworth, 1986) suggests that the participation of 'locals' or individual speculators is likely to increase in the future. Thus, the success of a new futures contract depends not only on a satisfactory demand for hedging but also on an adequate supply of speculative interest.

At this point it may well be asked why, if it is in the interest of the farmers to hedge their sales, private entrepreneurs have not already set up schemes of cooperative hedging. There seems to be at least five possible answers. There may be large economies of scale in hedging and private entrepreneurs may find it difficult to set up schemes of sufficient size to make them cost-effective. Setting up new schemes may be more risky than private entrepreneurs could be willing to accept, given that they are more risk averse than the governments. It is possible that no private entrepreneur has seriously thought of setting up such schemes (particularly in commodities in which future trading is currently thin or absent) or that private entrepreneurs in LDCs have less access to information on the feasibility of such schemes than their governments. Finally, it may be cheaper for the governments to hedge the sales of their farmers via their control over marketing boards than for private entrepreneurs in cooperative schemes.

It has been contended (Yamey, 1985, p. 19) that there would be no demand for hedging facilities for a commodity which cannot be stored at reasonable cost. This is not strictly correct. Although most demand for futures trading comes from stock-holders, producers also have an interest in hedging future sales of physicals, even when storage is not involved. Provided that the governments of LDCs were involved in hedging future sales, the volume of hedging would probably be sufficient to create futures markets even for perishable commodities.

Futures trading and buffer-stocks can be regarded as substitutes or alternative measures to achieve the objective of reducing risk to market participants. Once producers can hedge, using the futures markets, their need for stable commodity prices will be reduced. This is because knowing in advance the shortfalls in prices helps them to anticipate better income changes say in the next year and hence this itself reduces the precautionary balance they need to hold. (Note that because of unpredictable variation in yields, knowledge of the changes in prices reduce but do not remove uncertainty about income changes.) However, futures trading cannot eliminate problems associated with fluctuations of prices and income altogether. Since, given the credit worthiness of each country and its borrowing ability, the more borrowing potential reserved for meeting even (perfectly) anticipated shortfalls, the less is available for other purposes. Even with ideal future markets, LDCs would still benefit from measures such as buffer stocks if they could stabilise spot and futures prices and outputs or incomes. Hence in this sense, buffer stocks and futures markets can be complementary rather than competitive. This should not be taken to mean that the social benefits of buffer stocks exceed their costs, which could be substantial.

At present, there is active futures trading in cocoa, coffee, potatoes, wool, tin, copper and sisal, but not in tea, apples, and synthetic fibres. Until recently, they were absent in nickel and aluminium and have had a chequered career in cotton (Yamey, 1985, pp. 14-15). The predominant share of the world's commodity futures trading takes place in Chicago, New York and London, with the remainder in Sydney, France, Holland and Hong Kong. Since World War II, new futures contracts which have been introduced successfully in the US include live cattle and hogs, frozen pork bellies, fresh eggs, frozen concentrated orange juice, plywood and lumber. Contracts for molasses, dressed beef and frozen shrimps have also been introduced but failed (Yamey 1985, p. 15). With LDC governments' involvement, there is no obvious reason why commodities of interest to producers in LDCs such as tea, bauxite, cotton and wood, cannot attract a sufficient increase in futures trading to be successful.

It is important to repeat the point that the creation of new futures contracts will also benefit those market participants not directly involved in futures trading since futures prices provide both useful forecasts for future spot prices and a basis for fixing prices for contracts in actuals ahead of delivery dates. This means that in assessing the overall benefits of futures trading for each new commodity, account should be taken of gains to people other than those directly involved in futures trading via their governments. The gain in market transparency would be considerable because in futures markets trade takes place in public and prices are widely reported, unlike what happens in many private sales.

Governments acting on the behalf of producers is but one way of reducing hedging costs. Other measures recently proposed by UNCTAD, (1984, p. 37) include (i) setting up new futures markets in interested LDCs, (ii) inclusion of interested LDCs on governing boards of commodity exchanges in MDCs, (iii) new international legislation, (iv) better information on rules, regulations and national surveillance, (v) reduced margins for producers or payment of interest on these and (vi) better training facilities for LDC personnel. But if measures (ii) - (vi) merely lower hedging costs to LDC producers (e.g. reducing transaction costs and margins) without at the same time reducing operating costs for futures' markets, they would make it relatively unattractive for commodity experts to be involved in commodity futures markets, particularly new ones. The efficiency of these markets would suffer as a result. Moreover, high costs of setting up and operating commodity exchanges together with their requirements for an efficient internal and international communication system make most LDCs unsuitable locations for them. The exceptions are international trading centres such as Hong Kong and Singapore. It appears that the most practical way of lowering average costs of hedging to LDCs' producers is through direct action by LDC governments in hedging on their behalf.

CONCLUSION

An increase in market transparency would help participants to make better decisions and would incidentally reduce fluctuations in outputs and prices. Futures' markets help to increase market transparency largely because their prices and volumes of transactions are widely reported. Moreover, producers in LDCs could also reduce their risks by hedging if only futures' markets with longer maturity were developed for the commodities, such as tree crops, which they produce. One drawback of futures markets is that price instability may be increased in times of extreme shortage or surplus when nervous speculators tend to over-react to rumours. But, in general for storable commodities, the existence of future markets reduces price variations because stockholders find it less risky to transfer stocks from periods of surplus (low prices), to periods of shortage (high prices). Probably new contracts for commodities for which futures trading is currently lacking or inactive and contracts for longer maturities will be forthcoming once there is clear indication of sufficient demand for hedging facilities. Aggregate demand by producers for hedging of their future sales is at present small as the average transaction costs are too high for each one of them because individually their sales are too small. (Producers are active in only a few markets, chickens and eggs.) However, through cooperative arrangements or government agencies hedging volumes can be increased and average hedging costs reduced. The high cost of setting up and operating new futures markets and the requirement for special skills and communication systems make LDCs unlikely locations for them. Most of the UNCTAD proposals to encourage LDCs in futures trading would be in vain if, in seeking to reduce hedging costs to LDCs' producers, they destroy the incentives to other agents (brokers, financiers, speculators) to maintain or expand the markets for futures.

NOTES

1. World Bank and FAO estimates put costs at from $80 per ton in parts of South Asia to $150 in land-locked parts of Africa, compared with about $10 a ton offered to contracting buyers by the Canadian Wheat Board, (Bale and Southworth, 1982, p. 329).

2. See for example UNCTAD documents: general studies - TD/229/Supp. 2 (1979); TD/B/C.1/PSC/23 (1981); TD/B/C.1/253 (1984) and specific commodity studies - TD/B/C.1/PSC/19/Rev.1 (1984, Bauxite/Alumina/Aluminium); TD/B/C.1/PSC/22/Rev.1 (1984, phosphates) etc.

3. See annual address to the Board of Governors by Roberts, MacNamara, President, World Bank, Washington D.C., 26 September 1977, in Annual Meeting of the Board of Governors, Summary Proceedings.

4. See UNCTAD document (TD/6/Rev.1), The Kennedy Round; Estimated Effects on Tariff Barriers.

5. UNCTAD document TD/B/C.2/197, 'Transnational aspirations and expansion of trade in manufactures and semi-manufactures...'; UN document E/C.10/38, United Nations Transnational Corporations in World Development; a re-examination.

6. See Report of the Secretary-General (1977), document E/C.7/68, 'Minerals: Solvent Issues ...', paper submitted to the fifth session of the Committee on Natural Resources, Geneva, 9-20 May 1977.

7. See Commodities Research Unit Ltd., Study on the degree and scope for increased processing of primary commodities in developing countries prepared for UNCTAD, September 1975.

8. See UNCTAD document TD/B/C.1/162 'The Marketing and Distribution System for Bananas'.

9. See UNCTAD document TD/225/Supp. 3 (1979), p. 3, para. 6.

10. The profit function of the firm is:

$$R = P (1 - b) Q - C.Q$$

First-order condition for maximum profit is:

$$dR/dQ = P (1 - b) - C (1 + 1/a) = O \quad \text{or}$$
$$\underline{C/P = (1-b)a/(1+a)} \quad \text{Q.E.D.}$$

where $a = (C/Q) (dQ/dC)$.

11. This is however no longer a substantial part of the market.

12. Avramovic (1978), D., 'Common Fund: Why and what Kind?', <u>Journal of World Trade Law</u>, September - October.

13. See UNCTAD document TD/229/Supp.3 (1979), p.21, para. 53.

14. See UNCTAD documents (containing reports of the Committee on Commodities) TD/B/C.1/BSC/230-TD/B/C.1/ PSC/24, TD/B/C.1/246-TD/B/C.1/36 and TD/B/944-TD/B/ C.1/247.

Chapter Seven

SUMMARY OF FINDINGS

Primary commodity exports, even when oil is excluded, remain the chief source of foreign exchange for most developing countries. Manufactured exports are important and growing rapidly but for only about 10 LDCs are manufactures more than 50 per cent of exports. Many LDCs still earn the bulk of their foreign exchange from no more than three commodities. As growth in most of them still depends on their ability to pay for imports of capital goods, raw materials and/or fuels, they are rightly concerned about the trends and fluctuations in the prices and proceeds of the commodities they export. For the industrialised nations, interest focuses mainly on the risk of interruptions in the supply of imports of strategic minerals and on the complexities of agricultural protectionism.

TRENDS IN COMMODITY TRADE

In the last twenty years trade in primary products (excluding fuels) has experienced a decline in its share of world trade, in its share of exports from LDCs, in LDCs' share of world exports of primary products and in the trend in LDCs' surplus in the trade balance in primary commodities. However, these broad trends conceal within them a great diversity of growth rates for individual countries and products.

The decline in the share of LDCs in world exports of non-oil primary products can be a natural and desirable adjustment to changing comparative advantage. As their education and skill levels are raised, technology is acquired and capital accumulated, they begin to process raw materials and produce manufactures and so become less dependent on the export of primary products. But it can also be the result of attempts to force the pace of import substituting industrialisation by protection and overvalued exchange rates which damage incentives to farmers and exporters.

Shift-share analysis reveals that the decline in LDCs' share in world primary exports was partly due to their con-

345

centration on commodities which on average have lower growth rates than those exported by the rest of the world (i.e. LDCs had an unfavourable commodity-mix component) and partly due to their having on average lower export growth rates for each commodity than the rest of the world so that even if the rest of the world were to export the same commodities in the same proportions as the LDCs, its growth rate would still be higher than that of the LDCs (i.e. LDCs also had an unfavourable regional component).

Faster growth of domestic use (resulting from greater increase in population, income and domestic processing of raw materials) rather than slower growth of production in LDCs than elsewhere appear to have been the main reason for lower LDCs' export growth for most of the 18 IPC commodities. However, the agricultural policies (involving import restrictions and export subsidies) pursued by OECD countries and import-substituting policies followed by LDCs (which moved the domestic terms of trade against food production and export crops) played an important role in depressing the growth rates of primary exports in some LDCs (e.g. cocoa in Ghana).

EVIDENCE ON COMMODITY TERMS OF TRADE

The widespread adoption of inward-looking import substituting policies by LDCs was to a considerable extent due to the influence of the Prebisch-Singer hypothesis of secular deterioration in the terms of trade between the primary exports of LDCs and the manufactured exports of MDCs. However, on closer examination, theory cannot provide a clear indication of the direction in the long term trend in these terms of trade. Factors such as low income elasticities, population growth (low in MDCs but high in LDCs), increasing availability of synthetic substitutes for some natural materials, diminishing returns to the world's fixed land resources, etc., appear to suggest lower growth rates of both supply and demand for primary products. But this implies a lower share for primary products in the total value of world trade rather than a declining trend in the terms of trade of primary products.

The data on price trends do appear to confirm a deterioration in the primary terms of trade over the seventy years period starting from 1868 but do not support the hypothesis for the period 1900-70. However, there was a clear decline in the terms of trade for the two sub-periods 1900-38 and 1950-70. The paradox is explained by an upward shift in the primary terms of trade between 1939-49.

As most people would probably regard this shift in the 1940s as an isolated historical event due to war and its aftermath rather than as part of a regular long term cycle it is probably best to omit these years. Few economic forecasters would predict another such shift say in the 1990s on account of a shift in these terms of trade in the 1940s. On the balance of available evidence and a priori judgements, a decline in the terms of trade of primary products throughout the historical period 1868-1970 seems to be highly plausible. Problems of measurement of the terms of trade, especially the effect of quality changes and new goods must, of course, qualify any welfare conclusions from this. Moreover, even if it is accepted that the terms of trade of primary commodities declined secularly over the last hundred years, these terms of trade may or may not continue on that downward trend in the next hundred years. Indeed most long-term forecasters seem to anticipate an eventual effect of demand pressing against the limits of non-renewable natural resources which would certainly raise commodity prices.

Over the medium term (to 1995), World Bank forecasts are not encouraging for LDCs. The effects of a decline in the real prices of commodities exported by low income LDCs do justify concern, although it is difficult to draw clear welfare implications from such a decline. In the view of the Bank the prices of the non-oil commodities will be lower in real terms in 1995 than they were in 1980. The implied projected long term growth rate of real export earnings of LDCs from commodities is as low in 1995 as it was in the 1970s, i.e. about 1 per cent per annum.

EVIDENCE ON COMMODITY INSTABILITY

Price instability has caused concern because it is believed to raise risks to traders, producers and consumers and contributes to the instability of export earnings, imports, investment and government expenditure. These effects are expected to hinder economic growth. But, not all price changes are harmful. In a market system some price changes are necessary to provide signals to producers and consumers to take actions to prevent or reduce future shortages or surpluses.

Since a trend line fitted to actual prices appears to be a good approximation for the steady state growth path of prices reflecting long term growth of supply and demand, price instability in this study has been measured as some average of the deviations of price around a trend. A smooth exponential trend was chosen in preference to a moving average trend or a linear trend for a number of a priori and statistical reasons. In adopting this particular measurement of instability, we deliberately include both predictable and unpredictable movements around the trend in the measure. To measure instability as an average of deviations around a predictable value is to equate unpredictability with instability, to regard all predictable swings as preventable and/or harmless. But as even fully-anticipated shortfalls in prices or earnings are likely to cause problems, a measurement of instability which can serve as a useful guide to the magnitude of the instability problem should include both unpredictable and predictable swings around trends.

As the most unstable commodities in terms of prices and export earnings seem likely to be prime targets for international stabilisation programmes they need to be identified. But the evidence on the magnitudes of nominal and real price instability for 18 major commodities for the three decades 1951-60, 1961-70, 1971-80 shows that ranking changed dramatically from one decade to the next. Commodities which appeared relatively stable in one decade became relatively unstable in the next. These changes in the rankings across periods suggest that random factors rather than systematic characteristics (e.g. low/high price/income elasticities of demand/supply and market structures) were the main determinants of price instability. However, over the three decades as a whole the five most unstable commodities were sugar, sisal, cocoa, zinc and coffee.

Evidence on the ten core commodities confirms that the world export unit value (EUV) is more stable than the world market price (except for jute) particularly for the four most unstable commodities: sugar, hard fibres, coffee and cocoa. This suggests that the prices received by exporters for quantities traded outside the commodity markets were more stable than the quoted prices. This was particularly true for sugar where, of course, many special trading arrangements exist.

The EUV to the country is a better measure of the price received by each LDC for its commodity export than either the world market price or the world EUV. Evidence shows that there was considerable variation in the degree of instability of the EUVs experienced by different countries for all commodities but on average, the world EUV did not exaggerate the instability of prices received by individual countries.

On the other hand, earnings for each commodity appeared to be considerably more stable at world level than at the country level. The degree of earnings instability also varied widely across countries and volume instability across countries generally showed even greater variation than earnings instability. Thus, even when earnings and volume at world level are relatively stable, this can conceal severe instability for individual LDCs.

Evidence for the 1971-80 period confirms the view that the prices of commodities were more unstable than those of most manufactures exported by major industrial countries.

Comparing the means of the earnings instability indexes for 90 LDCs (excluding major oil exporters Saudi Arabia, Kuwait and Libya) with those for 19 MDCs for the three decades 1951-60, 1961-70 and 1971-80 reveals that LDCs' export earnings were considerably more unstable than those of MDCs in all three decades. The ratios of the means of instability of MDCs to that of LDCs were three-fifths, one-third and two-fifths in the above three decades respectively.

Causes of Instability

Although price and earnings instability are interrelated and may share common causes it is useful to examine them separately. Although large shifts in supply and demand and low price elasticities of supply and demand are responsible for price instability, large shifts in supply combined with low price elasticities contribute to earnings instability only to the extent that the price elasticity of demand departs from unity. With unit elasticity, supply shifts effect price but not earnings instability.

Price instability

Results from econometric studies confirm low price elasticities of supply and demand (between zero and 0.5). Low price elasticities are further confirmed by the fact that for the ten core commodities world volumes are considerably more stable than world unit values or prices.

Because of the familiar problem of identification in statistics it is difficult to infer from the volume and price instability or the covariance of their deviations from trends at world level whether demand or supply shifts are the predominant cause of market fluctuations. However, at individual country level supply shifts appear to have played a dominant role in determining each country's earnings instability.

Both supply and demand in the world market for a commodity are the residual difference between production on the one hand and consumption plus stock change on the other. Thus for each country, demands can be conceived as negative supply and vice versa. Hence, factors affecting production, consumption and stocks in each country would be determinants of export supply and demand shifts. Production of commodities tends to be sensitive to natural factors such as rainfall, temperature, pests; prices of inputs such as fertilisers, seeds and fuels and government policies concerning matters such as land tenure and tax. Strikes and civil disturbances can also cause serious disruptions to production. Consumption tends to respond strongly to changes in variables such as income, population, taste, technology and supply of substitutes. Changes in stocks are influenced considerably by changes in interest rates, storage costs and speculation about future commodity prices.

Since the world supply of (or demand for) exports are the sums of the differences between domestic production and consumption plus stock change in individual countries, a small change in production or consumption may lead to a pro-

349

portionately larger change in the quantity of exports supplied (or demanded). The adoption of variable trade levies (in the form of variable rates of import duties or export subsidies) in OECD countries has been an important contributing cause of the instability of the residual world markets.

For most commodities, price instability is aggravated by the long lags between the investment decision to expand output and the actual increase in output. The longer are such lags the more uncertain producers are about the expected profitability of their investment and the more probable are large mistakes. Forward contracts allow producers to know in advance of planting a crop the quantities they can sell at a fixed price to dealers or final buyers. However, difficulties may occur if either party fails to meet his obligation.

These difficulties are reduced by the use of future contracts which represent simply pieces of paper containing legally enforceable promises to deliver a given quantity of a specified quality of a given commodity on a given date at a given location. These future contracts can be traded and may change hands many times before the date of delivery arrives. One important advantage of futures trading to producers, consumers and merchants is that it enables them to hedge sales for future delivery at reduced cost thanks to the participation of speculators who are more willing to carry risks. By hedging a producer can know in advance what he would get for a fixed quantity delivered at some future date. Normally the average cost of hedging is the difference between the expected mean of future prices and that of the spot prices quoted in the physical markets.

However, a major disadvantage of the futures market is that through the sales/purchases of stocks, the spot prices of a commodity become sensitive to expectation about future spot prices, interest rates, exchange rates and general asset prices and can be made very unstable as a result of the buying and selling of speculators in times of large shortages or surpluses or violent swings in exchange rates or interest rates.

Earnings instability.
The causes of earnings instability at the individual country level suggested by a priori reasoning and investigated by many economists are (i) high commodity and geographical concentration of exports, (ii) specialisation in primary commodities, (iii) small economic size, (iv) a high degree of openness to trade and (v) a high rate of export growth. The results of the studies reviewed are seen to be sensitive to the time periods of investigation, the formulae used for measuring instability and/or concentration and the samples of countries chosen.

The evidence shows a very weak association between commodity concentration and instability. This is because: (a) countries tend to specialise in commodities which are relatively stable or whose fluctuations tend to be mutually offsetting, (b) LDCs tended to have a high degree of concentration and (c) there is considerable variation in the instability indexes of different commodities exported by these countries. However, the observed weak association between concentration and instability does not necessarily mean that countries whose exports are unstable cannot substantially reduce this by diversification. Evidence on the most unstable countries shows that there is considerable scope for reducing instability by diversifying into relatively stable products because their current export instability stems from their specialisation in relatively unstable products. As diversification for them would mean shifting out of unstable commodities into more stable ones this would generally reduce their earnings instability.

There is no clear evidence that geographical concentration causes instability. But cross-country analyses do yield support for the views that country size (in terms of total export or national income) and specialisation in manufactured exports are positively associated with more stable export earnings.

However, evidence from cross country regression analyses seems to yield little that is useful for policy. Despite the lack of a strong cross-country relationship between instability and commodity concentration, we have shown that many of the most unstable countries could actually reduce instability in their total export earnings by diversifying into more stable products. But in determining the commodity structure of its exports each country may be more concerned with dynamic comparative advantage and earnings growth than with instability. If there is a trade-off between these objectives, growth is likely to triumph. Finally, the finding that large countries tend to have more stable exports provides no help to the large number of small countries.

Consequences of instability

The evidence from time series analysis and country modelling taken along with a priori reasoning suggest that a large swing in exports, above or below trend would affect strongly, first, the export sector and then, if the export sector is large, the rest of the economy, unless offset by policy actions. Such offsetting policy actions supported by adequate reserves or external borrowing could substantially reduce these effects.

Time series analysis and country modelling have generally failed to establish a clear negative relationship between instability and growth. This suggests that the ratchet effects of instability on growth, which can be captured by time

351

series analysis, are either absent or weak. It does not mean that instability does not have substantial effects on growth by lowering the trends of variables effecting growth (such as the investment/income ratio or investment efficiency). It is simply that these effects are ones which time series by its nature cannot detect. They can be captured by cross country analysis, but it has other limitations.

Export instability may be only one, and not necessarily a powerful influence on economic growth and the responses to it of investment, imports and income may be very different for different countries. These facts make it most unlikely that the effects of instability on economic growth would consistently be revealed in different cross-country studies using different samples of countries and over different periods of time. Indeed, the results from published studies reveal on the whole a weak support for the belief that instability hinders growth but the results are shown to be sensitive to the samples of countries selected, the periods under investigation and the formulae used for measuring both instability and growth.

POLICIES FOR DEALING WITH INSTABILITY

Interest in commodity issues soared in the aftermath of the 1973/74 oil crisis period and the commodity boom and slump of 1972/3. MDCs were concerned about the threat to the security of supplies of a few key minerals, the risk of cartel actions by LDC suppliers following OPEC example and the contribution of widely fluctuating commodity prices to their domestic inflation.

The upsurge of interest among the LDCs led to their demands for a NIEO which then received serious consideration from the MDCs who also happened to be concerned about commodity instability and supply disruptions. Some of these demands found expression in the adoption in 1976, at UNCTAD IV, of several proposals for an Integrated Programme for Commodities. These involved the establishment of; (i) a Common Fund to provide assistance to International Commodity Agreements to finance buffer stocks for a number of storable commodities, (ii) a new additional facility for compensating commodity export shortfalls in LDCs, (iii) a framework for assisting LDCs to surmount obstacles to processing of raw materials before export and (iv) a framework to improve the access of LDCs' primary commodity exports to MDCs' markets. Although the main aim of (iii) and (iv) is to enable LDCs to increase their export earnings they could also help to stabilise them.

SUMMARY OF FINDINGS

The Common Fund
The main argument put forward for the Common Fund was that by providing ready financial assistance, it would encourage the negotiation of new ICAs and the re-negotiation of existing ones. Other arguments were that a large central fund could borrow on better terms than separate ones and that it could economise on the total finance required to the extent that there are offsetting changes in commodity prices so that when some ICAs are borrowing others could be repaying.

The Developing Countries' Group of 77 preferred a Common Fund with adequate financial resources of its own (independent of the ICAs) which it could lend to ICAs or to other agencies, e.g. to finance national stocks. The MDCs opposed such a strong Common Fund and proposed instead a pooling arrangement whereby the surplus funds of individual ICAs would be deposited with the Fund. After a prolonged negotiation, agreement was reached in June 1980 and the capital structure and mode of operation of the Common Fund which emerged were close to the MDCs' proposal and fell far short of the LDCs' idea. Instead of the $6 billion proposed for assisting the finance of ICAs' buffer stocks the core capital is only $330 million but with power to borrow from banks in addition. $280 million has been earmarked for the second window, financed by voluntary government contributions, to provide assistance for such purposes as research and development in primary commodities. However, although now ratified (February 1986), the Common Fund has yet to come into operation.

International Commodity Agreements
Ten years have passed since UNCTAD IV and yet only one new price stabilising agreement, that for natural rubber in 1982, has been concluded. Two other new agreements (for jute and tropical timber) have been negotiated but they involve no price provisions. Those agreements which existed before 1976 were negotiated but have become weaker now than before. The Tin Agreement, long acclaimed a success, has collapsed (November, 1985) leaving a tin market in total disarray.

A review of the recent history of ICAs reveals problems and failures and rarely successes. Only three ICAs made use of international buffer stocks. These were tin, cocoa and rubber, but the first two also provided for export quotas. Negotiations in these commodities have often experienced long delays and the recurrence of serious problems and severe difficulties have sometimes caused the suspension of economic provisions.

The problems facing ICAs in practice are both political and economic. The most common cause of delay in negotiation and breakdown of the agreements is the inherent conflict of interests between producers and consumers concerning the intervention prices. Often conflicts also exist between producers with different costs, prospects for expansion or diversification, etc.

Most agreements have many objectives but few provisions for their attainment apart from exchanges of information and price stabilisation. Even for this last and crucial objective, the methods used bear little resemblance to a textbook model. The reference prices are normally set by bargaining which may only be slightly influenced by rather informal price forecasts rather than set in accordance with frequent systematic forecasts which make efficient use of all available information. However even if actual ICAs were to use the best available forecasting technique and information to fix their reference prices, the chance of running out of either funds or stocks because of failure to distinguish between temporary and permanent shifts in supply or demands remains high. A combination of such technical failures combined with conflicts of interest appear to have brought about the collapse of the Tin Agreement.

In Chapter 5 the technical and financial implications of a buffer stock were examined by using a simple but plausible model whose parameters were assumed to be known. The model was used to generate alternative price paths associated with different types of supply and demand shifts and with and without buffer stocks operations. There we show that a buffer stock operating under the rather favourable situation of an ideal commodity market, ideal in the sense that its structural parameters are precisely known, could face enormous difficulties in attempting to stabilise prices around its long term equilibrium path. Thus, our experiments reinforce the conclusion emerging from our survey of the history of ICAs that it can be exceedingly difficult in practice to stabilise price via ICAs. If the ultimate objective is to assist LDCs to stabilise their export earnings there are better options. One such is various schemes for compensatory financing of export fluctuations.

Compensatory Financing
Two compensatory financing schemes - the compensatory financing facility (CFF) of the IMF and the EEC Stabex - were established in 1963 and 1975 respectively. The idea of having a third compensatory financing facility to complement these arose because of a belief that the two existing schemes were inadequate and/or unable to deal effectively with fluctuations at national and sectoral levels in individual LDCs.

IMF-CFF
Underlying a compensatory financing scheme such as the IMF-CFF is the belief that with a relatively stable import

capacity (defined as total foreign exchange inflows divided by an import price index), each country can maintain a steady flow of essential imports and this would enable it to insulate its domestic economy from export fluctuations by, for example, using changes in government expenditure to offset dips and booms in exports. This implies that the aim of stabilising foreign exchange receipts in real terms around a fairly long term trend. It also implies that each country should borrow from the facility only if it has a need (because of a balance of payment deficit) and should repay when and if it is financially able to do so without hardships i.e. when its balance of payments is in surplus. However, in practice most LDCs have for several reasons persistently experienced deficits in their balance of payments on current account, and so the 'balance of payments need test' is often inapplicable to them and the 'ability to repay test', had it existed, would result in insufficient repayment from them even over a long period.

The apparent objective of the IMF's CFF is the stabilisation of foreign exchange receipts in nominal (not real) terms around a medium (not long) term trend. Compensatory drawings from it are tied to export shortfalls (and optionally cereal import excesses) subject to a balance of payments test but repayments of these are not tied to export overages (i.e. earnings in excess of trend) or subject to any ability to repay test.

Since its establishment in 1963, various aspects of the CFF have been successively improved in 1966, 1975, 1979 and 1981. The major features affected are quota limits, base of shortfalls and the formula for calculating shortfalls. The base of shortfall, originally being total merchandise exports, was later expanded to include, at member countries' choice, earnings from services and/or cereal imports. Despite these improvements, the CFF has continued to incur many criticisms. While the change in the quota limits on CFF drawings produced a tenfold increase in the CFF's resources in nominal terms in the period 1963-81, in real terms the CFF's resources increased by only threefold because of the high rate of inflation. Furthermore, total IMF quotas as a proportion of LDCs' export earnings fell from 16 per cent in 1966-68 to 6 per cent in 1978-81.

The use of the five-year moving average centring on the shortfall year is difficult to defend logically. It requires forecasts for exports in two post shortfall years, making the calculated shortfalls unnecessarily sensitive to forecasting errors. Since an alternative more trouble-free method for estimating trend exists (e.g. the least-squares method), the persistence in using a trend estimation method which has encountered so many objections and faced so many problems is surprising.

355

It is widely recognised that giving compensation on the basis of shortfall from a nominal (rather than real) trend would often result in giving assistance to members when it is not needed and denying assistance when it really is. The basic aim of having a compensatory financing scheme is to provide short term external assistance to countries at the time it is needed (i.e. it is the timing rather than the total amount of assistance over time that is critical). This implies a need to regard the real purchasing power of exports as the key target for stabilisation. The repeated excuse for not changing over from nominal to real term calculations is that reliable and timely import price indexes are not available for most countries. Yet, comprehensive statistical information on import prices is available in the United Nations system and further improvements in the import statistics could be achieved with relative ease, particularly if, where necessary, countries receive technical assistance from an institution such as the World Bank or the IMF. In any case, the deficiency in the information on import prices is an argument for improving import statistics rather than one for continuing to provide compensatory financing services which do little or nothing to help countries to stabilise their real imports and income.

The present method for calculating shortfalls and the imposition of side conditions (e.g. the requirement of cooperation) which limit access to drawings cause each country to be unduly uncertain about whether and how much it may be entitled to draw from the CFF. Lack of automaticity in members' drawing right may deter many countries from using the CFF and reduces their willingness to incur the foreign exchange cost involved in domestic stabilisation which they are not sure they can recoup from the CFF.

EEC-Stabex

Stabex, established in 1975 and reviewed in 1980, is a commodity-specific compensatory financing system. It is limited to trade flows of mainly basic agricultural commodities from the African and Caribbean associates of the EEC. Stabex transfers have been a significant supplement to aid for many ACP countries because they are interest-free to all the outright grants to some. Also their uses have been shown to be rather beneficial to the countries receiving them. Nevertheless Stabex has several important limitations: (i) it is limited only to ACP countries and only for trade with the EEC (except for 13 small states); (ii) it covers merely agricultural products (including only 10 of the 18 IPC commodities); however, about seven minerals and metals were subsequently covered by a minerals facility (MINEX) which for the 1980-84 period had resources of 280 million ECUs; (iii) its method for calculating shortfalls tends to underestimate them, fails to take account of changes of import prices and represents a very short term trend over only four years and (iv) the resources at its disposal are very limited and have probably not improved in real terms since the start.

An Additional Facility

Since the establishment of the CFF in 1963, governments have shown interest in an additional compensatory financing facility to supplement the CFF. At the invitation of UNCTAD I, the World Bank staff prepared a study on such a scheme. The governments of USA, Sweden and West Germany each made their own proposals for a new scheme in 1975, 1977 and 1978 respectively.

UNCTAD V in 1979 commissioned a detailed study for the operation of a complementary facility to compensate for shortfalls in earnings of each commodity. UNCTAD VI in July 1983 reviewed a series of studies produced by the UNCTAD Secretariat on the new facility and recommended the setting up of an Expert Group to report on this facility. In December 1984, the Group produced a report containing descriptions of the nature, main characteristics and mode of operation of such a scheme in some concrete terms to help the governments to visualise and discuss how it could be designed.

The group's conclusions generally failed to reflect the basic principles which the UNCTAD Secretariat had proposed at UNCTAD V should form the basis of the new facility. These were: (i) the calculation of shortfalls in real terms around a long term trend, (ii) full compensation of the shortfall, (iii) no side conditions on compensation and (iv) terms of repayment and interest charges to be related to ability to repay. If the basic principles proposed by the UNCTAD Secretariat represent the aims of the LDCs, a new facility which embodied the features recommended by the Group would fail to satisfy them. Such a scheme would provide few attractions to most LDCs.

POLICIES FOR INCREASING LDCs' EXPORT EARNINGS

The main proposals for raising the foreign exchange earnings of LDCs from commodities are concerned with the removal of obstacles to facilitate the marketing of LDCs' primary products and the processing of primary products in LDCs before export. Of the obstacles to commodity trade, the one which appears to produce the most damaging effects on both LDCs and MDCs is the high and growing agricultural protection in MDCs, particularly in the European Community. Agricultural protection in the EC adversely affects not only primary producers in LDCs and other MDCs but also consumers and taxpayers in the Community. A reduction of agricultural protection in MDCs would raise the foreign exchange earnings

357

of LDCs and would at the same time benefit MDCs as a whole. At least in the short run, however, this would mean some increase in the world market prices of cereals, sugar and dairy products. For those LDCs which are net importers of these foodstuffs there would be an adverse shift in their terms of trade.

Increased LDCs' Processing of Raw Materials

The widespread interest in the increase of processing of primary products in LDCs was reflected in the adoption without dissent, at UNCTAD V, of a resolution to establish a framework of international cooperation to increase primary processing in LDCs. It is widely believed that many LDCs have potential comparative advantage in processing primary commodities they at present export in raw forms. It is also thought that they could earn much more foreign exchange by doing so.

Statistics show that MDCs' imports from LDCs were more concentrated on raw forms than those from other sources. Progress in LDCs' processing has been good for some commodities but poor or very poor for others. For example, for coffee, rubber, tobacco, manganese and phosphates processed forms remained low at 14 per cent in 1970-72 and in 1978-80, while for tin, leather, jute and cotton they rose from 81 per cent, 72 per cent, 70 per cent and 54 per cent respectively in 1970-72 to 90 per cent, 90 per cent, 87 per cent and 78 per cent respectively in 1978-80 but for copper and lead LDC processing actually declined. Overall the proportion of commodities in which over 50 per cent was processed in LDCs declined from three quarters in 1970-72 to three-fifths in 1978-80.

The changes in LDCs' market shares in the semi-processed and full-processed also varied considerably across commodities in these two periods.

Illustrative calculations by the UNCTAD Secretariat show that local semi-processing of the following ten commodities - copper, bauxite/alumina/aluminium, phosphate, natural rubber, cotton, jute, hides/skin, non-coniferous wood, cocoa and coffee - could raise the gross foreign exchange earnings of LDCs by $27.2 billion a year on the basis of 1975 trade figures, an increase of 152 per cent. The potential gains are greatest for bauxite, phosphate and natural rubber, where the ratios of additional gross foreign exchange earnings due to processing over the value of exports in raw form are 7.9, 2.6 and 2.2 respectively. They are quite substantial for cotton (1.9), hides and skin (1.7) and non-coniferous wood (1.7) but low for copper (0.4), cocoa (0.2) and jute (0.1) and negligible for coffee (0.04). For jute and copper, there is little scope for increasing foreign exchange earnings by increased processing largely because their shares of imports in raw forms by MDCs from LDCs were already very low (13 per cent and 29 per cent respectively). For coffee or cocoa, it is largely due to the relatively small value added in the processing of coffee and cocoa.

These results from the UNCTAD study are supported by the Joint World Bank and Commonwealth Secretariat Study for individual countries for rubber, tropical hardwood, cocoa, coconut oil, tea and bauxite. Of the agricultural commodities, value added and net foreign exchange earnings are highest for rubber, followed by tropical hardwood and tea (bags) and relatively low for cocoa and coconut oil.

Policies for increasing processing of raw materials in LDCs would largely involve assisting these countries to remove or surmount all kinds of barriers and obstacles such as tariff and non-tariff barriers raised by governments, entry barriers created by TNCs and market structures and general obstacles such as faulty domestic policies which handicap domestic processors vis-a-vis foreign rivals, lack of general and specific skills and technologies required for primary processing and restrictions on the transfer of technology imposed by TNCs. There is evidence that for the processing of most commodities some or all of these barriers and obstacles remain important at present and they would continue to be difficult to remove.

Improved Marketing of LDCs' Products

LDCs are concerned about the disproportionately low share of the final price received by their commodity producers. For example, according to estimates by the UNCTAD Secretariat, only 12 per cent of the price paid by consumers for bananas in 1971 was actually received by the growers and the percentage shares of LDCs' producers in the retail prices in France of iron ore, cocoa, jute, coffee and tea in the period 1967-72 were 8, 15, 32, 34 and 38 per cent respectively. The weak bargaining power of LDC producers has often been held responsible for their low share in the final price.

In most commodity markets there are, on the one hand a few large buyers, usually TNCs with powerful control over finance, transport, promotional services, information and distribution channels and on the other hand a large number of freely competing sellers with little market staying power. In so far as a firm has monopsonistic power, it can enhance its profit beyond a competitive (normal) level by restricting its purchases. The extent to which it can do so depends on the price elasticity of supply and the countervailing bargaining power of suppliers.

There are various forms which monopsonist buying may take in practice. A large international firm may obtain its supply of a commodity from its own plantations or subsidiaries in LDCs at a transfer price which it can fix below free market levels. It may buy direct from the producers of a number of LDCs (as one or two major buyers) often in the form of long-term contracts or from the commodity markets located in MDCs. In buying a commodity, each of a few large buyers may recognise the effect of its purchase on the commodity price and so may refrain from driving it up by competitive buying. Thus, in a market dominated by a few buyers, there is a strong incentive for them to collude and act collectively as a monopsonist to extend their joint and individual profits. In so far as they do exercise such power, the producers' share in the final price will necessarily be reduced, given the low price elasticities of supply in practice.

Where (and if) such practices exist then to improve the producers' share in the final price of commodities would require the adoption of policy measures to assist producers to participate more in the marketing of their products, to increase the number of buyers and/or to stimulate more competition among them and the establishment of marketing boards or producer associations to increase the collective bargaining power of sellers.

Agricultural Protection in MDCs

The Common Agricultural Policy (CAP) of the European Community, especially after enlargement to include Spain and Portugal, now represents by far the most serious barrier to agricultural trade. The average level of import tariffs on agricultural products rose from 36 per cent in 1956 to 69 per cent by the early 1970s in the EC as a whole. Over the same period, it doubled in Sweden and Norway and rose from 76 per cent to 103 per cent in Switzerland. Latest figures show that these trends continued through the 1970s in the EEC and also in Japan, where the average level of protection for several commodities rose from 70 per cent in 1974 to 300 per cent in 1978.

To make matters worse for foreign suppliers, agricultural protection in the EC takes the form of variable levies which have fluctuated tremendously from year to year, e.g. they ranged from 112 per cent to 571 per cent for milk powder between 1970 and 1977. This system has the effect of stabilising the agricultural prices in the EC but destabilising those prevailing in the free markets.

Apart from import levies, agricultural protection also takes the form of non-tariff barriers, quotas, exaggerated health restrictions, domestic subsidies and price supports and subsidised exports of food products. The level of agricultural protection is very high relative to the protection given to manufactures where nominal tariffs are generally less than 10 per cent.

The effects of the CAP are damaging not only to the LDCs and primary exporting MDCs (e.g. Australia, Canada,

New Zealand and the United States) in depressing and destabilising the free market prices of agricultural products but
also to the EEC member-countries themselves. Resources are
inefficiently used in the agricultural sectors which could earn
higher returns elsewhere and costs of food and raw materials
to consumers and firms respectively are higher than they
would otherwise be. We have examined in turn the various
strategic, environmental and social arguments which have
been put forward in support of the continuation of the CAP
and shown that none are really convincing. What has
preserved the CAP over the years has been the political
influences of its beneficiaries, i.e. the vested land, farming
and farm industry interests within the EC.

As far as LDCs are concerned, it has been estimated
that a fifty per cent reduction in trade barriers in the EEC
would increase their exports in 1977 values by 35 per cent or
$3 billion. Net food importing LDCs would, however, lose.
After allowing time for redirection of investment and income
effects, the gains to LDCs would probably be significant.

THE WORLD FOOD PROBLEM

Although for the world as a whole the production of food has
consistently increased at a faster rate than population over
the past twenty years and prices of wheat, rice and corn
have fallen in real terms, there has been some decline in the
rate of growth of output and an actual decrease in per capita
output in the low income LDCs, particularly in Africa. As
population has continued to rise fast there are more people
who are inadequately fed now than ten years ago.

To raise the food standards of undernourished people in
the poorest regions of the world, it may not be effective to
simply increase output or to give more aid to the governments
of the countries involved to enable them to pay for greater
amounts of food imports, since even during famines there has
often been sufficient food available within the affected
countries. The main cause of starvation has been that particular groups in the poor countries had no resources to pay
for food in years of bad harvests because of harvest failures,
lack of work, or increased prices for their staple foods.
Factors such as wars or civil strife and poor transport have
often made the distribution of famine relief difficult and
expensive.

In view of the skewed distribution of income both across
nations and within nations, it may be misleading to look at
food production at the world level or even at the country
level. It is more relevant to ascertain the target groups who
are at risk of hunger, facing either chronic or transitory
food insecurity. The best approach appears to be to target
help on such people, particularly where local food production

361

is vulnerable to the vagaries of the weather, to produce more of these products in which they have comparative advantage, be these food or non-food crops, semi-processed goods or simple manufactures in order to raise and stabilise their real incomes. In practice, because of market imperfections, trade barriers, transport difficulties and possible government restrictions in war conditions, poor people may find it difficult or excessively expensive to supplement their food consumption by buying food produced elsewhere. If this happens then the optimal interventions appear to be government provided work or income support given directly to people affected to help them to buy food. Sometimes because of lack of trading opportunities, they may have to be assisted to produce more food for their own need even if they appear to be less efficient in producing food than other cash crops for export or it is cheaper to give their governments money to import food.

THE WAY AHEAD

Progress in the implementation of policy proposals for dealing at the international level with the commodity problems of LDCs depends crucially on the continuation of MDCs' interest and cooperation. But the upsurge of MDCs' interest in 1974/75 turned out to be temporary. They soon realised that the necessary conditions for successful cartels are lacking for most of the minerals and, a fortiori, agricultural commodities with coffee a possible lone exception. The continuing weakening of OPEC's control over oil prices erodes further their remaining fears about cartel actions. Although the governments in MDCs continue to be rather concerned about domestic inflation and have retained costly measures (in terms of unemployment and loss of output and growth) to control it, they seem to assume that the inflationary effect of commodity price instability on their economies is small and has been exaggerated by supporters of the NIEO.

Their concern about the security of supplies of several key minerals has remained. But if they are worried about a sudden shortage of key minerals, the obvious course of action open to them would be to intensify their search for substitutes, to reduce their reliance on these minerals, to hold larger stocks of them and secure long term contracts with the few countries supplying them rather than making general NIEO type concessions to LDCs. As a consequence of the decline in MDCs' interest in these commodity issues, most of the UNCTAD proposals are likely to languish.

Despite the opposition of farming interests in France and Germany, it is likely that the EC will revise its common agricultural policy. This would not be because of any increase in the member countries' concern for the Third World but because of the costs to national budgets of growing stocks of unsold commodities in EC warehouses and export subsidies, and the political pressure which these give rise to from some adversely affected member-countries such as the United Kingdom. The ways in which the CAP is reformed can have very different effects on LDCs as exporters and importers of agricultural products. For example, a removal of protection on major food products would reduce food production in the EC, increase EC import of food, leading to a rise in world food prices which would benefit food exporting countries but would create problems for net food importing LDCs.

Theoretical reasoning and empirical evidence, largely from country modelling studies, clearly suggest that commodity instability need not be a problem for those countries which can afford to hold adequate reserves or borrow abroad to enable them to adopt domestic measures to insulate their economies from its effects. It can still cause considerable hardship to those poor countries which cannot afford to hold sufficient reserves or borrow easily from the international capital markets. But, even for these countries the failure of UNCTAD initiatives to establish an independent Common Fund with substantial financial resources of its own and the limited success of ICAs to stabilise commodity prices need not cause much concern because even if such measures had been established and even if fluctuations in the prices of storable commodities had been smoothed considerably, the extent this would help to stabilise the export earnings of these LDCs could well be very limited.

Our review of evidence and arguments suggests that the best way to help those countries most adversely affected by commodity instability is the provision of a generous international compensatory financing facility such as an appropriately revised IMF-CFF. To transform it into a satisfactory mechanism for tackling the instability problems at both macro and sectoral levels in the LDCs generally would involve an increase in the contributions of MDCs to the facility (largely to finance its interest subsidy account) by an amount which is small relative to their total aid to LDCs. For example, according to our calculations, the interest subsidy on CFF loans of 3.3 billion SDRs in 1981 was about 200 million SDRs. Assuming that all reasonable proposed reforms had been carried out in 1961 and the outstanding total debt had then increased four times, the resulting subsidy in 1981 would still have amounted to less than 1 billion SDRs. The real cost to the international community for stabilising the foreign exchange receipts of commodity exporters (excluding interest subsidy) via such a facility would be smaller still, as it is a matter of the MDCs creating a larger volume of paper money or credits.

The World Bank predictions of sluggish growth in the commodity export earnings of LDCs for the years up to 1995 may be too pessimistic. They are particularly sensitive to the assumptions about the underlying future growth rate of real GDP and inflation. If once MDCs can manage to control their domestic cost-push inflation and shift their attention to expansionary measures to hasten recovery, demands for commodities will revive and export earnings from commodities will probably grow at a much faster rate than the Bank forecast. Furthermore, as the level of unemployment in MDCs recedes and output accelerates, aid flows to LDCs may also rise not only absolutely but also relative to the MDCs' national income.

SUGGESTIONS FOR FURTHER RESEARCH

To improve understanding of commodity instability there is a clear need for further investigation into the causes of shifts in production, consumption and of changes in stock both for individual countries and for the world. Consumer demands for most food products are related to income, population and taste – none of which do fluctuate much from year to year and income elasticities for food are, in any case, mostly low. Hence violent annual swings in world prices of these commodities are due to shifts in production in both exporting and importing countries. Changes in the planted area in response to prices prevailing one or more years earlier may be partly responsible for the shifts in production. Better information flows among producers, consumers and traders concerning planted areas and planned production for a few years ahead would help to break the alternation of periods of high and low prices of the cob-web type.

The World Bank price projections do influence the plans of major producers. They should be as accurate as is possible in this uncertain world. Further research by the World Bank to improve their projections almost certainly pay good dividends in terms of better informed decisions. Special attention should be paid not only to the need to improve the specification and estimation of the models used, but also to the task of gathering better quality data and obtaining better forecasts of the variables which are assumed to be given, such as growth rates of real GDP in MDCs and LDCs, the trends of oil prices and prices of manufactures, the effects of technological changes and policy changes.

The evidence does suggest that for all commodities the export volumes of most countries fluctuate considerably more than the aggregate volume for the whole world. This reflects the tendency for volume to be rising in some countries while at the same time it is falling in others. This implies that for most countries, stabilising domestic producers' prices may do little to reduce the instability of producers' income. National income stabilisation schemes for individual export sectors would be required. As producers' incomes become more stable, it is possible that future production would also become more stable as farmers and mine directors may no longer respond so violently to short term price movements. Further research into the effectiveness of existing domestic stabilisation schemes, the end uses of compensatory loans and into ways in which such loans can be used to reduce the vulnerability of yields to weather conditions and pests, i.e. random shifts in supply, would also be useful to help to design policies to moderate commodity instability.

For those commodities for which futures markets exist, the determination of market prices (spot prices or prices of actuals) could be dominated at various times by speculation rather than by the real market forces. Sudden changes in current or expected interest rates and exchange rates could have pronounced effects on stock changes and market prices. We now have good descriptions of how these futures markets function. But it would be useful to have further research into the underlying relationships between spot prices and futures prices and factors determining the level and volatility of future prices. The fact that the income elasticity of demand for most commodities is considerably less than unity means that the share of commodities in the value of world trade or income is likely to fall steadily through time. For some commodities such as hard fibres, jute and tea which are almost entirely produced in LDCs, the decline in share may well be quite steep. This does imply that LDCs as a group should diversify away from such commodities. It does not necessarily follow that individual countries with relatively low costs of production for them should not expand such exports. There is a need for more cost-benefit studies for each commodity at both aggregate Third World level and country level to assist in the selection of projects which together determine an efficient future production plan. In carrying out a cost-benefit analysis for an individual country, it is important to make valid assumptions about the likely behaviour of rival producers.

There is also a need for further cost-benefit studies on the location of processing industries for primary products. While it is essential to state clearly all crucial assumptions, recognise explicitly their limitations as a partial equilibrium approach and/or piecemeal welfare approach and pay special attention to the need to remove some of the limitations, the importance of cost-benefit analyses for development or trade policies can hardly be overstated. Further research to improve methods of dealing with such difficult problems as equity (income distribution), externalities, scale economies and uncertainty should also have high priority.

Finally, the policies which seem best on the basis of economic analysis may not be adopted for political, social and/or military reasons. Hidden political motives may be stronger than apparent economic interests in determining the outcomes of most economic negotiations between governments. The search for practical solutions to economic problems facing primary producing LDCs and MDCs demands inter-disciplinary investigations of the complex interaction of political and economic factors in the determination of policies. Given the failure of commodity power, the search for progress on improving the economic prospects for LDCs' commodity trade probably depends on the identification of areas of mutual interest between, at least some, LDCs and MDCs. Economic research can help in that task by, for example, quantifying more accurately and objectively the likely benefits and costs to citizens and nations of the European Community of various possible reforms of the Common Agricultural Policy.

EPILOGUE

The world of trade in primary commodities is fraught with problems. Some stem from the very nature of the products involved. Demand and supply elasticities are low and their responses to price change usually lagged in complex ways, sometimes delayed for years. But many of the complexities and difficulties are man-made. The policies of governments in this area often seem particularly misguided if they intend to promote the welfare of their own citizens and avoid damaging the interests of other nations when there is no real conflict of national objectives. Yet the protectionist policies adopted by most of the industrially developed nations damage the interests of their own citizens as consumers of agricultural products. It also costs them jobs and incomes as producers of manufactures by lowering incomes and demand both at home and abroad.

Within many of the poor developing countries also government policies damage the interests of the majority of their citizens. Low fixed prices to farmers, overvalued exchange rates and heavily protected manufacturing industries all serve to harm the rural people, most of whom are poor and depend directly or indirectly on agriculture for their livelihood.

Most people in most countries would be better off if these market distortions in both the developed and developing countries were reduced or ended. One potentially important caveat (apart from the adjustment costs involved in any removal of trade barriers and subsidies) applies to LDCs which export commodities with low demand elasticities. If they simultaneously expand exports their revenues would fall. One solution would be for them to impose uniform ad valorem taxes on such exports. This would reduce supplies and raise prices while leaving the market free to operate so that efficient producers could earn higher profits and would expand while inefficient producers could be forced to contract. But at best this is itself a second best solution to the problem. A better one would be for the LDCs to remove all price distortions and for the MDCs to compensate the producers with economic aid for the loss of income caused by terms of trade shift.

If the problem of escalation of tariff and other barriers as the stage of processing rises were also tackled by abolishing or reducing the differential rates of protection accorded to the more processed forms of commodities, there would again be benefits to consumers in rich countries and producers in poor. These official barriers are well known and the gains, though probably not large, would be significant. There may be other obstacles to LDC processing e.g. freight rates may discriminate against them and there may be barriers to entry in some processing industries due to obligopoly or cartel arrangements between existing producers. There remains a need for hard evidence on such practices before policies can be formulated, but reduced barriers to trade in goods and services would of themselves tend to erode any such monopolistic practices by widening markets and facilitating new entry.

Instability

The reduction of protection would itself reduce instability in world prices. But those developing countries which are particularly vulnerable to instability in export earnings need further help. The most cost-effective way of providing such help would be through compensatory financing. That, if properly designed and operated, can smooth the flow of foreign exchange available to a country to enable it to pursue its own objectives.

If ad valorem tariffs on exports were designed so as to produce a particular average percentage rate over, say five years, but to fall more than proportionately in a year when prices fall and to rise more than proportionately when prices rise, this would automatically reduce fluctuations in the prices received by producers. It would not however take care of supply instability caused by weather, disease, strikes or other random shocks. It has been argued forcibly that to take care of producer income instability requires an additional complementary financing facility which would compensate the country for export shortfalls for each commodity. But this could actually destabilise a country's total earnings and is really an unnecessary complication. As long as the country has confidence that its total import capacity will be stabilised by an effective compensatory financing scheme it can undertake domestic action to smooth variations in each sector's revenues. That confidence could be provided by a reformed IMF CFF in which shortfalls were compensated in real terms on a more or less automatic and certain basis with repayments determined in the same way, i.e. they should be made when

367

real export earnings are above trend. The volume of resources available for the CFF should at least grow in line with the growth in value of world trade.

World Food Security

The world seems capable of producing enough food to meet world demand. But this does not mean that hunger will disappear. Even in the rich countries there is hunger because some people lack incomes and the social security systems fail them. Within most developing countries social security systems do not exist. Many people suffer chronic food insecurity because they lack the means to produce enough food or their incomes are inadequate and uncertain or the prices of their staple foodstuffs are too high and variable. Help needs to be targeted on these vulnerable groups. For those who are farmers the appropriate policies are likely to be to raise their productivity through better incentives and institutional reforms. Whether they should produce food or more cash crops depends on the structure of costs and prices which face them. It is important that these prices should represent marginal opportunity costs at the farmgate i.e. including transportation, so that in more remote areas self sufficiency in food production and local stocks would be encouraged. Children in both rural and urban areas may need to be protected by special programmes such as school milk and meals. Job creation through rural public work may be necessary if the stimulus to agriculture does not create enough jobs.

In urban areas higher food prices will harm the poor. Either increased incomes through more and better employment opportunities or subsidised food will have to be provided. If the latter, access should be restricted to the target groups e.g. by distribution through schools, clinics or food ration shops near the homes of the poor.

The causes of famine or acute intermittent food insecurity have to be diagnosed before remedies are proposed. Research has shown that many famines have occurred in countries where there were adequate supplies of food. When that happens the appropriate solution is often to provide income through public employment or other means to the starving so that they can buy food. It has the advantage over bringing in food from abroad in that it raises rather than lowers the incentives to local farmers to produce more food.

Of course, countries and remote regions within them do sometimes run short of food. Then national stocks of food (an expensive solution) or international liquidity to pay for food imports are the alternatives. Only if the political or financial risks of relying on the international market seem excessive should a nation follow the self-sufficiency route in production and stocks.

For most countries future risks of food crises probably would be most efficiently handled by increased food trade, better communications, financial reserves or adequate lines of credit, including the IMF's special facility for financing cereal imports, and some combination of traders' stocks and public international stocks.

APPLICATION OF COMPONENT ANALYSIS*

LDCs as a group have a decreasing share in total world commodity exports. This reflects the fact that their growth rate of total commodity export earnings is lower than that of the World. The difference between the LDCs growth rate (g_j) and that of the world (g) can be decomposed into two components: (i) the commodity-mix component (CMC) and (ii) the regional component (RC) of growth differential. The RC measures the extent to which the growth differential can be attributed to the regional factors specific to LDCs. The CMC measures the remaining part of the deficiency of LDCs' growth which is due to the 'wrong' commodity structure of their exports, i.e. they tend to specialise in the 'wrong' commodities - those with low world growth rates. To isolate the regional effects, LDCs' exports of individual commodities are each assumed to have the same growth rate as those of the world. This is done in order to compute a potential growth rate of LDCs' total commodity exports. The difference between this growth rate and the actual LDCs' growth rate is defined as the <u>RC</u> of the growth differential and the difference between it and the world growth rate is defined as the <u>CMC</u> of the growth differential.

THE MODEL

<u>Decomposition I</u>

$$GD_j = CMC_j + RC_j \qquad\qquad (1)$$

$$GD_j = g_j - g \qquad\qquad \text{(Growth differential)} \quad (2)$$

$$RC_j = \sum_i^n w_{ij} (g_{ij} - g_i) \qquad \text{(Regional component)} \quad (3)$$

---

*In Regional Economics this technique is widely known as the 'Shift-Share' technique.

$$CMC_j = \sum_i^n (w_{ij} - w_i) g_i \quad \text{(Commodity-mix component) (4)}$$

where –

$w_{ij} = X_{ij}{}^t / X_j^t$ $(t = \begin{cases} 0 \text{ for initial year weight} \\ 1 \text{ for terminal year weight} \end{cases})$

X_{ij} = export earnings of commodity i by regional group j;

$X_j = \sum_i^n X_{ij}$ = Total export region j (n = number of commodities).

$X_i = \sum_j^m X_{ij}$ = World export value of commodity i. (m = number of regional groups)

$X = \sum_i^m X_i$ = World total export

$w_i = X_i/X$

$g_{ij} = (X_{ij}^1 - X_{ij}^0) / X_{ij}^t$ (t is either 0 or 1)

(X_{ij}^1 and X_{ij}^0 refer to the

values of X_{ij} in the initial

terminal years respectively).

$g_i = (X_i^1 - X_i^0)/X_i^t$

Note:

$$g = \sum_i^n w_i g_i \quad \text{and} \quad g_j = \sum_i^n w_{ij} g_{ij}$$

(The choice of the initial year or terminal year as the base year (t) can significantly effect the results.)

Equations (1) - (4) above give only one possible decomposition. Three other are:

APPENDICES

Decomposition II

$$g_i - g = \sum_i^n (w_{ij} - w_i)g_{ij} + \sum_i^n w_i \ (g_{ij} - g_i) \tag{5}$$

Decomposition III

$$g_j - g = \sum_i^n (w_{ij} - w_i)g_{ij} + \sum_i^n w_{ij}(g_{ij} - g_i)$$
$$- \sum(w_{ij} - w_i) \ (g_{ij} - g_i) \tag{6}$$

Decomposition IV

$$g_j - g = \sum_i^n (w_{ij} - w_i)g_i + \sum_i^n w(g_{ij} - g_i)$$
$$+ \sum(w_{ij} - w_i)(g_{ij} - g_i) \tag{7}$$

The term on the right hand side of (6) and (7) may be called the interaction component (IC), which measures the extent to which regional group j specialises in exporting those commodities in which it has comparatively better growth performance.

Explanations for negative CMC
World demand for commodities which figure prominently in the export trade of LDCs has grown relatively slowly.

Explanations for negative RC
On average, growth rates of export earnings associated with individual commodities are lower for LDCs than the World. Since the difference between the growth rates of prices of the World and LDCs is likely to be very small, differences in the growth rates of earnings are largely due to the difference in growth rates of quantities. LDCs may have lower growth rates of quantities than those of the World because (i) protection policies in MDCs reduce MDCs' demand and increase MDCs'

supply, (ii) diversification, import-substitution and industrialisation policies in LDCs reduce their production and
hence export supply to the World and (iii) faster population
growth and income growth in LDCs (than in the World) speed up
the growth rate of their internal demand, leading again to a
reduction in their export supply (given production).

The interpretation of results is not always easy and the
results may depend a great deal on the choice of the base year
and the particular decomposition (I - IV).

APPENDIX B

EXTENDED JOHNSON MODEL

Let countries 1 and 2 represent respectively the primary
exporting regions (the periphery) and the manufacture exporting regions (centre). For convenience, the list of definitions
of symbols used is first given, to be followed by equations.

Definitions

X_1 = Demand for country 1's export by country 2.

X_2 = Demand for country 2's export by country 1.

P_1 = Price of country 1's good in terms of its currency.

P_2 = Price of country 2's good in terms of its currency.

Y_1 = Output of country 1, i.e. income valued in units of its
domestic good.

Y_2 = Output of country 2.

R = Exchange rate of country 1, expressing the number of
units of country 2's currency per unit of country 1's
currency.

$T = RP_1/P_2$ = Terms of trade of country 1, in terms of
country 2's currency.

$e_1 = \dfrac{Y_1}{X_2} \dfrac{dX_2}{dY_1}$ = Income - elasticity of country 1's demand
for country 2's export.

$e_2 = \dfrac{Y_2}{X_1} \dfrac{dX_1}{dY_2}$ = Income - elasticity of country 2's demand
for country 1's export.

$n_1 = \dfrac{-(1/T)}{X_2} \dfrac{dX_2}{d(1/T)}$ = Price - elasticity of country 1's demand
for country 2's export.

373

APPENDICES

$$n_2 = \frac{-T}{x_1} \frac{dX_1}{dT} \quad = \text{Price - elasticity of country 2's demand for country 1's export.}$$

$$B = \frac{TX_1}{X_2} \quad = \text{Ratio of country 1's export and import in country 2's currency.}$$

t = time and $\frac{dXi}{dYj}$ is the partial derivatives of X_i with respect to Y_j $(i,j = 1,2)$

Johnson suggests that an increase in B represents a 'real' improvement in the trade balance, whereas an increase in B* = $TX_1 - X_2$ represents a 'monetary' improvement in the trade balance. In considering the change in the trade balance he prefers the first criterion because 'real' balance is the more fundamental, and that changes in its money value arising from general movements in prices are more appropriately treated as gains or losses in purchasing power on capital account and also because it simplifies the argument and analysis (Johnson (1954), p. 98). Note that an increase in B implies an increase in B* only if initially B* = 0.

Import demand
By assuming no money illusion, so that the import demand for each product is homogenous of degree zero in the two prices and incomes, the demand functions may take the following simple form:

$$X_1 = f_1(T_1 \; Y_2) \tag{1}$$

$$X_2 = f_2(1/T, \; Y_1) \tag{2}$$

Terms of Trade
Johnson did not consider any change in the exchange rate (R) so that R needs not appear at all, provided that units of currency are so chosen that R = 1. Since we shall consider an induced change in R to restore trade balance, R has to be explicitly included in the definition of the terms of trade.

$$T = RP_1/P_2 \tag{3}$$

Real Trade balance on export/import ratio

$$B = TX_1/X_2 \tag{4}$$

Differentiating (4) with respect to t (time) to give:

$$\dot{B} = (1 - n_1 - n_2) \; \dot{T} + e_1 \; \dot{Y}_2 - e_2 \dot{Y}_1 \tag{5}$$

374

where $\dot{B}$, $\dot{T}$, $\dot{Y}_2$ and $\dot{Y}_1$, are the proportional growth rates of B, T, Y_2 and Y_1 respectively.

Differentiating (3) with respect to t and dividing through by T give:

$$\dot{T} = \dot{R} + \dot{P}_1 - \dot{P}_2 \qquad (6)$$

where $\dot{R}$, $\dot{P}_1$ and $\dot{P}_2$ are growth rates of R, P_1 and P_2 respectively.

Equation (5) above is basically the same as equation (1) in Johnson (1954). Initially, we shall follow Johnson to assume that $\dot{Y}_1$ and $\dot{Y}_2$ are <u>exogenously</u> determined by technical progress and capital accumulation. Thus, $\dot{Y}_1$ and $\dot{Y}_2$ may be conceived to be full capacity growth rates. In so far as a country has to reduce its income to correct a trade deficit under a fixed exchange rate, then actual income growth rate could be lower than this full capacity growth rate.

In the following analysis, we shall follow Prebisch-Singer to assume P_2 to be determined exogenously by para-market forces in country 2 and P_1 to be determined <u>exogenously</u> by productivity increase in country 1.

The effect of Prebisch-Singer's asymmetry of price responses

With the help of this model, let us now reconsider Spraos's contention that the asymmetry in the responses of prices to productivity increases along Prebisch-Singer's line would not by itself be sufficient to produce the deterioration in the terms of trade. Let us follow Spraos in the illustration to assume that

$$\dot{Y}_1 = \dot{Y}_2 \text{ and } e_1 = e_2 = 1 \text{ so that } e_1 \dot{Y}_1 = e_2 \dot{Y}_2$$

and equation (5) reduces to:

$$\dot{B} = (1 - n_1 - n_2) \dot{T} \qquad (7)$$

Suppose now owing to asymmetrical responses to productivity increases, P_1 falls, where P_2 remains constant and suppose the exchange rate is initially fixed, (e.g. the two countries pursue a fixed exchange rate regime), so that $\dot{R} = 0$, the terms of trade must deteriorate, i.e. $\dot{T} = \dot{P}_1 < 0$. It can be seen from (7) that a deterioration in the terms of trade would lead to an improvement in the real trade balance if the sum of elasticities, $n_1 + n_2$, exceeds unity but would lead to a worsening in the real trade balance if such sum falls short of unity.

Hence, in the Johnson Model and under a <u>fixed exchange rate</u> Prebisch-Singer's asymmetry could by itself produce the deterioration in the terms of trade, while the real trade balance improves or worsens depending on whether the sum of price elasticities exceeds or falls short of unity. Note that it is implicitly assumed that the export quantity of each product is determined by its respective demand, i.e. supply price elasticities are infinite.

Suppose now it is assumed that the exchange rate would appreciate ($\dot{R} > 0$) if the trade balance improves ($\dot{B} > 0$) and would depreciate ($\dot{R} < 0$) if the trade balance worsens ($\dot{B} < 0$), i.e. under a flexible exchange rate system. Let us consider first the case in which the sum of elasticities exceeds unity. In such a case, an initial $\dot{T} = \dot{P}_1 < 0$ suggests $\dot{B} > 0$. This would lead to $\dot{R} > 0$ which would in turn increase T. Thus, equilibrium trade balance requires:

$$\dot{B} = \dot{T} = \dot{R} + \dot{P}_1 = 0 \quad \text{or} \quad \dot{R} = -\dot{P}_1 > 0$$

In other words, Prebisch-Singer's asymmetry by itself would cause a proportionate increase in the exchange rate and would leave the terms of trade constant.

Let us now consider the case in which the sum of elasticities falls short of unity. In such a case, an initial negative $\dot{T}$ would lead to a negative $\dot{B}$ and a negative $\dot{R}$. A negative $\dot{R}$ would then reduce T and $\dot{B}$ further. Hence, we have a disequilibrium case. If to reverse $\dot{B} < 0$, country 1 increase R instead of reducing it (say because it is aware of the fact that the sum of elasticity falls short of unity and hence a deterioration in the trade balance requires an appreciation in the exchange rate). Then both $\dot{T}$ and $\dot{B}$ could be reduced to zero, and the asymmetry of price responses would again have the effect of raising the exchange rate, leaving the terms of the trade constant. Thus, under a <u>flexible exchange rate regime</u>, the (trade balance) equilibrium terms of trade is constant if the growth rate of demand induced by income increases in the two countries are the same (i.e. $e_1 \dot{Y}_1 = e_2 \dot{Y}_2$). However, under a <u>fixed exchange rate regime</u>, the asymmetry of price responses would lead to a deterioration in the terms of trade as well as in the trade balance of the periphery (if the sum of elasticities falls short of unity). Since in practice the burden of adjustment falls on the trade deficit countries, the periphery may then have to reduce its income growth (to reduce its imports) [5].

Hence, the asymmetry of price responses along Prebisch-Singer's line would harm the periphery not only via deterioration in its terms of trade but also possibly a lower growth rate of income than the rate permitted by productivity increase.

Terms of trade under conditions of trade balance equilibrium

Setting $\dot{B}$ in equation (5) to zero and solving for $\dot{T}$, we would obtain the (trade balance) equilibrium terms of trade under flexible exchange rate:

$$\dot{T} = (e_2 \dot{Y}_2 - e_1 \dot{Y}_1)/(n_1 + n_2 - 1) \qquad (8)$$

where $\dot{Y}_1$ and $\dot{Y}_2$ are full capacity growth rates of income.

It can be seen from equation (8) that the equilibrium terms of trade would depend on income elasticities (e_1, e_2), price elasticities (n_1, n_2) and income growth rates ($\dot{Y}_1$, $\dot{Y}_2$).

If the sum of price elasticities exceeds unity, then the greater (smaller) is the income elasticity of the demand for country 1's export relative to that of its import demand and the higher (lower) is the growth rate of income in country 2 relative to its lower growth rate, the more (less) favourable is the movement in its equilibrium terms of trade.

The importance of income elasticities can be illustrated by the following numerical example. Let $\dot{Y}_1 = \dot{Y}_2 = 2.5$ per cent per annum, $n_1 + n_2 = 1.5$, and $e_2 = 0.8$. The terms of trade can be seen to deteriorate at the rate of 1.0 per cent per annum. Thus, a rate of deterioration of the term of trade equal to the prevailing rate over the 1870s-1938 period could be brought about by a small difference in the income elasticities as <u>above</u>. Furthermore, if the sum of price elasticities is $\overline{1.25}$ instead of 1.5, the difference in the income elasticities could be only 0.1 (instead of 0.2) to produce the same rate of deterioration in the terms of trade. In practice income elasticity of demand for primary commodities may not only be low but also fall over time owing to (i) the operation of Engels' law in foodstuffs and (ii) the effect of technical progress on the supply of synthetic substitutes for natural products and on the raw material content of manufactures. Hence, in terms of the Johnson model, where price elasticities of supply are assumed infinite at exogenously given prices, the primary terms of trade could be expected to deteriorate at an increasing rate over time if the growth rates of the periphery and the centre are the same.

Sum of price elasticities less than unity

If the sum of price elasticities falls short of unity, then to correct a trade deficit, country 1 should increase the exchange rate, i.e. $\dot{R} > 0$ if $\dot{T} < 0$. In such a case, the equilibrium trend in the terms of trade would paradoxically be the higher, the lower (higher) is the growth in the demand for country 1's export (import). However, in practice, it is difficult to imagine any country would raise its exchange rate to correct a trade deficit. Furthermore, the relevant price elasticities here are long-term rather than short-term, and while the sum of short-term price elasticities could plausibly be less than unity, the sum of long-term ones would most probably be greater than unity. Hence, although this case yields interesting theoretical implications, it is unlikely to be important in practice.

Capital accumulation, technical progress, economies of scale and diminishing returns

In the context of the Johnson Model capital accumulation, technical progress and economies of scale in each country could be reflected in raising its income growth rate and diminishing returns to land would have the effect of lowering its income growth. Hence, the argument that the future primary terms of trade would improve because of limits to growth resulting from diminishing returns associated with the fixed stocks of land-based resources would also suggest a lower growth rate of productivity in the primary exporting region. This illustrates once again the fact that improvement (deterioration) in the terms of trade by itself does not have clear welfare implication.

APPENDIX C

PROJECTIONS BEYOND 2000

Limits-to-Growth.

The 'limits-to-growth' arguments may be summarised as follows. The prevailing social value is inherently unstable because it possesses the characteristics of fast growth, environmental limits and feedback delays. Since fast growth persist owing to feedback delays, the physical system temporarily expands well beyond its ultimately sustainable limits. During this period of overshoot, the short-term efforts required to maintain the excess population and capital are likely to erode or delete the resource base. The environmental carrying capacity will then be reduced as a consequence so that it can support only a much smaller population and lower material standard of living than would have been' possible before the overshoot. The result is an <u>uncontrollable decline</u> to lower levels of population and capital. (See <u>Dyamics of Growth in a Future World</u>, the technical report on World 3.)

These conclusions clearly call for urgent actions to reduce capital and population growth, to protect the earth's resource base. However, most economic and political decisions made today are based implicitly on a world view which is in direct conflict with the taking of these actions. The contemporary dominant view is that physical growth can and should continue; that technology and the price system can eliminate scarcities with little delay; that the resource base can be expanded but never reduced; that the solution of short-term problems will yield long-term results; and that population and capital, if they must ever stabilise will do so automatically, and at an optimal level. (See Meadows et.al. (1974), pp 561-63)

The 'limits-to-growth' conclusions are based on a global model, World 3, of the long term relationships between population, resources and the environment. This model describes the general patterns of causation by which these three factors interact and feedback on one another. It is general and strategy-orientated and makes no attempt to develop specific detailed analysis. In particular it deals with problems at global level rather than those of specific regions. Furthermore, many of its assumptions are controversial, e.g. it assumes that technology cannot alleviate natural limits. It neglects fossil fuels and social factors such as income distribution and international order, which may produce limiting problems well before actual physical limits are encountered and fails to allow for changes in the nature of economic growth which may reduce its dependency on limiting resources.

Mankind at the turning point

The conclusion of the second report of the Club of Rome are based on the Mesarovic-Pestel model. While World 3 treats the world as a one system which is projected to collapse in the middle of the next century if present trends continue and to prevent such a collapse, an immediate slowdown of economic growth is recommended, the Mesarovic-Pestel model views the world as a system of interacting regions and projects possible collapse at regional levels rather than at a global level. However, it suggests that such collapse will be felt throughout the entire world because of the close linkage between the regions.

The conclusions of the second report of the Club of Rome, however, are apparently not supported by clear references to the model form used to generate them. There are numerous ways that a model such as this one can be rigged to produce an outcome. For example, in one version of the model, it is assumed that new materials for nuclear power were available in unlimited quantities, yet this assumption has not been made known, nor is the problem caused by the generation of nuclear power discussed. It is conceivable that half a dozen equally controversial assumptions exist, unidentified, in the model's computer program. Thus, the most serious criticism of the model lies in its inadequate documentation and proof of validation. No statistical test results nor evidence of the model's ability to reproduce historical patterns of behaviour can be found anywhere in the accessible documentation. (See Global 2000 Report, p. 608)

APPENDICES

THE NEXT 200 YEARS

The Hudson Institute stresses the very temporary nature of the
current population phenomenon (abnormal growth) in a longer-
term perspective. It contends (p.30)

> '... despite ... the anticipated twenty-fold increase in
> world population over the 1776-2176 period, any expec-
> tations of exponential population growth continuing over
> appreciable periods of time can only be a delusion, at
> best a rather naïve extrapolation of an unusual human
> experience into the indefinite future without a real
> understanding of the dynamic forces involved. To those
> who cry out that this exponential growth must stop, the
> answer is that it does in fact appear to be stopping now,
> and not for reasons associated with desperate physical
> limitations to growth'.

According to the Hudson Institute, the rate of economic growth
will continue to be positive but gradually decrease more
because of a slowing pace of demand than because of increasing
difficulties in obtaining physical supplies. Population growth
will level off because of such factors as modernisation,
literacy, urbanisation, affluence, safety, good health and
birth control, and governmental and private policies reflecting changing values and priorities.
   The Hudson Institute is concerned that the beliefs and
attitudes in creating resistance to growth may not only impede
the resolution of our current problem but perhaps also lead to
the kind of disasters everyone wants to prevent, i.e. that
these beliefs will become in effect self-fulfilling proph-
ecies.
   Conclusions of the Hudson Institute serve to reinforce
the current world view held by most western governments
discussed earlier. They simply rationalise the present pre-
occupation with short-term economic problems, associated with
inflation and business cycles while leaving the future long-
term problems of over-population, resource base depletion and
pollution to the future generations to deal with. Although
many of the arguments of the Hudson Institute appear plausible, the conclusions are not based on any formal model
involving relationship between crucial factors as is the case
in the other studies and hence have not gained as much serious
attention as these other studies. Indeed, in a System Research
Centre paper of September, 1977, Mesarovic and Pestel reported
testing scenarios from The Next 200 Years, using their model,
and found the Hudson Institute's conclusions full of errors.
For example, they questioned the validity of the Hudson
Institute statement concerning the ease of adjustment to a
sudden disappearance of oil reserves, as they found it impos-
ible to design any energy programme in Western Europe and

Japan which could within ten years reduce energy demand and
increase energy production from non-petroleum sources sufficiently to compensate for the loss of the Persian Gulf by
1987.

APPENDIX D

MEAN AND VARIANCE OF A LOG-NORMAL VARIABLE

The estimate of a log-linear trend by least-squares method
presupposes the following time series model:

$$x_t = a + bt + u_t \tag{1}$$

where $x_t = \log X_t$ and u_t is the residual term which is assumed
to have the following properties:

$$E(u_t) = 0 \tag{2}$$

$$E(u_t u_{t-s}) = \begin{cases} 0 \text{ for } s = 0 \\ \sigma^2 \text{ for } s \neq 0 \end{cases} \text{for all } t \tag{3}$$

i.e. u_t is assumed to have zero expected mean, constant
variance and zero covariance (non-autocorrelated).

$E(u_t) = \int_{-\infty}^{\infty} u_t f(u_t)dt$, where $f(u_t)$ is the probability density
of u_t.

The above assumptions (2) and (3) are required for the least-
squares method to yield unbiased and efficient estimates. On
the basis of (1) above, the trend is given by

$$\hat{X}_t = e^{a + bt} \tag{4}$$

and the actual value may be expressed as follows:

$$X_t = \hat{X}_t U_t \tag{5}$$

where the multiplicative error

$$U_t = e^{u_t} = (X_t/\hat{X}_t) \tag{6}$$

Assuming that u_t has a normal distribution with mean 0 and
variance σ^2, i.e. $u_t \sim N(0, \sigma^2)$, can we say anything about the
distribution of U_t? It can be shown that U_t has a log-normal
distribution with expected mean

$$\mu_U = e^{\frac{1}{2}\sigma^2} \tag{7}$$

381

APPENDICES

and variance

$$\sigma_U^2 = e^{\sigma^2} (e^{\sigma^2} - 1) = e^{2\sigma^2} - e^{\sigma^2} \tag{8}$$

Since the expected mean of U_t is $e^{\frac{1}{2}\sigma^2}$ rather than $e^0 = 1$, the expected mean of X_t is:

$$EX_t = e^{\frac{1}{2}\sigma^2} \hat{X}_t \tag{9}$$

which is greater than $\hat{X}_t$ because $e^{\frac{1}{2}\sigma^2} > 1$, for $\sigma^2 > 0$. This implies that stabilising (fully or partially) X_t will reduce its expected mean, a consequence which has to be taken into account when the desirability of stabilisation is considered.

An unbiased estimate of σ^2 is given by:

$$\hat{\sigma}^2 = \frac{1}{n-2} \sum_{t=1}^{n} \tilde{u}_t^2 \tag{10}$$

where $\tilde{u}_t$ is the least-squares estimate of the residual u_t and n is the sample size. Since σ^2 is the only remaining parameter of both u_t and U_t (given that u_t has zero expected mean), it may be useful to have an unbiased estimate of it. One can then use $\hat{\sigma}^2$ to estimate the expected mean and variance of U_t, using equations (7) and (8) respectively. One useful measure of the variation of U_t is its coefficient of variation, given by

$$C_U = \sigma_U / \mu_U = \sqrt{e^{\sigma^2} - 1} \tag{11}$$

By replacing σ_u by $\hat{\sigma}_u$ in (11), we can obtain an unbiased

estimate of C_U of U_t, i.e.

$$\tilde{C}_U = \sqrt{e^{\hat{\sigma}^2} - 1} \tag{12}$$

$\tilde{C}_U$ is a possible instability index : it measures the variation of U_t or the ratio $X_t / \hat{X}_t$.

Massell has used $\hat{\sigma}^2$ as an instability index, even though it has no clear interpretation, apart from being the log-variance of U. Now consider our instability index I_3:

$$I_3 = \sqrt{\frac{1}{n} \sum_{t=1}^{n} \left[\frac{x_t - \hat{X}_t}{\hat{X}_t} \right]^2} = \sqrt{\frac{1}{n} \Sigma wt^2} \tag{13}$$

382

where $w_t^2 = \left(\dfrac{X_t - \hat{X}_t}{\hat{X}_t}\right)^2 = (U_t - 1)^2 = U_t^2 - 2U_t + 1$ (from (5) above)

$$\therefore \ Ew_t^2 = E\{U_t^2 - 2U_t + 1\} = EU_t^2 - 2EU_t + 1$$
$$= e^{2\sigma^2} - 2e^{\frac{1}{2}\sigma^2} + 1 \tag{14}$$

Since $\text{Log } U_t^2 = 2u_t \sim N(0, 4\sigma^2)$, $EU_t^2 = e^{2\sigma^2}$

and $Ew_t = E(U_t - 1) = e^{\frac{1}{2}\sigma^2} - 1$ (15)

$$\therefore \ \sigma_w^2 = Ew_t^2 - (Ew_t)^2 = e^{2\sigma^2} - 2e^{\frac{1}{2}\sigma^2} + 1 - (e^{\frac{1}{2}\sigma^2} - 1)^2$$
$$= e^{2\sigma^2} - e^{\sigma^2} = e^{\sigma^2}(e^{\sigma^2} - 1) \tag{16}$$

We can see that σ_w^2 given by (16) is identical to σ_U^2 given by (8). In other words, the percentage deviation of X from its trend has the same variance as the ratio of X to its trend. Little can be gained by using the coefficient of variation C_U rather than the standard error σ_U, since μ_U in $C_U = \sigma_U/\mu_U$ is itself a function of the same parameter σ^2. Since w refers to the percentage deviation of a variable from its trend, it is more meaningful to use the variance of this percentage as an index of instability. Hence, replacing σ^2 by $\hat{\sigma}^2$ in equation (16) should provide us with an instability index which is at the same time an unbiased estimate of the variance of the percentage deviation from trend. See Table A.1. below for different values of $\hat{\sigma}_w$ and $\hat{\mu}_w$ associated with different values of $\hat{\sigma}$.

It can be seen that I_3^2 in (13) will provide a biased estimate of σ_w^2. The bias would not be eliminated even if $(n/n-2)$ I_3^2 is used instead of I_3^2, because $\bar{w} = (1/n)\Sigma w_t \neq 0$. However, in practice, people may be interested to know the mean percentage deviation around a trend rather than to know what is an unbiased estimate of the variance of this percentage deviation. Hence I_3 is used in preference to $\hat{\sigma}_w$, even though it is a biased estimate of σ_w.

Table A.1

$\hat{\sigma}$	0.80	0.70	0.60	0.50	0.40	0.30	0.20	0.10
$\hat{\sigma}_w$	1.30	1.02	0.79	0.60	0.45	0.32	0.21	0.10
$\hat{\mu}_w$	0.38	0.28	0.20	0.13	0.08	0.05	0.02	0.005
$\tilde{s}_w$	1.36	1.05	0.81	0.62	0.46	0.32	0.21	0.10

$$\tilde{S}_w = \sqrt{Ew_t^2} = \sqrt{\sigma_w^2 + \tilde{\mu}_w^2}.$$ S_w^2 may be considered to be the expected mean of $(\overline{n-2})I_3^2$ Hence $E(I_3) = \sqrt{\dfrac{n-2}{n}} \cdot S_w$; with $\tilde{S}_w = 0.81$, $\tilde{I}_3 = \tilde{S}_w \sqrt{\dfrac{n-2}{n}}$ would be 0.72 and 0.77 for n equal 10 and 20 respectively.

APPENDIX E

THREE SIMPLE MARKET MODELS

Conventional Model

<u>Demand</u> : $q = a - bp + u$ (I.1)

<u>Supply</u>: $q = c + dp + v$ (I.2)

where q, p, u and v are quantity, price, demand shift and supply shift respectively, a and c are constants and b and d are price elasticities of demand and supply respectively. All variables (q, p, u and v) are in logarithms. Solving equations (I.1) and (I.2) simultaneously for p and q gives:

$$p = \frac{a - c}{b + d} + \frac{u - v}{b + d} \tag{I.3}$$

$$q = \frac{bc + da}{b + d} + \frac{bv + du}{b + d} \tag{I.4}$$

The logarithm of revenue is:

$$r = p + q = \frac{(1 + d)a - (1 - b)c}{b + d} + \frac{(1 + d)u - (1 - b)v}{b + d} \tag{1.5}$$

The variances of p, q and r are:

$$\text{Var } p = \frac{1}{(b + d)^2} [\text{Var } u + \text{Var } v] \tag{I.6}$$

$$\text{Var } q = \frac{1}{(b + d)^2} [d^2 \text{ Var } u + b^2 \text{ Var } v] \tag{I.7}$$

$$\text{Var } r = \frac{1}{(b + d)^2} [(1 + d)^2 \text{ Var } u + (1 - b) \text{ Var } v] \tag{I.8}$$

384

Lemma 1:

Given:

$$q_t + k\, q_{t-1} = w_t \qquad\qquad (1)$$

then:

$$\text{Var } q = \frac{\text{Var } w}{1 - k^2} \qquad\qquad (2)$$

Proof of Lemma 1:

Multiplying through equation (1) by q_{-1} and taking expectation give:

$$\text{Cov } (q,\, q_{-1}) + k\, \text{Var } q = 0$$

or

(since $E(q_{-1}{}^w) = 0$)

$$\text{Cov } (q,\, q_{-1}) = -k\, \text{Var } q \qquad\qquad (3)$$

Squaring both sides of (1) and taking expectation give:

$$E(q^2 + k^2 q_{-1}{}^2 + 2kqq_{-1}) = Ew^2 \qquad\qquad (4)$$

Since $E(q^2) = E(q_{-1}{}^2) = \text{Var } q$, equation (4) can be expressed:

$$(1 + k^2)\, \text{Var } q + 2k\, \text{Cov } (q,\, q_{-1}) = \text{Var } w \qquad\qquad (5)$$

Substituting (3) into (5) and dividing through by $1 - k^2$ give equation (2).

Cob-Web Model:

$$q = a - bp + u \qquad\qquad (\text{Ass. Cov } (u,\, u_{-1}) = 0) \quad (\text{II.1})$$

$$q = c + dp_{-1} + v \qquad (P_{-1} \text{ is p lagged by one period}) \quad (\text{II.2})$$

Equating (1) and (2) and rearranging give:

$$p + \frac{d}{b}\, p_{-1} = \frac{a - c}{b} + \frac{u - v}{b}$$

Stability requires $d < b$

or

$$p + k\, p_{-1} = w \qquad\qquad (\text{II.3})$$

385

APPENDICES

where $k = \dfrac{d}{b}$ and $w = \dfrac{a - c}{b} + \dfrac{u - v}{b}$

Var $w = \dfrac{1}{b^2}$ [Var u + Var v], assuming Cov $(u,v) = 0$.

Since $1 - k^2 = 1 - (d/b)^2 = (b^2 - d^2)/b^2$

$$\text{Var } p = \frac{\text{Var } u + \text{Var } v}{b^2 - d^2} \qquad \text{(by Lemma 1)} \qquad (II.4)$$

Similarly: $q + \dfrac{d}{b} q_{-1} = [\dfrac{d}{b}a + c] + [\dfrac{d}{b}u_{-1} + v]$

$$\text{Var } q = \frac{d^2 \text{ Var } u + b^2 \text{ Var } v}{b^2 - d^2} \qquad (II.5)$$

Since $r = p + q$,

$$r + \frac{d}{b} r_{-1} = [\frac{1 + d}{b} a + \frac{b - 1}{b} c] + [\frac{u + du_{-1}}{b} + \frac{b - 1}{b} v]$$

$$\text{Var } r = \frac{(1 + d)^2 \text{ Var } u + (b - 1)^2 \text{ Var } v}{b^2 - d^2} \qquad (II.6)$$

Nerlovian Adjustment-Lag Model

$$q = a + gq_{-1} - bp + u \qquad (III.1)$$

$$q = c + hq_{-1} + dp + v \qquad (III.2)$$

Solving for p, q and r gives:

$$p - kp_{-1} = \frac{1}{b+d} [u - hu_{-1} - v + gv_{-1}]$$

$$q - kq_{-1} = \frac{1}{b+d} [du + bv] \qquad (III.3)$$

$$r - kr_{-1} = \frac{1}{b+d} [(1 + d) u - hu_{-1} - (1 - b) v + gv_{-1}]$$

where $k = \dfrac{dg + bh}{b + d}$

The variances of p, q and r are then:

$$\text{Var } p = \frac{(1 + h^2) \text{ Var } u + (1 + g^2) \text{ Var } v}{(b + d)^2 - (dg + bh)^2} \tag{III.4}$$

$$\text{Var } q = \frac{d^2 \text{Var } u + b^2 \text{ Var } v}{(b + d)^2 - (dg + bh)^2} \tag{III.5}$$

$$\text{Var } r = \frac{[(1 + d)^2 + h^2] \text{ Var } u + [(1 - b)^2 + g^2] \text{ Var } v}{(b + d)^2 - (dg + bh)^2} \tag{III.6}$$

Note: While b and d represent both short-run and long-run price elasticities of demand and supply respectively in the conventional and cob-web models, they represent only short-run elasticities in the adjustment-lag model.

APPENDIX F

THE MODEL

Consider a country exporting commodities. The percentage deviation (U_{it}) of the export proceeds (X_{it}) of commodity i from its trend ($\bar{X}_{it}$) is defined as follows:

$$U_{it} = (X_{it} - \bar{X}_{it})/\bar{X}_{it} \tag{1}$$

and the percentage deviation of (U_t) of total export proceeds from its trend as follows:

$$U_t = (X_t - \bar{X}_t)\bar{X}_t \tag{2}$$

From (1) and (2) we obtain the following equation relating the instability of total exports to the weighted instability of the individual exports:

$$U_t = \sum_i^m w_{it} U_{it} \tag{3}$$

where $w_{it} = \bar{X}_{it}/\bar{X}_t$ and m is the number of commodities which make up the country's exports. Given that

$$X_t = \sum_i^m X_{it} \tag{4}$$

387

APPENDICES

and assuming that

$$\bar{X}_t = \sum_i^m \bar{X}_{it} \tag{5}$$

then the variance of U_t, which can be taken as a measure of the degree of instability, is

$$S_t^2 = E(U_t^2) = \sum_i^m \sum_j^m w_i w_j V_{ijt} \tag{6}$$

where $V_{ijt} = E(U_{it} U_{jt}) = \begin{cases} S_{it}^2 \text{ for } i = j \\ C_{ijt} \text{ for } i \neq j \end{cases}$ $\tag{7}$

S_{it}^2 and C_{ijt} are the variance of U_{it} and covariances of U_{it} and U_{jt} respectively S_t^2 would vary over time, not only because S_{it}^2 and C_{ijt} vary over time, but also because w_{it} ($i = 1...,m$) also vary over time as different commodities may be expected to have different trends in export proceeds.

To simplify the analysis, let us assume that S_{it}^2 and C_{ijt} remain constant at S_i and C_{ij} respectively so that S_t still varies over time only because w_{it} vary. Furthermore, to avoid the complications involving the presence of positive or negative covariances, we consider first the neutral case in which they are all zero. Equation (6) above becomes:

$$S_t^2 = \sum_i^m w_{it}^2 S_{it}^2 = C_t^2 \tilde{S}_t \tag{8}$$

where

$$C_t^2 = \sum_i^m w_{it}^2 \tag{9}$$

and

$$\tilde{S}_t^2 = \sum_i^m v_{it} S_i^2 \tag{10}$$

388

$$(v_{it} = w_{it}^2 \big/ \sum_{i}^{m} w_{it}^2 \; ; \; \text{hence,} \; \sum_{i}^{m} v_{it} = 1)$$

Thus the variance of U_t can be seen to be equal to the product of the concentration index and a weighted average of the variance of U_{it} with the weight being

$$v_{it} = w_{it}^2 \big/ \sum_{i}^{m} w_{it}^2$$

Equations (8) - (10) above provide us with the necessary exact mathematical framework to consider each of the causes listed above.

APPENDIX G

AN INTEGRATED ACTUALS AND FUTURES MODEL

List of variables and definitions
Endogenous variables

D = quantity of actuals demanded (consumption)

S = quantity of actuals supplied (production)

A = changes in stocks of actuals

A^S = supply of futures by hedging arbitrageurs

A^D = net demand for futures by speculators

P = spot (actuals) price

P^f = futures price (3 month-maturity)

Exogenous variables

P^e = expected spot price in 3 months' time

r = 3 month interest on finance for stock holding

THE SPOT OR ACTUALS MARKET

Demand for actuals

$$D = a_1 - a_2 P \hspace{3cm} (a_1, \, a_2 > 0) \hspace{2cm} (1)$$

APPENDICES

Supply of actuals

$$S = b_1 + b_2 P \qquad (b_1, b_2 > 0) \qquad (2)$$

$$(a_1 > b_1)$$

Equilibrium condition in actuals market

$$D + A = S \qquad (3)$$

Let b* and d* represent the long-run price elasticities of demand and supply, then b* and d* are related to b, d and the lag-coefficients g and h as follows:

$$b* = (1 - g)b \qquad (III.7)$$

$$d* = (1 - h)d \qquad (III.8)$$

Hence suppose the long-run price elasticities in the three models are the same and g = h = 0.5, then the short-run price elasticities in the adjustment lag model are only half of the corresponding ones in the other two models.

THE FUTURES MARKET

Supply of futures

Let us assume that merchants hedge stocks purchases (sales) by selling (buying) equivalent amounts in the futures market. Arbitrageurs see profits in buying per stocks now and simultaneously selling a futures contract as long as $P^f > p(1 + r)$ and vice versa. So the supply of futures contracts equals the demand for stocks. Hence,

$$A^S = c_1 [P^f - P(1 + r)] \qquad (4)$$

$$A = A^s \qquad (5)$$

For simplicity, it is assumed that only merchants deal in the futures market, producers and consumers do not and that futures contracts are not resold. In practice contracts may change hands many times before the delivery date.

Demand for futures

The demand for futures comes from speculators who expect the spot price in 3 months' time will exceed the present price for 3 months' futures. As long as $P^e > P^f$ they will buy futures. Their demand is therefore related to P^e and P^f, say:

$$A^D = d_1 (P^e - P^f) \qquad (6)$$

In practice, the turnover of the futures trading may be five to ten times as large as the value of trading in actuals. Hence speculators among themselves determine futures price, with arbitrageurs probably playing a minor role. In such a case, d_1 in (6) is large relative to c_1. In the limit, we can replace P^f in (4) by P^e and simplify the model as a result. Hence this model may be more general and complicated than necessary.

Equilibrium condition in futures market

$$A^S = A^D \qquad (7)$$

Since we have seven endogenous variables (unknowns) and seven equations, we can solve for each endogenous variable in terms of the two exogenous variables, P^e and r.

Substituting (1), (2), (4) and (5) into (3) and solving for P gives:

$$P = \frac{a_1 - b_1 + c_1 \, P^f}{a_2 + b_2 + c_1 \, (1 + r)} \qquad (8)$$

Equation (8) gives P in terms of P^f at which the actuals market is in equilibrium.

Substituting (8) into (4) and the result and (6) into (7) and solving for P^f give:

$$P^f = \frac{c_1 \, (1 + r) \, (a_1 - b_1) + [a_2 + b_2 + c_1 \, (1 + r)] \, d_1 \, P^e}{[a_2 + b_2 + c_1 \, (1 + r)] \, (d_1 + c_1) - c_1^2 \, (1 + r)} \qquad (9)$$

Equation (9) gives P^f in terms of P^e at which both actuals and future markets are in equilibrium. We shall assume the denominator positive so that $P^f > 0$.

For P > 0, we also assume $a_1 > b_1$. From (9) we can see that:

$$\frac{dP^f}{dP^e} > 0.$$

It can be shown

$$\frac{dP}{dP^e} > 0; \quad \frac{dA}{dP^e} > 0; \quad \frac{dD}{dP^e} < 0 \text{ and } \frac{dS}{dP^e} > 0.$$

From (8):

$$\frac{dP}{dP^e} = \frac{dP}{dP^f} \, \frac{dP^f}{dP^e} > 0, \text{ since } \frac{dP}{dP^f} > 0$$

391

APPENDICES

From (3):

$$\frac{dA}{dP^e} = \left(\frac{dS}{dP} - \frac{dD}{dP} \right) \frac{dP}{dP^e} > 0$$

since:

$$\frac{dS}{dP} - \frac{dD}{dP} = b_2 + a_2 > 0$$

From (1) and (2):

$$\frac{dD}{dP^e} = - a_2 \frac{dP}{dP^e} < 0 \text{ and } \frac{dS}{dP^e} = b_2 \frac{dP}{dP^e} > 0.$$

Note that as $d_1 \to \infty$, $P^f \to P^e$.

Thus an increase in the expected future spot price, P^e, would raise futures price, demand for stocks, spot price and production of actuals and reduce the consumption of actuals. An increase in the interest rate is equivalent to a reduction in the sum of the supply and demand's slopes, $a_2 + b_2$. It can similarly be shown that an increase in r reduces demand for stocks, hence futures supply, prices and production and raises consumption.

APPENDIX H

COMMODITY MODEL USED IN SIMULATION EXPERIMENTS

List of variables

Endogenous variables

D = demand

S = supply

K = private stocks

P = price

Exogenous variables

X = demand shift

Z = supply shift

392

Data for X and Z are generated by the following equations:

$$X_t = e_1 t + e_2 \sin(e_3 t) + e_4 + e_5 U_t$$

$$Z_t = f_1 t + f_2 \sin(f_3 t) + f_4 + f_5 V_t$$

U_t, $V_t \sim N(0,1)$. A sequence of 50 values each for U_t and V_t is obtained from a table of normal random numbers. Subscript t denotes times in years.

All variables are logarithms, except for U_t and V_t.

The equations

Demand

$$D = a_1 + a_2 D_{t-1} - a_3 P_{t-1} + a_4 X_t \tag{1}$$

Supply

$$S = b_1 + b_2 S_{t-1} + b_3 P_{t-1} + b_4 Z_t \tag{2}$$

Private Stocks Supply

$$K_t = \text{Log}_e \{\exp(K_{t-1}) + \exp(S_{t-1}) - \exp(D_{t-1})\} \tag{3}$$

Private Stocks Demand

$$P_t = c_1 + c_2 P_{t-1} - c_3 (K_t - D_t) \tag{4}$$

$$(a_1, a_2, a_3, a_4, b_1, b_2, b_3, b_4, c_1, c_2, c_3 > 0)$$

where $\exp(K_{t-1})$ stands for the exponential of K_{t-1} etc.

(Note $\exp(K_{t-1})$ represents the level of stocks, whereas K_{t-1} represents its logarithm.)

With initial values for D, S, K and P suitably chosen and the time series of X and Z, equations (1) - (4) can be used recursively to generate time series for D, S, K and P without buffer stocks operations.

BUFFER STOCKS

$\hat{P}_t$ = reference price level - projected trend value one year ahead

$P_t^c = \hat{P}_t + \log_e (1 + m)$ = ceiling price level

$P_t^f = \hat{P}_t - \log_e (1 + m)$ = floor price level

APPENDICES

(In experiments 1 and 2, m = 15 per cent when the buffer stocks partially stabilise price.)

The calculation of $\hat{P}_t$ is explained in the text.

In the absence of buffer stocks' activities, price is determined in equation (4), given demand, supply and private stocks determined by (1) – (3). Equation (4) is the inverse form of the demand for stocks, whose original form is:

$$K_t = (c_1 + c_2 P_{t-1} - P_t)/c_3 + D_t \qquad (4)^*$$

Suppose P_t, the market price without buffer stocks' purchase, is lower than P^f. For price to rise to P_t^f, K_t has to fall to K_t^f, the level determined by (4)* with P_t^f replacing P_t. To reduce private stocks from K_t to K_t^f, the buffer stocks must purchase the quantity exp (K_t) – exp (K_t^f). Note that both K_t and K_t^f are in logarithms. In other words, the size of the stocks purchased equals the difference between the level of private stocks people wish to hold at the floor price and the actual level prevailing at the beginning of the year (defined to be last year stocks plus the excess of last year supply over demand). Stock sales can similarly be determined when market price without stocks sales exceeds the ceiling price.

Table A.1: Component Analysis : Commodity Mix and Regional Components of Developing and Developed Countries (1971-81)

Developing Countries

$g_j = 220.8$ $G = 238.7$ $GD_j = -17.9$ $CMC = -4.4$ $RC = -13.5$

Commodity	w_{ij}	w_i	$w_{ij} - w_i$	g_i	$(w_{ij} - w_i)g_i$
Vegetable oils	7.4	14.5	-7.1	316.7	-22.4
Bovine meat	3.4	7.2	-3.8	292.6	-11.0
Iron ore	5.8	8.8	-3.1	181.9	-5.6
Copper	12.0	13.2	-1.2	115.4	-1.4
Phosphate R.	1.3	1.5	-0.1	371.3	-0.5
Cotton	11.3	11.4	-0.1	186.0	-0.3
Manganese O.	0.6	0.6	0.0	141.5	-0.1
Hard fibre	0.8	0.7	0.1	109.0	0.1
Jute	3.5	2.5	1.0	51.3	0.5
Timber	8.2	8.0	0.2	268.1	0.6
Bauxite	1.3	1.0	0.3	239.4	0.8
Tea	3.2	2.3	0.8	171.1	1.4
Bananas	2.9	1.9	1.1	143.1	1.5
Tin	3.4	2.5	0.9	283.6	2.6
Cocoa	4.2	2.5	1.9	199.5	3.3
Nat. rubber	5.2	3.2	2.0	249.8	5.0
Sugar	11.0	9.1	1.9	450.6	8.8
Coffee	14.9	9.2	5.8	213.0	12.3

Commodity	g_{ij}	g_i	$g_{ij}-g_i$	w_{ij}	$w_{ij}(g_{ij}-g_i)$
Sugar	366.6	450.6	-84.3	11.0	9.3
Cotton	127.1	186.0	-58.9	11.3	-6.6
Bovine meat	113.0	292.6	-179.6	3.4	-6.1
Coffee	198.7	213.0	-14.8	14.9	-2.2
Cocoa	182.7	199.5	-16.7	4.2	-0.7
Tea	156.1	171.1	-15.0	3.2	-0.5
Jute	42.8	51.3	-8.5	8.5	-0.3
Manganese O.	117.1	141.5	-24.4	0.6	-0.1
Bananas	141.1	143.1	-2.0	2.9	-0.1
Bauxite	242.9	239.4	3.5	1.3	0.0
Tin	290.2	283.6	6.6	3.4	0.2
Hard fibre	135.8	109.0	26.8	0.8	0.2
Nat. rubber	254.3	249.8	4.4	5.2	0.2
Phosphate R.	467.7	371.8	96.3	1.3	1.3
Timber	287.5	268.1	19.4	8.2	1.6
Iron ore	222.8	181.9	40.9	5.8	2.4
Copper	138.1	115.4	22.8	12.0	2.7
Vegetable oils	363.1	316.7	46.5	7.4	3.5

$$CMC_j = \sum_i (w_{ij} - w_i)g_i \quad ; \quad RC_j = \sum_i w_{ij}(g_{ij} - g_i) \quad ;$$

Table A.1: (Continued)

Developed Countries

$g_j = 287.7$ $g = 238.7$ $GD_j = 49.0$ $CMC_j = 8.4$ $RC_j = 40.7$

Commodity	w_{ij}	w_i	$w_{ij} - w_i$	g_i	$g_i(w_{ij} - w_i)$
Coffee	0.9	9.2	-8.3	213.0	-17.7
Sugar	5.7	9.1	-3.4	450.6	-15.2
Nat. rubber	0.2	3.2	-3.0	249.8	-7.4
Cocoa	0.1	2.5	-2.4	199.5	-4.8
Tin	1.1	2.5	-1.4	283.6	-3.9
Cotton	9.7	11.4	-1.7	186.0	-3.1
Tea	0.8	2.3	-1.5	171.1	-2.6
Bananas	0.4	1.9	-1.5	143.1	-2.1
Phosphate R.	1.0	1.5	-0.5	371.3	-1.7
Bauxite	0.6	1.0	-0.4	239.4	-1.0
Jute	1.0	2.5	-1.4	51.3	-0.7
Timber	7.9	8.0	-0.1	268.1	-0.2
Manganese O.	0.6	0.6	0.0	141.5	0.0
Hard fibre	0.8	0.7	0.0	109.0	0.0
Copper	15.7	13.2	2.5	115.4	2.8
Iron ore	12.7	8.8	3.9	181.9	7.0
Bovine meat	14.3	7.2	7.1	292.6	20.8
Vegetable oils	26.6	14.5	12.1	316.7	38.3

Commodity	g_{ij}	g_i	$g_{ij}-g_i$	w_{ij}	$w_{ij}(g_{ij}-g_i)$
Copper	84.0	115.4	-31.3	15.7	-4.9
Timber	254.7	268.1	-13.4	7.9	-1.1
Iron ore	174.3	181.9	-7.6	12.7	-1.0
Hard fibre	56.0	109.0	-53.0	0.8	-0.4
Nat. rubber	124.1	249.8	-125.8	0.2	-0.3
Bauxite	221.2	239.4	-18.2	0.6	-0.1
Jute	46.6	51.3	-4.7	1.0	0.0
Tin	283.0	283.6	-0.6	1.1	0.0
Tea	175.2	171.1	4.2	0.8	0.0
Bananas	173.4	143.1	30.3	0.4	0.1
Phosphate R.	401.9	371.3	30.6	1.0	0.3
Manganese O.	213.3	141.5	71.8	0.6	0.4
Cocoa	2229.5	199.5	2030.1	0.1	1.2
Vegetable oils	323.3	316.7	6.7	26.6	1.8
Coffee	665.8	213.0	452.7	0.9	3.9
Cotton	279.0	186.0	93.0	9.7	9.0
Bovine meat	359.4	292.6	66.8	14.3	9.5
Sugar	837.5	450.6	386.9	5.7	22.1

$GD_j = CMC_j + RC_j = g_j - g$; $g_j = \sum_i w_{ij} g_{ij}$; $g = \sum_i w_i g_i$

Source of data: UNCTAD Secretariat

Table A.2: Trends in World Trade in Selected Primary Commodities : 1961-80 (percentages)

Commodity	Export Value for LDCs in 1980 ($US billion)	Share of developing countries in world exports (average 1961-1980)	Average annual rates of growth: 1961-1980				
			Export value		Export quantity		Export unit value
			World	Developing countries	World	Developing countries	
Food Cereals							
Wheat	.8	5.4	10.0	8.5	3.4	2.4	6.4
Maize	1.0	15.5	15.4	10.1	8.6	3.4	6.3
Rice	2.1	42.6	9.6	6.3	2.3	-0.3	7.1
Livestock products							
Bovine meat	1.2	22.4	14.0	8.5	5.0	n.a	9.1
Fruit and spices							
Bananas	1.1	88.1	7.2	7.7	3.1	3.4	4.0
Pepper	.3	97.1	10.7	10.6	3.8	3.8	6.6
Oil-seeds and oils							
Groundnuts	.3	63.1	4.9	-0.4	-3.9	-8.4	9.2
Groundnut oil	.2	74.9	8.9	7.9	1.8	1.1	7.0
Copra	.2	99.7	-0.1	-0.1	-5.6	-5.6	5.5
Coconut oil	.7	86.3	13.7	13.6	7.0	7.0	6.3
Palm oil	1.9	94.3	18.2	18.1	10.6	10.6	6.9
Palm kernels	.06	99.7	-2.3	-2.4	-6.9	-6.9	4.9

Palm kernel oil	.2	80.6	15.9	19.0	8.6	11.0	6.7
Olive oil	.2	37.2	9.7	10.0	2.7	3.6	6.8
Soya beans	1.1	13.0	17.7	37.6	10.2	28.7	6.8
Soya bean oil	.5	16.4	17.1	66.3	10.3	58.4	6.2
Sunflower oil	-	12.9	13.1	21.0	6.6	12.1	6.7
Sugar	8.0	83.9	11.9	12.0	2.2	2.4	9.5
Beverages							
Tea	1.4	79.9	5.6	4.6	2.5	1.8	3.0
Cocoa	2.8	96.7	11.8	11.6	-0.2	-0.4	12.1
Coffee	11.8	94.5	11.3	11.0	1.3	1.1	9.8
Agricultural raw materials							
Cotton	3.4	54.3	7.1	5.6	1.0	-0.6	6.0
Wool	.2	15.9	2.7	-0.1	-1.9	-4.6	4.7
Sisal	.1	95.3	-0.4	-0.4	-5.9	-5.5	5.9
Jute	.2	95.2	-1.7	-2.0	-4.0	-4.1	2.3
Rubber	4.3	96.3	7.5	7.8	2.7	2.9	4.7
Non-coniferous wood	5.8	61.0	13.3	14.6	6.2	6.5	6.7
Tobacco	1.6	38.5	8.0	8.9	2.7	3.4	5.1
Minerals, ores and metals							
Phosphate rock	1.0	63.3	13.9	14.1	5.3	4.7	8.2
Manganese ore	.2	49.3	12.8	10.0	0.3	-2.1	11.0
Iron ore	3.2	39.6	9.6	9.3	6.1	5.7	3.3
Bauxite	.8	83.7	10.1	9.2	4.9	3.2	5.0
Alumina	1.1	36.2	19.0	14.2	14.4	8.7	4.2

Table A.2: (Continued)

Copper ore	1.2	60.5	17.0	17.7	10.9	11.5	5.5
Copper blister[a]	.9	51.6	5.1	4.1	-0.5	-1.3	5.6
Refined copper[a]	3.1	82.0	5.1	6.0	1.9	3.1	3.2
Tin ore and concentrates	.2	83.9	4.7	2.4	-3.8	-6.0	8.9
Refined tin	2.2	80.2	11.3	12.7	1.8	2.8	9.4

Source: UNCTAD secretariat calculations.

[a] Relates to 1970–1979

Table I.1: Instability and Commodity Concentration Indices of Developing Countries 1962-77

		INDEX 1	INDEX 2	INDEX 3	INDEX 4	EFR1	EFR2	GC1	GC2	GC3	SHAPE	M
1	Algeria	23.17	24.93	25.05	21.25	1.34	3.64	65.63	54.98	50.00	1.67	4
2	Angola	23.78	27.11	31.64	15.90	-3.72	-8.34	66.59	49.54	30.15	45.80	11
3	Benin	23.19	31.77	49.73	26.39	-6.06	-9.29	67.24	56.60	44.72	76.46	5
4	Botswana	49.30	36.00	42.64	49.67	7.83	7.87	98.79	75.72	70.71	26.14	2
5	Burundi	53.03	33.43	25.75	54.16	5.68	8.08	94.45	74.24	70.71	96.96	2
6	Cape Verde	51.39	37.14	34.03	52.35	2.89	3.55	92.02	73.49	70.71	7.85	2
7	Central Africa Emp.	28.13	25.21	22.22	27.53	-0.89	-2.74	56.24	49.29	40.82	59.74	6
8	Chad	27.12	33.74	49.24	27.91	-5.94	-1.94	88.77	67.71	57.74	85.24	3
9	Comoros	44.20	34.03	28.21	45.15	-0.08	-1.10	82.16	62.26	50.00	13.31	4
10	Congo	21.55	20.48	26.72	19.35	0.23	-1.59	69.66	53.02	35.36	37.50	8
11	Egypt	18.67	17.59	26.61	19.05	-1.04	-4.61	85.15	64.19	50.00	58.55	4
12	Ethiopia	31.12	19.70	33.08	38.73	3.60	-11.74	83.58	62.20	44.72	62.83	5
13	Gabon	22.96	23.20	23.91	23.20	-3.55	-4.03	69.11	58.29	57.74	25.91	3
14	Guana	26.88	26.37	29.65	24.40	-4.45	-6.00	81.78	61.48	44.72	74.76	5
15	Guadaloup	19.50	20.13	20.13	15.99	0.06	0.06	71.34	70.71	70.71	81.17	2
16	Guinea-Bissau	31.42	62.11	115.64	30.59	-10.42	-8.41	95.79	70.99	57.74	66.14	3
17	Guinea	98.67	72.16	36.00	97.64	-2.00	-2.73	76.55	58.16	44.72	54.84	5
18	Ivory Coast	39.60	35.91	32.03	27.26	-1.18	-0.22	55.29	49.69	40.82	78.35	6
19	Kenya	62.59	49.02	25.23	52.16	1.11	9.50	63.48	52.06	37.80	41.10	7
20	Liberia	13.54	17.29	31.71	12.27	-1.96	-3.80	76.51	57.89	40.82	91.85	6
21	Madagascar	27.25	22.63	22.16	28.97	-1.92	-3.62	66.14	49.88	33.33	50.25	9
22	Malawi	21.79	19.16	21.65	19.73	0.57	3.60	62.04	51.03	37.80	85.78	7
23	Mali	54.41	50.98	53.51	45.51	-3.38	7.15	71.89	57.92	44.72	52.32	5
24	Martinique	36.37	32.02	21.04	34.47	-2.77	-3.20	87.63	72.29	70.71	60.89	2
25	Mauritius	42.50	29.33	22.96	42.61	1.43	2.12	97.73	75.34	70.71	85.14	2
26	Morocco	65.08	49.95	24.79	62.42	-2.06	-5.42	81.26	59.08	35.36	44.56	8

#	Country											
27	Mozambique	29.06	25.87	20.39	18.95	1.00	7.91	44.49	39.64	33.33	52.32	9
28	Niger	41.89	28.30	23.69	42.52	2.98	2.84	94.58	70.35	57.74	31.29	3
29	Nigeria	14.81	14.07	15.00	14.93	-1.75	-2.66	58.13	47.95	40.82	12.81	6
30	Rhodesia	35.64	30.67	20.68	29.78	-1.08	2.94	74.66	56.44	40.82	28.49	6
31	Rwanda	54.03	39.05	35.52	53.46	-0.64	-0.78	82.23	71.18	70.71	90.21	2
32	Sao	22.98	20.00	18.92	21.94	-0.97	-1.34	83.14	65.51	57.74	97.89	3
33	Senegal	42.62	49.44	50.57	34.56	-1.40	-1.18	79.61	70.05	70.71	58.09	2
34	Sierra Leone	18.36	22.87	23.29	22.76	-2.38	-3.34	52.50	50.24	50.00	32.47	4
35	Sudan	15.03	29.80	72.88	20.51	-4.11	-7.48	77.93	64.38	57.74	73.41	3
36	Swaziland	44.81	38.94	38.48	44.22	-5.01	-6.67	91.28	67.16	50.00	54.76	4
37	Togo	45.64	33.61	22.56	45.07	-0.39	-0.97	61.72	52.12	44.72	91.22	5
38	Tunisia	51.03	45.18	34.93	38.87	-1.41	-1.49	63.93	53.07	44.72	29.45	5
39	United Republic Cameroon	28.39	27.07	25.76	18.04	-1.77	-1.60	52.48	42.75	33.33	70.80	9
40	United Republic Tanzania	29.03	24.71	26.87	24.11	-0.13	4.22	49.93	43.66	33.33	56.74	9
41	Uganda	26.29	17.87	16.36	29.62	0.50	-5.08	71.78	54.57	37.80	89.36	7
42	Upper Volta	31.48	20.72	26.01	50.60	6.00	0.10	72.51	62.25	57.74	37.29	3
43	Zaire	22.57	20.16	20.36	24.05	-2.01	-6.49	74.29	54.46	30.15	82.08	11
44	Zambia	28.66	30.16	40.08	29.34	-5.16	-5.46	97.91	70.90	50.00	91.47	4
45	Afghanistan	64.93	54.94	51.79	62.47	-4.75	-5.79	89.48	72.77	70.71	16.60	2
46	Bangladesh	48.62	43.41	41.51	47.50	-4.60	-5.55	90.66	73.09	70.71	84.27	2
47	Burma	30.21	26.63	30.42	26.30	-1.97	-2.71	68.77	53.01	31.62	80.15	10
48	Democratic Yemen	39.48	38.88	39.60	31.71	-2.60	-3.17	56.55	50.14	44.72	5.69	5
49	Cyprus	34.00	35.12	40.81	32.39	-6.75	-9.65	93.45	69.80	57.74	12.19	3
50	Fiji	32.31	26.64	23.94	30.61	-1.03	0.64	89.51	68.09	57.74	69.45	3
51	French Polynesian	40.76	53.77	54.95	31.79	0.41	0.62	78.51	70.76	70.71	29.04	2
52	Hong Kong	52.91	48.93	48.28	41.62	1.65	2.15	62.52	57.87	57.74	1.82	3
53	India	16.84	20.35	23.62	20.02	-3.50	-7.79	43.17	37.23	31.62	35.35	10
54	Indonesia	43.26	43.15	38.68	24.38	-1.10	-0.95	48.05	41.14	35.36	31.16	8
55	Iran	25.50	22.52	23.17	25.33	-0.31	-0.33	89.96	72.90	70.71	1.16	2
56	Jordan	64.38	62.33	80.74	61.72	-9.62	-12.50	92.66	67.94	50.00	31.38	4
57	Kampuche	41.51	28.29	33.29	35.85	8.00	17.36	61.85	49.11	40.82	75.13	6

Table I.1: (Continued)

58	Korea Republic	40.57	28.54	28.88	53.56	8.23	8.14	79.58	70.84	70.71	3.70	2
59	Lao	45.69	46.68	54.04	42.69	-4.77	-6.18	72.40	59.71	50.00	54.53	4
60	Lebanon	48.53	41.52	36.44	46.14	-0.07	1.06	71.89	60.55	57.74	2.69	3
61	Malaysia	28.60	30.04	37.67	16.36	-2.06	-2.01	53.70	47.45	37.80	70.92	7
62	New Hebrides	47.14	38.41	31.27	43.61	-2.30	-1.78	80.23	60.52	44.72	61.34	5
63	Pakistan	20.39	12.43	18.55	29.19	3.95	-2.00	65.54	56.61	50.00	38.81	4
64	Papua New Guinea	43.81	37.86	35.17	32.66	-0.02	0.66	53.07	45.99	44.72	68.00	5
65	Philippines	23.63	21.39	27.80	17.18	1.17	6.73	48.23	41.38	35.36	69.68	8
66	Samoa	40.32	40.82	40.86	31.18	-0.88	-0.87	63.07	57.74	57.74	90.82	3
67	Singapore	34.27	34.75	35.89	24.60	-0.44	-0.58	54.91	47.12	40.82	6.48	6
68	Solomons	36.81	36.70	44.43	31.22	-4.55	-6.49	72.71	63.77	57.74	70.16	3
69	Sri Lanka	17.91	17.52	20.80	16.42	-2.33	-2.08	73.29	59.01	50.00	75.94	4
70	Syrian Arab Republic	24.82	21.65	30.05	25.16	0.31	-2.08	94.07	70.09	57.74	30.72	3
71	Thailand	32.63	30.56	32.70	19.26	0.42	8.55	43.57	39.10	31.62	61.39	10
72	Tonga	31.77	36.22	37.32	32.15	0.07	0.06	79.37	70.82	70.71	72.54	2
73	Yemen	54.34	46.98	45.98	45.70	-4.37	-6.38	69.01	60.90	57.74	84.72	3
74	Antigua	93.09	72.44	66.64	90.30	-3.47	-4.26	84.39	71.57	70.71	4.31	2
75	Argentina	28.02	34.75	46.54	24.63	-5.34	-14.80	54.97	44.50	35.36	30.73	8
76	Belize	57.14	52.17	59.68	54.09	-8.92	-12.86	89.03	67.87	57.74	55.85	3
77	Bolivia	20.71	17.86	15.57	19.04	-0.18	4.02	75.55	56.12	37.80	73.63	7
78	Brazil	21.45	29.30	26.15	21.57	-1.98	-0.50	47.95	39.39	27.74	58.65	13
79	Chile	22.55	21.15	20.74	21.21	-3.15	-3.71	91.68	73.39	70.71	72.52	2
80	Columbia	22.67	28.48	28.74	30.92	-2.69	-1.74	83.58	60.87	37.80	71.04	7
81	Costa Rica	29.76	30.58	45.08	24.69	-5.12	-8.16	58.15	48.08	37.80	71.38	7
82	Cuba	43.42	35.46	30.94	43.11	-3.43	-4.60	97.31	70.56	50.00	72.29	4
83	Dominica	14.94	13.90	18.55	15.23	-0.70	-0.86	91.76	69.02	57.74	62.70	3
84	Dominican Republic	35.50	30.76	29.74	36.37	-2.68	-6.63	64.35	50.25	37.80	77.81	7
85	Equador	19.17	22.96	32.50	18.41	-1.10	-4.10	59.18	50.69	40.82	48.09	6

	Index 1	Index 2	Index 3	Index 4	EFR1	EFR2	GC1	GC2	GC3	Share	M
86 El Salvador	47.47	36.41	30.69	44.20	1.01	6.29	75.50	58.37	44.72	67.57	5
87 Grenada	24.93	47.42	73.84	21.15	11.54	10.93	70.80	59.40	57.74	49.51	3
88 Guatemala	44.80	40.87	23.78	34.01	-2.41	-3.05	60.57	48.96	37.80	65.15	7
89 Guyana	33.75	28.82	23.81	26.96	-1.66	-0.46	61.31	50.63	40.82	75.26	6
90 Hawaii	31.93	28.15	25.57	28.23	-1.03	0.22	61.46	49.01	37.80	70.47	7
91 Honduras	29.18	31.19	31.40	23.17	-2.27	-8.97	59.01	48.48	31.62	68.29	10
92 Jamaica	19.38	21.81	23.97	17.44	-1.80	-5.90	65.89	56.10	44.72	44.21	5
93 Mexico	16.08	15.11	16.36	18.14	0.53	-2.84	44.19	38.03	27.74	33.89	13
94 Nicaragua	30.82	28.47	13.20	24.37	1.69	10.59	52.01	45.01	33.33	71.27	9
95 Panama	11.74	13.88	25.25	20.29	-0.05	-6.94	78.43	59.87	44.72	47.67	5
96 Paraguay	59.90	49.56	48.00	39.96	3.63	9.37	46.11	39.99	37.80	54.15	7
97 Peru	13.49	12.79	10.88	15.25	0.22	3.64	45.59	39.89	35.36	59.69	8
98 St Ritts	44.03	38.52	41.29	43.82	-4.82	-8.32	98.97	72.60	57.74	91.14	3
99 St Lucia	26.26	24.33	26.74	24.45	-2.76	-2.97	82.95	65.42	57.74	72.72	3
100 St Vincent	29.01	27.18	37.01	29.79	-3.53	-5.07	85.54	66.51	57.74	56.48	3
101 Surinam	15.50	15.88	19.07	13.88	0.44	2.92	81.51	61.20	44.72	38.41	5
102 Trinidad	34.37	28.99	26.13	32.63	-2.35	-3.57	84.11	65.39	57.74	4.36	3
103 Uruguay	25.37	25.70	28.12	26.07	0.59	0.52	86.30	71.97	70.71	29.27	2
104 Venezuela	17.55	17.82	24.95	17.83	-1.26	-3.97	86.30	66.35	57.74	4.44	3
105 Turkey	25.24	21.10	24.05	20.85	1.22	4.51	65.61	54.65	37.80	43.58	7
Mean	26.10	23.89	24.94	24.13	-0.87	-1.10	54.43	43.86	36.77	34.59	23
Std Dev	20.24	17.60	19.58	19.05	3.02	4.89	34.21	26.99	24.05	24.05	

Index 1, Index 2 and Index 3 are instability indices associated with the shares used in the calculation of Gini-coefficients GC1, GC2 and GC3 respectively, whereas EFR1 and EFR2 are the differences between Index 1 and Index 2 and between Index 1 and Index 3 respectively which are due to correlations not equal zero. Index 4 is Index 1 with all correlations (between pairs of goods) equal zero. Share refers to percentage share of the commodities included here in total export earnings and M is the number of commodities exported by the country.

BIBLIOGRAPHY

Adams, F.G. and Behrman, J. (1982) Commodity Exports and Economic Development: The Commodity Problem, Goal Attainment and Policy in Developing Countries, Lexington Books, D.C. Heath, Lexington, Mass.

Adams, F.G., Behrman, J.R. and Roldan, R.A. (1979) 'Measuring the Impact of Primary Commodity Fluctuations on Economic Development: Coffee and Brazil', American Economic Review, 69, No. 2

Adams, F.G. and Klein, Sonia (1978) (eds.) Stabilising World Commodity Markets: Analysis, Practice and Policy, Lexington Books, D.C. Heath, Lexington, Mass.

Adams, F.G. and Priovolos, T. (1981) 'Commodity Exports, Economic Development and Policy: Coffee and Brazil', Unpublished Report to USAID, Philadelphia: Wharton Econometric Forecasting Associates Inc.

Adams, F.G., Behrman, J.R. and Lasaga, M. (1980) 'Commodity Exports and NIECO proposals for Buffer Stocks and Compensatory Finance: Implications for Latin America' in W. Baer and M. Gillis (eds.), Export Diversification and the New Protectionism: the Experiences of Latin America, University of Illinois, Urbana

Advisory Council (1985) Draft Report, Food Security in Africa, Dublin, November

Ady, P. (1969) 'International Commodity Policy' in E. Stewart (ed.), Economic Development and Cultural Change, Edinburgh University Press, Edinburgh

Arrowsmith, J.M. (1972) 'The Effect of the Post-War Tin Agreement on the Stability of Tin Prices and Export Proceeds', University of Michigan, Department of Economics, Discussion Paper No. 44

Ashworth, Fiona Gordon-Ashworth (1984) International Commodity Control: A Contemporary History and Appraisal, Croom Helm, London

- (1986) 'The Commodity Futures Markets', Bank of England, Quarterly Bulletin, vol. 26, No. 2

Avramovic, D. (1968) 'Common Fund: Why and What Kind?'

Journal of World Trade Law, 12, No. 5
- (1982) 'Commodity Price Instability: a Note' in R. French-Davis and E. Tironi (eds.), Latin America and the New International Economic Order, Macmillan Press, London, New York etc.
Bacha, E.L. (1978) 'An Interpretation of Unequal Exchange from Prebisch to Emmanuel', Journal of Development Economics, Vol. 5, 319-30
Balassa, B. (1978) 'Exports and Economic Growth: Further Evidence', Journal of Development Economics, Vol. 5, No. 2
- (1981) The Newly Industrialising Countries in the World Economy, Pergamon
Baldwin, R.E. (1955) 'Secular Movements in the Terms of Trade', American Economic Review, Papers and Proceedings, May, Vol. 45, 259-69
- (1966) Economic Development and Growth, John Wiley, New York
Bale, M.D. and Duncan, R.C. (1983) 'Food Prospects in the Developing Countries: A Qualified Optimistic View', The American Economic Review, Vol. 73, No. 2, May, 244-8.
Bale, M.D. and Southworth, V.R. (1982) 'World Agricultural Trade and Food Security: Emerging Patterns and Policy Directions', Wisconsin International Law Journal, Proceedings of the 1982 Symposium, United States Agricultural Export Policy, Vol. 1, 24-41
Bale, M. and Koester, U. (1983) 'Maginot Line of European Farm Policies', The World Economy, December, p. 381
Bale, M. and Lutz, E. (1978) 'Trade Restrictions and International Price Instability', World Bank Staff Working Paper, No. 303, October
Bates, R.H. (1981) Markets and States in Tropical Africa, The Political Basis of Agricultural Policies, The Regents of the University of California
Beckerman, W. (1985) 'How the Battle Against Inflation was Really Won', Lloyds Bank Review, January 1985
Behrman, J.R. (1977) International Commodity Agreements: An Evaluation of the UNCTAD Integrated Commodity Programme, Overseas Development Council, Washington DC
- (1978) Development, the International Economic Order and International Commodity Agreements, Perspectives on Economics Series, Addison-Wesley Publishing Company, Reading, Mass.
- (1978) 'International Commodity Structures and the Theory Underlying International Commodity Market Models' in F.G. Adams and J.R. Behrman (eds.), Econometric Modelling of World Commodity Policy, Lexington Books, D.C. Heath, Lexington, Mass.
- (1978) 'The UNCTAD Integrated Commodity Program: An Evaluation' in F.G. Adams and Sonia Klein (eds.),

Stabilising World Commodity Markets: Analysis, Practice and Policy, Lexington Books, D.C. Heath, Lexington, Mass.

- (1979) 'Commodity Agreements' in W.R. Cline (ed.), Proposals for a New International Economic Order: An Economic Analysis of Effects on Rich and Poor Countries, Praeger for Overseas Development Council, New York

- (1979) 'The Gains from Pooling Finances Across International Commodity Agreements', Modern Government/ National Development

- (1979) 'International Buffer Stock Commodity Agreements to Stabilise Prices: the Impact on Foreign Exchange Available to Developing Countries', Modern Government/ National Development

- (1981a) 'Segmented Markets for Latin American Primary Commodity Exports: Implications of Available Estimates for Identifying Dominant Source of Market Disturbances, Policies to Exploit Market Power and Some Econometric and Modelling Questions', Integracion Latinoamericana

- (1981b) 'Comment on "Distributional Effects of International Commodity Price Stabilisation"', Journal of Policy Modelling, 3

- (1981c) 'Comment on "The Importance of Supply and Demand Variations in Earnings Instability"', Mimeo, University of Pennsylvania, Philadelphia

Behrman, J. and Tinakorn, P. (1978) 'Evaluating Integrated Schemes for Commodity Market Stabilization' in F.G. Adams and J.R. Behrman (eds.), Econometric Modelling of World Commodities Project, Lexington Books, D.C. Heath, Lexington, Mass.

- (1979) 'The Impact of the UNCTAD Integrated Commodity Program on Latin American Export Earnings' in W. Labys, M. Ishaq Nadiri and J. Nunez del Arco (eds.), Commodity Markets in Latin American Development: A Modelling Approach, Ballinger Publishing Company and National Bureau of Economic Research, Cambridge, Mass.

- (1979) 'Indexation of International Commodity Prices through International Buffer Stock Operations', Journal of Policy Modelling, 1, No. 1

Beissner, K.H. and Hemmer, H.R. (1981) 'The Impact of the ECs Agricultural Policy on its Trade with Developing Countries', Intereconomics, March/April

Bell, R.T. (1979) 'Theories of the Terms of Trade of Less Developed Countries: A Critical Survey', Economia Internazionale, Vol. 32, 200-17

Bhagwati, J. (1957-58) 'Immiserizing Growth: A Geometric Note', Review of Economic Studies, Vol. 25, 201-5

- (1968) 'Distortions and Immiserizing Growth: A Generalisation', Review of Economic Studies, Vol. 35, 481-5

- (1973) 'The Theory of Immiserizing Growth: Further Applications' in A.K. Connolly and A. Swoboda (eds.),

International Trade and Money, Allen and Unwin, London
Bird, G. (1978) 'An Analysis of the Welfare Gains from Special Drawing Rights', Economia Internazionale, XXXI
- (1979) 'The Terms of Trade of Developing Countries: Theory, Evidence and Policy', Economia Internazionale, Vol. 32, 399-413
Blackwell, B. (1985) 'The World Economy', A Quarterly Journal on International Affairs, Trade Policy Research Centre, London, Vol. 8, No. 1, March
Body, R. (1982) Agriculture: The Triumph and the Shame, Temple Smith, London
Brandt, W. (Chairman) (1980) North-South: A Programme for Survival, Report of the Independent Commission on International Development Issues, Pan Books, London and Sydney
Brooks, E.M., Grilli, E.R. and Waelbroeck, J. (1977) 'Commodity Price Stabilization and the Developing World', World Bank Staff Working Paper, No. 26, Washington DC
Brown, A. (1979) 'On Measuring the Instability of Time Series Data: A Comment', Oxford Bulletin of Economics and Statistics, 41, No. 3
Brown, C.P. (1974) 'International Commodity Control through National Buffer Stocks: Case Study of Natural Rubber', Journal of Development Studies, January
- (1975) Primary Commodity Control, Oxford University Press, Oxford
- (1980) The Political and Social Economy of Commodity Control, Macmillan Press, London, New York etc.
Brundell, P., Horn, H. and Svedberg, P. (1981) 'On the Causes of Instability of Export Earnings', Oxford Bulletin of Economics and Statistics, 43, No. 3
Caine, S. (1958) 'Comment', Kyklos, Vol. XI, Fasc. 2
Clark, C. (1942) The Economics of 1960, Macmillan Press, London
Coppock, J.D. (1962) International Economic Instability, McGraw-Hill Publishing Company, New York
Corbett, H. (1974) 'Raw Materials: Beyond the Rhetoric of Commodity Power', Trade Policy Research Centre, London
Crowson, P.M. (1982/83) Minerals Handbook
Cuddy, J.D.A. (1978a) 'Commodity Stabilization: Its Effects on Producers and Consumers', Resource Policy, March
- (1978b) 'Financial Savings from the Common Fund', Weltwirtschaftliches Archiv, 3
- (1978c) 'The Common Fund and Earnings Stabilization', Journal of World Trade Law, 12, No. 2
- (1979a) 'Raw Materials: Commodity Agreements, Integrated Programme, Common Fund and Export Receipts Stabilization' in J. Rey (ed.), Le Role de L'Europe dans le Nouvel Ordre Economique International, Universite Libre de Bruxelles, Bruxelles

BIBLIOGRAPHY

- (1979b) 'Compensatory Financing in the North-South Dialogue', Journal of World Trade Law, 13, No. 1
- (1979c) 'Raw Materials: Commodity Agreements, Integrated Programme, Common Fund and Export Receipts Stabilization' in J. Rey (ed.), Le Role de L'Europe dans le Nouvel Ordre Economique International, Universite Libre de Bruxelles, Bruxelles
Cuddy, J.D.A. and Della Valle, P.A. (1978) 'Measuring the Instability of Time Series Data', Oxford Bulletin of Economics and Statistics, 40, No. 1
Dadone, A.A. and Di Marco, L.E. (1972) 'The Impact of Prebisch's Ideas on Modern Economic Analysis' in L.E. di Marco (ed.), International Economics and Development: Essays in Honour of Raul Prebisch, Academic Press, New York and London, pp. 15-34
Democoq, M. (1984) 'The Rationale and Modalities for Compensating Export Earnings Instability', Development and Change, 15, 3 July
Diaz-Alejandro, C. (1982) 'International Finance: Issues of Special Interest for Developing Countries' in R. Ffrench-Davis and E. Tironi, (eds.), Latin America and the New International Economic Order, Macmillan Press, London etc.
Dick, H., Gupta, S., Mayer, T. and Vincent, D.P. (1983) 'The Short-Run Impact of Fluctuations in Primary Commodity Prices on Three Developing Economies: Colombia, Ivory Coast and Kenya', World Development, Vol. 11, No. 5
Dick, H. and Rodemer (1983) 'Financial Implications of a Sweeping CAP Reform', The World Economy, March
Donaldson, G. and Lewis, C.M. (1983) The Trade and Marketing Dimension to Food Security in Developing Countries, AGREP Division Working Paper No. 80, September
Duggan, J.E. (1979) 'On Measurement of the Instability of Time Series Data', Oxford Bulletin of Economics and Statistics, 41, No. 3
Van Duyne, C. (1975) 'Commodity Cartels and the Theory of Derived Demand', Kyklos, 28
Eckbo, P.L. (1975) 'OPEC and the Experience of Previous International Commodity Cartels', MIT Energy Laboratory Working Paper No. 75-008WP
United Nations Economic Commission for Latin America (ECLA) (1962), Economic Bulletin for Latin America, October
Edwards, R. and Hallwood, P. (1980) 'The Determination of Optimum Buffer Stock Intervention Rules', Quarterly Journal of Economics, XCIV
Eicher, C.K. (1986) 'Transforming African Agriculture', The Hunger Project Paper, No. 4, January
Eicher, C.K. and Staatz, J.M. (1985) Food Security Policy in Sub-Saharan Africa, Department of Agricultural Eco-

nomics, Michigan State University

Ellsworth, P.T. (1956) 'The Terms of Trade Between Primary Producing and Industrial Countries', Inter-American Economic Affairs, Vol. 10, 47-65

Emmanuel, A. (1979) 'The Dynamics of Unequal Exchange/ Unequal Development', Paper presented to the ELEMEP Conference on Dependency in March 1979 at the London School of Economics

Erb, G.F. (1978) 'North-South Negotiations and Compensatory Financing', Overseas Development Council, Washington DC

Erb, G.F. and Schiavo-Campo, S. (1969) 'Export Instability, Level of Development and Economic Size of Less Developed Countries', Oxford Bulletin of Economics and Statistics, 31

European Communities (1975) 'The Lome Convention. The Stabilization of Export Earnings', Information, Development and Co-Operation, Commission of the European Communities, General Directorate for Information, document 94/75

- (1981) 'Comprehensive Report on the Export Earnings Stabilization System Established by the Lome Convention for the Years 1975-1979', Commission of the European Communities, Brussels, SEC (81) 1104

EEC, Yearbook of Agricultural Statistics, various issues

FAO, (Food and Agricultural Organisation) Commodity Review and Outlook, 1979-1980 (Rome 1979), pp. 112-14

- (1981) Agriculture: Toward 2000, Rome

- (1982) Director-General's Report on World Food Security: A Reappraisal of the Concepts and Approaches, Committee on World Food Security, Eighth Session, Rome, 13-20 April 1983

- (1985) 'World Food Security: Selected Themes and Issues', FAO Economic and Social Development Paper 53, Food and Agriculture Organization of the United Nations, Rome

Felder, G. (1982) 'On Exports and Economic Growth', Journal of Development Economics, 12

Findlay, R. (1980) 'The Terms of Trade and Equilibrium Growth in the World Economy', American Economic Review, Vol. 70, 291-9

- (1981) 'The Fundamental Determinants of the Terms of Trade' in S. Grassman and E. Lundberg (eds.), The World Economic Order: Past and Prospects, Macmillan Press, London and Basingstoke, pp. 425-63

Finger, M. and Derosa, D. (1978) 'Commodity-Price Stabilization and the Ratchet Effect', The World Economy, 1, No. 2

- (1980) 'The Compensatory Finance Facility and Export Instability', Journal of World Trade Law, 14, No. 1

Fisher, B.S. (1972) The International Coffee Agreement: A

411

Study in Coffee Diplomacy, Praeger, New York

Flanders, M.J. (1964) 'Prebisch on Protectionism: An Evaluation', Economic Journal, Vol. 74, 305-26

Fleming, M. et al. (1963) 'Export Norms and Their Role in Compensatory Financing', IMF Staff Papers, X

Ford, D. (1977) 'Simulation Analyses of Stabilization Policies in the International Coffee Market', Mimeo, Wharton Econometric Forecasting Associates Inc., Philadelphia

-    (1978) 'An Econometric Model of the World Coffee Economy: Version 2', Wharton Econometric Forecasting Associates Inc., Philadelphia

Fox, W.A. (1974) Tin: The Working of a Commodity Agreement, Mining Journal Books Ltd., London

Gelb, A.H. (1979) 'On the Definition and Measurement of Instability and the Costs of Buffering Export Fluctuations', Review of Economic Studies, 44

Gemmil, G.T. (1985) 'Forward Contracts or International Buffer Stocks? A Study of Their Relative Efficiencies in Stabilising Export Earnings', The Economic Journal, June

Gibson, B. (1980) 'Unequal Exchange: Theoretical Issues and Empirical Findings', Review of Radical Political Economics, Vol. 12 (Fall number), 15-35

Glezakos, C. (1973) 'Export Instability and Economic Growth: A Statistical Vertification', Economic Development and Cultural Change, 21

-    (1983) 'Instability and the Growth of Exports', Journal of Development Economics, 12

-    (1984) 'Export Instability and Economic Growth: Reply', Economic Development and Cultural Change, 32, No. 4

Goreux, L.M. (1980) Compensatory Financing Facility, International Monetary Fund, Pamphlet Series No. 34, Washington DC

-    (1981) 'Compensatory Financing for Fluctuations in the Cost of Cereal Imports' in A. Valdes (ed.), Food Security for Developing Countries, Westview Press, Boulder, Colorado

Green, C. and Kirkpatrick, C. (1980) 'Insulating Countries against Fluctuations in Domestic Production and Exports: An Analysis of Compensatory Financing Schemes', University of Manchester, Department of Economics, Discussion Paper No. 16

-    (1982) 'The IMF's Food Financing Facility', Journal of World Trade Law, 16

Grondona, L. St. Clare (1976) Economic Stability is Attainable, Hutchinson Benham, London

Gulati, I.S. (1980) 'Compensatory Financing: Inadequacy of Present Arrangements and New Proposals' in A. Sengupta (ed.), Commodities, Finance and Trade: Issues in North-South Negotiations, F. Pinter, Oxford

Gulbrandson, O. and Lindbeck, A. (1973) The Economics of the Agricultural Sector, Alinquist and Wicksell, Stockholm, p. 38

Haberler, G. (1961) 'Terms of Trade and Economic Development' in H. Ellis (ed.), Economic Development of Latin America, St. Martin's Press, New York, pp. 275-97

Hallwood, P. (1977) 'Interactions between Private Speculation and Buffer Stock Agencies in Commodity Stabilization', World Development, April

Harberger, A.C. (1957) 'Some Evidence on the International Price Mechanism', Journal of Political Economy, Vol. 65, 506-21

Harling, K. (1983) 'Agricultural Protectionism in Developed Countries: Analysis of Systems of Intervention', European Review of Agricultural Economics, 10, 223-47

Harrod, Sir Roy (1976), Preface to Grondona

Heady, C.J. (1981) 'Alternative Theories of Wages in Less Developed Countries: An Empirical Test', paper presented to the SSRC Development Economics Study Group on 27 November

Helleiner, G.K. (1966) 'Marketing Boards and Domestic Stabilization in Nigeria', Review of Economics and Statistics, 48

- (1980) International Economic Disorder: Essays in North-South Relations, Macmillan Press, London and Basingstoke

- (1981) Intra-Firm Trade and the Developing Countries, Macmillan Press

Hermann, R. (1982) 'The Effects of Partial International Price Stabilization on the Stability of National Export Earnings', Universitat Kiel, Kiel, Institut fur Agrarpolitik und Marktlehre, Diskussionsbeitrage, No. 46

- (1983) 'The Compensatory Financing System of the International Monetary Fund: An Analysis of its Effects and Comparisons with Alternative Systems', Forum Reports on Current Research in Agricultural Economics and Agribusiness Management, No. 4 (Kieler Wissenschaftsverlag Vauk)

Hewitt, A. (1983) STABEX: 'An Evaluation of Economic Impact over the First Five Years', World Development, December

Hildreth, C. (1977) 'What do we Know about Agricultural Producers' Behaviour under Price and Yield Instability', American Journal of Agricultural Economics, December

Hindley, B. (1985) 'Commodity Markets in their Policy Content', How Commodity Futures Markets Work, (Thames Essays), Trade Policy Research Centre

Hirsch, V. (1977) Rich Man's Poor Man's and Everyman's Goods, J.C.B. Mohr (Paul Siebeck), Tubingen, p. 121

House of Lords Select Committee on Commodity Prices (1977) 'Report', 18 May

Howarth, R.W. (1985) Farming for Farmers?, The Institute of Economic Affairs, Hobart Paperback 20

Hyde, F.L. (1963) 'A Critique of the Prebisch Thesis',

Economia Internazionale, Vol. 16, 463-87
IBRD (1965) Supplementary Financial Measures: A Study Requested by UNCTAD - 1964, Washington DC
-    (1979a), 'Stabilization of Export Earnings', Summing up by the Managing Director of the Discussion at the Meeting of the Committee of the Whole of the Development Committee 79/3
-    (1979b) Stabilization of Export Earnings, A Further Study Prepared by the Staff of the International Monetary Fund and the World Bank, revised, Washington DC
Imlah, A.H. (1950) Journal of Economic History, Vol. 10, 170-94
International Monetary Fund (1963) Compensatory Financing of Export Fluctuations, Washington DC, February
Isserlis, L. (1938) 'Tramp Shipping Cargoes and Freights', Journal of the Royal Statistical Society, Vol. 101, 53-146
Iwasaki, Y. and Konama, H. (1978) 'Japanese STABEX Arrangement with South-East Asia', International Development Center of Japan, Working Paper No. 10
Jenkins, T.N. (1982) 'The Benefits to the ACP Countries of the EEC-ACP Export Earnings Stabilisation Scheme', Journal of Agricultural Economics, XXXIII
Johnson, D.G. (1973) World Agriculture in Disarray, Macmillan Press
Johnson, H.G. (1955) 'Economic Expansion and International Trade', Manchester School of Economic and Social Studies, Vol. 23, pp. 95-112
-    (1959) 'Economic Development and International Trade', Nationalokonomisk Tidsskrift, Vol. 97, 253-72
-    (1967) Economic Policies Toward Less Developed Countries, Brookings Institution, Washington DC
-    (1968) 'The Gains from Exploiting Monopoly or Monopsony Power in International Trade', Economica, Vol. 35, 151-6
-    (1977) 'Commodities: Less Developed Countries' Demands and Developed Countries' Responses' in J. Bhagwati (ed.), The New International Economic Order: The North-South Dialogue, MIT Press, Cambridge, Mass. and London
Kaldor, N. (1964) 'Stabilizing the Terms of Trade of Under-Developed Countries', Economic Bulletin for Latin America, Vol. 8, 1-7
-    (1976) 'Inflation and Recession in the World Economy', Economic Journal, Vol. 86, No. 344, December, pp. 703-14
Kaln, H., Brown, W. and Martel, L. (1979) The Next 200 Years, Associated Business Programmes, London
Katrak, H. (1973) 'Commodity Concentration and Export Fluctuation: A Probability Analysis', Journal of Development Studies, 9, No. 4
Kemp, M.C. (1955) 'Technological Change, the Terms of Trade and Welfare', Economic Journal, Vol. 65, 457-73

Kenen, P. and Voivodas, C. (1972) 'Export Instability and Economic Growth, Kyklos, 25, 791-804
Kindleberger, C.P. (1956) The Terms of Trade: A European Case Study, Technology Press of MIT and John Wiley, New York and London; Chapman and Hall, London
- (1958) 'The Terms of Trade and Economic Development', Review of Economics and Statistics Supplement, Vol. 40, pp. 72-85, February
Kingston, J. (1976) 'Export Concentration and Export Performance in Developing Countries, 1954-67', Journal of Development Studies, 12
Knapman, B. and Schiavo-Campo, S. (1983) 'Growth and Fluctuations of Fiji's Exports, 1875-1978', Economic Development and Cultural Change, 32, No. 1
Knudsen, O. and Parnes, A. (1975) Trade Instability and Economic Development, Lexington Books, D.C. Heath, Lexington, Mass.
Knudsen, O. and Yotopoulos, P. (1976) 'A Transitory Income Approach to Export Instability', Food Research Institute Studies, XV, Washington DC
Koester, U. (1985) 'Regional Co-operation in the Food Sector', Mimeo of paper given to 19th International Conference of Agricultural Economists, Malaga, Spain, September 1985
Labys, W.C. (1978) 'Bibliography of Commodity Models' in F.G. Adams and J.R. Behrman (eds.), Econometric Modelling of World Commodity Policy, D.C. Heath, Lexington and Toronto
Labys, W.C. and Granger, C.W.J. (1970) Speculation, Hedging and Commodity Price Forecasts, Lexington Books, D.C. Heath, Lexington, Mass.
Labys, W.C. and Pollak, P.K. (1984) Commodity Models for Forecasting and Policy Analysis, Croom Helm, London
Labys, W.C. and Thomas, H.C. (1975) 'Speculation, Hedging and Commodity Price Behaviour: An International Comparison', Applied Economics, Vol. 7
Laird, S. and Yeats, A.J. (1986) 'Empirical Evidence Concerning the Magnitude and Effects of Developing Country Tariff Escalation', Discussion Paper
Lam, N.V. (1980a) 'Export Instability, Expansion and Market Concentration: A Methodological Interpretation', Journal of Development Economics, 7
- (1980b) 'Export Instability, Growth and Primary Commodity Concentration', Economia Internazionale, XXXIII, No. 1
Lancieri, E. (1978) 'Export Instability and Economic Development: A Reappraisal', Banca Nazionale del Lavoro Quarterly Review, 125
- (1979) 'Instability of Agricultural Exports', Banca Nazionale del Lavoro Quarterly Review, 130
Lasaga, M. (1981) The Copper Industry in the Chilean

Economy, An Econometric Analysis, Lexington Books,
D.C. Heath, Lexington, Mass.

Lawson, C. (1974) 'The Decline in World Export Instability, A
Reappraisal', Oxford Bulletin of Economics and Statistics,
36

—   (1980) 'Changes in the Export Instability of Less
Developed Countries: A Dissenting Note', Banca
Nazionale del Lavoro Quarterly Review, 132

Lawson, C.W. and Thanassoulas, C. (1981) 'Commodity Con-
centration and Export Instability: A Missing Link on
Hunting a Snack?', Bulletin of the Oxford Institute of
Economics and Statistics, pp 201-6

League of Nations (1945) Industrialisation and Foreign Trade,
Geneva

Lee, K.H. (1977) 'Export Structure and Export Instability',
The Developing Economies, XV, No. 3

Lerdau, E. (1962) 'Some Notes on the Terms of Trade and
Economic Development', Quarterly Journal of Economics,
Vol. 76, 464-70

Lewi, W.A. (1952) 'World Production, Prices and Trade,
1870-1960', Manchester School of Economic and Social
Studies, Vol. 21, 139-91

—   (1953) 'Economic Development with Unlimited Supplies of
Labour', Manchester School of Economic and Social
Studies, Vol. 21, 139-91

—   (1965) 'Economic Development and World Trade' in
E.A.G. Robinson (ed.), Problems in Economic Development, Macmillan Press, London, pp. 483-95

—   (1972) 'Reflections on Unlimited Labour' in L.E. Di Marco
(ed.), International Economics and Development: Essays
in Honour of Raul Prebisch, Academic Press, New York
and London, pp. 75-96

Lim, D. (1974) 'Export Instability and Economic Development:
The Example of West Malaysia', Oxford Economic Papers,
March

—   (1976) 'Export Instability and Economic Growth: A
Return to Fundamentals', Oxford Bulletin of Economics
and Statistics, 38, No. 4

—   (1980) 'Income Distribution, Export Instability and
Savings Behaviour', Economic Development and Cultural
Change, 28, No. 2

Lin, W.N. (1977) 'Measuring Aggregate Supply Response
under Instability', American Journal of Agricultural
Economics, 59, No. 5

Lira, R. (1980) 'The Impact of Copper in the Chilean
Economy' in W.C. Labys, M.I. Nadiri and J. Nunez de
Arco (eds.), Commodity Markets and Latin American
Development: A Modelling Approach, Ballinger Publishing
Company for National Bureau of Economic Research,
Cambridge, Mass.

Little, I.M.D. and Mirrlees, J.A. (1969) Social Cost Benefit

Analysis. Manual of Industrial Project Analysis in Developing Countries, Vol. II, OECD, Paris

Lloyd, P.J. and Procter, R.G. (1983) 'Commodity Decomposition of Export-Import Instability', Journal of Development Economics, 12

Lofchie, M.F. and Commins, S.K. (1984) 'Food Deficits and Agricultural Policies in Sub-Saharan Africa', The Hunger Project Papers, No. 2, September

Lord, M.J. (1979) 'The UNCTAD Integrated Program: Export Stabilization and Economic Growth in Latin America' in W. Labys, M.I. Nadiri and J. Nunez del Arco (eds.), Commodity Markets in Latin American Development: A Modelling Approach, Ballinger Publishing Company for National Bureau of Economic Research, Cambridge, Mass.

- (1981) 'Distributional Effects of International Commodity Price Stabilization: Do the Aggregate Gains Apply to Individual Countries?', Journal of Policy Modelling, 3, No. 1

Love, J. (1977) 'The Decline in Export Instability?', Oxford Bulletin of Economics and Statistics, 39

MacBean, A.I. (1966) Export Instability and Economic Development, George Allen and Unwin, London

- (1978) A Positive Approach to the International Economic Order. Part I: Trade and Structural Adjustment, British-North American Committee, London

MacBean, A. and Balasubramanyam, V.N. (1978) Meeting the Third World Challenge, 2nd ed., Macmillan Press for Trade Policy Research Centre, London

MacBean, A. and Nguyen, D.T. (1980) 'Commodity Concentration and Export Earnings Instability: A Mathematical Analysis', Economic Journal, 90

Maizels, A. (1968) 'Review of Export Instability and Economic Development', American Economic Review, 58

Massell, B. (1964) 'Export Concentration and Fluctuations in Export Earnings: A Cross-section Analysis', American Economic Review, 54

- (1969) 'Price Stabilization and Welfare', The Quarterly Journal of Economics, LXXXIII, No. 2

- (1970) 'Export Instability and Economic Structure', American Economic Review, 60

Mathews, A. (1985) The Common Agricultural Policy and the Less Developed Countries, Gill & Macmillan, Trocaire, 1985

Mathieson, D. and McKinnon, R. (1974) 'Instability in Under-Developed Countries: The Impact of the International Economy' in P.A. David and M.W. Reder (eds.), Nations and Households in Economic Growth, Academic Press, New York

Mayer, T. (1979) 'Exporterlosinstabilitat, Einkommens-schwankungen und Sparen in Entwicklungslandern' (Export Earnings Instability, Income Fluctuations and

417

BIBLIOGRAPHY

Savings in Developing Countries), Die Weltwirtschaft, No. 1

- (1980) 'Zum Zusammenhang zwischen Exporterlosschwankungen und Investitionsguterimporten in ausgewahlten Entwicklungslandern' (On the Relationship between Fluctuations of Export Earnings and Imports of Investment Goods in Selected Developing Countries), Konjunkturpolitik, Berlin, Vol. 26
- (1982a) 'Export Instability and Economic Development: The Case of Columbia', Weltwirtschaftliches Archiv - Review of World Economics, Vol. 118
- (1982b) 'Export Diversification as a Counter to Export Instability', Institut fur Weltwirtschaft an der Universitat Kiel, Kiel Working Paper, No. 145
- (1983) 'Instabile Exportmarkte und Wirtschaftliche Entwicklung: Der Fall Kolumbien' (Unstable Export Markets and Economic Development: The Case of Columbia), Kieler Studien 178, J.C.B. Mohr, Tubingen

McNicol, D.L. (1977) Commodity Agreements and Price Stabilization: A Policy Analysis, Lexington Books, D.C. Heath, Lexington, Mass.

Meade, J.E. (1964) 'International Commodity Agreements' in Proceedings of the United Nations Conference on Trade and Development, Vol. III, Commodity Trade, United Nations publication, Sales No. E64.II.B.13

- (1976) 'A Strategy for Commodity Policy', Scandinavian Journal of Economics

Meadows, D.H. and D.L. (1972) The Limits to Growth, Universe Books, New York

Meier, G.M. (1963) International Trade and Development, Harper and Row, New York and Evanston

Mesarovic, M. and Pestel, E. (1975) Mankind at the Turning Point, Hutchinson, London

Michaely, M. (1962) Concentration in International Trade, North Holland Publishing Co., Amsterdam

Moran, C. (1983) 'Export Fluctuations and Economic Growth', Journal of Development Economics, 12

Morgan, T. (1959-60) 'The Long-Run Terms of Trade Between Agriculture and Manufacturing', Economic Development and Cultural Change, Vol. 8, 1-23

- (1963) 'Trends in Terms of Trade and Their Repercussions on Primary Producers' in R. Harrod and D. Hague (eds.), International Trade Theory in a Developing World, Macmillan Press, London

Morrison, T. and Perez, L. (1976) 'Analysis of Compensatory Financing Schemes for Export Earnings Fluctuations in Developing Countries', World Development, Vol. 4, No. 8

Muller, J.C. (1980), 'The Stabex System in Lome II', The Courrier: Africa-Caribbean-Pacific-European Community, No. 62

Murray, D. (1978) 'Export Earnings Instability: Price, Quan-

tity, Supply, Demand?', Economic Development and Cultural Change, 2
- (1978) 'Statistical Measurement of Export Earnings Instability', Malayan Economic Review, 23, I
Naya, S. (1973) 'Fluctuations in Export Earnings and Economic Patterns of Asian Countries', Economic Development and Cultural Change, July
Newbery, D.M.G. and Stiglitz, J.E. (1981) The Theory of Commodity Price Stabilization. A Study in the Economics Risk, Clarendon Press, Oxford
Nguyen, D.T. (1979a) 'The Implications of Price Stabilization for the Short-Term Instability and Long-Term Level of LDCs' Export Earnings', Quarterly Journal of Economics, Vol. XCIII
- (1979b), 'The Effects of Partial Price Stabilization on Export Earnings Instability and Level: Implications for the North-South Negotiating Process' in A. Sangupta (ed.), Commodities, Finance and Trade: Issues in North-South Negotiations, F. Pinter, Oxford
- (1979c) 'The Sign of Covariance of Price and Quantity and the Predominant Cause of Market Instability', mimeographed, University of Lancaster, Lancaster
- (1980) 'Partial Price Stabilization and Export Earning Instability', Oxford Economic Papers, 32
Nurkse, R. (1959) Patterns of Trade and Development, Wiksell Lectures, Almqvist and Wiksell, Stockholm
Nziramasanga, M.T. and Obidegwu, C. (1981) 'Primary Commodity Price Fluctuations and Developing Countries: An Econometric Model of Copper and Zambia', Journal of Development Economics, Vol. 9, No. 1, 89-119
Oberhansli, H. (1980) 'Stabex und Inflation. Die Funktionstuchtigkeit des Stabilisierungsystems bei Geldentwertung', Aussenwirtschaft, 35
Obidegwu, C.F. and Nziramasanga, M. (1981) Copper and Zambia: An Econometric Analysis, Lexington Books, D.C. Heath, Lexington, Mass.
Okun, A.M. (1962) Proceedings of the Business and Economic Statistics Section, American Statistical Association
Organization of American States (1962) Final Report of the Group of Experts on the Stabilization of Export Receipts, Doc. 59, revision 4, April, and Proposed Articles of Agreement of the International Fund for Stabilization of Export Receipts, Doc. 64, revision 4, April
Perez, L. (1976) 'Commodity Exports and Economic Development in Primary Producing Countries', Mimeo, USAID, Washington DC
Pobukadee, J. (1980) 'An Econometric Analysis of World Copper Market', Mimeo, Wharton Econometric Forecasting Associates Inc., Philadelphia
Perry, W.L. (1970) 'Changing Labour Markets and Inflation', Brooklings Papers on Economic Activity, pp. 411-48

BIBLIOGRAPHY

Porter, R. (1970) 'On Placing the Blame for Primary Product Instability', International Economic Review, 11, No. 1

Prebisch, R. (1950) 'The Economic Development of Latin America and Its Principal Problems', Economic Bulletin for Latin America, 1962, Vol. 7, 1-22 (first published as an independent booklet by UN, ECLA in 1950)

— (1951) 'The Spread of Technical Progress and the Terms of Trade' in UN, Economic Survey of Latin America, 1949, United Nations, Department of Economic Affairs, New York, pp. 46-61

— (1959) 'Commercial Policies in Underdeveloped Countries', American Economic Review, Papers and Proceedings, Vol. 49, pp. 251-73

— (1963) 'Development Problems of the Peripheral Countries and the Terms of Trade', Part C, Chapter 1, in UN, Towards a Dynamic Development Policy for Latin America, United Nations, New York

— (1964) 'Towards a New Trade Policy for Development', Report by the Secretary General of UNCTAD, United Nations, New York

— (1976) 'A Critique of Peripheral Capitalism', CEPAL Review (UN, ECLA), Vol. 1, 9-76

Prosterman, R.L. (1984) 'The Decline in Hunger-Related Deaths', The Hunger Project Papers, No. 1, May

Priovolos, T. (1981) Coffee and the Ivory Coast: An Econometric Study, Lexington Books, D.C. Heath, Lexington, Mass.

Radetski, M. (1976) 'The Potential for Monopolistic Commodity Pricing by Developing Countries' in G.K. Helleiner (ed.), A World Divided: The Less Developed Countries in the International Economy, Cambridge University Press, Cambridge

— (1978) 'Market Structure and Bargaining Power: A Study of Three International Mineral Markets', Resources Policy

Rangarajan, C. and Sundararajan, V. (1976) 'Impact of Export Fluctuations on Income - A Cross-Country Analysis', Review of Economics and Statistics, 58

Ravenhill, R. (1984) 'What is to be Done for Third World Commodity Exporters? An Evaluation of the STABEX Scheme', International Organization, 38, No. 3

Reynolds, L.D. (1963) 'Domestic Consequences of Export Instability', The American Economic Review

Salant, S.W. (1983) 'The Vulnerability of Price Stabilization Schemes to Speculative Attack', Journal of Political Economy, Vol. 91, No. 1

Sampson, G.P. and Snape, R.H. (1980) 'Effects of the EEC's Variable Import Levies', Journal of Political Economy, Vol. 88, No. 5

Sapsford, D. (1985) 'The Statistical Debate on the Net Barter Terms of Trade Between Primary Commodities and Manufactures: A Comment and Some Additional Evidence',

Economic Journal, Vol. 95, 781-8

Savvides, A. (1984) 'Export Instability and Economic Growth: Some New Evidence', Economic Development and Cultural Change, April

Schloss, H.H. (1977) 'Declining Terms of Trade: Myth or Reality', Economia Internazionale, Vol. 30, pp. 466-9

Schuh, G.E. (1985) Strategic Issues in International Agriculture, Draft, 4th April

Sen, A. (1982) Poverty and Famines, Clarendon Press, Oxford

Sheehey, E. (1977) 'Levels and Sources of Export Instability: Some Recent Evidence', Kyklos, 30, No. 2

Singer, H. (1950) 'The Distribution of Gains between Investing and Borrowing Countries', American Economic Review, Papers and Proceedings, Vol. 40, pp. 473-85

— (1958) 'Comment' on Kindleberger's 'The Terms of Trade and Economic Development', Review of Economics and Statistics, Supplement, Feb. 1958, Vol. 40, pp. 85-8

— (1974-5) 'The Distribution of Gains from Trade and Investment Revisited', Journal of Development Studies, Vol. 11, 376-82

Siri, G. (1980) World Coffee Prices and the Economic Activity of the Central American Countries, Unpublished report to USAID, Wharton Econometric Forecasting Associates Inc., Philadelphia

Smith, G. (1979) 'Commodity Instability: New Order or Old Hat' in R. Amacher et al. (eds.), Challenges to a Liberal International Economic Order, American Enterprise Institute for Public Policy Research

Smith G.W. and Schink, G.R. (1976) 'The International Tin Agreement: A Reassessment', Economic Journal, 86

Soutar, G. (1977) 'Export Instability and Concentration in the Less Developed Countries', Journal of Development Economics, 4

Spraos, J. 'The Theory of Deteriorating Terms of Trade Revisited', Greek Economic Review, December, Vol. 1

Spraos, J. (1980) (The Statistical Debate on the Net Barter Terms of Trade Between Primary Commodities and Manufactures: A Comment and Some Additional Evidence', Economic Journal, Vol. 90, pp. 107-28

— (1985) 'The Statistical Debate on the Net Barter Terms of Trade: A Response', Economic Journal, Vol. 95, p. 789

Stein, L. (1977a) 'Export Instability and Development: A Review of Some Recent Findings', Banca Nazionale del Lavoro Quarterly Review, 122

— (1977b) 'Export Instability and Economic Development', Banca Nazionale del Lavoro, September

Stephens, C. (1980) 'The Lome Convention: A Good Deal for Industry?', Multinational Business, No. 1

Stern, R.M. (1976) 'World Market Instability in Primary

Commodities', Banca Nazionale del Lavoro, June
Tan, G. (1983) 'Export Instability, Export Growth and GDP
    Growth', Journal of Development Economics, 12
Tangermann, S. (1979) 'Agricultural Trade Relations Between
    the EC and Temperate Food Exporting Countries',
    European Review of Agricultural Economics, Autumn
Tebsa, L.G. and Higinbotham (1976) 'Organised Futures
    Markets: Costs and Benefits', Journal of Political
    Economy, October
Tuong, H.D. and Yeats, A. (1976) 'A Note on the Measure-
    ment of Trade Concentration', Bulletin of the Oxford
    Institute of Economics and Statistics, pp. 299-309
Turnovsky, S.J. (1974) 'Price Expectations and the Welfare
    Gains from Price Stabilization', American Journal of
    Agricultural Economics, November
-   (1978) 'The Distribution of Welfare Gains from Price
    Stabilization: A Survey of Some Theoretical Issues' in
    F.G. Adams and S.A. Klein (eds.), Stabilizing World
    Commodity Markets, Lexington Books, D.C. Heath,
    Lexington, Mass.
UNCTAD (1964) 'Compensatory Financing to Counter the
    Effects of Deterioration in the Terms of Trade', Chapter
    III, Section A, of the Report by the Secretary-General
    of the United Nations Conference on Trade and Develop-
    ment, Towards a New Trade Policy for Development,
    United Nations publication, Sales No. E.64.II.B.4
-   (1967a) 'Intergovernmental Group on Supplementary
    Financing: Report on its First Session', TD/B/C.3/41
-   (1967b) 'Intergovernmental Group on Supplementary
    Financing: Report on its Second Session', TD/B/C.3/44
-   (1974a) 'An Integrated Programme for Commodities',
    TD/B/C.1/166
-   (1974b) 'An Integrated Programme for Commodities: A
    Common Fund for the Financing of Commodity Stocks',
    TD/B/C.1/166/Supp. 2 and Corr. 1
-   (1974c) 'An Integrated Programme for Commodities: The
    Role of Multilateral Commitments in Commodity Trade',
    TD/B/C.1/166/Supp. 3
-   (1974d) 'An Integrated Programme for Commodities:
    Compensatory Financing of Export Fluctuations in Com-
    modity Trade', TD/B/C.1/166/Supp. 4
-   (1975a) 'Recent Developments in International Commodity
    Arrangements Relevant to the Elaboration of an Inte-
    grated Programme for Commodities', TD/B/C.1/185 and
    Corr. 1
-   (1975b) 'A Common Fund for the Financing of Commodity
    Stocks: Amounts, Terms and Prospective Sources of
    Finance', TD/B/C.1/184 and Corr. 1 and Add. 1 and
    Add. 1/Corr. 1
-   (1975c) 'Indexation', TD/B/563
    (1975d) 'International Arrangements for Individual Com-

modities within an Integrated Programme', TD.B/C.1/188
- (1975e) 'Measures for Individual Commodities', TD/B/C.1/194
- (1975f) 'An Integrated Programme for Commodities: The Impact on Imports, Particularly of Developing Countries', TD.B/C.1/169
- (1976) 'Preservation of the Purchasing Power of Developing Countries' Exports', TD/184/Supp. 2 and Corr. 1
- (1978) 'Compensatory Financing for Export Fluctuations', TD.B/C.3/152/Rev. 1 and Corr. 1
- (1979a) 'Compensatory Financing: Issues and Proposals for Future Action', TD/229/Supp. 1 and Corr. 1
- (1979b) 'The Processing Before Export of Primary Commodities: Areas for Further International Co-operation', TD/229/Supp. 2
- (1979c) United Nations on Trade and Development, The Processing Before Export of Primary Commodities: Areas for Further International Co-operation, TD/229/Supp. 2, Geneva
- (1980a) Agreement Establishing the Common Fund for Commodities, TD/IPC/CF/CONF/25 and Corr. 1, United Nations publication, Sales No. E.81.II.D.8 and corrigendum
- (1980b) 'Complementary Facility for Commodity-Related Shortfalls in Export Earnings, Conference Resolution 125 (V)', TD/B/C.1/214 and Corr. 1
- (1981a) 'Complementary Facility for Commodity-Related Shortfalls in Export Earnings: A Feasibility Study by the UNCTAD Secretariat', TD/B/C.1/222
- (1981b) 'Estimates of Commodity-Related Shortfalls and Overages in Export Earnings', UNCTAD/CD/242 and Add. 1-3
- (1982a) 'Selected Issues in the Negotiation of International Commodity Agreements: An Economic Analysis', study by A. Maizels, TD/B/C.1/224
- (1982b) 'Complementary Facility for Commodity-Related Shortfalls in Export Earnings: Agreed Conclusions 19 (S-I) of the Committee on Commodities', TD.B/C.1/234
- (1982c) 'Review of Stabex and SYSMIN', TD.B/C.1/237
- (1982d) 'Protectionism and Structural Adjustment in the World Economy', TD/B/888/Rev. 1
- (1983) 'World Commodity Trade: Review and Outlook', TD/B/C.1/236, 1 May
- (1983a) 'Commodity Issues: A Review and Proposals for Further Action', TD/273 and Corr. 1 and 2
- (1983b) 'Protectionism and Structural Adjustment', Protectionism and Structural Adjustment in Agriculture, TD/B/939, March
- (1983c) 'Review of the Operation of the Compensatory Financing Facility of the International Monetary Fund',

TD/B/C.1/243
- (1983d) Trade and Development Report, Table IV
- (1983e) World Commodity Trade
- (1983f) 'Protection and Structural Adjustment, Non-Tariff Barriers Affecting the Trade of Developing Countries ...: The Inventory of Non-Tariff Barriers', TD/B/940
- (1984a) 'Compensatory Financing of Export Earnings Shortfalls: Background Report by the UNCTAD Secretariat', TD/B/AC.37/3 and Corr. 1
- (1984b) 'Report of the Expert Group on the Compensatory Financing of Export Earnings' Shortfalls', TD/B/1029 and TD/B/1029/Add. 1
- (1984c) Document TD/B/C.1/252
- (1984d) 'Protectionism and Structural Adjustment', An Improved and More Efficient Safeguard System, TD/B/978
- (1984e) United Nations on Trade and Development, Studies in the Processing, Marketing and Distribution of Commodities, TD/B/C.1/PSC/1/Rev. 1 to TD/B/C.1/PSC/39/Rev. 1, Geneva
- (1986a) 'Protectionism and Structural Adjustment, Problems of Protectionism and Structural Adjustment, Part I, TD/B/1081, January
- (1986b)'Protectionism and Structural Adjustment', Problems of Protectionism and Structural Adjustment, Part II, TD/B/1081, January
United Nations (1951) Measures for International Economic Stability. Report by the Group of Experts, E/2156-ST/ECA/13, United Nations publication, Sales No. 1951.II.A.2
- (1961) International Compensation for Fluctuations in Commodity Trade, E/3447-E/CN.13/40, United Nations publication, Sales No. 61.II.D.3
- (1962) 'Stabilization of Export Proceeds through a Development Insurance Fund. Study by the Secretariat', E/CN.13/43
- (1982) Population Bulletin of the United Nations, No. 14, 'Infant Mortality: World Estimates and Projections, 1950-2025'
- (1985) Yearbook of International Commodity Statistics, United Nations Conference on Trade and Development, Geneva, United Nations, New York
US Council on Environmental Quality and Department of State (1982) The Global 2000 Report to the President, Penguin
Valdes, A. and Hayssen, J. (1979) Trade Liberalisation in Agricultural Commodities and the Potential Foreign Trade Benefits to Developing Countries, International Food Policy Research Institute, Washington, February
Valdes, A. and Zeitz, J. (1980) 'Agricultrual Protection in OECD Countries: Its Cost to Less-Developed Countries', International Food Policy Research Institute, Research Report No. 21, Washington DC, December

Varon, B. and Takeuchi, K. (1974) 'Developing Countries and Non-Fuel Minerals', Foreign Affairs, April

Vincent, D. (1981) 'Multisectoral Economic Models for Developing Countries: A Theoretical Framework and an Illustration of their Usefulness for Determining Some Implications of UNCTAD Proposals for Commodity Market Reforms', Institut fur Weltwirtschaft und der Universitat Kiel, Kiel Working Paper No. 117

Voivodas, C. (1974) 'The Effect of Foreign Exchange Insta- bility on Growth', The Review of Economics and Stat- istics, Vol. LVI, No. 3

De Vries, J. (1975) 'Compensatory Financing: A Quantitative Analysis', World Bank Staff Working Paper No. 228, Washington DC

Wachter, M.L. (1976) 'The Changing Cyclical Responsiveness of Wage Inflation', Brookings Papers on Economic Activity, pp. 115-68

Wall, D. (1976) The European Community's Lome Convention: STABEX and the Third World's Aspirations, Trade Policy Research Centre, London, Guest Papers, No. 4

Waugh, F.V. (1944) 'Does the Consumer Benefit from Price Instability?', Quarterly Journal of Economics, 58

- (1964) 'Does the Consumer Benefit from Price Insta- bility?', Quarterly Journal of Economics, 58

Wilson, P. (1977) 'Export Instability and Economic Develop- ment - A Survey. Part I: The Theory', Warwick Eco- nomic Discussion Paper No. 107, Warwick University

- (1983) 'The Consequences of Export Instability for Developing Countries - A Reappraisal', Development and Change, Vol. 14, No. 1

World Bank (1980) World Development Report

- (1982) World Development Report

- (1983) Case Studies on Industrial Processing of Primary Products, Vol. I and Vol. II, New York

- (1984a) World Development Report

- (1984b) 'Price Prospects for Major Primary Commodities', Vol. I: Summary and Implications, Report No. 814/84

- (1984c) 'Price Prospects for Major Primary Commodities', Vol. II: Food Products and Fertilizers, Report No. 814/84

- (1984d) 'Price Prospects for Major Primary Commodities', Vol. IV: Metals and Minerals, Report No. 814/84

- (1985) Ensuring Food Security in the Developing World: Issues and Options, Draft, 15 May

- (1986) World Development Report

World Food Council (1984a) Progress Toward the Eradication of Hunger, A Multilateral Decade for Food 1974-1984, Report by the Executive Director

- (1984b) Progress Toward the Eradication of Hunger, A Multilateral Decade for Food 1974-1984. Executive Summary and Conclusions

BIBLIOGRAPHY

- (1984c) The World Food and Hunger Problem: Changing Perspectives and Possibilities, 1974-1984, An Independent Assessment Presented to the World Food Council

Yamey, B.S. (1985) 'Scope for Futures Trading and Conditions for Success' in How Commodity Futures Markets Work, Thames Essays, Trade Policy Research Centre

Yeats, A.J. (1981) 'Agricultural Protectionism: An Analysis of Its International Economic Effects and Options for Institutional Reform', Trade and Development, Winter

- (1984) 'On the Analysis of Tariff Escalation: Is there a Methodological Bias Against the Interest of Developing Countries?', Journal of Development Economics, pp. 77-88

- (1985) 'A Note on the Functioning of International Commodity Price Stabilization Agreements in Periods of Fluctuating Monetary Exchange Rates', Mimeo, UNCTAD, Geneva

INDEX

Note: *Commodities are not entered separately but can be found under general categories e.g. metals and minerals, food etc.*

INDEX

balance of payments, disequilibrium
   model of 45–6, 373–8
Balassa, B. 28, 310
Baldwin, R.E. 84, 261
Bale, M.D. 5, 26–7, 261, 271
Bangladesh 263
   commodities market instability 107–8,
      110–12, 117, 403
barriers *see* protectionism; tariffs
Bates, R.H. 266
Behrman, J.R. 2, 12, 125–6, 158–9,
      167–71, 180
Belgium/Belgium–Luxembourg 59, 84
   commodities market instability 105–12,
      118
Benin 117, 212, 402
Bernstein, B. 83
Bhagwati, J. 29
bias criterion 170
Body, R. 4, 5–6
Bolivia 107, 110, 117, 255, 404
   primary commodity instability policies
      184, 196
boom and slump 11
borrowing 151–2
Bosson 260, 304–5
Box–Jenkin ARIMA method 93
Brazil
   agriculture 266, 278
   commodities market instability 104–12,
      118, 127, 172, 404
   metals and minerals 255, 256, 258,
      260
   trade 1, 16, 28, 266, 278
Brundell, P. 135, 137, 146, 147
Buffer Stock Financing Facility (BSFF)
      204
buffer stocks 183–96, 271, 393–4
Burma 26, 117, 197, 403
Burundi 2, 17, 117, 403

Caine, Sir S. 155
callable capital 288
Cameroon 107, 110, 118, 403
Canada
   agriculture 5, 264, 276–7, 290
   commodities market instability 106,
      109, 116, 119
   primary commodity instability policies
      186, 197, 258
   protectionism 317
   trade 48, 75, 277, 310, 321, 360
CAP *see* Common Agricultural Policy
capacity *see* supply
capital
   accumulation 378

paid-in and callable 288
Caribbean *see* Central America and West
      Indies
carrying capacity of earth 78
cartels 2, 41, 317
   see also transnationals
Carter, J. 9, 65
causes of commodities market instability
      116, 119–48
   empirical evidence 136–47
   policy implications 147–8
   theoretical considerations 132–6,
      387–9
Central African Republic 118, 402
Central America and West Indies
   agriculture 276, 334; food 263, 270,
      278
   commodities market instability 104,
      106–11, 117–18, 138–40, 144,
      166, 172, 404–5
   instability policies *see* Stabex
   metals and minerals 256, 260
   trade 1, 16, 278
centrally planned economies
   agriculture 6, 29, 261
   prospects and policies 261, 337
   trade 14, 17–18, 20–2, 102, 107, 112;
      component analysis 21–2; with
      LDCs 28–9
   see also individual countries
centre and periphery concept 41, 43–4,
      373
CFF *see* Compensatory Financing
      Facility
Chad 117, 402
Chile
   commodities market instability 106,
      109, 117, 166, 172, 173, 404
   metals and minerals 254, 255
China 27, 255
   agriculture 39, 261
   commodities market instability 107–8,
      110–12
chronic food insecurity 264
Club of Rome projections 65, 77, 78,
      83, 379
CMC *see* commodity mix component
Cob–Web market model 120, 385–6
collectives *see* co-operatives
Colombia 278
   commodities market instability 104,
      106, 109, 112, 118, 128, 174, 404
commission fee 338
commodities *see* concentration;
      instability policies; instability;
      projections; terms of trade; trade

428

Printed in the United States
by Baker & Taylor Publisher Services